Population Migration in
The European Union

Population Migration in The European Union

Edited by

PHILIP REES

JOHN STILLWELL

ANDREW CONVEY

MAREK KUPISZEWSKI

University of Leeds, UK

JOHN WILEY & SONS

Chichester · New York · Brisbane · Toronto · Singapore

Copyright © 1996 Editors & Contributors
Published 1996 by John Wiley & Sons Ltd,
Baffins Lane, Chichester,
West Sussex PO19 1UD, England

National   01243 779777
International (+44) 1243 779777

Other Wiley Editorial Offices

John Wiley & Sons, Inc., 605 Third Avenue,
New York, NY 10158-0012, USA

Jacaranda Wiley Ltd, 33 Park Road, Milton,
Queensland 4064, Australia

John Wiley & Sons (Canada) Ltd, 22 Worcester Road,
Rexdale, Ontario M9W 1L1, Canada

John Wiley & Sons (SEA) Pte Ltd, 37 Jalan Pemimpin #05-04,
Block B, Union Industrial Building, Singapore 2057

Library of Congress Cataloging-in-Publication Data

Population migration in the European Union / edited by Philip Rees ...
    [et al.].
            p. cm.
    Includes bibliographical references (p.) and index.
    ISBN 0–471–94968–X (hard : alk. paper)
    1. Migration, Internal—European Union countries. 2. European
Union countries—Emigration and immigration. I. Rees, P. H.
(Philip H.), 1944–
HB2041.P66 1996
304.8'2'094—dc20   95–24756
                                                        CIP

British Library Cataloguing in Publication Data

A catalogue record for this book is available from the British Library

ISBN 0–471–94968–X

Typeset in 10/12pt Palatino by Saxon Graphics Ltd, Derby.
Printed and bound in Great Britain by Bookcraft (Bath) Ltd, Midsomer Norton.
This book is printed on acid-free paper responsibly manufactured from sustainable foresta-
tion, for which at least two trees are planted for each one used for paper production.

Contents

List of Tables   vii

List of Figures   xi

List of Contributors   xv

Acknowledgements   xvii

Preface
Harri Cruijsen   xix

1 Introduction: Migration in an Integrated Europe   1
Philip Rees, John Stillwell, Andrew Convey and Marek Kupiszewski

PART 1   INTERNATIONAL MIGRATION PATTERNS

2 Extra-Union Migration: the East–West Perspective   13
Marek Kupiszewski

3 Extra-Union Migration: the South–North Perspective   39
Allan Findlay

4 Migration Flows Between the Countries of the European Union: Current Trends   51
Michel Poulain

5 Redefining the Front Line: the Geography of Asylum Seeking in the New Europe   67
Vaughan Robinson

PART 2   INTERREGIONAL MIGRATION PATTERNS: NATIONAL
         PERSPECTIVES

6 Migration in Belgium: Temporal Trends and Counterurbanization Patterns
Michel Poulain   91

7 Changing Patterns of Net Migration in Denmark: an Explanatory Analysis
Sven Illeris   105

8 Interregional Migration Patterns and Processes in Germany
Hansjörg Bucher and Hans-Peter Gatzweiler   123

9 Greece: Population Change Components and Internal Migration
Georgios Papadakis and John Stillwell   145

10 **Spain: Return to the South, Metropolitan Deconcentration and New Migration Flows**   175
Juan Romero González and Juan M. Albertos Puebla

11 **Migration in France Between 1975 and 1990: a Limited Degree of Decentralization**   191
Brigitte Baccaïni and Denise Pumain

12 **Ireland: the Human Resource Warehouse of Europe**   207
Russell King, Ian Shuttleworth and James Walsh

13 **The Pattern of Internal Migration: the Italian Case**   231
Alberto Bonaguidi and Valerio Terra Abrami

14 **The Netherlands: from Interregional to International Migration**   247
Hugo Gordijn and Leo Eichperger

15 **Recent Trends in Regional and Urban Dynamics in Portugal**   261
João Peixoto

16 **Migration between NUTS Level 2 Regions in the United Kingdom**   275
John Stillwell, Philip Rees and Oliver Duke-Williams

PART 3   IMPACTS OF MIGRATION ON POPULATION DEVELOPMENT

17 **Migration and Policy in the European Union**   311
Andrew Convey and Marek Kupiszewski

18 **Projecting the National and Regional Populations of the European Union Using Migration Information**   331
Philip Rees

References   365

Index

List of Tables

1.1   The national administrative divisions used in the NUTS classification   3
2.1   Number of migrants to Germany reported by various statistical agencies, 1987–90   14
2.2   Asylum seekers from Eastern Europe lodging their applications, 1983–92   18
2.3   Migration of *Aussiedler* into West Germany, 1985–91   22
2.4   The changes in the East European population living in EU countries in the 1980s   25
2.5   Nationalities ranked by percentage shares of total population   27
2.6   General economic characteristics of East European and EU countries   31
3.1   The Mediterranean, 1990—a demographic and economic divide   44
3.2   Stock of foreign population, 1980 and 1990   47
3.3   Stock of foreign population for selected nationalities, 1990 ('000s)   48
4.1   Migration exchanges between the member states of the European Union, 1990   54
4.2   Estimation of the migration exchanges between the countries of the European Union, 1990   55
4.3   Mobility rate, volume and net migration for each member state of the European Union in 1990   56
4.4   Weighted differences between observed and expected migration flows   60
4.5   The most important weighted deviations between observed flows and expected flows   61
4.6   The most marked disequilibrium between migration flows between pairs of countries   62
6.1   Variation in the distance decay parameter by age group, 1979–82 and 1988–92   98
7.1   Population of Danish *amter*, 1970–93   106
7.2   Population change and its components by *amter*, 1966–92   109
7.3   Age-specific migration rates, 1990   111
7.4   Internal net migration by age group in selected areas and years, 1965–90   112
7.5   Regional distribution of employment, 1960–90   113
7.6   Population in the Copenhagen region, 1970–93   114
7.7   Population change and its components, 1973–92   117

7.8   Internal net migration by age group, 1973–90   119
7.9   Age distribution of population in core communes, 1973–92   120
7.10   Number of dwellings in the Copenhagen region, 1970–92   121
8.1   Components of population change, 1990–2000   138
9.1   Correlation coefficients for population change rates (PCR) against natural
        change rates (NCR) and net migration rates (NMR), 1980–91   165
9.2   Population, 1981 and net migration, 1976–81, by area type   167
9.3   In-migration and immigration by area type, 1976–81   168
9.4   Net migration by age and area type, 1976–81   169
9.5   Interregional migration to and from Anatoliki Sterea and Nisia and
        between all other regions, 1984   172
10.1   Net migration by region, 1961–90   178
10.2   Relationship between net migration and settlement size, 1980–1 and
        1989–90   181
11.1   Annual average regional net migration rates by age group, 1982–90   195
11.2   Evolution of the population of city centres and peripheries, 1975–90   197
11.3   Goodness of fit and parameter values for gravity models applied to inter-
        regional migration, 1975–82 and 1982–90   200
12.1   Emigration, unemployment and labour market characteristics, 1971 and
        1980–90   214
12.2   Gross migration outflow for 1987–8 classified by the socio-occupational
        group of the head of household from which the emigrant left   214
12.3   Changing regional pattern of Irish emigration, 1981–91   218
12.4   Economic status of 1990 school leavers by region   219
12.5   Migration and population change by region, 1971–91   221
12.6   Distribution of intercounty migrants 1980–1 according to occupational
        status   225
12.7   Rural–urban and urban–rural migration by region, 1985–6   226
13.1   Long-term evolution of internal migration in Italy, 1956–87   232
13.2   Regional net migration, 1977–8 and 1987–8   234
13.3   Interregional distribution patterns for Lombardy and Campania, 1977–8
        and 1987–8   236
13.4   Metro/non-metro migration shifts, Turin and Milan metropolitan areas,
        1977–8 and 1987–8   238
13.5   Intermetropolitan net migration shifts, Turin and Milan metropolitan
        areas, 1977–8 and 1987–8   239
14.1   Migration between types of municipalities, 1972–92   255
15.1   Population change and its components by NUTS 2 region, 1970–81   264
15.2   Population change and its components, and urbanization rates by region,
        1981–91   265
16.1   Migration coefficients, NUTS 2 regions, 1991–2   286
16.2   Correlations between NHS migrations and Census migrants for flows
        between NUTS 2 regions by age and gender, 1990–1   292

16.3   Ratios and regression parameters for NHS migration flows versus Census
        migrant flows for NUTS 2 regions, by age, 1990–1   293
16.4   Migration rates at different spatial scales, 1991 Census, Great Britain   296
16.5   Net migration flows by broad age group, 1991 Census   300
16.6   Migration coefficients for broad ages and macroregions, 1991 Census 302
16.7   A grouping of NUTS 2 regions by interaction pattern, 1990–1   304
17.1   Conditions for the issuing of work permits and residence permits for non-
        EU citizens residing in selected EU member states   322
18.1   Projections of the population of the European Union (EUR-12)   332
18.2   Mortality assumptions (life expectancies at birth) for selected EU member
        states: alternative projections   341
18.3   Fertility assumptions for selected EU member states   343
18.4   External migration assumptions for selected EU member states (annual net
        migration)   347
18.5   Intermember state migration flows for the EU: synthetic estimates for
        1982, 1986–8   349
18.6   The income scenario adopted for interregion migration in the EU   351
18.7   The counterurbanization/urbanization scenario adopted for interregion
        migration in the EU   352
18.8   The projected populations of the member states of the European Union,
        1990–2020   354
18.9   DEMETER projections: highest and lowest regions   356
18.10   Top and bottom ten NUTS 1 regions under variant interregion migration
        scenarios, percentage change 1990–2020   357
18.11   Projected populations of NUTS 1 regions under variant migration
        scenarios, 2020   360

List of Figures

1.1   Demographic regimes in European Union regions, 1991   6
4.1   Relationship between the rate of migration and the population at risk   57
4.2   Time series of migration flows between selected countries, 1981–91 (corrected data)   63
4.3   Time series of migration flows between selected countries, 1981–91 (corrected data)   64
5.1   Number of refugees in the world, 1962–92   68
5.2   Principal sources of the world's refugees and asylum seekers, 1993   74
5.3   Number of asylum seekers in the industrialized world compared to major refugee flows elsewhere in the world, 1991 and 1992   76
5.4   Refugee populations by country, 1991   77
5.5   Top 20 contributors to international refugee aid agencies, 1992   78
5.6   Number of applications for asylum made to countries of the EC and EFTA, 1982–92   79
5.7   Source and number of refugees making asylum applications in 10 European countries, 1988–92   80
5.8   Source and number of refugees making asylum applications in 10 European countries,1988–92, broken down by country of application   81
5.9   Human fallout from the Yugoslavian crisis: outward flows and destinations 1991–3   82
6.1   Change in the standardized index of total migration (M) and the index of interlinguistic migration (L), 1948–92   93
6.2   Total migration by sex and age, 1992   94
6.3   Total migration rate by sex and five-year age groups from 65, 1992   95
6.4   Comparison of migration rates, 1970 and 1992   96
6.5   Decomposition of migration by age into local, regional or interregional components, males, 1992   97
6.6   Evolution of migration flows between Brussels and Flemish and Walloon Brabant, 1964–91   99
6.7   Net migration between Brussels and its neighbours, computed as in-migration to Brussels, 1964–91   100
6.8   Covariation between the number of counterburbanizing migrations, the cost of buying property (houses and building plots), the cost of construction and the interest rate, 1964– 91   101
6.9   In-migrations, out-migrations and migration balance by age, Charleroi, 1988–93   102

6.10   Belgian communes with positive net migration for ages 15–24,
        1988–92   102
6.11   Belgian communes with positive net migration for ages 25–39,
        1988–92   103
6.12   Zones of attraction and repulsion in Flanders and Wallonia,
        1988–92   104
7.1   Net migration (in thousands) between groups of *amter*, 1950–69   107
7.2   Total net migration (in thousands), 1970–92   108
7.3   Annual population change rate by type of municipality, 1966–92   115
7.4   Total net migration (in thousands) in the Copenhagen region,
        1973–92   116
8.1   Regional population change, 1979–89   124
8.2   Gross interregional in-migration rates in Western and Eastern Germany,
        1952–89   125
8.3   Net interregional migration rates, all ages, 1980–9   126
8.4   Net interregional migration rates, ages 18–29, 1980–9   128
8.5   Net interregional migration rates, ages 50 and over, 1980–9   129
8.6   Main out-migration flows from eastern to western *Länder*, 1991   130
8.7   Balance of international migration in the unified Germany,
        1950–2000   132
8.8   Nationality of migrants entering the Federal Republic of Germany,
        1965–89   132
8.9   Structure of the interregional migration model   134
8.10   Population change in the western and eastern *Länder* of Germany,
        1989–2000   138
8.11   Regional population change, 1989–2000   139
8.12   Spatial effects of international migration, 1990–2000   140
8.13   Age structure change in the western and eastern *Länder* of Germany,
        1989–2000   141
9.1   NUTS 1 and 2 regions of Greece   146
9.2   National population change, 1980–92   147
9.3   Regional population totals, 1992   149
9.4   Annual population change rates by region, 1980–92   150–2
9.5   Population change rates by region, 1991   153
9.6   Age pyramids for Voreio Aigaio, 1980 and 1992   154
9.7   Natural change and net migration rates, 1980–91   156
9.8   Natural increase rates by region, 1980–91   158–60
9.9   Natural increase rates by region, 1991   161
9.10   Net migration rates by region, 1980–91   162–4
9.11   Net migration rates by region, 1991   165
9.12   Net migration rates by age and region, 1976–81   170–1
10.1   NUTS 2 and 3 regions of Spain   176
10.2   Annual net migration rates, 1961–70, 1971–80 and 1981–90   177

10.3   Annual net migration rates, 1981–5 and 1986–90   183

10.4   Short-distance intraprovincial migrations, 1988–90   187

11.1   NUTS 1 and 2 *régions* of France   192

11.2   Annual net migration rates by *région*, 1982–90   194

11.3   Net migration rates by population size of settlement, 1968–90   196

11.4   Annual net migration rates for selected age groups, 1982–90   198

11.5   Indices relating to gravity model residuals, 1975–82 and 1982–90   203

11.6   Indices relating to gravity model residuals, ages 20–9 and 60+,
        1982–90   204

12.1   Components of population change, 1946–91   209

12.2   Annual estimates of net migration, 1945–92   213

12.3   Net annual migration rates by county, 1971–91   220

12.4   Patterns of intercounty migration rates, 1980–1   223

12.5   Migration to and from Dublin as a percentage of total intercounty migra-
        tion, 1980–1   224

13.1   Age profiles of gross and net migration rates for the northwestern macro
        region, 1980–2   241

13.2   Age profiles (standardized) of south to northwest and northwest to
        south migration rates, 1980–2   242

13.3   Age profiles of migration rates from Campania to north and from
        Lombardy to south, 1977–9 and 1989–90   243

14.1   Division of the Netherlands into COROP regions   249

14.2   Migration in the Netherlands, 1960–92   250

14.3   Migration by age and gender in the Netherlands, 1972–4 and
        1988–90   250

14.4   Netherlands international migration by age and gender (forecast),
        1992   251

14.5   Net migration as a percentage of total migration, 1972–9   252

14.6   Net migration as a percentage of total migration, 1987–92   253

14.7   Arrival/departure ratio, age group 15–24, 1987–92   254

14.8   Arrival/departure ratio, age group 65+, 1987–92   254

14.9   Population density by COROP region, 1990   255

14.10   Net migration by age group for centre, ring and periphery, 1972–3,
        1981–3 and 1990–2   256

14.11   Three scenarios for future demographic development, 1992–2015   258

15.1   NUTS 2 and 3 regions of Portugal   262

16.1   NUTS 2 regions of the United Kingdom   276

16.2   Migration level, time series index, 1983–96   279

16.3   Net migration balances, NUTS 2 regions, 1983–92   280

16.4   Net migration balances, main gaining and losing regions,
        1983–92   281

16.5   Net migration rates, NUTS 2 regions, 1991–2   282

16.6   Out-migration rates, NUTS 2 regions, 1991–2   284

16.7   In-migration rates, NUTS 2 regions, 1991–2   285
16.8   Primary interregional net migration flows, 1983–92   287
16.9   Secondary interregional net migration flows, 1983–92   288
16.10   Tertiary interregional net migration flows, 1983–92   289
16.11   Migration rates for migrants resident in Britain by gender, 1990–1   295
16.12   Migration rates by age for a variety of spatial scales, Great Britain,
         1990–1   295
16.13   A comparison of migration rates for a variety of spatial scales with the
         national standard, Great Britain, 1990–1   298
16.14   Interaction pattern groupings, 1991 Census   303
18.1   The hierarchical structure of the ECPOP projection model for NUTS 1
         regions   337
18.2   Population change, 1990–2020: zero scenario versus constant internal
         migration scenario   362

List of Contributors

Brigitte Baccaïni
Institut National d'Etudes Démographiques, 27 Rue du Commandeur, 75675 Paris Cedex 14, France.

Alberto Bonaguidi
Dipartiménto de Statística e Matemática Applicata All'Economía, Università Degli Studi di Pisa, Via Ridolfi 10, 56100 Pisa, Italy.

Hansjörg Bucher
Bundesforschungsanstalt für Landeskunde und Raumordnung, Postfach 20 01 30, D 53131, Bonn, Germany.

Andrew Convey
School of Geography, University of Leeds, Leeds LS2 9JT, UK.

Oliver Duke-Williams
School of Geography, University of Leeds, Leeds LS2 9JT, UK.

Leo Eichperger
Rijksplanologische Dienst, Ministerie van Volkshuisvesting, Ruimtelijke Ordening en Milieubeheer, Rijnstraat 8, 2515 XP, Den Haag, The Netherlands.

Allan Findlay
Department of Geography, The University of Dundee, Perth Road, Dundee DD1 4HN, UK.

Hans-Peter Gatzweiler
Bundesforschungsanstalt für Landeskunde und Raumordnung, Postfach 20 01 30, D 53131, Bonn, Germany.

Juan Romero González
Departamento de Geografía, Facultad de Geografía/Historia, Universidad de Valencia, Apartat 22060, 46080 Valencia, Spain.

Hugo Gordijn
Rijksplanologische Dienst, Ministerie van Volkshuisvesting, Ruimtelijke Ordening en Milieubeheer, Rijnstraat 8, 2515 XP, Den Haag, The Netherlands.

Sven Illeris
Department of Geography, Socioeconomic Analysis and Computer Science, Roskilde University, PO Box 260, 4000 Denmark.

Russell King
School of European Studies, Arts Building,University of Sussex, Falmer, Brighton BN1 9QN, UK.

Marek Kupiszewski
School of Geography, University of Leeds, Leeds LS2 9JT, UK.

Georgios Papadakis
10 Midias Street, 162 32 Byron, Athinai, Athens, Greece.

João Peixoto
Gabinete de Estudos Demográficos, Instituto Nacional de Estatística, Av. António José de Almeida, 5/P-1078 Lisboa Codex, Portugal.

Michel Poulain
Département de Sciences Politiques et Sociales, Université Catholique de Louvain, 1 Place Montesquieu, boîte 17, B-1348 Louvain-la-Neuve, Belgium.

Juan M. Albertos Puebla
Departamento de Geografía, Facultad de Geografía/Historia, Universitad de Valencia, Apartat 22060, 46080 Valencia, Spain.

Denise Pumain
Institut National d'Etudes Démographiques, 27 Rue du Commandeur, 75675 Paris Cedex 14, France.

Philip Rees
School of Geography, University of Leeds, Leeds LS2 9JT, UK.

Vaughan Robinson
Department of Geography, University of Wales Swansea, Singleton Park, Swansea SA2 8PP, UK.

Ian Shuttleworth
Department of Geography, School of Geosciences, Queen's University of Belfast, Belfast BT7 1NN, UK.

John Stillwell
School of Geography, University of Leeds, Leeds LS2 9JT, UK.

Valerio Terra Abrami
Demographic Statistics, Istituto Nazionale di Statistica (ISTAT), viale Liegi, 13, I-00198, Rome, Italy.

James Walsh
Department of Geography, St. Patrick's College, Maynooth, County Kildare, Ireland.

Acknowledgements

The authors wish to thank support staff at the University of Leeds for their help in bringing the book to fruition. Maureen Rosindale, Jo Shorrocks and Christine Hudson helped with the word-processing involved. Alistair French and Alison Manson of the Graphics Unit used their expertise to produce the attractive maps and graphs in the book. The editors had assistance with translation from Chloe Rees and Françoise Convey.

Throughout the book the authors use statistics produced by the various demographic and statistical offices of the European Union member states. We are grateful for all the efforts that such offices put into the preparation of time series on population and migration which are intensively used in the book. Although virtually all of the tables and figures contained heavily derived and processed information, we acknowledge that the copyright to the raw data resides with the statistical offices. We trust they will find the uses to which their data has been put of some considerable interest.

Preface

Most Europeans like change and diversity. The continuous refinements of already complex social, economic, political and technological systems, the ongoing renaissance of local, regional and national cultures, the continuous reshaping of the physical environment, the ever growing plurality of life styles, all these phenomena express deeply rooted beliefs and wishes in our societies summarized in the very old saying 'a change of food whets the appetite'.

Strongly related to this, most Europeans move several times during their lives. Recent estimates based on the population estimates held in the early 1990s indicate that in the European Union at least 25 million people change their place of main residence each year. This implies that internal migration is by far the most important demographic phenomenon in numerical terms. In the 15 member states of the European Union in 1994 only 4 million babies were born, only 3.7 million people died, only 2 million immigrants entered from outside and only 1 million people emigrated.

However, internal migration has only been studied in a fragmentary fashion. Internationally comparable studies are lacking and with the growing interest in a 'Europe of the Regions' (formerly recognized in the Treaty of Maastricht), this situation needs to change.

That is why this book is produced at the right time and with the right approach. The approach is decentralized and exploratory with some common guidelines, so that the authors, experts on internal migration in their countries, could present a full account of national findings but without losing sight of international similarities. In addition and essential for a wider understanding of spatial mobility, there are chapters devoted to international migration, which has been in recent years, as we all know, the 'hottest' demographic issue. The book ends with highly relevant discussions of the relationship between migration and policy and of the use of migration information for making demographic projections.

I am convinced that many Europeans (and non-Europeans) will enjoy this international variety. It demonstrates once more that our ways of living are full of change and diversity.

Harri Cruijsen
Eurostat

1 Introduction: Migration in an Integrated Europe

PHILIP REES, JOHN STILLWELL, ANDREW CONVEY and
MAREK KUPISZEWSKI

1.1 WHY REGIONAL MIGRATION IS IMPORTANT

The ratification of the Treaty on European Union at the end of 1993
marked an important step in the process toward further integration.
(Bruce Millan writing in the Foreword to CEC, 1994).

One of the concerns of the European Union (EU) since its inception, emphasized in
the changes introduced in the Treaty of Maastricht, has been to foster more even
development across the regions of its member states. The EU has in place a set of
Structural Actions (financed from the Structural and Cohesion Funds) which will
grow in relative importance over the 1990s. In 1993, Structural Actions comprised
31 per cent of the Community budget, but by 1999 they will constitute 36 percent of
the EU budget (CEC, 1994, Table 17, p.126). The regional development policies of
the EU aim at enabling the poorest regions of the EU to close the gap with the richer
regions. The key criteria used in monitoring the success of this drive towards convergence are the gross domestic product per capita and the unemployment rate of
the regions. In both measures a role is played by the regional population: the total
number is used to work out GDP per capita and the numbers in the labour ages are
employed as part of the calculation of unemployment rates. Knowledge of the current
level and future direction of change in regional populations is thus a vital ingredient
both in the preparation of regional policies and in the evaluation of their impact.

This book examines one important aspect of the development of regional populations across the EU—the role that migration plays in population redistribution.
Why is there a need to examine the nature of migration at a regional scale? First, the
migration component is crucial in determining the direction of population change
for regions, and its importance increases as the regional scale shrinks. For example,
natural increase rates (birth rates less death rates) across EU regions (a mixture of
NUTS 1 and NUTS 2 areas) reported in 1991 in Eurostat (1994, Table 1.2) range
from a minimum of –7.3 per 1000 per annum to a maximum of 9.6 per 1000,
whereas the equivalent range for net migration rates is from –12.8 to 37.4 per 1000,
a range three times as large.

Second, migration between regions has played a key role in redistributing

Population Migration in the European Union. Edited by Philip Rees, John Stillwell, Andrew Convey and Marek
Kupiszewski. © Editors and contributors. Published 1996 John Wiley & Sons Ltd.

population from those of labour surplus to those of labour deficit. The long-standing flow of labour migrants from the southern regions of Italy to the northern and the more recent migration streams out of the new *Länder* of eastern Germany into the country's western regions are two clear examples of such redistribution.

Third, relatively little attention has been paid to date to a proper comparative examination of internal migration within the European Union. Recent works on European migration have focused on international migration, particularly on flows from outside the EU to member states (King 1993b, King 1993c; Fassmann and Münz 1994). It is clear that three types of migration at regional scale should be distinguished: migration flows between the region and countries outside the EU; migration flows between the region and other EU member states; and migration flows between the region and other regions within the same member state. This partitioning of migration streams was used in the regional population projections carried out by Rees, *et al.* (1992) which are reviewed in Chapter 18. Chapter 4 of this volume provides an account of the migration exchanges between member states.

Fourth, there exists a need to examine migration at a regional scale across Europe in order to form a clear view on the direction and nature of change in migration flows. The pace and selectivity of migration has varied dramatically over recent decades. All of the national chapters in Part 2 place emphasis in their analysis on both long-run and short-run shifts in migration pattern. Some of these shifts are well known: the turnaround in migration pattern in the 1970s from one of urbanization to one of counterurbanization in northern member states has been well documented, but the chapters on Italy, Spain and Portugal suggest that the process of change has only just started in those southern countries.

Fifth, this knowledge about trends in regional migration is needed to inform development of the migration scenarios entered into population forecasts. Current practice at both national and EU level is to assume that the patterns of the latest period for which migration data are available persist without change into the future (eg NEI, 1994a; CEC, 1994). The insights embodied in the national chapters of this book should enable future forecasters to develop better scenarios of change in patterns of regional migration

1.2 ORGANIZATION OF THE BOOK

The aim of this book is to report on the migration of people within the European Union and in particular within member states of the EU at regional level. At its core are the 11 chapters of Part 2 (from Chapter 6 on Belgium to Chapter 16 on the United Kingdom) which describe migration at regional scale within each member state. The national chapters are arranged in the alphabetical order normally used in European Union publications which follows the international convention for the letters used on automobiles visiting foreign countries. So, for example, the chapter on migration in Spain is placed before that on migration in France because E (for España) precedes F (for France) in the alphabet. Each chapter has been written by an expert or team of experts from the country concerned. The authors were provided with general guidelines for the information and insights that would be useful to convey to a general audience, but no strict framework of regions or topics has been imposed. As a result each chapter contributes both common and unique elements in the analysis of migration at regional level.

Table 1.1 The national administrative divisions used in the NUTS classification

Member state	NUTS 1		NUTS 2		NUTS 3	
Belgium (B)	**Régions**	3	**Provinces**	9	**Arrondissements**	43
Denmark (DK)		1		1	Amter	15
Germany (D)	**Länder**	16	**Regierungsbezirke**	40	Kreise	543
Greece (GR)	Groups of development regions	4	**Development regions**	13	Nomoi	51
Spain (E)	Agrupación de comunidades autonomas	7	**Comunidades autonomas** **+ Mellila y Ceuta**	17 1	**Provincias**	50
France (F)	ZEAT +DOM	8 1	**Régions**	22 4	Départements	96 4
Ireland (IRL)		1		1	Planning regions	9
Italy (I)	Gruppi di regioni	11	**Regioni**	20	Provincie	95
Luxemburg (L)		1		1		1
Netherlands (NL)	Landsdelen	4	**Provincies**	12	**COROP-Regios**	40
Portugal (P)	Continente	1	**Comissãoes de coordenação regional**	5	Grupos de Concelhos	50
	Regioes autônomas	2	**Regioes autônomas**	2		
United Kingdom (UK)	Standard regions	11	**Groups of counties**	35	Counties/Local authority areas	65
EUR12		71		183		1044

Note: 1 The divisions marked in bold are the units used in the national chapters

Source: adapted from CEC (1994, Table A.1, p. 173)

The regional frameworks adopted in the national chapters vary. Table 1.1 sets out the general scheme called *Nomenclature des Unités Territoires Statistiques*, abbreviated as NUTS, used by the Statistical Office of the European Communities (Eurostat) to collate and publish regional statistics. Within the table, identified in bold, are the units used in each national chapter. Where appropriate a map providing a key to the regions used is included in the national chapter. Most chapters use regions at NUTS level 2, except where this level provides inadequate regional delimitation when NUTS 3 regions are used (as in the chapters on Belgium, Spain,

Ireland and the Netherlands). In Belgium and Ireland regions smaller than NUTS level 3 are also used in some analyses. Most of the regional divisions are used for administrative purposes, though some are unique to the NUTS system (eg the NUTS 2 regions in the UK).

The national analyses of Chapters 6 to 16 form the core of the book, but either side of that core are chapters which examine migration themes of EU-wide importance. The chapters in Part 1 provide reviews of four aspects of international migration affecting EU member states.

Chapter 2 brings together the most recent information on migration flows into the European Union from the countries of Central and Eastern Europe. The late 1980s and early 1990s witnessed the birth of completely new migration streams into the EU, particularly into Germany. Chapter 3 looks at the migration exchanges between Third World countries of the 'South' and the EU which have a longer history than East–West flows but which have undergone recent profound change in the relationships among the countries involved. Chapter 4 puts together a picture of the migration flows among member states of the EU, highlighting their neglected importance and the rather imprecise nature of the statistical data about them. While migrants in Chapter 4 move freely and easily among EU member states in well-ordered career paths, the migrants described in Chapter 6 arrive at the EU's doorstep in varying degrees of distress, requesting shelter. This chapter provides a graphic account of the growing numbers and widening origins of refugees and asylum seekers who look to enter the EU to escape the harmful situations they encounter in their home countries.

The final part of the book, consisting of two chapters, attempts an overview across the EU of two migration themes. Chapter 17 examines the way in which policy has influenced, in the recent past, migration across the EU's internal and external borders. Chapter 18 reviews the ways in which recent projections of EU national and regional populations have been prepared and, in particular, how knowledge of migration flows and trends has been fed into regional projections.

We have omitted from the book consideration of regional patterns in the three new member states which joined the EU on 1 January 1995, namely Austria, Finland and Sweden. Their membership applications were still under consideration by the EUR12 member states and by their own electorates during the gestation period of the book. Should this volume be successful enough to warrant a second edition towards the end of the century, the additional EFTA members could be included relatively easily as all have well-developed population and migration statistics at regional scale and plenty of experts on population migration within their countries. By 2000, however, it might be necessary to include a further four chapters covering the Czech Republic, Slovakia, Hungary and Poland!

1.3 OVERVIEW OF FINDINGS

It will be helpful for many readers to provide a short overview of findings of the book. This is not meant as a comprehensive summary because each chapter is packed with rich analyses and arguments, but rather as an encouragement to read further if some of the general remarks provoke curiosity.

1.3.1 THE DEMOGRAPHIC REGIMES OF EU REGIONS

Using population statistics for 1991 collated by the Statistical Offices of the European Communities (Eurostat 1994, Tables 1.2, 1.4), it is possible to produce very rough estimates of the components of change for a mixture of EU NUTS 1 and NUTS 2 regions (Figure 1.1). This figure characterizes the current regimes of population change in EU regions, showing that the different types can be found across a wide number of member states. The regimes identified are the eight categories formed by combining gains and losses for the three demographic components of natural change, net internal migration and net external migration.

Some caveats about the reliability of the classification are in order. The data are for only one year in time, and many situations identified may be very short run. The statistics are not complete and are not fully comparable. Some crude assumptions have been made simply to fill the whole map. For example, no comprehensive statistics were available in 1994 for migration to and from the eastern *Länder* of Germany (though the best estimates of the Federal Forecasting Agency are reported in Chapter 8). The internal migration estimates for France are based on the intercensal period 1982–90 rather than any annual period. All of the net external migration estimates are residuals produced by subtracting the net internal migration rate estimate from the net total migration rate (itself usually produced by subtracting natural increase from population change). Any statistical errors therefore accumulate in the net external migration estimate.

Because of these difficulties, only simple dichotomies of gain and loss in each component have been used to classify regional demographic regimes. Denmark, Ireland and Luxemburg have been treated as individual regions with gains and losses to other EU members treated as internal migration (using data from Chapters 7 and 12 and estimates from Rees, *et al.* 1992, Table 4).

Each of the eight classes formed by the logical division procedure has member regions. The two largest classes are regions with natural gains, net internal losses and net external gains (36 regions in regime C) and regions with gains in all components (33 regions in regime A). Between seven and 12 regions fall in each of the other regimes except for the class where all three components are negative (regime H), which has just two members.

No demographic regime is confined to one member state although regime G (natural loss, net internal loss and net external gain) is concentrated in Germany and regime E (natural loss, net internal gain and net external gain) in Italy. Even the most favoured growth regime (A) is found in nine out of 12 member states. Figure 1.1 thus makes the case for an integrated study of population development and migration trends across the European Union. The chapters in this book make a considerable start on such an endeavour.

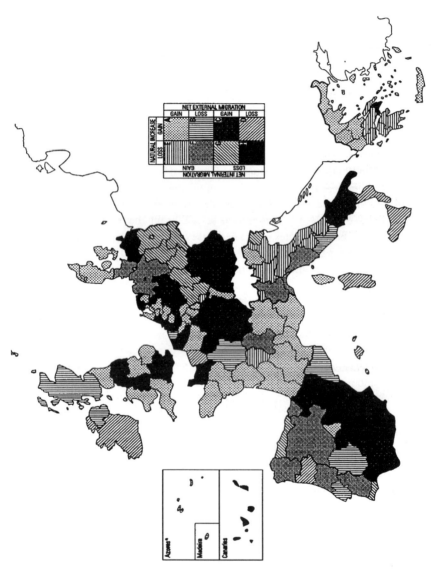

Figure 1.1 Demographic regimes in European Union regions, 1991

1.3.2 EXTRA-UNION MIGRATION

The potential for continuing migration into the EU from both the countries of Eastern Europe and from the developing world is revealed to be very considerable in the analyses of Chapters 2, 3 and 5. The policy response has been to restrict the right to immigrate into EU member states to fewer and fewer people. Fortress Europe has raised the drawbridge for asylum seekers, refugees and the poor. In all three chapters the authors argue for a more enlightened and humanitarian approach to the pressures for immigration into the EU.

1.3.3 INTER-EU MEMBER STATE MIGRATION

Chapter 4 provides an estimate of intermember state flows of about 600 000 a year. These migrants are free, by and large, to move in response to labour demands and career opportunities. The economic and administrative centre of the EU (the Brussels–Luxemburg–Strasbourg axis plus adjacent Dutch and German regions) will continue to attract migrants from the periphery, particularly the well educated. Former working-class migrants may return to peripheral regions as these regions develop, and peripheral regions with favourable environments may build up their attraction to retirement migrants.

1.3.4 INTERREGIONAL MIGRATION PATTERNS: NATIONAL PERSPECTIVES

In the national chapters, several common processes can be seen at work but at varying degrees dependent on the country being studied.

1.3.4.1 The importance of both a long-term and short-term time perspective

Migration trends are subject both to long-term shifts and to short-term fluctuations, and a time series perspective is essential in the study of regional migration patterns. A good example of long-term shifts is the secular decline in migration between the Flemish- and French-speaking areas of Belgium, reflecting the polarization of the two linguistic communities (Chapter 6). The importance of short-term variations in the conditions affecting migration are illustrated by the close ties between interregional migration level and housing/labour market cycle traced in both Belgium (Chapter 6) and in the United Kingdom (Chapter 16).

1.3.4.2 Major migration flows related to level of regional development

Migration responds to major disparities in economic development among regions consequent on structural differences, ongoing changes in activities and their differing attractiveness to mobile firms and new enterprises. The major migration streams from southern to northern Italy (Chapter 13), from northern to southern France (Chapter 11) and from eastern to western Germany (Chapter 8) are examples, though the economic circumstances in both sending and receiving regions are peculiar to the national situations. A fourth example is the continuing emigration stream from peripheral regions and countries such as Ireland towards the economic centre of the EU (Chapter 12).

1.3.4.3 The counterurbanization turnaround

The role of internal migration in redistributing population towards regions with lower population densities is examined in most national chapters. In some countries, such as the UK (Chapter 16), the migration process over the past two decades has been dominated by 'de-metropolitanization'—severe losses of migrants from all metropolitan areas to neighbouring or distant non-metropolitan regions. Counterurbanization is the dominant process in Belgium (Chapter 6), Denmark (Chapter 7) and the UK (Chapter 16) and significant in France (Chapter 11), Italy (Chapter 13) and Germany (Chapter 8). There is now strong evidence of its emergence in selected regions in Spain (Chapter 10) and signs of a start in Portugal (Chapter 15). In Denmark, on the other hand, it may have run its course (Chapter 7).

1.3.4.4 The role of external migration

The gains through external migration are a vital contribution to sustaining population growth in German regions (Chapter 8), in Dutch regions (Chapter 14) and for central Copenhagen (Chapter 7). Across Europe immigrants from outside the EU appear to replacing native out-migrants in the largest cities: this is a process particularly well developed in the London, Paris and Randstad regions.

1.3.4.5 Age effects

Where authors have examined migration patterns by age, there is a common finding (Chapters 6, 11 and 16) that the young (in the leaving home or starting career ages) are swimming against the general migration tide. They still move to the large metropolises, from which older cohorts are leaving, to take up the opportunities for higher education and entry-level jobs that are concentrated in such places. The Ile de France, for example, experienced massive migration losses in the 1982–90 period in all age groups except for those aged 20–9 (Table 11.1). At the other end of the age spectrum, several chapters examine the level and pattern of migration of the elderly. Compared with previous work, the importance of retirement age migration is reduced and that of migration after retirement ages enhanced. A privileged minority of retirees are able to cash in their housing chips in metropolitan areas and move to pleasanter, lower-density places, but a majority of the elderly face the life course changes (illness, infirmity, loss of a spouse, diminution of income) that trigger migration (Chapters 6, 16).

1.3.5 THE IMPACT OF MIGRATION ON POPULATION DEVELOPMENT

The book concludes with two reviews of topics across the EU. Chapter 17 looks at the policies that are in place both nationally and by agreement at EU level for regulating the flow of migrants both into and within the EU. Migration policies have always been crucial for long-term population development. The second review in Chapter 18 examines the methods and assumptions used to forecast EU regional populations, incorporating natural change and both external and internal migration components. A clear demonstration of the importance of intra-EU migration, both between member states and between regions, is provided through a comparison of scenarios with and without intra-EU migration components (Figure 18.2).

Both with respect to migration policy and to population forecasting practice, we (the chapter authors) are critical of the current position. A shift in policy towards the 'liberal' consensus of authors in the current volume is, in the short term, unlikely but perhaps some attention will be paid to the pleas, but the insights of the analyses reported in this book could well provide a vital ingredient in improving the methodology for forecasting the evolution of EU regional populations.

Part 1

INTERNATIONAL MIGRATION PATTERNS

2 Extra-Union Migration: The East–West Perspective

MAREK KUPISZEWSKI

Over the last decade all developed European countries have witnessed increasing migrational pressure on their boundaries. New migration streams emerged after the fall of communism in the former USSR and Eastern Europe. The aim of this chapter is therefore to discuss the contribution of former Soviet and Eastern European countries to the overall increase in migration inflow to Western Europe, in particular to European Union members. This cannot be done satisfactorily without a brief examination of the availability and quality of the data on international migration.

The terms 'Eastern Europe' or 'East' in this chapter will denote all European countries of the former Soviet bloc; the terms 'Western Europe' or 'West' will usually denote the European Union unless stated otherwise.

2.1 DATA AVAILABILITY AND QUALITY

In Europe the availability and quality of demographic data, despite all complaints, are usually very good. The only exception is data on international migration. There is a lack of an agreed definition of 'international migrant' and the practice of registration of migrants differs from country to country. Even within the European Union reports from receiving and sending countries may differ by a factor of 10 in a single year. For example, in 1988 Germany reported that 12 210 of its citizens migrated to France, but France acknowledged only 1 114 Germans (Poulain *et al.* 1991a). Table 2.1 shows that the situation is even worse when one tries to assess the magnitude of flows between countries of Eastern and Western Europe. As an example we may consider the data on migration from Eastern Europe to Germany, as reported by relevant national East European and German statistical offices, which differ in the extreme case of migration from Poland in 1990 by a factor of 32.

Apart from the lack of an international harmonization of definitions, these discrepancies between numbers of migrants reported by sending and receiving countries are due to the fact that all East European statistical offices counted in their official statistics only migrants who left legally (SOPEMI 1994). A condition for the registration of an international migration was that the migrant had received a

Population Migration in the European Union Edited by Philip Rees, John Stillwell, Andrew Convey and Marek Kupiszewski. © Editors and Contributors. Published 1996 John Wiley & Sons Ltd.

Table 2.1 Number of migrants to Germany reported by various statistical agencies,1987–90

According to respective East European Statistical Offices		
From	Hungary[b]	Czechoslovakia[c]
1987	6389	717
1988	4864	719
1989		1021
1990		
According to the German Statistisches Bundesamt[a,d]		
From	Hungary	Czechoslovakia
1987	8938	9101
1988	12 966	11 978
1989	15 372	17 130
1990	18 400	21 000

[a] to West Germany only
[b] all emigrants irrespective of destination, both legal and overstayers
[c] to East and West Germany
[d] including *Aussiedler*

Source: SOPEMI 1992

permit for the migration prior to leaving the country. As the process of getting a permanent emigration permit was protracted and often humiliating, a majority of emigrants preferred to apply for a tourist passport and not reveal their willingness to emigrate. This allowed them to keep their options open in case they were unsuccessful in settling in a foreign country. More details on this issue can be found in SOPEMI (1992) and Okólski (1991). Redei (1992) provides a description of the situation in Hungary; Kupiszewski (1993) describes the position in Poland.

Those who have chosen to cross boundaries on tourist passports and have tried to regularize their status in the country of destination have not appeared in the statistics of permanent emigrants. The data on these migrants have been captured only by the Ministries of Internal Affairs: In all East European countries, when crossing a state boundary, it was necessary to fill in a form with information on identification and on destination, itinerary and planned duration of stay abroad and to hand it over to a border guard. On return a similar form was required, and exit and return forms were matched and compared. It was therefore fairly simple to keep track of all citizens staying abroad and, in particular, those overstaying. Ministries of Internal Affairs kept these data but refused to publish them. Only recently did it become possible to use some data on boundary crossing and overstayers from Poland (see Kupiszewski 1993). Similar data have been released in the Commonwealth of Independent States (CIS) (Boubnova 1992).

These data may be misleading with respect to the destination of the migrants, as some destinations were perceived as 'better' in terms of chances of receiving a tourist passport than others and therefore were selected more frequently by applicants. It was often the case that a country of destination shown in the form was just a transitional country on the way to extra-European destinations (Fassman and Münz 1990).

In the second half of the 1980s and the beginning of the 1990s there were dramatic political and, consequently, legal changes in all former communist countries. In Poland and Hungary communist governments gradually increased the degree of freedom. In other countries, the bloodless revolution of 1989 brought radical changes. Currently all East Europeans are allowed to keep their passports at home and travel at will. As a consequence of democratization of political systems, existing forms of registration of transborder flows have been abandoned, but, like in Western Europe, no other systems of monitoring have been introduced.

Other potential sources of information on international migration are the statistical registers of the receiving countries. They are fairly exact, as large proportions of migrants who left their country on tourist passports tried either to get asylum or a work permit. However, these sources do not give any idea of the extent of clandestine and illegal migration and their comparability is limited, owing to the variety of definitions of 'migrant' and 'migration' adopted. Another problem with these data is that they are either not published or published as 'grey' publications. They are often highly aggregated, in varying tabulations and for various periods in time, which makes it difficult to use them. In general, however, they provide the most reliable information on international emigration from Eastern Europe, both during the communist era and at the present time.

In some countries limited data could be obtained from the national censuses of sending countries. Data on international migration were not available until the most recent censuses held in the late 1980s and early 1990s. It is possible, as Korcelli (1992a) for Poland, Redei (1992) for Hungary and Pavlik (1991) for the former Czechoslovakia have noted, to get a crude idea of the size of outflow, both legal and clandestine, by comparison of the results of the census with the results of the current registration. One cannot be sure, however, to what extent the differences are due to registration errors, census errors or international migration.

The data used in this chapter are no better than the data available world-wide: definitions of the various events are not always compatible and data are collected over varying periods of time. Therefore the comparisons must be conducted with caution.

2.2 THE EXISTING SITUATION

The last decade has witnessed a number of changes in the European migration scene. The most important one is quantitative: we have observed the increase in the volume of migration and in the stock of foreign population. For example, during the decade 1980–90 the latter increased in Denmark from 101 600 to 160 600; in Germany from 4 453 300 to 5 241 800 and in Italy from 298 700 to 781 100 (SOPEMI 1992).

There were also important geographical changes: the traditional emigration countries of Southern and Eastern Europe became both emigration and immigration countries (Salt 1991). For Eastern Europe this is a new phenomenon. In the past there were small contingents of labour immigrants from 'brother' countries, in particular in East Germany, the former Soviet Union and the then Czechoslovakia (Grzeszczak 1989). However, these workers were under strict police surveillance, enjoyed limited rights and in many cases lived in closed precincts. Another novelty is that Eastern Europe became a 'stop-over' for numerous illegal migrants from Africa and Asia.

The new wave of travellers and migrants is hard to control and difficult to manage. It consists of short-term travellers, illegal migrants, asylum seekers, regular labour migrants and long-term migrants who sometimes seek permanent stay permits in the host country and eventually apply for citizenship. Various categories of migration will be discussed below, giving the opportunity to present other aspects of the change in European migration.

2.2.1 ILLEGAL MIGRATION

Illegal migrants come predominantly from the former Soviet Union, Romania and Bulgaria, but Poland,[1] Albania[2] and the other countries of Eastern Europe also contribute their fair share. Recently illegal emigration from the former Yugoslavia increased rapidly (Okólski 1994). The ultimate target of the illegal emigrants, especially from the former Soviet Union, Romania and Bulgaria, are the countries of Western Europe, in particular Germany, but some East European countries are also quite desirable destinations.

From the point of view of Western Europe, it is important to note that even the more prosperous East European countries are severely impoverished and not attractive destinations in comparison with Western Europe. For many illegal migrants, these countries are in fact nothing more than stepping stones on the way to the West (SOPEMI 1994). Usually migrants try to get from the Czech Republic, Poland or Hungary to Germany and Austria, often with political asylum in mind. As they usually have little chance of obtaining visas, they try to cross the boundary illegally on a large scale. The boundary crossings are often organized by 'professional' guides, who persuade villagers from Romania to travel legally to Poland or the Czech Republic and then illegally to Germany where, according to them, everyone can obtain a well-paid job. These migrants often sell their homes in order to have some cash to start with and then end up homeless. Some idea of the magnitude of illegal migration is indicated by the following statistics: within the first nine months of 1992, Polish border guards along a 78-kilometre stretch of boundary with Germany intercepted 9178 persons (including 8133 Romanians and 395 Bulgarians) trying to cross the boundary illegally (Markiewicz 1992a) and during the whole of 1992 30 390 were arrested in connection with an attempt to cross boundaries illegally (Okólski 1994). The problem is aggravated by the fact that East European governments cannot afford the repatriation of illegals: those caught red-handed are registered, asked to go home and released. However, they do not return home; instead they try to get across the border again and again.

The Germans have tried to curb illegal inflow with spectacular and decisive action. *Gazeta Wyborcza* (1992) reports on the expulsion of only 244 out of 60 000

Romanians threatened with forced repatriation, but since 1992 the number of expelled Romanians (mainly Romanian Gypsies) has increased to some 30 000. Expulsion of some 60 000–100 000 Croats originally from 'safe' areas of Croatia is under way (*Migration News* 1994b) and deportation of some 60 000 Serbs, Montenegrians and Kosovo Albanians was put on hold only due to a protracted negotiations (*Migration News* 1994c). However, only the recent changes to Paragraph 16 on asylum law of the German Constitution, coupled with bilateral agreements being negotiated or signed with its neighbours on the repatriation of asylum seekers and illegal migrants to a 'safe country' from which they have arrived (all countries surrounding Germany are deemed to be safe) will make the 'German option' much less attractive. This policy has apparently been efficient: in the RFE/RL *Daily Report* of 20 July 1993 a sharp drop in the number of illegal border crossings from Poland (to 10 038 in the first half of 1993) is cited, but the discrepancy in the standard of living will remain an important factor attracting illegal migrants for years to come.

2.2.2 ASYLUM SEEKERS AND REFUGEES

The growth in the number of asylum seekers is one of the most important features in the changes to international migration patterns in the last decade. In Denmark, asylum seekers increased from 200 in 1980 to 4600 in 1991 and to 6121 in 1993, in Germany from 107 800 to 438 200 in 1992 (though these decreased in 1993 to 322 600) and in Italy from 3100 in 1983 to 28 000 in 1991 but this figure also decreased to 1075 in 1993 (SOPEMI 1992; Commission of the European Communities 1994). In the whole of Europe the number of applicants jumped from 67 000 in 1983 to over a half of a million in 1991 (Hovy 1992) but has decreased slightly in the last two years (Commission of the European Communities 1994). Simultaneously the share of asylum seekers in Europe originating from Eastern Europe has been growing. Until 1986, the percentage of applicants who were European stood below 27 per cent. From 1987, it has fluctuated to well over 30 per cent, in 1988 going as high as 39.6 per cent. In nine European Union countries: Belgium, France, Germany, Greece, Italy, the Netherlands, Portugal, Spain and the United Kingdom, these proportions were even higher (Hovy 1992). Since only a marginal proportion is from outside the former Soviet bloc, this means that the overall increase is due to the number of applicants from the Eastern European countries. Contrary to the recent general trend of decreasing numbers of asylum seekers in Europe (UNECE 1993a), the rise of applications from Eastern Europe is apparent. The increase was from 128 000 in 1989 to 175 000 in 1992 (Table 2.2). The latter data do not include applications from the former Yugoslavia and, as such, are much lower than in reality.

Before 1989, for political reasons, all asylum claims by citizens of communist Eastern Europe were almost routinely accepted in the West. The major sending country was Poland with the number of applicants growing regularly until 1988, at a moderately reduced rate in 1989 and then dropping rapidly in 1992 and 1993. A similar trend can be observed for Hungarian, Czech and Slovak asylum seekers.

18

Table 2.2 Asylum seekers from Eastern Europe lodging their applications, 1983–92

	Albania	Bulgaria	Czechoslovakia	Hungary	Poland	Romania	USSR	Yugoslavia	Other European
1983	551	323	4769	2166	5605	3211	133	931	1292
1984	384	408	5256	2232	10968	3528	96	984	144
1985	480	420	4860	3150	14 310	4500	150	2070	60
1986	287	451	4797	4141	20 910	7093	123	2788	369
1987	232	348	5104	6902	20 938	6670	10 092	7656	116
1988	182	546	4641	6006	44 317	10 647	546	24 024	182
1989	256	8064	7424	3456	33 920	47 232	1280	26 112	384
1990									
1991[a]	26 158	15 094	1873	646	5899	50 872	12 000		
1992[a]	8394	33 203	3109	1163	5979	111 346			

[a] Data for 1991 and 1992 refer to applications in European Community countries
Source: Hovy 1992; Commission of the European Communities 1994

There is no doubt that the political changes that occurred after 1989 in Poland, Hungary and the former Czechoslovakia will make it very difficult for anyone from these countries to claim the right to political asylum in future.

The decrease in the number of applications originating in Visehrad Group countries has been offset by the increase in applications from other former Soviet bloc countries. Since 1989 the most important sending country has been Romania (47 000 applications lodged in Europe in 1989, 111 000 in EC countries in 1992). The shares of Bulgaria and Albania (respectively 33 000 and 8000 applications lodged in EC countries in 1992; Table 2.2) have increased substantially, albeit from a much lower level. Despite the fact that in all these countries democratically elected governments are in place, it may be in some cases justified for other countries to grant asylum to members of some national groups (such as Hungarians and Gypsies from Romania, Turks from Bulgaria or Greeks from Albania), or to political dissidents. The willingness to apply for asylum may be enhanced by the appalling economic situation, which constitutes a major push factor.

The successor states of the former Soviet Union are also a major source of asylum seekers and refugees. At present they are confined to the territory of the Commonwealth of Independent States, in particular to Russia (Öberg and Boubnova 1993), and are beyond the scope of this chapter.

Between 1983 and 1990 the main destination for the East European asylum seekers was Germany (around 175 000 applications) and the second largest destination was Austria (65 000). Large numbers (over 20 000) of applicants also chose Hungary, Italy, the former Yugoslavia and Sweden (Hovy 1992). It is symptomatic that former communist countries almost exclusively attracted applicants from their geopolitical region of Europe. Virtually all applications lodged in Hungary came from Eastern Europe, in particular from the former Yugoslavia, though most recently there are reports of growing numbers of Chinese asylum seekers applying there (Redei 1992). Among West European countries Austria (84.9 per cent), Italy (70.2 per cent) and Germany (35.2 per cent) had the highest proportions of European applicants among their asylum seekers.

According to UNECE (1993a), the war in the former Yugoslavia caused five million refugees and displaced persons to seek safe shelter (data as of October 1993). They came mainly from Bosnia-Herzegovina and Croatia. UNHCR offered assistance to 4.3 million, mainly in Bosnia-Herzegovina (UNHCR 1993), and around 0.7 million fled to other countries (UNECE 1993a). The vast majority sought to settle in Germany, which took 244 000 by March 1993, although not all applied for asylum. Other countries accepting refugees from the former Yugoslavia are in order of numerical importance: Switzerland (87 000), Sweden (70 000), Austria (65 000), the United Kingdom (47 000) and Hungary (29 000) (UNECE 1993b). Apart from Germany and the United Kingdom, the countries of the European Union have shown little interest in admitting Yugoslav refugees. Many Yugoslavs do not meet the definition of asylum seeker as set out in the 1951 Geneva Convention, but they are war refugees and displaced persons. This makes their situation particularly difficult from a legal point of view. Rapid outflow from former Yugoslavia has been a phenomenon of the last three years and has already generated the largest wave of refugees in Europe since World War II.

It is clear that with the progress in the creation of democratic systems to replace mono-party communist rule and with the strengthening of healthy market economies Eastern Europe will cease to produce asylum seekers. The problem is that currently only three countries, the Czech Republic, Hungary and Poland, have made some economic progress, but even they still have a very long way to go. Virtually all other East European countries, and above all, the successor states of Soviet Union, are in a desperate economic situation and in years to come will remain important sources of applicants for asylum.

On the other hand decisive changes in asylum policies have occurred in European Union countries over the last three years. The most important are: signing the Dublin convention; harmonizing asylum laws and expulsion policies (Commission of the European Communities 1994, SOPEMI 1994); the introduction on 1 July 1993 of the Germans' new Asylum Law, which uses a concept of 'safe countries' from which no asylum applications may be accepted (SOPEMI 1994); the negotiation of bilateral agreements on readmission between Germany and Poland (1993), the Czech Republic (1993) and Romania (1992) (SOPEMI 1994) with more negotiations under way; increasing the number of staff dealing with asylum requests; and reducing the access of asylum seekers to the labour market during the period while their applications are being processed (France) (SOPEMI 1994). France reported that the voluntary repatriation scheme introduced in 1991, aimed at helping unsuccessful asylum seekers to return home, was failing (SOPEMI 1992). All these measures have reduced the number of unsuccessful applications and speeded up the process of expulsion of those abusing the system. The results of these measures will be more visible in the years to come as potential asylum seekers gain more knowledge about the new, more restrictive regulations.

2.2.3 LABOUR AND LONG-TERM MIGRATION

Long-term labour migrants form another significant category of population moving to Western countries and to certain countries of Eastern Europe. Since the mid-1980s Europe has experienced a general increase in the volume of long-term migration. This has mainly been due to family reunions, as the stocks of foreign labour have been relatively stable (Salt 1991). It is likely that a part of the official labour migration has been replaced by a clandestine inflow, but it is very difficult to substantiate such speculation.

These general trends are similar to those observed in the inflow from the East, with the main difference being that since the late 1980s a very rapid increase in migration from the former communist bloc has been observed. Okólski (1991) provides some evidence of the increasing official outflow from Poland, Romania and Hungary, although the last country does not have any great importance as a source of migrants. There were also some sporadic brief waves, as with the emigration of some 352 000 Turks and Pomaks from Bulgaria to Turkey during 1990, of whom

138 000 returned to Bulgaria (SOPEMI 1991); Vasileva (1992) cites 369 839 emigrants with 159 937 returning before 10 September 1990. These differences in the data are probably due to the different periods of time for which the statistics were assembled.

Vishnevsky and Zayonchkovskaya (1992) quote Goscomstat data on net international migration in the former Soviet Union for the period from 1961 to 1990. Until 1970, net migration was positive but later showed constant negative values. Record losses of 203 700 were noted in 1989, but these more than doubled (to 412 700) in 1990. The vast majority of these migrants aimed to go to Israel (187 000 in 1990), (Holt 1991) and then to Western Europe and North America. However, those East European countries which are more successful in the process of economic transition, such as Hungary, Poland and the Czech Republic, also received their share.

After the dissolution of the former Soviet Union this sort of data was no longer available. However, the Russian Federation noted a substantial positive balance of migration (plus 268 000), (UNECE 1993a) in the first half of 1993 due exclusively to inflow from the non-Russian territories of the former Soviet Union. Russia still reports losses to Germany and Israel, though these are lower than in previous years (UNECE 1993a).

In the West the traditional destinations for long-term and labour migrants from Eastern Europe have remained unchanged for decades. The primary targets are Germany and Austria and then Italy, France and the Nordic countries. The USA and Canada remain important as traditional destinations, especially for Poles and Ukrainians who have a long history of resettlement and have well-established communities in these countries.

The most important destination is Germany. SOPEMI (1992) reports that German net migration gains from Eastern Europe doubled each year between 1986 and 1989, rising from 63 100 to 460 600, before stabilizing below half a million a year. According to the Statistisches Bundesamt (1991) the inflow to Germany in 1989 was 1 112 000 migrants, consisting of 377 000 migrants who claimed to be ethnic Germans (*Aussiedler*),[3] 250 000 legally migrating foreigners, 121 000 asylum seekers and 344 000 migrants from East Germany (*Ubersiedler*),[4] who until the unification of Germany in 1990 counted as international migrants (Kemper 1993, after Sommer and Fleischer 1991).

Aussiedler form the largest group of immigrants to Germany. Between 1985 and 1993[5] there were 1 788 000 of them, originating predominantly from Poland (37 per cent), the former Soviet Union (48 per cent) and Romania (13 per cent) (Table 2.3). The number of *Aussiedler* from Poland peaked in 1989, reaching over a quarter of a million. Since then, there has been a sharp decrease in the inflow from Poland (40 129 in 1991 and only 5228 in 1993), but this was partially offset by a rapid increase in the number of *Aussiedler* from the former Soviet Union and Romania (Statistisches Bundesamt 1991 and 1992; Bundesverwaltungsamt 1993, 1994). The inflow from the former Soviet Union increased from 8222 in 1985 to 195 567 in 1992. Over the last two years of the period this inflow accounted for 85 and 94 per

Table 2.3 Migration of *Aussiedler* into West Germany, 1985–91

Country of origin	1985	1986	1987	1988	1989	1990	1991	1992[a]	1993[b]
Poland	22 075	27 188	48 419	140 226	250 340	113 253	40 129	17 742	5228
Former USSR	8222	10 052	19 815	47 572	98 134	147 455	147 320	195 576	181 167
Bulgaria	7	5	12	9	46	27	12		
Former Yugoslavia	191	182	156	223	11 496	530	450	199	
Romania	14 924	13 130	13 990	12 902	23 387	107 189	32 187	16 146	5190
Former Czechoslovakia	757	882	835	949	2027	1324	92,	460	
Hungary	485	584	579	763	1618	1038	925	354	
Other countries	69	64	44	29	34	11	27	199	260
Total	46 730	52 087	83 850	202 673	387 082	370 827	221 977	230 565	191 845

[a] For 1992 Bulgaria is included in 'Other countries'
[b] All countries for which data is not given are included in 'Other countries'; data for the period from January till November 1993

Source: Statistisches Bundesamt 1991, 1992; Bundesverwaltungsamt 1993, 1994

cent respectively of the total inflow of *Aussiedler* and virtually dominated the scene. It is in fact the only source from which we have not observed a marked decrease in the number of immigrants in 1992 and 1993. Inflows from other countries approximately halved in 1992 in comparison to 1991 and reduced even further in 1993.

It is clear that an important prerequisite for this massive inflow of migrants is the German constitutional law (Article 116 of the German Constitution), which grants German citizenship to anyone who is able to prove German origin. In Poland, the former Soviet Union and Romania there exist substantial groups who can do so. These people are quite keen to resettle in Germany, some due to their feeling that they belong to the German nation, others clearly because their countries are in a disadvantageous economic situation. Many of them do not speak any German (Kemper 1993) and have no link whatsoever with German culture. The German Ministry of Labour has taken on the expensive task of converting them into real Germans. Given the differences in culture and mentality between Eastern Europe and Germany, this is no doubt a job for generations to come (Hessenberger 1994).

The policy of granting instant citizenship to *Aussiedler* is in sharp contrast to the policy of no naturalization for second- or even third-generation non-German migrants, who were born and brought up in Germany and who, linguistically and often to large extent culturally, are German.

A new and important development on the migration scene has been the revival of guestworker arrangements between some countries of the European Union and Eastern Europe. Germany is in the forefront of these changes and has introduced the following new regulations (Schütte 1994).

2.2.3.1 Contracts for services

This is when a company in Eastern Europe may second its employees for a period of between 12 and 24 months to do specific work in Germany. These contracts are not limited by the situation in the German labour market, but the number of employees is limited by quotas. Agreements have been signed with Poland, Hungary, Bulgaria, Romania, the Czech and Slovak Republics, Slovenia and Croatia. Agreement with Yugoslavia is suspended due to the UN embargo. Currently quotas are for 73 590 workers: 31 710 allocated to Poland, 13 220 to Hungary, 6360 to Romania, 5260 to Croatia with the rest distributed among other countries of the region.

2.2.3.2 Traineeships

These allow employment of 18- to 40-year-old East Europeans in Germany for a period of between 12 to 18 months with the aim of developing transferable skills. Hungary, Poland, the Czech and Slovak Republics, Albania, Bulgaria, Lithuania, Latvia, Romania and Russia are eligible. However, the scale of this employment is limited: in 1992 there were 5057 trainees from all these countries.

2.2.3.3 Seasonal workers

These can be employed for a period of between three and 12 months in specific sectors of the economy (currently limited to hotels, restaurants, agriculture including the food-processing industry and saw mills). At the moment agreements are in place with Poland, the Czech and Slovak Republics, Romania and Hungary. In 1992 there were 212 000 seasonal workers from these countries.

2.2.3.4 Cross-boundary commuters

Workers from specific areas along the boundaries with Poland and the Czech Republic are allowed to work in Germany on the condition they either return home daily or do not spend more than two consecutive days in Germany.

France and Belgium have made a step in the same direction by signing similar agreements, but their scope is very limited. For example, the French–Polish agreement allowed 8210 seasonal workers and 100 on-the-job trainees to work in France in 1991 and 1992. Over the same period of time Belgium allowed 50 on-the-job trainees (Okólski 1994).

All the changes discussed above have resulted over the last decade in some changes in the numbers of East European population in European Union countries. Table 2.4 demonstrates that, apart from Germany, sizeable East European populations exist in the United Kingdom, France, Italy and also in Sweden and Austria. In Spain and Germany, for which more detailed data are available, the increase in numbers of East Europeans, especially Poles and Romanians, has been prominent. In Germany the East European population has grown much faster than all other foreigners. It seems that the East European population has also increased in Denmark, Greece and Italy, although the data available are quite fragmented. The only country which has actually experienced a reduction in its East European population is France. It is, however, very difficult to make any comparisons between countries due to the different definitions of 'foreign population' adopted across Europe.

2.3 THE FUTURE OF EAST–WEST EUROPEAN MIGRATION

Some factors influencing international migration are predictable only to a limited extent. One can mention here the political situation and closely linked with it, ethnic and religious relations, economic development, demographic imbalances and finally migration policy development. This section of the chapter offers an analysis of these factors and their possible impact on changes in international migration between East and West Europe. An assessment of the feasibility of a more formal numerical forecasting is made at the end.

2.3.1 ETHNICITY, NATIONALISM AND WARS

2.3.1.1 Nationalism and the impact of the ethnic composition of populations on international mobility

Nationalism of all kinds has turned out to be a major factor causing unrest, disturbances, riots and even wars in postcommunist Europe. Nationalism has an enormous impact on migration, constituting a very powerful push factor. The degree of national homogeneity prejudges, to some extent, the probability of frictions

Table 2.4 The changes in the East European population living in EU countries in the 1980s

Country	Belgium	Denmark	France	Germany	Greece	Italy	Luxembourg	Netherlands	Portugal	Spain	UK
As close as possible to 1980											
Albania				4100[e]							
Bulgaria											
Czechoslovakia	600[s]										
Hungary		970[j]		26 900[e]						61[n]	
Poland	7600[s]		64 800[h]	21 100[e]				3184[i]		115[n]	
Romania				87 600[e]						53[n]	
Former Yugoslavia	5900[i]	7300[k]	62 500[h]	12 300[e]	460[o]			14 100[z]		88[n]	
Former USSR				6500[e]		5000[t]				59[n]	
Total (E. Europe and former USSR)											53 000[b]
As close as possible to 1990											
Albania			800[u]	11 400[d]							
Bulgaria	500[t]		2000[u]	46 700[t]		27 000[v]					
Czecho-Slovakia	700[t]		2900[u]	35 100[d]							
Hungary	4800[t]									188[m]	
Poland		47 000[u]	46 300[g]	241 300[d]		16 996[a]				613[m]	
Romania			5700[u]	53 100[d]		7500[u]				779[m]	
Former Yugoslavia	5800[a]		51 700[g]	652 500[f]	1892[p]	29 800[u]	1500[c]	13 500[a]		416[m]	
Former USSR	900[t]	10 000[u]	4300[u]	8100[u]						402[m]	
Total (E. Europe and former USSR)											57 000[a]

The sources from which data for this table have been assembled vary enormously as the statistics of international migration vary from country to country. It was impossible to acquire data for a uniform period of time. Therefore the direct comparison of the data provided across various countries should be made with caution.

Sources:
a SOPEMI 1992, data for 1990
b SOPEMI 1992, data for 1984
c SOPEMI 1992, data for 1985
d SOPEMI 1992, data as on 30 September 1990
e SOPEMI 1992, data as on 30 September 1983
f SOPEMI 1992, data for 1987
g SOPEMI 1992, according to the Census held on 6 March 1990
h SOPEMI 1992, according to the Census held on 4 March 1982

i SOPEMI 1992, data for 1990
j Stpiczynski 1992, data for 1980
k SOPEMI 1994, data for 1982
l Baldwin-Edwards (1991), data for 1988
m Instituto Nacional de Estadística, 1992, data for 1990
n Instituto Nacional de Estadística, 1992, data for 1981
o National Statistical Service of Greece 1990, data for 1987
p National Statistical Service of Greece 1991, data for 1989

q Okólski 1991, data for 1981
r Okólski 1991, data for 1990
t SOPEMI 1994, data for 1991
u SOPEMI 1994, data for 1990
v SOPEMI 1994, data for 1990
x SOPEMI 1994, data for 1991
z SOPEMI 1992, data for 1980
z SOPEMI 1992, data for 1980

between the national groups inhabiting a particular country. However, historical resentments are equally important. Table 2.5 shows the five largest national groups in republics of the former Soviet Union and in the states of Eastern, Central and South Eastern Europe (for the sake of brevity collectively referred to as Eastern Europe). It is clear that the countries of Central–Eastern Europe are not experiencing serious problems at the moment, either because they are very homogeneous (as in the case of Poland or Hungary) or they are able to settle existing conflicts peacefully, as the Czechs and Slovaks have done so far. Despite a sizeable and allegedly badly treated Hungarian minority in Slovakia, no substantial emigration from this area has occurred. It is likely that this lack of a tradition of out-migration will hold down emigration levels in future. It is, however, possible that a limited outflow of Slovak Hungarians to Hungary and probably to the West may occur.

A much more explosive situation exists in the Balkan peninsula and in Romania. Before the present civil war started, the share of the largest group (the Muslims) in Bosnia-Herzegovina was as low as 44 per cent (Table 2.5). Other former Yugoslav republics had lesser percentages but still had large numerical minorities. Albania, Bulgaria and Romania, with the shares of Albanians, Bulgarians and Romanians respectively being between 90 and 85 per cent, are more homogeneous (Table 2.5).

The register of existing or potential national conflicts in these two regions is very long. In the former Yugoslavia, apart from war torn Bosnia-Herzegovina and to lesser extent Croatia and Serbia, there are at least three areas of potential friction: Macedonia, which is in dispute with Greece over its name and has unresolved conflicts with Greece and Bulgaria; Voivodina, where only half of the population is Serb and 18.9 per cent is Hungarian[6]; finally Kosovo, where war between suppressed Albanians (over 77 per cent of Kosovo's population during the last Census in 1981[7] and increasing extremely quickly) and Serbs seems to be imminent. Albania, the poorest country in Europe, might easily be dragged into this conflict which would make the Yugoslav war international. If these potential conflicts turn into reality they will trigger large waves of refugees, perhaps hundreds of thousands or even millions of persons. The geographical location of Kosovo and Macedonia, combined with the existing conflict in Bosnia, will probably protect Western Europe from additional refugee migrants for a while. But nothing will protect Greece, Albania and Bulgaria, which are all ill-prepared to give shelter to a large number of new migrants.

By Balkan standards, Albania is a fairly homogeneous country—made up of 90 per cent Albanians and only 8 per cent Greeks, the second largest nationality. But this minority is another potential source of unrest, as it is backed by the government of Greece, which has laid claim to part of Northern Epirus, and by the Greek Orthodox Church. Potential emigration of Albanian Greeks will be, no doubt, directed to Greece as there exist ethnic links and a network of immigrants who arrived over the last couple of years.

Romania, which has been much more stable than countries in the Balkan Peninsula, has her own troubles, as a result of the presence of the Hungarian minority in Transylvania. This conflict has deep historical roots and is being aggravated

Table 2.5 Nationalities ranked by percentage shares of total populations

Area	Total pop. ('000s)	First nationality	(%)	Second nationality	(%)	Third nationality	(%)	Fourth nationality	(%)	Fifth nationality	(%)	Cum.% of top 5
Former USSR	285 743	Russian	50.8	Ukrainian	15.5	Uzbek	5.8	Belorussian	3.5	Kazakh	2.8	78.5
Russia	147 022	Russian	81.5	Tatar	3.8	Ukrainian	3.0	Chuvash	1.2	Dagestanian	1.2	90.6
Ukraine	51 452	Ukrainian	72.7	Russian	22.1	Jewish	0.9	Belorussian	0.9	Moldavian	0.6	97.2
Belorussia	10 152	Belorussian	77.9	Russian	13.2	Polish	4.1	Ukrainian	2.9	Jewish	1.1	99.2
Moldova	4335	Moldavian	64.5	Ukrainian	13.8	Russian	13.0	Jewish	1.5	Belorussian	0.5	93.2
Lithuania	3675	Lithuanian	79.6	Russian	9.4	Polish	7.0	Belorussian	1.7	Ukrainian	1.2	98.9
Latvia	2667	Latvian	52.0	Russian	34.0	Belorussian	4.5	Ukrainian	3.5	Polish	2.3	96.2
Estonia	1566	Estonian	61.5	Russian	30.3	Ukrainian	3.1	Belorussian	1.8	Jewish	0.3	97.0
Georgia	5401	Georgian	70.1	Armenian	8.1	Russian	6.3	Azerbaydzhanian	5.7	Ossetian	3.0	93.3
Azerbaydzhan	7021	Azerbaydzhanian	82.7	Russian	5.6	Armenian	5.6	Dagestanian	3.3	Kabardinian	0.6	97.7
Armenia	3305	Armenian	93.3	Azerbaydzhanian	2.6	Russian	1.6	Ukrainian	0.3			
Kazakhstan	16 464	Kazakh	39.7	Russian	37.8	German	5.8	Ukrainian	5.4	Uzbek	2.0	90.8
Uzbekistan	19 810	Uzbek	71.4	Russian	8.3	Tadzhik	4.7	Kazakh	4.1	Tatar	2.4	90.9
Kirghizstan	4258	Kirgiz	52.4	Russian	21.5	Uzbek	12.9	Ukrainian	2.5	German	2.4	91.7
Tadzhikistan	5093	Tadzhik	62.3	Uzbek	23.5	Russian	7.6	Tatar	1.4	Kirgiz	1.3	96.1
Turkmenistan	3523	Turkmen	72.0	Russian	9.5	Uzbek	9.0	Kazakh	2.5	Tatar	1.1	94.1
Slovenia	1963	Slovenian	91.0	Croat	3.0	Serb	2.0	Muslim	1.0			
Croatia	4784	Croat	78.0	Serb	12.0	Muslim	0.9	Hungarian	0.5			
Serbia & Montenegro	10 642	Serb	63.0	Albanian	14.0	Montenegrin	6.0	Hungarian	4.0			
Bosnia-Herzegovina	4364	Muslim	44.0	Serb	33.0	Croat	17.0					
Macedonia	2174	Macedonian	67.0	Albanian	20.0	Turk	4.0	Serb	2.0			
Albania	3285	Albanian	90.0	Greek	8.0							
Bulgaria	8869	Bulgarian	85.3	Turkish	8.5	Gypsy	2.6	Macedonian	2.5	Armenian	0.3	99.2
Hungary	10 333	Hungarian	96.6	German	1.6	Slovak	1.1	Romanian	0.2			
Romania	23 170	Romanian	89.1	Hungarian	8.9	German	0.4					
Czechoslovakia	15 725	Czech	62.9	Slovak	31.8	Hungarian	3.8	Polish	0.5	German	0.3	99.3
Poland	38 386	Polish	97.6	German	1.3	Ukrainian	0.6	Belorussian	0.5			

Sources: First Book of Demographics (1992); *The CIA World Factbook* (NISS Wide Area Information Server, 1993)

by Romanian nationalists. It has already contributed to the inflow of Romanian Hungarians to Hungary (Szoke 1992) and will, no doubt, continue to do so in future.

Gypsies, who are particularly numerous in Romania, Hungary, Bulgaria and Slovakia, constitute a separate problem. Their presence does not cause any direct large-scale problem, but they are disliked by local communities and tend to flee *en masse* to the West (Barany 1992). Given the traditional mobility of Gypsies and the fairly strong incentives to move, it will be difficult to discourage potential migrants. However, there are signs that some governments are prepared to take tough measures against this group, as recent expulsions of Romanian Gypsies from Germany show.

An extremely explosive situation exists in the former Soviet Union, with around a half a dozen local conflicts heating up the political atmosphere. These conflicts have already generated substantial streams of refugees. Öberg and Boubnova (1993) estimate that there are 600 000 refugees in the CIS. If the conflicts are globalized, we may have to deal with an unmanageable tidal wave instead of a stream of people. In 1991, Poland worked out plans for the reception of some six million refugees from the former Soviet Union, in what turned out to be a futile exercise. In fact Segbers (1991), quoting forecasts from two to 25 million emigrants from the former Soviet Union, calls them all 'best guesses' not based on any firm evidence.

In nine out of the 14 former republics, Russians are the second largest nationality, with a share as high as 22.1 per cent in populous Ukraine and well over 30 per cent in Estonia, Latvia and Kazakhstan (Table 2.5). They are the third largest group in Moldova, Armenia, Tadzhikistan and Georgia. Altogether, the Russians living in non-Russian republics number 25 million plus some eight million living in autonomous regions of the former Russian republic. The collapse of the Soviet empire has dramatically changed the situation of Russians in the non-Russian republics, now successor states of the Soviet Union. From being a better educated and politically privileged nationality with an access to the best jobs and cultural and educational amenities, they have been turned into unwanted foreigners against whom on some occasions an armed hand has been raised, as in the case of Moldova.

In the Baltic states, efforts are being made by the governments to limit the political rights of the Russians, but not so as to cause any decisive response from the Russian state (Brubaker 1992). In the former Central Asiatic republics national differences are aggravated by religious differences. These will remain so with the growth of influence of militant Moslems. The growing conflict in Tadzhikistan is a good example. The fact that, in general, the Russians do not speak local languages (*Post-Soviet Geography* 1993) does not help them to gain acceptance by the locals. Also the collapse of some branches of industry, such as the coal industry in the Ukraine, which is dominated by Russian labour, may put certain large Russian communities under threat.

For the Russians, one possible response to this situation is to emigrate. Due to the division of labour along national lines massive emigration of the Russian population would be an economic catastrophe for many successor states. But step-by-step replacement of Russian specialists is feasible. A slow stream of outflow of Russians from non-Russian republics started more than a decade ago (Vishnevsky and Zayonchkovskaya 1992), and the outflow from the successor states has accelerated recently. For example the Russian population in Tibilisi reduced due to migration by 18.3 per cent over four years (1989–93) (Gachechiladze and Bradshaw 1994).

The natural destination for these migrants will be Russia. But Russia already has serious problems with the dislocation of troops withdrawn from Eastern Europe and the prospect for any economic assistance to those Russians returning will be bleak. They may also be perceived as strangers or even foreigners in Russia. It is clear that they will try to find their way to the West—initially to Poland and Hungary and then to Western Europe. Available reports (Kuba Kozlowski 1994; Redei 1992) suggest that the process has already started but has not yet gained momentum.

The representatives of other nations in the former Soviet Union show varying propensities to migrate. They often adopt a 'stepping stones' strategy, moving first to a Central European country with the intention to moving on to the West (SOPEMI 1994, Kuba Kozlowski 1994). The most determined of these transit migrants may arrive in Western Europe fairly soon, but there is no sign that their number will be very high. Central European countries try to create their own protective systems with a limited degree of success. Hungary and Poland have recently held major international conferences focused on this issue. The phenomenon has been discussed in length in a series of papers which appeared in issues 23, 24 and 25 of volume 3 of *RFE/RL Research Reports.*

2.3.1.2 Return to the country of origin

Another wave of ethnic migration is emigration of those who identified themselves as nationals of one of the states outside the former Soviet empire, which has been in place for a relatively long time, but has only recently gained momentum. According to the 1989 Census of Population in the former Soviet Union, there were 2 038 000 Germans, 1 126 000 Poles, 374 000 Bulgarians, 358 000 Greeks, 171 000 Hungarians and 47 000 Finns (after Chesnais 1993). A reliable count of minorities is difficult to achieve (Liebich 1992). Numbers given by the Census are usually lower than those given by national organizations or interested third countries. For example, Korcelli (1992b) refers to Polish estimates of somewhere between two and three million Poles in the former USSR; Gasior (1990) speaks of two to four million.

Only Greece and Germany have received a substantial number of this category of migrants. Greece took almost 20 000 Pontic Greeks during the 18 months starting on 1 January 1990 (SOPEMI 1992) and an unknown number of emigrants from Albania who are encouraged by the Greek government to return home (SOPEMI 1994).

The importance of the migration of 'Germans' living in Eastern Europe to Germany has been emphasized earlier in the chapter. Here the future of that migration stream is assessed. Öberg and Boubnova (1993) say that 52 per cent of

Soviet Germans do not use German as their native language and it is unlikely that this group is perceived as German in Germany. The German government, already in political trouble because of immigration, would like to reduce the inflow as much as possible. Various projects to create German enclaves in the CIS have been put forward, but they all are costly and some, such as the creation of a German zone in the Kaliningrad area, are politically unacceptable. An attempt to recreate German settlement in Ulyanovsk on the Volga river cost Russia 48.6 million roubles (between 1990 and 1992) and 9000 hectares of land, while Germany contributed in kind constructing a school, bakery and factory for cheese production. As a result 1535 Germans from Kazakhstan, Kirghizstan, Ukraine and Siberia moved there rather than to Germany (Markiewicz 1993), which is as little as 1.05 per cent of those who settled in Germany in 1991. A similar scheme has been launched by the Ukrainian government (*The Economist* 29 August 1992). The combined efforts of the Ukrainian, Russian and German governments to create better conditions for resettlement within the CIS have not been particularly successful. However, they are extremely important, as they pave the way for limiting migration in the future.

2.3.1.3 Existing diaspora and chain migration

The existence of a large diaspora of nationals abroad can also facilitate and stimulate chain migration. It is enough to say that approximately 12 million Poles and their descendants live outside Poland (Stpiczynski 1992), mainly in Germany, Austria, France, Italy and the United Kingdom and outside Europe in North America. Czech and Slovak communities exist in Germany, France, Austria and Switzerland (Van de Kaa 1993). Although there are between two and 3.5 million (*Rzeczpospolita* 1992) Hungarians outside Hungary, emigration does not have much appeal to Hungarians in Hungary (Dövenyi 1992). On the contrary, it is likely that there will be a sizeable migration to Hungary. Among the nations of the former Soviet Union, large groups of Ukrainians and Armenians are located all over the world and this may be an important stimulus to migration.

Summarizing, it seems that the emigration of ethnic minorities will continue in the future for at least two reasons. First, there still exists a huge German population as discussed above, especially in the former Soviet Union but also in other countries, which is willing to emigrate. The second reason is the swelling of ethnic emigration by friendship and kinship links. The experience shown with emigration of Germans from Poland shows clearly that, paradoxically, in the late 1980s, the more Germans emigrated from Poland, the larger the emigration stream became, although in the long term the process is probably self-limiting, as the data for the early nineties show (see Table 2.3).

2.3.2 ECONOMIC DISCREPANCIES – A MAIN PUSH FACTOR

2.3.2.1 Wealth does matter

It is widely agreed that international migration is very sensitive to economic

Table 2.6 General economic characteristics of East European and European Union countries

Country	GDP per capita 1991[f]	Real GDP per capita 1989[g]	Life expectancy at birth 1991[f]	Human Development Index 1990[c]	Maternal mortality rate (per 100 000 live births) 1990[c]	Unemployment rate 1992
Albania	800[b]		72.2[c]	0.791	100	
Bulgaria	1840		72	0.865	40	16.0[d]
Former Czechoslovakia	2470		72	0.897	14	
Czech Republic						3.2[d]
Slovak Republic						12.1[d]
Hungary	2720	6245	70	0.893	21	11.6[d]
Poland	1790	4770	71	0.874	15	13.3[d]
Romania	1390		70	0.733	210	5.5[d]
Former Yugoslavia	3060[a]	5095	73	0.857	11	
Former USSR	3518[a]		70.6[c]	0.873	45	
Belgium	18 950	13 313	76	0.950	4	10.3[e]
Denmark	23 700	13 751	75	0.953	4	11.1[e]
France	20 380	17 164	77	0.969	13	10.2[e]
Germany	23 650	14 507	76	0.955	8	7.7[e]
Greece	6340		77	0.901	7	9.2[e]
Ireland	11 120	7481	75	0.921	3	17.2[e]
Italy	18 520	13 608	77	0.922	6	10.7[e]
Luxembourg	24 980[c]	16 537	74.9[c]	0.929	2	1.5[e]
Netherlands	18 780	13 351	77	0.968	14	6.8[a]
Spain	12 450	8723	77	0.916	7	22.5[e]
United Kingdom	16 550	14 610	75	0.962	11	10.1[a]
Portugal	5930	6259	74	0.850	14	4.0[e]
Eastern Europe and USSR	2469[c]		71.0[c]		48	
European Community	15 495[c]	12 860	75.9[c]		11	10.1[e]

Sources: [a] World Bank 1992, data for 1990
[b] *Geographical Digest 1992–93,* 1992; data for 1989
[c] UNDP 1992, data for 1990
[d] Boeri 1994
[e] OECD 1993
[f] World Bank 1993
[g] UNDP 1992

incentives (Greenwood and McDowell 1992). The disparities in the standards of living between Eastern and Western Europe are quite substantial (see Table 2.6). The per capita GDP of the better off East European countries is comparable to that of Portugal, but the gap between the richest EU member state and the poorest Eastern European country is enormous. Luxembourg has 46 times the per capita income of Albania. The majority of Western countries have a per capita GDP between three and 15 times higher than in Eastern Europe. Life expectancy at birth is 4.9 years longer in the West, and the maternal mortality rate is more than four times lower. Okólski (1991) shows that similar discrepancies exist in housing conditions and in the work time required to purchase consumer goods. Differences in the salaries and wage levels (Rhode 1993) also contribute strongly to the differences in wealth on the both sides of the former Iron Curtain. The level of out-migration will undoubtedly be influenced by the rate of development of the East European economies in the near future. It is beyond the scope of this chapter to provide economic predictions. *The Economist*'s surveys of Eastern Europe and Russia (*The Economist* 13 March 1993 and 5 December 1992 respectively) give very positive accounts of changes and propose a fairly optimistic outlook for Hungary, Poland and the former Czechoslovakia, though a rather less encouraging picture of other countries' performance and prospects is painted. Already there is some evidence of the influence of the economy on migration behaviour: Hryniewicz, *et al.* (1992) have shown that, since the introduction of a market economy in Poland, the international brain drain from research institutions and universities has been replaced by an internal brain drain, in which research and teaching staff have taken lucrative jobs in the commercial sector. The bottom line is, however, that as long as the disparities in standards of living are as huge as we observe at present, the flow of migrants is inevitable.

2.3.2.2 Unemployment at the source and job opportunities at the destination

Table 2.6 shows that unemployment levels in the East and West are similar. However, it must be stressed that in Eastern Europe, where for the 50 years before the fall of communism unemployment had been virtually non-existent, this phenomenon is very shocking. For the well-being of families it is much more dangerous than in the West, as in the East many employed live on the brink of poverty and do not have any resources which could allow for their survival in bad times. One should also bear in mind that unemployment is, as with migration, age selective: the last-in–first-out rule applies almost everywhere. School leavers, in particular those with vocational training, are in a difficult situation. Since 1990, unemployment has increased in all the countries of Eastern Europe, including the former Soviet Union, more or less in line with economic transformation, and will probably continue to rise for several years, which must tend to push substantial numbers of people out of their countries.

The level of unemployment in the East will have an impact on decisions to emigrate. It is likely that the labour market at the destination will be split into two segments: low-paid, low-status jobs and professional jobs. For those aiming at the former segment the decision to migrate may be fairly insensitive to the level of unemployment in receiving countries, as they will seek jobs in segments of the market completely unattractive to the native population. Owing to their low level of education and limited ability to extract and process information, they may not be informed about the real situation in the receiving country. They will have, however, to compete with migrants from other parts of the world, in particular from Third World countries, which, given recent increases in migration, will be a hard task.

Those aiming at the 'better' segment of the labour market may be unwilling to migrate unless they have secured an appropriate job in the West. They will be sensitive both to the unemployment level in the receiving country and to the intervening opportunities in their own country, as a study by Hryniewicz *et al.* (1992) has clearly demonstrated. These migrants are not desperate to migrate; they seek to improve their living conditions and work environment (Kurcz and Podkanski 1991). The rapid proliferation of modern production and services requiring a high degree of skill and knowledge in Eastern Europe may have an important impact on this category of migrants.

It should also be noted that highly skilled migrants often downgrade their professional career and take jobs requiring much lower qualifications than they actually hold. This observation has been confirmed by questionnaire research in the country of origin (Hryniewicz *et al.* 1992) and at the destination (Lewandowska 1991). This practice may in future prevent some potential migrants from emigrating, in particular if combined with an increase in the number of well-paid, highly skilled jobs in the East.

Many authors question the value of qualifications of East Europeans on the West European labour market. Given the numerous and successful careers of academic research staff in West European and American Universities (Korcelli 1992a) and in the high-technology commercial sector this is probably not a problem for the highly skilled. However, this category of migrants is, in terms of their share in the overall volume of migrants, marginal. For the rest the problem does exist, as stated for example by Kemper (1993) in relation to Soviet Germans and by Lewandowska (1991) in relation to Polish emigrants. Coleman (1993b) points out that the demand for specific qualifications in the West will be met to a very limited extent by the supply from the East. What may make the situation even worse is that often professional and vocational qualifications issued in one country are not accepted in another. This problem has not been fully resolved within the European Union (Convey and Kupiszewski 1994), let alone with regard to other countries.

2.3.3 DEMOGRAPHIC DISCREPANCIES

A recent UN projection of the world population (UN 1991b) forecasts that between 1990 and 2010 we will have to face a 2 per cent reduction in the labour force in Western Europe.[8] Strictly speaking the forecast refers to the population aged between 15 and 60 for women and 15 and 65 for men. It does not take into account either extended—sometimes up to 23–24 years of age—periods of education, nor varying labour force participation ratios. Sophisticated analysis of the phenomena may be found in Coleman (1992). Germany—migration Mecca for many East Europeans—will undergo the most profound structural changes losing 18.2 per cent of its labour force (Dzienio and Drzewieniecka 1992). On the other hand in South and North Europe the existing labour force will grow respectively by 1.3 per cent and 3.6 per cent. In Eastern Europe and the former Soviet Union forecast growth will be even faster: 9.1 per cent and 16.5 per cent. Poland will account for 54 per cent of the growth of the labour force in Eastern Europe.

Purely demographic changes will be enhanced by structural transformations — East European economies have a high proportion of their labour force employed in agriculture. Employment in this sector will probably shrink, as has happened in the more developed European countries, and part of the labour released will have serious trouble in finding employment. Therefore, on the supply side, there will be a pressure to go. However on demand side, in the West, it is doubtful that there will be many jobs to take up. It is likely, as Coleman (1992) argues, that governments will try to offset labour force losses by the liquidation of unemployment, by retraining and by increasing female labour force participation before they allow foreigners to enter. Political pressure from the right and extreme right as well as experiences gained in the 1960s and 1970s, with guest workers who refused to go home when they were not needed any more, will enhance these policies.

2.4 POLICY RESPONSES

Policy responses in the West have been firm: Western countries do not want more migrants. Asylum laws have been tightened, in particular in Germany, and the number of staff processing asylum applications has been increased in Germany, France and the United Kingdom (SOPEMI 1994). Asylum procedures have been streamlined: for example, in the Netherlands most cases can be handled within 24 hours (*Migration News* 1994e). In Austria new authorities responsible for dealing with refugees have been set up (UNECE 1993b). Many countries have signed bilateral agreements on readmission, making step-by-step migration illegal as well as the inflow of asylum seekers more difficult (*Migration News* 1994d). Applications from asylum seekers coming from a safe country (virtually the whole of Europe except the former Yugoslavia and some areas of the former Soviet Union) are rejected as a matter of course. The acceptance rate for asylum applications is very low: 19.7 per cent in France and around 5 per cent in Italy, between 3 and 5 per cent in Norway (SOPEMI 1994) and below or around 5 per cent in Switzerland, Sweden and Germany, all data for 1992 (Mihalka 1994). In some cases the low acceptance rate is accompanied by an increase in exceptional residence permits for humanitarian reasons, as for example in the United Kingdom and Switzerland (SOPEMI 1994). Germany decided to expel 60 000–100 000 Croats (*Migration News* 1994b) and considers the same with respect to other nationals of former Yugoslavia (*Migration News* 1994c). Germany also repatriated around 30 000 Romanians and Romanian Gypsies and is negotiating a deportation agreement with Turkey, with the aim of removing some of the Kurds (*Migration News* 1994d).

There is also a clear tightening of visa requirements with more countries introducing very strict rules on issuing stay and transit visas to citizens of states known for high propensities to emigrate (SOPEMI 1994). The Schengen group of countries, a subset of EU member states, postponed for several years the opening of internal frontiers between their states until the information system designed to track and control foreign immigrants could be properly operated (see Chapter 17 for a more detailed discussion).

Internal control of labour markets is also on the increase. France, for example, requires employers to notify the administration about the employment of foreigners and penalizes them for employing illegal migrants. Simultaneously penalties have been increased for smuggling and accommodating undocumented foreigners (SOPEMI 1994). Belgium requires employers to notify the National Social Security Office prior to employing a foreigner and requires employees in the construction sector to be in possession of identification documents (SOPEMI 1994). Similar measures were taken in Germany (*Migration News* 1994a). In various countries stricter rules have been imposed on subcontracting, which up to recently provided a convenient way for employers to bypass employment restrictions (SOPEMI 1994, *Migration News* 1994a).

Changes in naturalization laws have proceeded in two directions: Germany, Italy and Belgium have made it easier to acquire citizenship for second-generation migrants, in recognition of their sizeable and long-established foreign populations. At the same time, Italy has made it more difficult for the first generation of migrants to become naturalized by increasing the period of residency required from five to ten years (SOPEMI 1994).

All these measures will decrease the number of all categories of migrants and travellers from Eastern to Western Europe. As a result some more successful countries of Central Europe, such as Hungary, Poland or the Czech Republic, may face increasing pressure by migrants from the economically less-developed countries of the former Soviet empire.

2.5 COULD WE FORECAST THE NUMBERS OF MIGRANTS?

Forecasting internal migration is a tricky business. Forecasting international migration is an even more difficult task but theoretically feasible in very stable conditions, which, of course, do not exist at present. The problem with forecasting East–West migration is this lack of stability. Politically, the region is involved in sophisticated transition processes. Economic stability is limited. Probably only demographic processes (understood narrowly as fertility and mortality) are stable, although a war can easily destabilize them. Attempts to apply specific theories of migration are of limited help. Öberg and Wils (1992 p.1) state: 'There is of course no scientific method to predict either flows or events that will influence them...' However, they recognize that theory is useful in explanation of existing flows.

Let us take just two examples. Who in 1986 or 1987 would have predicted that roads on the Hungarian–Austrian border would be jammed with East German 'Trabbies' heading for West Germany? Who at the same time would have predicted that over half a million Yugoslav Moslems, Serbs and Croats would be knocking on the doors of Western Europe, not as guest workers but as expellees? Certainly not very many people and definitely not those who have the power to take political decisions.

Despite these limitations, press reports, research publications and speeches of politicians are full of statements forecasting the numbers of migrants. The only problem is that they are normally completely unfounded on facts. The various predictions differ by an order of magnitude. Segbers (1991) quotes estimates of emigration from the former Soviet Union of between two and 25 million.

What can really be said about the future of East–West migrations? We may envisage some structural changes—a reduction in the number of asylum seekers from Central–East Europe being offset by the rapid increase from the former Yugoslavia and a not so rapid but still high flow from Romania. There is also the possibility of an increasing inflow of Albanians, of citizens of the Baltic states and above all from the successor states of the Soviet Union. Changes in asylum policy may reduce the flows of economic asylum seekers. Labour migration may remain high with a fairly stable geographical structure. The migrational behaviour of inhabitants of the former Soviet Union remains an enigma. Up to now, outflow from this area has been high in real terms, albeit low in comparison to the migration potential. The economic recovery of Central–East Europe provides a good prospect for a reduction of these flows, but high unemployment will probably hamper this trend. Another important factor in future will be chain migration. It is likely that the late 1980s and early 1990s have seen the peak of migration. It is, however, certain that the overall level of migration from the East to West will remain high for a long time and that Western Europe will have to learn how to live with this phenomenon.

2.6 CONCLUSIONS

Eastern Europe has around 410 million inhabitants. The majority of these live in relative poverty when compared with those living in the Western world. Political instability, ethnic frictions, unemployment and poor economic conditions force many of them to migrate. Currently they emigrate at a rate of slightly less than one million a year (Öberg and Wils 1992 for the period 1990–1). An inflow of that size is difficult for the West to accept, mainly for political and economic reasons. It also causes demographic and, more important, human capital losses in the East. It is a vital interest for the whole of Europe to curb these migrations and the only way to do that is to remove push factors in the East. As the Yugoslav war has proved, the international community is powerless in the case of ethnic conflicts, but it can help develop the economies of the region—mainly by removing barriers in free trade. It is naïve to believe that the alternative policy—more barbed wire and watch towers —will help in the long term.

NOTES

[1]Poles 'specialize' in overstaying abroad. For example, W. Spirydowicz, an official from the Consular Department of the Polish Ministry of Foreign Affairs stated that there were around 150 000 Poles residing illegally in Greece (interview with E. Pawelek Pieszo, bez paszportu i pieniedzy, Zycie Warsawy, 16 June 1992).
[2]Albanians mainly migrate to Italy and Greece. The latter country is often chosen by Albanian Greeks. *RFE/RL Daily Report* no. 121, 29 June 1993 quotes a Greek official claiming that there are 150 000 illegal Albanian immigrants in Greece. Three days later the same source (*RFE/RL Daily Report* no. 124, 2 July 1993) reported that illegal Albanians are being expelled from Greece at a rate of 3000 a day.
[3]Detailed characteristics of *Aussiedler* are given in Fleischer and Pröbsting (1989).

[4]German law recognized at that time *Aussiedler* (citizens of other countries who are ethnic Germans) and *Ubersiedler* (Germans who lived in the German Democratic Republic).

[5]Until the end of November 1993.

[6]Thus almost all Hungarians have fled from Voivodina to Hungary (*Mniejszosci traktowac nowoczesnie,* Interview with Geza Entz, Secretary of State for Hungarians Abroad, *Rzeczpospolita,* 12 June 1992.

[7]The most recent census in the former Yugoslavia did not cover Kosovo due to the tense political situation. It is also likely that the Serb authorities preferred not to have data from this area.

[8]In this section the terms 'Western', 'Eastern', 'Northern' and 'Southern' Europe follow the division adopted in UN projections

3 Extra-Union Migration: The South–North Perspective

ALLAN FINDLAY

3.1 INTRODUCTION

In 1946, Kirk, having assessed demographic trends in inter-war Europe and having considered the potential labour demand created by postwar reconstruction and subsequent economic growth, predicted a boom in international migration. By 1980, the immigrant stocks in Germany stood at 4.7 million persons and in France at 3.7 million, reflecting the mass migrations which had taken place to these and other industrialized countries of north-west Europe during the 1950s and 1960s. The bulk of these migrants came from the states of the Maghreb, Yugoslavia and Turkey. From 1973 onwards, faced with very different economic and social circumstances, Western European countries introduced very restrictive labour immigration policies which militated strongly against further mass labour migration, although family reunion policies allowed overall migrant stocks to continue to grow.

In the early 1990s, predictions were once again being made of a new era of mass migration. This, it was claimed, might be on an even greater scale than the flows of the 1950s and 1960s. R. King (1993a, p.22) and Lutz (1991), basing their projections on, among other factors, the gap between the demographic growth rates of the countries of Western and Southern Europe and those of the countries to the South of the Mediterranean, saw interesting historical parallels which they believed justified the view that a new phase of mass migration was under way.

This chapter seeks to consider the future of mass migration to Europe as much as to dwell upon the past. It focuses attention particularly on South to North migration. Many other erudite reviews of the level and significance of immigration from the South into Europe already exist (Castles and Miller 1993; Collinson 1993; R. King 1993b; Montanari and Cortese 1993; Livi-Bacci 1993). As a consequence, there is no need here to rehearse once again in detail the historical evolution of immigration to Western Europe. What is useful in the context of this book is to re-examine the underlying explanations of South to North migration. The reason for this is that the conflicting interpretations which exist of patterns of immigration to Europe, although arising from a more or less widely agreed empirical base, produce very different expectations of what will happen in the future. As is so often the case in

Population Migration in the European Union Edited by Philip Rees, John Stillwell, Andrew Convey and Marek Kupiszewski. © Editors and Contributors. Published 1996 John Wiley & Sons Ltd

social science, it is not the empirically verifiable events which are of greatest significance but rather the meaning which is attached to them.

The chapter commences with a brief comparison of neo-classical economic interpretations and Marxian perspectives on immigration to Europe. This is followed by a consideration of the grounds which might be presented for anticipating a fresh migrant influx and the alternative labour market situations which might emerge. Throughout the chapter the term 'South' is used to refer to all less developed countries outside Europe rather than more narrowly to the countries on the southern shore of the Mediterranean.

3.2 MIGRANTS, MARKETS AND MARX

The neo-classical economic view interprets migration flows as a response to labour market inequalities of supply and demand. Classical economists of the 18th and 19th centuries advocated the principle of free trade, including the unrestricted movement of labour, goods and capital. Thus, international labour immigration was seen as a rational economic response by markets and individual decision makers which ensured an equalization of returns to labour between two or more labour markets in which uneven supply or demand for labour had emerged. The neo-classical position recognized, in addition, the existence of certain imperfections within the market, not least of which is introduced by the intervention of the state itself. From this perspective the state exists to create conditions in which its autonomous citizens can freely pursue their own activities within the market. Advocates of this position will probably suggest that the state should adopt an utilitarian view of immigration and emigration. If the state needs labour, immigration may offer one means to provide the requirements of the market without encountering the inflationary pressures on wages which follow from situations of fixed labour supply and rising labour demand.

It was just such a situation which has been identified as existing in Western Europe in the 1950s and 1960s. Fertility rates dropped rapidly, cutting off the future supply of labour to the market from natural population growth. At the same time, rapid economic growth was translated into a sustained increase in demand for labour. This has been interpreted by some as producing the potential for wage inflation which was only countered by increasing female participation rates and international labour immigration (Jones and Smith 1970). Taking a similar position with regard to the interpretation of international migration, but applying his ideas to the situation of the 1990s, Salt (1993, p.25) concludes that: 'unlike the 1950s and 1960s, when migration into North West Europe was primarily demand driven, present pressures for movement stem mainly from excess supply'. The reasons why Salt sees a switch from labour demand to labour supply as the driving mechanism behind migratory pressures will be discussed later in this chapter. For the moment, the salient point is that neo-classical views of migration offer one interpretation of why mass immigration took place in the 1950s and 1960s and they also provide a basis for projecting what might happen in the very different labour market circumstances of Western Europe in the 1990s.

The same migration trends are explained in a very different fashion by Marxist and Marxian writers. The Marxian perspective draws its understanding first and foremost from the view that: 'surplus population... becomes a condition for the existence of the capitalist mode of production. It forms a disposable industrial reserve army, which belongs to capital just as if the latter had bred it at its own expense' (Marx 1976, p.784).

From this position, Marxist analysts interpret international labour migration as a means for a capitalist state to draw on reserve armies of labour from other states. In particular, Miles (1987) has explored three mechanisms by which the European guest worker system of the 1950s and 1960s produced conditions of 'unfree labour' which were of benefit to the state: first, the externalizing of reproduction costs such as education and training; second, the competitive replacement of workers from one country by those from another and third, the creation of clandestine reserve armies of labour through the effects of the work and residence permit systems in creating a division within the immigrant workforce between those entering legally and those in clandestine employment because of their inability to gain or renew their permits.

Just as the era of mass migration to Western Europe from the South is viewed from this perspective as a structured event related to the way in which mass production was organized in capitalist states, so also Marxist authors interpret the end of mass migration in 1973–4 as more than the outcome of one historically specific event such as the economic recession which followed the raising of oil prices by certain Arab states. To quote from Castles and Miller (1993, p.77): 'The ending of organized recruitment of manual workers was not a mere conjunctural phenomenon, but rather a reaction to fundamental restructuring of the labour process and of the world economy.'

The economic restructuring referred to by Castles and Miller is evident in the empirical material relating to European labour markets in the 1970s. White (1986) has shown, for example, that although the 1973 oil crisis undoubtedly brought to an end the period of continuous economic growth which most European countries had been enjoying for several decades, by 1976 economic recovery had been achieved. All West European economies were once again enjoying positive economic growth, but this was neither translated into a significant rise in labour demand nor into a return of mass migration.

In 1976, Britain recorded economic growth of 3.9 per cent and Germany a growth rate of 5.6 per cent. Throughout the rest of the 1970s, sustained economic growth was enjoyed across Western Europe, but unlike the period prior to 1973, economic growth was not associated with a strong growth in labour demand. Instead, unemployment rates soared in the late 1970s and early 1980s reflecting the consequences of economic restructuring in these economies. Industrial structures were reorganized, elements of production were relocated and new patterns of investment within Europe were undertaken which involved a switch to more capital intensive methods. As a consequence of these changes, the freeze on policies favouring labour immigration remained in place throughout the 1970s, and some governments moved to introduce policies favouring migrant repatriation (Lawless, et al. 1982).

From a Marxian perspective economic restructuring reflected a new international division of labour. The new phase of capital accumulation was based on the existence of an integrated global economy, organized in relation to the ability of large firms to co-ordinate production systems carried out at many different locations and permitting the spatial separation of labour-intensive tasks from managerial and research functions. The effect of these changes in production was, according to Massey (1984) and others, to encourage the headquarters' functions of large firms to shift increasingly towards global cities such as London and Paris, while labour-intensive production processes relocated in branch plants in the peripheral regions of the older industrial nations and in the low-cost sites of certain labour-surplus countries in the developing world. The effect on migration patterns in Europe was a reduction in the attraction of the older urban regions and a return migration of some migrants to the peripheral and now revitalized economies of Southern Europe. Strachan and King (1982) and Horner et al. (1987) have described how, for example, the 1980s witnessed a reversal of migration flows to regions as far apart as southern Italy and western Ireland. In more abstract terms, Fielding (1993) notes that the change in production regimes associated with the new international division of labour has been just as influential in producing return migration as was the earlier production regime in generating mass immigration.

Once again, the interesting point here with regard to the Marxian perspective is not whether Fielding's position is correct with respect to its interpretation of every aspect of the migration events recorded in Europe in the 1980s, but what it implies about the determinants of future immigration to Western Europe from the South. Unlike the neo-classical view, it would suggest that shifts in production regimes are the key determinant of shifts in migration trends, rather than changes in the supply and demand for labour, and Sunley (1992) and other analysts writing from this perspective do suggest that production regimes have changed once again in the 1990s. Lipietz (1993) points, for example, to the declining size of large corporations as evidence of the crisis of hierarchically organized mass-production systems. He also identifies the emergence of new types of industrial districts based on flexible forms of accumulation as representing more than a trend towards sub-contracting and proposes that the emergence of networks of small high-technology firms partly accounts for the patterns of endogenous industrialization which have been witnessed in parts of Southern Europe. If these new forms of flexible accumulation reflect a genuine departure from the production systems established under the so-called 'orthodoxy' of the new international division of labour (Lipietz, 1993), then they also would imply the possibility of a new phase in the migration history of the economies involved. To quote from Fielding once again, the new forms of production which have emerged in the context of patterns of flexible accumulation 'seem to be as inimical to mass migration as they are to mass production and mass consumption' (Fielding 1993, p. 14).

If this analysis is correct, then Europe by the end of the 1990s will face a curious set of simultaneous circumstances—substantial visible ethnic minority groups remaining in the older industrial regions from the era of mass immigration in the 1950s and 1960s, high levels of indigenous unemployment in the older industrial regions resulting among other factors from the effects of new international divisions of labour and third, the growth of new industrial districts offering opportunities for wealth creation but not resulting in many new jobs. At the same time, demographic forces and economic circumstances will contrive to make the economies of the South increasingly unattractive, thus raising the potential desire of citizens from these countries to seek entry to the North.

It is in these circumstances that international frontiers between North and South not only serve to maintain international inequalities through the regulation of trade and financial flows (Zolberg 1989, p. 406) but also serve as barriers to individuals seeking through the migration process to sell their labour power in countries where their labour can earn higher wages. Before considering whether migration policies can really act as a control on pressure for international population transfers from poor to rich countries, the chapter considers in more detail the nature of the demographic and economic divide represented by the Mediterranean Sea.

3.3 THE MEDITERRANEAN – A DEMOGRAPHIC AND ECONOMIC DIVIDE

The Mediterranean Sea marks one of the sharpest demographic and economic divides currently to be found on the world map. To the north lie countries whose demographic growth is extremely low and whose standard of living is among the highest in the world. To the south of the Mediterranean lie the countries of North Africa, with rates of natural increase which are extremely high and whose economies, while not uniformly weak, provide their populations on average with incomes worth only 6 per cent of the value of incomes in Western Europe.

Given the difficulty of comparing national census data from different countries, the generalizations made in the previous paragraph are derived from a study of the data sets provided by the United Nations World Population Prospects, as assessed in 1990, and from the World Bank Atlas. Table 3.1 gives greater detail of the spatial contrasts which are evident even from a summary examination of the data. Perhaps most striking is the column of Table 3.1 which shows population doubling time. This is a measure of the number of years until the population will double, assuming a constant rate of natural increase. It is a useful indicator of the potential population growth of a country or region but should not be used as a forecast of the actual doubling time, since it does not include reasonable assumptions about trends in fertility and mortality.

Table 3.1 shows a strong similarity between the countries of Europe in terms of their rates of natural increase. Most were scarcely growing at all, due to a combination of low fertility and mortality. In extreme cases, such as Germany, total fertility

Table 3.1 The Mediterranean, 1990—a demographic and economic divide

Region	Rate of Natural Increase (per annum)	Population Doubling Time (years)	Gross National Product per Capita ($US)
Northern Europe	0.2	286	16 370
Example: UK	0.2	330	14 750
Western Europe	0.2	388	17 330
Example: Germany[1]	0.0	–	17 830
Southern Europe	0.2	290	9830
Example: Italy	0.1	1155	15 150
North Africa	2.7	25	1100
Example: Morocco	2.5	28	900
West Africa	2.9	24	330
Example: Burkina Faso	3.3	21	310

Note 1: No doubling time is given for Germany because its rate of natural increase is slightly negative

rates had fallen by 1990 to as low as 1.5, well below the replacement level of 2.1. Other Northern and Western European countries facing virtual demographic stagnation include Austria, Denmark, Italy and the Netherlands, with total fertility rates of 1.4, 1.6, 1.4 and 1.6. Variations in the doubling times among these countries arise because of differences in the levels of net immigration. In all cases the countries of Northern, Western and Southern Europe can be said to have entered a phase of demographic stagnation.

The implications of these demographic trends for Europe are not only that total population numbers have stabilized but that the age structure has changed. Low fertility levels combined with high life expectancies have contributed towards the ageing of their population structures. For example, in France and the Netherlands, life expectancy at birth in 1990 had risen to 77 years while 13 per cent and 14 per cent of their populations were over 65 years of age. The percentage of elderly in the populations of all the European Union countries is projected to rise to over 21 per cent of the total over the next 20 years.

The countries of north Africa provide a starkly different demographic picture to that in Europe. As Islamic countries, the North African states share high fertility rates (Fargues 1988) even though some of them such as Libya have enjoyed oil wealth and moderate levels of national income. Algeria, for example, had a total fertility rate of 5.4 in 1990, despite having an above average gross national product per capita of $US2170. Across North Africa, high fertility rates combine with low levels of mortality to produce high rates of population growth. In many cases the very youthful population structures of these countries produce crude death rates

(CDR) far lower than those of Europe. For example, Tunisia's CDR in 1990 was only 7 per 1000 compared with a CDR of 11 in Germany and 12 in the UK. Overall, the high rates of natural increase in North Africa produce population doubling times of only 25 years for these countries, or less than a tenth of the doubling time for Southern Europe. It is not surprising that these statistics, when taken along with the economic differential between the relative prosperity of the economies on the two sides of the Mediterranean, have produced fears in Western and Southern Europe about the prospect of a migrant invasion from the South over the next few decades.

Concern over the prospect of massive South to North migration flows is increased when a wider definition of 'South' is adopted, for indeed the countries of North Africa are neither the poorest nor the most rapidly expanding states in demographic terms. Colonial linkages between West and South European states and their colonial territories throughout the developing world produced significant migration linkages in the past which if sustained would mean the South to North transfer of peoples across an even greater demographic and economic divide. Table 3.1 includes data for just one such region: West Africa. It can be seen here that average income levels are much lower than in North Africa, producing an even greater gap with Western Europe. Income levels in Western Europe are 50 times the level of those in West Africa, with the unevenness in levels of GNP per capita being even greater for the poorer states of ex-colonial West Africa such as Burkina Faso, Guinea-Bissau, Nigeria and Sierra Leone. In these countries, very high fertility is producing very high population growth rates and, as in Burkina Faso, population doubling times of just over 20 years.

The result of these contrasting demographic regimes between North and South is particularly stark when expressed in terms of the relative age structures of their respective populations. In 1990, the OECD countries of Europe had 13 children under 15 years of age for every 10 people over 65 years. In sub-Saharan Africa the equivalent figures were 159 children for every 10 old people (Golini *et al.* 1993). Some debate exists as to the future demographic path or paths which developing countries will follow, but whether or not fertility levels fall, the existing youthful population structures of these countries will ensure that the cohorts of potential parents will continue to grow rapidly over the next few decades.

If the demographic statistics presented above are considered as indicators of future labour supply, then they imply stagnant and declining labour supplies in Western Europe over the next three decades as the populations of these countries age and as declining numbers in the youthful cohorts produce a reduction in the supply of new entrants to the labour market. For example, in the United Kingdom, there were only 2.6 million persons in the 16–19 age cohorts in 1994, nearly a million less than a decade before. Inversely, in the countries of the developing world, the very high fertility levels will produce a burgeoning labour supply of young persons entering the active age cohorts and seeking work. This contrasting labour supply situation combines with stark differences in the economic prospects of the two realms. In 1990, the European countries of the North were not only much richer than those of the South, their economies were growing more rapidly, thus increasing the economic gap. In the 1980s not only was economic growth in the South slower than in the North, but large numbers of countries, particularly in sub-Saharan Africa, experienced net economic decline. Foreign debt crippled many of these economies, diverting key resources to repaying international loans rather than being used for investment in development projects. Egypt, for example, with a GNP per capita of only $US630, had a debt level in 1988 which was equal to $US995 per inhabitant.

According to Lutz *et al.* (1991), the combination of demographic and economic inequalities which have been described above provide the basis for an unprecedented South to North migration into Europe. They predict an annual immigration into Europe of 1.5 million persons, an immigration surge far greater than anything experienced by Western Europe in the 1950s or 1960s. That this scale of immigration should actually occur seems improbable for a variety of reasons, but what is certain is that the demographic and economic gap between the North and South shores of the Mediterranean has produced and will continue to produce an exceptionally high potential for international migration.

Whether or not the potential for a new era of mass migration will be translated into reality seems to depend on the one hand on one's ideological position and on the other hand on whether there is any evidence that state policies concerning immigration can actually influence events to any great extent. The neo-classical economic position outlined in the first part of this chapter would seem to suggest that the massive inequalities between North and South should, other things being equal, generate new migration flows through the increased supply of labour available in the developing world. This economic position would, however, be mediated by the role of the state seeking to restrict migration on other grounds such as the social and political considerations linked with mass migration. It thus becomes pertinent to turn briefly to the policy motives of recent European migration legislation and also to the issue of the effectiveness or otherwise of attempts to alter immigration trends.

3.4 IMMIGRATION POLICY AND PRACTICE

In a detailed analysis of immigration policies in western Europe, White (1986) has argued that political movements towards the abandonment of the guest worker system of the 1960s and the endorsement of the repatriation policies of the 1970s had their root in the months and years preceding the 1973–4 crisis. In other words, the economic crisis of 1973–4 provided a pretext for political intervention in Western Europe's migration system, rather than being the underlying cause of the policy change. For example, in Britain, the Immigration Act of 1971 had its origins in Britain's changing position *vis-à-vis* the Commonwealth and the European Community (Sarre 1989), while in Switzerland a restrictive policy on immigration was adopted as early as 1970. These and other examples indicate that restrictions on immigration, particularly from countries of the South, were primarily initiated in the early 1970s in response to political and social pressures relating to the size of certain visible immigrant groups rather than as a direct function of economic forces.

Ironically, state immigration policies and immigration trends seldom appear to be consistent with one another. In Western Europe in the 1980s, despite the existence of highly restrictive immigration policies, there was a continual growth in the stocks of foreign population in almost every country (Table 3.2). This was the case not only because of rising levels of immigration from Eastern Europe but also because of continued growth in the numbers of people from traditional labour migration countries in the South. For example, in Belgium, the number of Moroccans rose by one-third between 1980 and 1990. In France, the stock of Moroccans, Tunisians and migrants from sub-Saharan Africa increased considerably between 1982 and 1990, while in the Netherlands, the number of Turks rose by over 40 per cent. In Germany, the increase was also considerable, with the number of Turks rising from 1.5 million in 1980 to 1.7 million in 1990 (Table 3.3)

Table 3.2 Stock of foreign population, 1980 and 1990

Country	% Foreign 1980	% Foreign 1990	Foreign Population 1990 ('000s)
Austria	3.7	5.3	413.4
Belgium	–	9.1	904.5
Denmark	2.0	3.1	160.6
Finland	0.3	0.5	26.3
France	–	6.4	3607.6
Germany	7.2	8.2	5241.8
Italy	0.5	1.4	781.1
Luxembourg[1]	25.8	27.5	104.0
Netherlands	3.7	4.6	692.4
Norway	2.0	3.4	143.3
Sweden	5.1	5.6	483.7
Switzerland	14.1	16.3	1100.3
United Kingdom	–	3.3	1875.0

Note 1: Figures for 1989 (Source: OECD 1992, p.31)

The most significant increases in South to North migration have not, however, been in the traditional destination regions of Northern Europe, but in Southern Europe. The main destination countries of the late 1980s and early 1990s were Italy, Spain, Greece and Portugal. Unfortunately the limited system of recording migration statistics in these countries, combined with the clandestine nature of many of the moves, makes it extremely difficult to arrive at precise assessments of the scale or composition of these new migration flows. In Italy, for example, recent estimates put the foreign population at 1.1 million persons, of which 880 000 are believed to be from the developing countries (Montanari and Cortese 1993). The majority of

Table 3.3 Stock of foreign population for selected nationalities, 1990 ('000s)

Country of Immigration	Country of Origin			
	Algeria	Morocco	Tunisia	Turkey
Belgium	10.7	141.6	6.3	84.9
France	619.9	584.7	207.5	201.5
Germany	6.7	67.5	25.9	1675.0
Netherlands	–	156.9	2.6	203.5

Source: OECD 1992, various tables

these new immigrants are estimated to be illegal immigrants entering the country through family contacts, friends or on tourist visas.

Other reasons for the growth of Europe's immigrant stock from the developing countries at a time of increasingly restrictive labour immigration policies include the rising importance of family reunification among migrant communities. While European countries were able to set their migration policies firmly against further labour immigration, humanitarian concerns such as the right of existing migrants to be joined by their families and close relatives have meant that in practice considerable levels of legal immigration have continued to take place from the developing world. OECD statistics show that during the 1980s the dependency ratios of migrant communities in Western Europe changed significantly as family reunification proceeded. Of course not all who entered under family reunification rules remained outside the labour market, so that even though policies were in place to restrict all further labour immigration, it is not entirely surprising to discover that the operation of other migration channels led to a net increase not only in migrant stocks but also in the migrant labour force (OECD 1992).

Another reason why migrant stocks rose during the 1980s despite stringent anti-labour immigration policies, was the rise in the number of asylum seekers entering Western Europe from the developing countries. For example, in Norway, the large number of refugees entering the country (especially from Vietnam, Iran, Sri Lanka and the Philippines) accounted for much of the growth in migrant stocks, while in Sweden, the number of Iranians and Chileans grew very rapidly (up 39 000 and 20 000 respectively in 1990 against 3000 and 7000 in 1980). In these and other West European countries, the flow of asylum seekers soared during the 1980s. On the one hand, rising political instability in many parts of the developing world increased the number of persons fleeing from fear of persecution, while on the other hand, the closing of alternative migration channels encouraged potential labour migrants from war-torn countries to attempt to enter Western Europe through the refugee route. For policy makers in Western Europe, this dual influence created a severe dilemma in trying to stem the tide of asylum seekers. Most states claimed to continue their policies of recognizing asylum seekers in line with the now outdated definitions of the 1951 UN Convention on refugees, while at the same time introducing new legislation to restrict the scale of refugee immigration and in particular to ensure that so called 'economic migrants' seeking to enter under asylum rules would be excluded. Fuller details of the dilemmas facing Western Europe with regard to developing appropriate policies to deal with the world's refugee crisis have been discussed elsewhere in this book. The pertinent issue relative to this chapter is, however, the more general point that despite restrictive labour immigration policies, the countries of Western Europe experienced a net growth of immigrant stocks during the 1980s because migrants continued to arrive through family reunification and asylum channels. Policies to close off one channel of migration only added to pressure for immigration via other channels. The net effect was that, by 1990, foreigners made up 16 per cent of the total population of Switzerland, 9 per cent of the population of Belgium and 8 per cent of the population of Germany (Table 3.2). Countries such as the United Kingdom, although having a fairly low proportion of the total population made up of foreigners (3.3 per cent), nevertheless had a significant foreign stock in absolute terms (1 875 000).

An interesting feature of migration trends during the 1980s, which has not been drawn out so far, is that an important change in the composition of the migrant stocks of Western Europe took place when analysed by the nationality of migrants. Despite an increased freedom of movement between EU countries during the decade, the proportion of foreigners from other EU countries declined significantly, especially in Belgium, France and the Netherlands (Findlay, in press). Thus, as migration policies seeking to restrict labour immigration from the South seemed to be failing to have much effect, policies to facilitate labour exchanges within the EU were also running contrary to intra-EU migration trends.

Various conclusions might be drawn from the preceding discussion. The most obvious conclusion would seem to be that labour migration policies in themselves are incapable of reversing fundamental migration trends. If this is evident in terms of trends in the legally registered migrant populations of Europe, how much stronger would be the case if the size of clandestine migrant populations were known. Salt (1993) notes that Italy alone has 600 000 clandestine migrants (mainly from Tunisia and Algeria) and Spain a further 300 000 (mainly from Morocco).

To say that even the most vigorously enforced immigration policy cannot halt a migration trend is not to say that it has no effect. There seems little doubt that, in the absence of Western Europe's restrictive immigration regime, many more migrants from the developing world would have sought to enter the wealthier economies of the region. It also seems evident that the countries of Southern Europe have only recently become aware of their new status as immigration destinations and that scope exists for considerably more stringent policing of their borders and of access to their labour markets. Enforcing restrictive immigration policies in Southern Europe will not, however, be easy, given the scale of their informal economies. For example, controlling illegal immigration to Italy is difficult, given the estimated 20 per cent of the GDP which is derived from so-called 'informal activities' (Collinson, 1993).

There seems little scope for immigration policies in Western Europe to become much more restrictive in terms of their intentions. Instead, the rest of the 1990s will see greater efforts being made to enforce existing migration policies, as well as much time being devoted to achieving international harmonization of policies on immigration. This latter goal will be difficult to achieve, since migration policy remains at its heart an issue relating to national identity (Parekh 1994). Unfortunately very little time seems likely to be devoted to evaluating either the economic desirability or effectiveness of sustaining Europe's restrictive immigration policies.

The evidence presented in this chapter supports the view that restrictive immigration policies seem doomed to be increasingly ineffective as pressures for migration mount from the South. Yet despite this, little attention has been given to the potential of policies aimed either at reducing the pressure for emigration in the South or at developing migration policies to match the economic processes of an era of flexible accumulation. Until European immigration policy makers recognize the underlying motors driving international migration processes and direct themselves to the causes rather than consequences of South to North migration, they seem likely to continue to design reactive and partial policies. The changing world in which Western Europe is positioned demands not only new theories of South to North migration but also new approaches to migration policy formulation.

3.5 CONCLUSION

This chapter has tackled only a few dimensions of South to North migration. Important issues such as the segregation of ethnic minority groups in certain parts of the housing and labour markets of Western Europe, evidence of increasing racism across Europe at a time of growing nationalism and issues such as changing policies on the integration of immigrant communities have not been investigated. Instead attention has focused on the changing forces accounting for international migration to Europe from the developing world. It has been shown that the pressures for immigration have never been greater, while arguably the changing nature of production processes has created an economic regime inimical to further mass migration. These tensions, when set in the context of rising social and political pressures to police the frontiers of Europe against further legal immigration, help to explain why immigration has been one of the most frequently debated topics on the international political agenda in the early 1990s (OECD 1993). Neither political talk nor the development of yet more authoritarian tools to enforce Europe's restrictive immigration policies will halt immigration from the South. It is ironic that Western European governments, in the aftermath of the demolition of the Berlin Wall and the removal of the Iron Curtain, seem set on erecting new and moderately ineffective barriers to immigration along their southern shores. Their efforts should be directed to a greater extent to dealing with the causes of the new international migration waves which will affect Europe in the first half of the 21st century.

4 Migration Flows Between the Countries of the European Union: Current Trends

MICHEL POULAIN

4.1 INTRODUCTION

Analysis of migration flows among the 12 countries of the European Union cannot be done without a preliminary examination of the available sources of data, their respective reliability and their level of comparability. Without doubt, international migration is the most difficult demographic phenomenon to grasp and for which methods of data collection are the most diverse. Because migration is not an event sanctioned by acts of Parliament, the statistical tools used are of various types. First, the administrative files or population records such as those in seven EU countries (Germany, Belgium, Denmark, Spain, Italy, Luxembourg, the Netherlands) constitute an administrative tool which, in order to assign a residence to each individual, establishes compulsory registration of changes of address. A statistical collection carried out starting from these registers has the potential to provide all the desired demographic information on international migration. The situation varies according to country, eg Spain does not record international emigration, Luxembourg does not give the country of destination or of origin and the Italian data suffer from obvious under-registration.

Looking separately at the system of recording the population, only the United Kingdom uses a specific data-gathering tool, an enquiry into migration called the *International Passenger Survey (IPS)*. On the basis of an appropriate survey, carried out principally at airports, the IPS allows you to estimate the number of people entering the UK with the intention of staying there at least a year, having resided abroad for at least a year. It also lets you estimate the number of people leaving the country after having lived there at least one year with the intention of residing abroad for a minimum of one year. Unfortunately, the report does not include migration exchanges with the Republic of Ireland which are the largest flows. The estimates of small migratory flows from this sample survey are subject to uncertainty and their reported levels fluctuate greatly from one year to the next.

The question asked in many European censuses about place of residence at a certain date in the past, whether one year ago, five years or at the time of the last census,

Population Migration in the European Union Edited by Philip Rees, John Stillwell, Andrew Convey and Marek Kupiszewski. © Editors and Contributors. Published 1996 John Wiley & Sons Ltd.

theoretically allows you to calculate the number of international immigrants in the corresponding period. However, it is very rare for figures to be available giving the distribution of international immigrants by country of residence one or five years ago or at the last census. The Labour Force Survey also asks a question about place of residence one year prior to the survey and about the place of residence of emigrants, but the sampling rate and the rarity of the phenomenon mean that it is not possible to produce satisfactory estimates of migratory flows by country of origin or destination. Finally, for France, Greece, Ireland and Portugal, and also for emigration out of Spain, there are no available data describing the origin or destination of migrants. Nevertheless, a few statistics are published for these countries, but they deal only with a specific sub-population (eg Spanish emigrants assisted by their country or foreign immigrants workers in France who have undergone a medical examination).

While the availability of data and methods of data gathering vary noticeably from country to country, so do the criteria for defining international immigrants and emigrants. Only the UK's *International Passenger Survey* adopts the definition of the United Nations (UN 1980). In other surveys, the principal criterion is the intention to settle in the country or the intention to leave. Less often, the survey refers to the predicted length of stay, and the periods of reference are from three to six months, occasionally one year. Moreover, these criteria vary depending on whether you are considering nationals, EU nationals or nationals of other countries. In this last case, the criteria include residency permits for immigrants. The Economic Commission for Europe in Geneva and the Statistical Office of the European Communities (Eurostat) in Luxembourg, conscious of the difficulty of following the evolution of international migratory movements, have undertaken an analysis and harmonization of the defining criteria for international migrants, with a view to achieving a consensus on the use of common criteria, independently of the systems of data collection.

The problem of the reliability of collected data is further aggravated because, as all demographers agree, data collection for migration suffers most from underregistration. In direct relation to the advantages or disadvantages of registering or not registering a change of residence, there is a clear under-registration of spatial mobility, which particularly affects international emigration. For example, national or local administrations, in order to maintain or increase their population figures, benefit from recording new arrivals quickly and delaying or simply omitting to record those leaving. Also, it is often in the interests of individual emigrants to register quickly in their new country of residence, whereas they hesitate to sign off from the country they leave, hoping to maintain links there. Immigration is normally better recorded than emigration. Both are more accurately counted where there is a centralized system of population registration rather than a decentralized system operating at a local administrative level or no system at all.

Despite the different systems of data collection, the countries which don't supply any data, the lack of common criteria and the variable reliability of collection processes, we will try to analyse migratory currents between the countries of the

European Union. However, the risk of misinterpretation due to the unreliability of some data must be borne in mind.

4.2 THE AVAILABLE DATA

In the case of migratory flows, every movement between country A and country B can be measured using the emigration from A to B and also the immigration to B from A. Thus, a similar international migratory flow will be measured, in principle, by the two countries involved and the two figures obtained should coincide. As shown by the double matrix in Table 4.1, for 12 EU countries (EUR-12) the immigration figures in non-italics are systematically different from the emigration figures in italics directly below. This presentation, in the form of a double matrix, shows flows for which no figures are available (28 cases out of 132), those for which there is only one figure, whether for immigration or emigration (68 cases out of 132) and finally those where both figures are available and can be compared (36 cases out of 132). In these cases, the weakness of agreement can be seen: only four flows differ by a margin of less than 10 per cent; whereas there are 12 cases, or a third, where the observed difference is greater than 100 per cent, ie the ratio of the lower figure to the higher is more than two.

Only a harmonization of the criteria for identifying migrants and an improvement in the reliability of data collection in the countries concerned can improve this situation. Such a process of harmonization will without doubt take a long time and could probably only lead to more reliable and comparable data by the beginning of the 21st century. The five northern European countries have given themselves more than 10 years to attain harmonization, starting from similar computerized registers of population.

Without waiting for the result of such a process of harmonization and in order to suggest a first summary analysis of intra-European migratory flows, we have used a mathematical method of estimation which produces the best estimate of a migratory flow by taking into consideration all the figures from the double matrix in Table 4.1. Based on the estimate of relative qualifying factors for either immigration or emigration, the value of the flow of proposed migration is assumed to be that which could be measured if all countries measured their migratory movements in the way the best countries do, that is, in the way that Germany, Denmark, the Netherlands and the UK enumerate their immigration (Poulain 1993b). A supplementary method allows one to make estimates for migration flows for which there is only one measurement. Finally, starting with rough figures and estimating indirectly and 'unofficially' the immigration flows of certain countries, in Table 4.2 we show estimates of migration flows for which neither of the countries concerned published official figures. It goes without saying that the confidence interval which brackets this group of estimates increases greatly if you only use one information source and base it on rough estimates. In Table 4.2 the data calculated from the figures for immigration and emigration are shown in bold type, data estimated from only one

Table 4.1 Migration exchanges between the member states of the European Union, 1990. The numbers in the table in normal type, preceded by the letter 'D', are the figures provided by the country of immigration. *The numbers in the table in italic type, preceded by the letter 'O', are the figures provided by the country of emigration.*

Destination

1990 Origin		B	DK	D	GR	SP	F	IRL	I	L	NL	P	UK	Total
Belgium	D		361	4332		920	6572		2096	1198	5335		5761	18 805
	O		156	3050	373	1584		78	2079		3804	484	1774	21 152
Denmark	D	289		3148		153			236		425		2657	6908
	O	483		2441	245	767	1293	129	528	224	475	114	3827	10 526
F.R. Germany	D	3645	2051			3784			13 198		978		17 542	50 007
	O	4323	2066		15 243	9732	14 594	2569	37 004	964	9083	3794	12 819	112 191
Greece	D	661	230	27 589		15			778		886		1449	31 608
	O													0
Spain	D	1438	837	8065					1155		2314		12 635	26 444
	O													0
France	D	7355	954	17 158		4034			4930		2958		19 221	56 610
	O													0
Ireland	D	255	155	3878		50			209		587			5134
	O													0
Italy	D	2616	511	39 679		454	5277			1145	1494		3072	47 826
	O	3181	217	26 098	520	1353		43			870	139	3564	42 407
Luxembourg	D	911	124	1068		47			256		192		386	2984
	O													0
Netherlands	D	5847	447	9281		646			824	259			2476	20 061
	O	6929	327	6921	449	2126	2526	378	1070			551	4650	26 186
Portugal	D	1539	124	7805		696			265		883		696	12 008
	O													0
United Kingdom	D	2564	3130	18 071		2398			3648		7176			36 987
	O	5016	1518	19 393	423	8174	16 417	3119	2984		3942	1088		58 955
Total	D	27 120	8563	136 282	16 880	12 277			25 499	2592	26 702		60 134	296 577
	O	19 932	4128	54 853		22 152	40 107	3119	41 586		14 370	5686	24 860	250 265

Table 4.2 Estimation of the migration exchanges between the countries of the European Union, 1990

Destination

1990 Origin	B	DK	D	GR	SP	F	IRL	I	L	NL	P	UK	Total
Belgium		338	4476	730	1993	12 859	153	2172	2344	5516	947	5227	36 755
Denmark	484		3109	240	687	1268	127	543	220	474	112	3731	10 994
F.R. Germany	4411	2066		15 766	10 575	15 085	2655	34 737	996	9787	3922	17 287	117 287
Greece	1132	202	29 277		53	2064	40	1707	151	924	35	1553	37 118
Spain	2463	736	8558	233		3477	564	2534	225	2413	1168	13 367	35 738
France	12 599	839	18 208	2860	14 160		1500	10 817	3207	3084	1529	20 334	89 137
Ireland	437	136	4115	314	176	3517		459	119	612	97	35 000	44 982
Italy	2866	483	38 873	1127	1585	11 441	93		2482	1549	301	3185	63 985
Luxembourg	1560	109	1133	67	165	1852	65	562		200	2323	408	8444
Netherlands	7134	439	9752	557	2314	3136	469	1136	322		684	4517	30 460
Portugal	2636	109	8282	142	2443	11 543	30	581	9632	921		736	37 055
United Kingdom	5083	2828	19 452	508	8694	19 701	19 628	3791	961	6868	1306		88 819
Total	40 805	8285	145 235	22 544	42 845	85 943	25 324	59 038	20 659	32 347	12 424	105 325	599 204

measurement are in normal type and estimates derived from indirect and unofficial estimates of immigration are in the shaded boxes. Finally, we have managed to fill almost the whole matrix of 132 migratory exchanges between 12 EU (EUR-12) member states. Only flows between Ireland, Greece and Luxembourg were not able to be evaluated, but their small size would hardly alter our conclusions.

4.3 MIGRATION FLOWS BETWEEN EU COUNTRIES IN 1990

First of all, some comments are necessary about the global level of intra-community mobility. In 1990, 600 000 people migrated between two EU countries: this represents about one person in 500. This is a relatively small number, if you consider that, among the 600 000 migrations, more than a third are between adjacent countries and a significant proportion of these are of short distance and do not coincide with what we think of as international migration.

Table 4.3 Mobility rate, volume and net migration for each member state of the European Union in 1990

| Origins | Migration Numbers | | | Population | |
	Entries	Departures	Total	Net	(in '000s)
Belgium	40 805	36 755	77 560	4050	9947
Denmark	8285	10 994	19 279	−2709	5135
F.R. Germany	145 235	117 287	262 522	27 948	62 514
Greece	22 544	37 078	59 622	−14 534	10 120
Spain	42 845	35 738	78 583	7107	38 924
France	85 943	87 637	173 580	−1694	56 652
Ireland	23 754	44 982	68 736	−21 228	3503
Italy	59 038	63 985	123 023	−4947	57 285
Luxembourg	20 659	8444	29 103	12 215	388
Netherlands	32 347	30 460	62 807	1887	14 892
Portugal	12 424	37 025	49 449	−24 601	9871
United Kingdom	105 325	88 819	194 144	16 506	56 548
Total	599 204	599 204		0	325 779

| Origin | Migration Rates (per 10 000) | | | |
	In	Out	Total	Net
Belgium	41	37	78	4
Denmark	16	21	38	−5
F.R. Germany	23	19	42	4
Greece	22	37	59	−14
Spain	11	9	20	2
France	15	15	31	0
Ireland	68	128	196	−61
Italy	10	11	21	−1
Luxembourg	532	218	750	315
Netherlands	22	20	42	1
Portugal	13	38	50	−25
United Kingdom	19	16	34	3
Total	18	18	37	0

Is it possible to compare the differences between observed and expected flows? Use of absolute or relative differences between these two sets of values is not satisfactory. In fact, the absolute differences will be largest where a large number of migrations are recorded, ie for countries with large populations, whereas the relative differences will favour the migratory flows of countries with small populations. A more satisfactory intermediate solution is to compute a Chi square distance by dividing the absolute difference by the square root of the estimated flow. Table 4.4 supplies the range of these weighted variables, while Table 4.5 shows the most significant variations in relation to the standard of reference, whether positive or negative variations.

A first finding is easily explained: flows between neighbouring and contiguous countries are, in the majority of cases, higher than the expected values. This is the case principally between Belgium, Luxembourg, the Netherlands and France. Despite the contiguity between Germany and the above four countries, the flows between these countries and Germany are comparatively less important.

Except for the effect of spatial contiguity, the exchanges between Portugal and Luxembourg clearly outweigh the others, as do those between the United Kingdom and Ireland. In the latter case, there is obviously spatial contiguity between the Republic of Ireland and Northern Ireland but not with Great Britain. But estimates indicate that most of the exchanges between the United Kingdom and the Republic of Ireland take place with England. Exchanges between Greece and Germany, France and Portugal and Luxembourg and Italy are also greater than the expectation based on the standard of reference.

Among the flows which are somewhat weaker than expected are exchanges between Italy and Spain and between the United Kingdom and Italy.

4.5 THE MOST SIGNIFICANT IMBALANCES

By taking from Table 4.4 the difference of the weighted variables for a migration flow between two countries and the counter-flow, you obtain a new index which is the ratio of the net flow between the two countries divided by the square root of the estimated flow. This index lets you compare the migratory exchanges between each pair of countries independently of the size of their populations. Table 4.6 gives the values of this index in descending order by highlighting the most significant imbalances (the first column corresponds to the country with an in-migration balance).

The biggest imbalances are found between Portugal and Luxembourg, ahead of the exchanges between Ireland and the United Kingdom and those of Greece and Germany. The relationship between Portugal and France as well as that between Italy and Luxembourg are also worth mentioning. The flows Portugal–Luxembourg, Ireland–United Kingdom, Greece–Germany, Portugal–France and Italy–Luxembourg are significantly greater than the opposite flows. The larger size of the emigration flow from Italy to Luxembourg compared to the flow Luxembourg–Italy is the only relic of the significant emigration of Italians to north-

Table 4.4 Weighted differences between observed and expected migration flows

Origin

Destination	B	DK	D	GR	SP	F	IRL	I	L	NL	P	UK
Belgium		0	5	2	-11	149	-5	-26	458	144	12	24
Denmark	8		21	-6	-18	-15	1	-32	57	-2	-12	41
F.R. Germany	4	-1		178	-44	-55	31	71	66	46	-3	-40
Greece	18	-8	387		-50	-28	-5	-35	24	-2	-24	-37
Spain	-2	-16	-60	-47		-92	-11	-101	12	-23	-27	-10
France	145	-25	-35	-15	-4		-31	-73	253	-34	-36	-7
Ireland	14	2	70	5	-24	61		-24	37	14	-9	929
Italy	-15	-33	98	-44	-19	-69	-34		192	-55	-56	-125
Luxembourg	303	26	77	8	6	141	19	34		26	455	22
Netherlands	196	-3	45	-14	-25	-33	7	-60	46		-9	-14
Portugal	78	-12	65	-20	-2	128	-4	-52	1904	-2		-49
United Kingdom	22	20	-26	-53	-49	-11	505	-121	68	17	-39	

Table 4.5 The most important weighted deviations between observed flows and expected flows (flows between contiguous countries are indicated in bold)

Origin	Destination	Deviation
The most important flows		
Portugal	Luxembourg	1904
Ireland	**United Kingdom**	**929**
United Kingdom	**Ireland**	**505**
Belgium	**Luxembourg**	**458**
Luxembourg	Portugal	455
Greece	F.R. Germany	387
Luxembourg	**Belgium**	**303**
France	Luxembourg	253
Netherlands	**Belgium**	**196**
Italy	Luxembourg	192
F.R. Germany	Greece	178
Belgium	**France**	**149**
France	**Belgium**	**145**
Belgium	**Netherlands**	**144**
Luxembourg	**France**	**141**
Portugal	France	128
The least important flows		
Spain	Italy	−101
Italy	Spain	−109
United Kingdom	Italy	−121
Italy	United Kingdom	−125

western Europe that followed World War II. These days, only Portugal, Ireland and, to a lesser extent, Greece, are countries of emigration, the favoured destinations being Luxembourg and France for the Portuguese, the United Kingdom for the Irish and Germany for Greeks. As regards immigration, Luxembourg registers a largely positive balance not only for Italians and Portuguese but also for Belgians and the French. Only Germany has a positive migratory balance in relation to Luxembourg, but its balance is negative with Spain and to a lesser extent with the Netherlands.

4.6 THE EVOLUTION OF SOME INTRA-EUROPEAN MIGRATION FLOWS DURING THE 1980s

Are intra-European migration flows stable or have they undergone changes in recent years? A precise analysis is unfortunately not possible except between countries which give annual statistics for immigration and emigration. Therefore we will look at Belgium, Denmark, Italy, the Netherlands and the United Kingdom, with some reservations about this last country, given the great variability of published figures from year to year. It will not be possible to see for certain whether Ireland, Portugal and Greece have always registered a deficit compared with other EU countries or if Luxembourg has always been attractive. However, we can highlight two clear trends:

Table 4.6 The most marked disequilibrium between migration flows between pairs of countries

Between	And	Index
Luxembourg	Portugal	1449
United Kingdom	Ireland	424
F.R. Germany	Greece	209
France	Portugal	164
Luxembourg	Italy	158
Luxembourg	Belgium	155
Luxembourg	France	112
Spain	France	88
F.R. Germany	Portugal	68
Belgium	Portugal	66
Greece	Italy	57
Belgium	Netherlands	52
Luxembourg	United Kingdom	46
United Kingdom	Spain	39
F.R. Germany	Ireland	38
Luxembourg	Denmark	31
Netherlands	United Kingdom	31
F.R. Germany	Italy	27
Spain	Portugal	26
F.R. Germany	Denmark	23

Note: Net migration is into the country cited in the first column of the table

1. First, the Italian situation in relation to Germany, Belgium and Denmark shows a decrease in favourable flows to Italy, suggesting people returning. This decrease, associated with the maintaining, albeit rather weakly, of Italy's emigration flows, leads to an inversion of the migratory balance, an inversion which appears in 1985 in the Netherlands, and in 1988 in Belgium and Denmark. In Germany the inversion is not complete since the negative migratory balance is reabsorbed but does not become positive: the net flow has been almost nil since 1986. Figures 4.2a and 4.2b illustrate the trends for the Netherlands and Germany.

2. The migratory exchanges between Germany, Belgium, Denmark and the Netherlands globally show an increase in migratory exchanges between these four countries particularly in 1990 and 1991. In other respects, a certain hierarchy appears, more clearly in 1990 and 1991. Belgium has favourable flows from the Netherlands and Denmark whereas between Belgium and Germany a balance is achieved after a long period where the situation had favoured Germany. Exchanges between Germany and the Netherlands stay balanced during this period, while the exchanges between these two countries and Denmark are unfavourable to Denmark. Figures 4.3a, 4.3b and 4.3c show these recent changes regarding exchanges between Belgium and Germany, Germany and Denmark and Belgium and the Netherlands.

Unfortunately, the poor quality of available statistical data prevents the extension of this approach to all intra-European migratory exchanges.

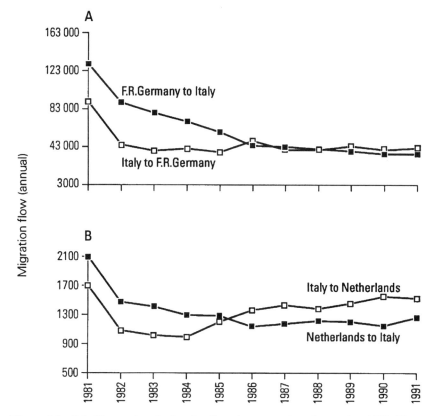

Figure 4.2a & b Time series of migration flows between selected countries, 1981–91 (corrected data)

4.7 CONCLUSION

This current analysis of migration flows between the 12 EU countries should be looked at through a wider lens, of time as well as space. First of all, attention is limited to the postwar period; the current situation is a continuation of two distinct phases.

1. The first, prior to 1973, which is characterized by massive migration of workers from countries supplying labour and situated in the south of the EU towards the countries of the northwest which demanded labour.
2. The second, following this, with much weaker intra-community migration, as much because of a disappearance of demand and the adoption of more restrictive immigration policies by north-west European countries as because of economic development which progressively affected all the southern countries. In so far as the partial statistical data used are a reflection of the whole of intra-

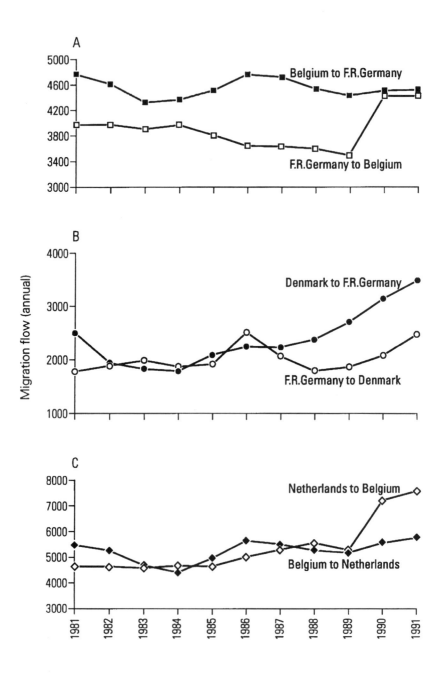

Figure 4.3a, b, c Time series of migration flows between selected countries, 1981–91 (corrected data)

5 Redefining the Front Line: the Geography of Asylum Seeking in the New Europe

VAUGHAN ROBINSON

5.1. INTRODUCTION

It is difficult to estimate the number of refugees in the world today. Different organizations define refugees in different ways, and there is a wide variety of methods
of collecting and collating data. Despite this, working estimates now suggest that
numbers lie somewhere between 18.2 million (UNHCR 1994) and 17.6 million
(USCR, 1993). More important than the gross total, however, is the rate of increase,
with the world having seen a dramatic growth in the number of refugees since the
mid-1970s. As Figure 5.1 demonstrates, and taking 1960 as a starting point, it took
16 years for the first doubling in numbers of refugees in the world (1.4 million to
2.8 million) but only three years for the next and six years for the subsequent doubling. During 1991 alone, the net number of refugees grew by 3300 people per day.
Thus even on numerical grounds alone the world's refugees have become a major
issue. According to USCR (1993) in some countries, such as Namibia and Djibouti,
refugees and resettled refugees now form almost a quarter of the entire population.
However, refugees are not just numbers, and what makes the refugee issue all the
more pressing is that many of the millions who are now refugees have experienced
human rights violations, persecution, famine and physical hardship, loss of kin and
friends, dispossession and mental trauma. What is equally clear is that these experiences will have resonances possibly for the remainder of those individuals' lives
(for example see Beiser 1993). There can thus be little doubt that the whole issue of
refugees and in particular the questions of how to protect them and how to reconcile
their aspirations with the opportunities on offer in countries of first asylum or resettlement is one of the main challenges facing the international community in the
closing stages of the 20th century.

This chapter contains four main sections which address this issue and its ramifications for Europe. The first charts the development of the world refugee crisis and
demonstrates how what was once a European problem has now become a global
challenge, but how, in addition, Europe has become increasingly myopic in the last
few years as the crisis has returned to its geographical roots. The second tries to set

Population Migration in the European Union Edited by Philip Rees, John Stillwell, Andrew Convey and Marek
Kupiszewski. © Editors and Contributors. Published 1996 John Wiley & Sons Ltd.

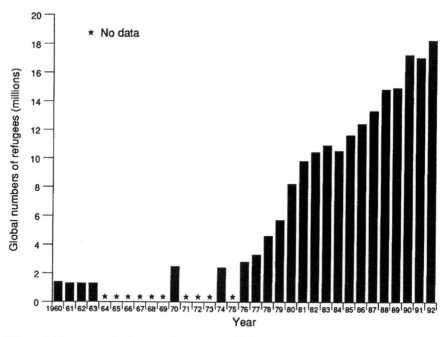

Figure 5.1 Number of refugees in the world, 1962–92

Europe's contemporary plight in a global context and again demonstrates how Europe has increasingly focused on its own concerns while those of others are equally pressing. The next section looks in greater detail at the flows of refugees into Western Europe and their changing sources, and then disaggregates these data by individual country of destination. The fourth describes how Western Europe has responded to the new flows of refugees, and how it is now taking combined action to define a new set of perimeter defences not unlike those of the motte and bailey castles of yore.

5.2 THE CHRONOLOGICAL DEVELOPMENT OF A WORLD REFUGEE CRISIS

5.2.1 ESTABLISHING A FRAMEWORK, 1921–50s

Although the media might have us believe that refugees are essentially a phenomenon of the last two decades and that the legislation and structures designed to respond to their plight are the product of the last decade, this is far from the truth. Much of the thinking, the most influential piece of legislation and the main body responsible for protecting and resettling refugees can trace their origins back to World War II or even earlier.

World War I, the collapse of the Ottoman Empire and the dislocation brought about by the Russian Revolution all led to calls for intergovernmental action on refugees and forced migrants. This took the form of the appointment of a High Commissioner by the League of Nations with special responsibility for Russian refugees. Fridjof Nansen took up his post in 1921 and established several principles which have been retained in modified form until today. He argued for an international response to national refugee crises, for voluntary repatriation as the preferred long-term solution to refugee episodes and for the principle of 'non-refoulement', by which refugees would not be repatriated to their countries of origin against their wishes. The Nansen Medal and Nansen Passport are further reminders of the seminal contribution of Fridjof Nansen in this formative period.

In 1933, the League of Nations again took the initiative in establishing a High Commission for Refugees leaving persecution in Nazi Germany. Not only did the Commission concern itself with the issues arising from flight, but it also took it upon itself to address the reasons for flight, campaigning for both protection and an end to persecution.

World War II marked a significant turning point in refugee matters, for not only had the allies to contend with their guilt over the Holocaust, but they faced the task of accommodating and resettling some 60 million displaced persons within Europe. Their response was to establish first the UN Relief and Rehabilitation Agency and then to replace this in 1947 with the International Refugee Organization which acted outside the UN. Finally when, in 1950, the IRO's mandate expired, it was itself replaced by the United Nations High Commission for Refugees (UNHCR) which came into being in January 1951 and has remained the core agency dealing with refugee matters ever since.

Finally, in 1951, the UN proposed a formal legal definition of a refugee which has been used as the basis for deciding who should be eligible for receiving the benefits granted legal refugees ever since, albeit with subsequent modification. Some would even argue that the 'Convention' definition, as it is now known, has taken on even greater significance in the 1990s than in any other decade since its inception. What is particularly pertinent to the present discussion, however, is that the original 1951 definition applied only to those refugees generated within Europe. Non-Europeans were not officially added to the legal definition until the 1967 Bellagio Protocol, and some countries (such as Malta and Turkey) have still not become signatories to this amended definition.

During this first phase, in which institutions, responsibilities and definitions were being formulated and codified, Europe was both the instigator and beneficiary. Definitions applied to European refugees only and agencies were formed specifically to rehabilitate and resettle those dislocated by the war in Europe. Preferred policy on resettlement was formulated against the background of the need to reconstruct shattered economies, cities and infrastructure at a time of labour shortage in many countries. Nations thus turned the refugee 'problem' into an opportunity and enthusiastically recruited and resettled refugees as a means of satiating their demand for pliable and non-unionized labour. Britain's European Volunteer Workers scheme which operated between 1947 and 1951 was an excellent example of the synergy between demand for labour and the need to resettle refugees from the camps of Western Europe (Tannahill 1958). The decision to offer residence to the Polish exiles dispossessed by the Yalta conference was another (Robinson, forthcoming). That immigration policy and refugee policy could be dovetailed so effectively and easily was a happy coincidence and one predicated on the fact that refugees were overwhelmingly white and European and often Christian and skilled.

5.2.2 GLOBALIZATION AND THE MORAL HIGH GROUND, 1960s AND 1970s

While the first phase had seen Europe addressing what was thought to be a European problem, the second phase saw a marked shift in the locus of refugee production. Refugees were still encouraged to leave the East and migrate to the West as a way of confirming the moral superiority of the latter and reminding the world of the human rights violations of the former, but numbers were generally limited and apart from the major waves leaving Hungary in 1956, Czechoslovakia and Poland in 1968 and the GDR prior to the erection of the Berlin Wall, their impact was slight.

The major transformation of the period was the growth in refugee numbers in the Third World. Decolonization by European states created power vacuums and inappropriate national boundaries and groupings, and the superpowers responded by supporting their strategic interests with arms sales which effectively militarized the Third World. At the same time, population growth in LDCs began to accelerate to its peak of 2.05 per cent per annum during the 1960s and when this was combined with the growing debt crisis in the Third World, dependence upon volatile world markets for sales of primary products and the shock waves of the first energy crisis of 1973, the wealth gap between first and third worlds sharpened markedly. So too, did the rate of land degradation and the decline in average agricultural landholdings in the LDCs (Harrison 1993). Not surprisingly, this powerful mix of rapid population growth, competition for diminishing resources and political dominance, and ethnic and racial tensions contrived to create conditions conducive both to human rights violations and the wholesale marginalization of population groups. Refugee flows from Bangladesh, Ghana, the Congo, Burundi and Uganda served to prove the point.

The changing nature of the refugee 'problem' prompted other changes. In 1969 the Organization of African Unity proposed an alternative and broader definition of what constituted a refugee, based more upon the experience of Third World countries rather than postwar Europe. Equally, as the plight of refugees in the 'South' became more widely known and more graphically portrayed by the media, a consensus began to develop in advanced societies that there needed to be a global response to such episodes, led by the West. While this initially took the form of funded assistance to refugees in, or near, their place or origin, the Vietnam war brought about a sea change in attitudes. American guilt over the war, the public self-criticism which was characteristic of the period and the well-publicized suffering of the Boat People all combined radically to affect attitudes towards refugees in the West. The ideas of international 'burden-sharing' and extra-regional resettlement of refugees both grew in favour, and over one million South East Asians have now been permanently resettled in the West, many through private sponsorship schemes relying upon public goodwill (see Lanphier 1993 and Robinson 1993). In retrospect this combined effort over a period of five years represents perhaps the high-water mark of international collaborative effort and humanitarianism towards refugees.

5.2.3 KNOCKING ON THE DOOR, 1980s

The third phase began at different times in different countries dependent upon their geographical location. What marks it off as a distinct period is the change in balance between quota refugees and spontaneous refugees. Whereas in the 1970s the West had selected refugees (often for their labour market skills or their assimilability) and had agreed to resettle them in predetermined numbers at specific times, thereby regulating all aspects of the flow, the situation in the 1980s was very different. The spread of cheap air travel, the progress of the mass media in the Third World and the chain effect of previous migrations served to empower many refugees, who opted to take matters into their own hands rather than waiting for an offer of quota resettlement. In the 1980s refugees simply arrived in the West and claimed asylum at the airport or port. In some countries this development was greeted with shock and brought about a profound rethink of refugee admission criteria. Refugees were no longer a group who could be kept at arms length and screened and selected. Instead they were the Vietnamese arriving by boat in Darwin, Australia and stepping ashore ready to begin a new life (Robinson 1993) or the Tamils landing at Heathrow or arriving off the coast of Canada.

While in another decade the arrival of spontaneous refugees might have been accepted, in the 1980s this was not to be the case. The economic downturn resulting from the two oil shocks and the rise of the Pacific Rim economies had left most Western economies in deep recession and with rising unemployment. Labour migration had been sharply curtailed through progressively more restrictive legislation and the extreme right had begun to re-emerge in countries such as the United Kingdom and France. The arrival of migrants from overseas colonies or Southern Europe in the previous two decades had stoked racism, which was increasingly being expressed not only through discrimination but also through racial harassment and attacks.

Spontaneous refugees from the Third World were thus arriving, expecting to be treated on humanitarian criteria but were instead being seen as both black and potential and unwelcome labour migrants. The language of refugee definition changed, and increasingly asylum seekers were labelled economic migrants or economic refugees. Governments moved to bring immigration and refugee legislation into line, and the discourse increasingly began to resemble that of the 1960s when coloured labour migration was at its peak. Refugee numbers became an important topic of national interest, the proportion of refugees granted convention status was seen as the litmus test of how many were 'proper refugees' and the media began to discuss the issue of illegals who outstayed their permits or disappeared when their application was not successful. Politicians began to talk tough about refugee policy and countries took unilateral action which simply and temporarily displaced refugee flows to other destinations. In short the humanitarianism and collaboration of the 1970s had been replaced by complacent xenophobia and self-interest in the 1980s.

While the West responded in this way, the refugee crisis continued to develop. The number of refugees in the world rose from 5.7 million in 1979 to 14.9 million in 1989. During this phase the preferred 'durable solution' recommended by UNHCR and Western governments was no longer long-distance and permanent resettlement in the West but localized and temporary resettlement in countries which adjoined the source region. The refugee problem had been contained and kept at a distance from the 'North'.

5.2.4 SQUARING THE CIRCLE, 1990s

No sooner had the policy of arms length containment been formulated than circumstances rendered it obsolete. The rapid and unexpected melting of the Cold War, the global law and order deficit that followed and the hurried reunification of Germany changed the perceived source of refugees yet again. East–West migration took on much greater salience and threatened to overwhelm certain countries. As Salt (1993) notes, various estimates of the expected outflow from the former Soviet Union alone amounted to between two million and 11 million. Within this total there are significant numbers of refugees seeking asylum from the explosive rebirth of ethnic nationalism in the East, as groups try to fill the ideological and power vacuums left by the crumbling of communist regimes, and historical regional enmities re-emerge. In parallel we have seen a process of ethnic sorting within Eastern Europe, personified by the Yugoslav civil war but also evident in internal migration patterns within the former Soviet Union (Zayonchkovskaya *et al.* 1993), in the migration of *Aussiedler* back to the reunited Germany (Hofman and Heller 1992; Jones 1990; Jones and Wild 1992) and in the return of ethnic Hungarians from Romania (Poulton 1992).

However, circumstances were no more positive for these potential asylum seekers than they had been for the previous wave of spontaneous refugees from the Third World. All of Western Europe had been plunged into a deep recession by the close of the 1980s and unemployment levels had risen further. The former guest worker groups throughout Europe had entered a period of family creation and reunion which translated into growing ethnic minority populations. And the extreme right was resurgent throughout most of Western Europe (Hainsworth 1992), not only in the polls but also in direct street action such as the attacks upon refugee hostels in Germany. Ethnic nationalism and the migration of 'preferred ethnics', such as the *Aussiedler*, also intensified the ingroup–outgroup distinctions which had been implicit in previous periods.

The result of this coincidence of circumstances has been that Europe has again been faced with a refugee crisis of its own, in which spontaneous refugees have only to travel relatively short distances to cross international boundaries and enter the industrialized core of Europe. However, unlike the 1940s and 1950s, there is neither the demand for their labour, nor is there the humanitarian desire to assist their resettlement or the geopolitical value to be gained from hosting those fleeing communist regimes. What has resulted has been the redefinition of 'deserving' and 'undeserving' refugees and the application of many of the restrictions which had previously been devised to limit the access of Third World (black) asylum seekers to fellow Europeans. Equally there has been an introspective redefinition of the refugee crisis as a European refugee crisis as opposed to a world refugee crisis. Inevitably, this further marginalizes and reduces the possibilities for the increasing number of Third World refugees, who are now seen, in Europe, as even less deserving.

Former countries of asylum have thus sought exclusion, even tighter containment of refugees in their *source locale* and an abrogation of the principle of *non-refoulement*, while also falling back on a self-interest rationale summarized as follows: 'Why, the reasoning goes, should outside countries who are not to blame for the human rights abuses and political violence that cause refugees to flee be forced to shoulder the refugee burden? ...Should there not be some way to redirect the problem back to its source?' (Frelick 1993, p.6).

5.3 REFOCUSING UPON A WORLD PERSPECTIVE

The section above has described how over the last five years Europe has gradually developed myopia in its view of the world refugee crisis and how the former Yugoslavia has come to seem more immediate and important than the Sudan. Before we can engage in analysis of circumstances within Europe—the purpose of this book — we need to establish the veracity of Europe's claim to be hosting a refugee crisis.

Figure 5.2 is based upon data from the United States Committee for Refugees (USCR). Its definition of refugees is in some respects broader than the 1951 Convention definition but in others narrower. It defines refugees as those 'who require international protection and/or assistance...[and are]...unable or unwilling to repatriate due to fear of persecution and violence in their homelands'. However, they specifically exclude 'refugees permanently resettled in other countries'. Figure 5.2 maps the main sources of those 16 579 800 refugees in need of protection as of 1 January 1993. It demonstrates that while the Yugoslav crisis accounted for some 10.7 per cent of those refugees in existence in the preceding 12 months, Europe is not a major source of refugees (total 11.9 per cent) on a par with Africa (34.3 per cent), South and Central Asia (34.2 per cent), or even the Middle East (17.2 per cent). Clearly then while Europe does have a significant part to play in the contemporary world refugee crisis, it is by no means central to the crisis as a source of refugees. Data from 1986, not graphed here, would underscore this conclusion to an even greater extent. At that time, the USCR did not even list Europe as a significant source of refugees.

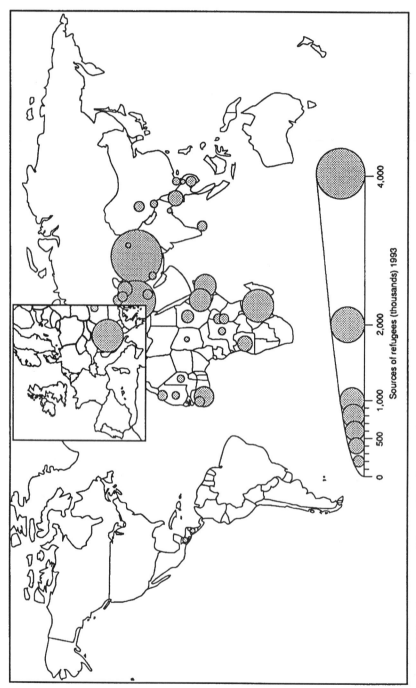

Figure 5.2 Principle sources of the world's refugees and asylum seekers, 1993

If Europe still only generates about one in eight of the world's refugees, despite the current crises in former Yugoslavia and the former Soviet Union, does it have a more significant role to play as a destination for asylum seekers from elsewhere? Again, the answer is dependent upon the time period selected. Figure 5.3 collates 1993 UNHCR data and charts the destination of asylum seekers created by the most significant refugee flows to occur in 1991 and 1992 and compares this with the number of asylum applications received by major industrialized nations over the same period. It reveals that countries within Europe—especially West Germany (with 694 000 applicants)—have been important as destinations over this period, particularly when compared with other industrialized nations such as Canada (68 000), the United States (160 000), Australia (20 000) or Japan (500). Nevertheless other—less affluent—countries have fared much worse in relative terms, with Iran receiving 1.4 million refugees, and Guinea, Kenya and Bangladesh accepting nearly a quarter of a million refugees each. As we noted above, though, the early years of this decade have been exceptional for Europe and it is therefore perhaps more useful to look at the cumulative total of refugees accepted for settlement in each country. Figure 5.4, which is based upon UNHCR collation of government estimates for the period up to 1 January 1992, indicates how, within Europe, Germany again stands out as having resettled a relatively large number of refugees (383 900). Most other Western European nations have totals of well under 50 000 with the exceptions of France (170 000), Sweden (238 400) and the United Kingdom (100 000). All of these figures are, however, dwarfed by those of a string of African and Asian countries such as Malawi (981 000), the Sudan (729 200), Zaire (483 000), Ethiopia (527 000), Guinea (548 000) Iran (4.4 million), Pakistan (3.1 million), let alone the United States (482 000) and Canada (538 100).

The data above suggest that while Europe is playing an increasing role as a generator of refugees and a significant role as a destination for asylum seekers, its plight is not unique or even exceptional. Indeed relative to its wealth and population size, Europe has until recently managed to avoid a proportionate share of the human fall-out from the world refugee crisis. Clearly the current panic about refugee numbers and flows in Western Europe is just that. Equally the views that Europe is 'full' or being 'swamped' or that the 'life-boat is in danger of sinking' are relative and based upon a myopic and unhealthy preoccupation with parochial concerns.

Finally we might need to qualify this conclusion somewhat if a broader definition of assisting refugees is used. Some countries might choose to meet their perceived obligations through financial assistance rather than through resettling families and individuals. Figure 5.5 graphs the relative contribution of the top donors to international refugee aid agencies. Not only is the EU the second largest contributor as a block, but 13 of the 19 individual countries mentioned are from Western Europe. Indeed when converted into donations per head of population, European countries fill the top seven places with countries such as Norway and Sweden donating $14 per head per year against the $2 per head of the leading non-European contributor, Oman. Taking an even narrower focus, if contributions to UNHCR alone are considered, then Western Europe funded fully 67 per cent of the organization's entire budget in 1992.

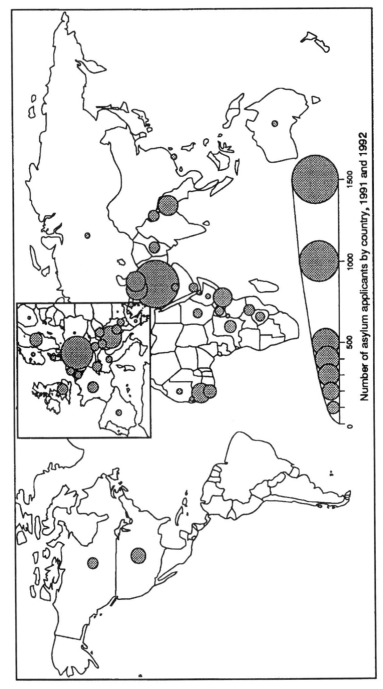

Figure 5.3 Number of asylum seekers in the industrialized world compared to major refugee flows elsewhere in the world, 1991 and 1992

77

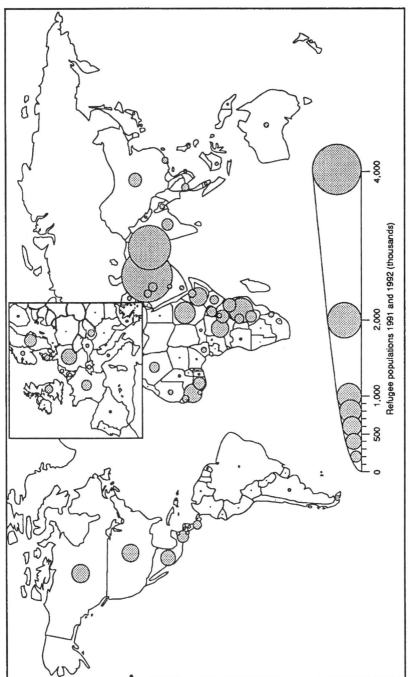

Figure 5.4 Refugee populations by country, 1991

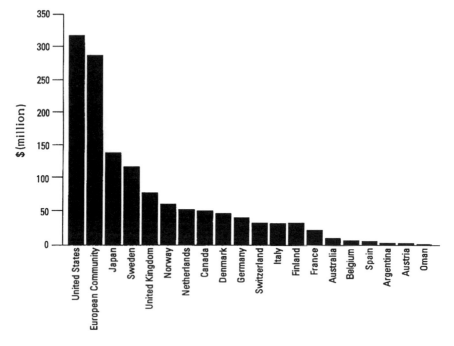

Figure 5.5 Top 20 contributors to international refugee aid agencies, 1992

5.4 WESTERN EUROPE

Although it has been argued that Western Europe should not be viewed as a special case, there can be no doubt that the last 20 years have seen a dramatic growth in demand for asylum in Europe. There were fewer than 13 000 applicants per year for asylum (in EC or EFTA countries) in the early 1970s compared with 687 000 in the last full year for which we have estimates, 1992 (see Figure 5.6). What is also noticeable is that the growth in numbers has been steady, albeit with less spectacular growth in 1987 and more rapid growth in each year since 1989. Finally, Figure 5.6 also shows that demand for asylum has not been restricted to the EU countries but has also been characteristic of former EFTA nations.

Inevitably there has been a parallel growth in the bureaucracy needed to process such applications and in both the cost of administration and waiting times. Salt (1993) notes how the number of pending cases grew from 159 000 in 1985 to 900 000 in 1991 and how there are now 20 000 administrators and caseworkers involved in refugee work in Western Europe. The cost of staff, legal aid, translators, reception centres, social aid and removal expenses has also grown from $2.4 billion in 1985 to $7.5 billion in 1991. UNHCR, too, has seen its expenditure in Europe grow sharply. Its budget for that region in 1992 was $328 million, up from $27 million the previous year (UNHCR 1994).

As the Yugoslav crisis has clearly shown, refugee episodes develop rapidly, and,

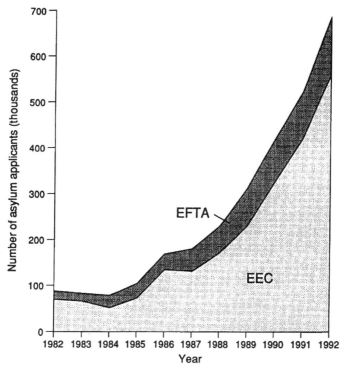

Figure 5.6 Number of applications for asylum made to countries of the EC and EFTA, 1982–92

as a result, there is great temporal volatility in the source of refugees seeking asylum in resettlement countries. This has been particularly true of Western Europe which has received several waves and many vintages (Kunz 1973) of refugees over the last two decades. Figure 5.7 shows the main source of refugees applying for asylum in 16 leading European (EC and EFTA) countries over the period 1988–92. This represents only a snapshot over a limited time-period but nevertheless demonstrates how at any one point in time Europe is experiencing the final vintages of earlier waves as well as the first vintages of newly breaking waves. In Europe's case we can identify waves from a variety of directions, namely, Chile (up to 1988), Poland (1988–90), Lebanon (1988–90), Iran (1988–92), the former Yugoslavia (1988 to date), Turkey (1988 to date), Sri Lanka (1988 to date), Zaire (1988 to date), Romania (1988 to date) and Iraq (1992 to date). Taken together, these waves have produced a five-year pattern (1988–92 inclusive) in which between 40 to 50 per cent of applicants are from Europe, 10 per cent are from Africa, very few are from Latin America or South-east Asia and a declining proportion are from the Middle East (about 10 per cent in 1988–90 falling to 2 per cent in 1992). Comparison of these percentages with Figure 5.2 demonstrates that the regional origins of Europe's asylum applicants are not representative of all refugees found in the world today.

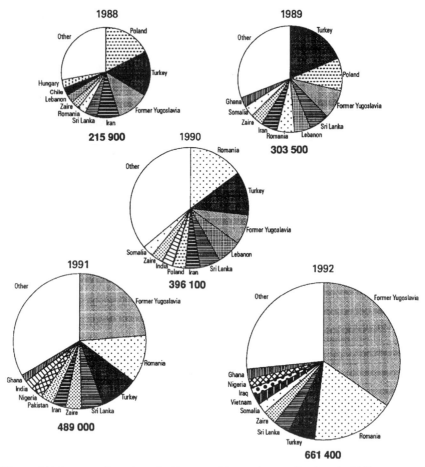

Figure 5.7 Source and number of refugees making asylum applications in 10 European countries, 1988–92

While in an ideal world refugee admission policy would be driven solely by notions of humanitarianism and need, in practice this is never the case. Admissions are instead determined by the troika of national foreign policy interests, national domestic politics and cost. Although Europe espouses collective ideals in the foreign policy arena, in practice it is not yet a cohesive entity, and different countries still retain traditional allegiances and national policies. As Figure 5.8 demonstrates, there has been a common response to certain external events, most notably the dissolution of the communist bloc. Having worked persistently for four decades to bring an end to Communism, all of Western Europe has had to accept the consequences of achieving this goal, and, in the short term, most governments have retained the mindset that the best response is to allow people to flee into exile (the so-called 'exilic bias'). Hence, all 10 countries have accepted former Yugoslavs,

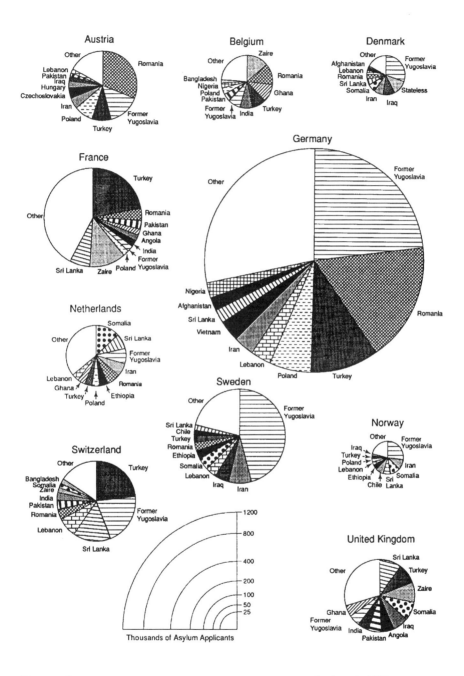

Figure 5.8 Source and number of refugees making asylum applications in 10 European countries, 1988–92, broken down by country of application

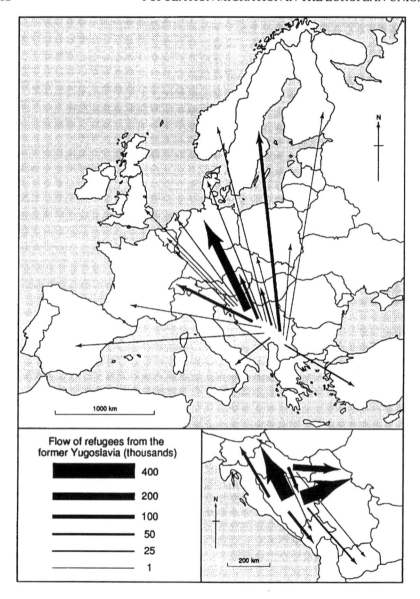

Figure 5.9 Human fallout from the Yugoslavian crisis: outward flows and destinations, 1991–3
Source: USCR (1993)

eight have accepted Romanians, seven have taken Poles and one has taken Czechs and Hungarians. Even within this 'collective' foreign policy response, there have been variations. Because of its geographical location, Austria has admitted Hungarians and Czechs as well as former Yugoslavs, Romanians and Poles. The United Kingdom, on the other hand, because of its geographical location (among other factors) has been little involved in the Eastern Europe exodus. Foreign policy considerations are also reflected in the presence of those from Turkey, Iran and Iraq, for again the West is signalling by means of its refugee policy its condemnation of a hostile regime and its support for the adversaries of that regime, namely those who oppose Saddam Hussein. The admission of Vietnamese by many European countries—only the tail-end of which is captured in Figure 5.8—can also be attributed to foreign policy and the need to maintain pressure on communist regimes. However, outside these 'collective' responses, there are also individualistic reasons which might account for variations in policy among countries. Historical, and particularly colonial, links are important since they engender a feeling of responsibility and create migrant communities overseas which are able to act as pressure groups, facilitators or conduits for information for later arrivals. Britain's past links with India, Pakistan, Ghana and Somalia are examples, as is Belgium's former association with Zaire. The commitment which certain countries have to humanitarian ideals is another. It is significant that Norway and Sweden have very similar profiles as source countries and accept refugees from Somalia, Ethiopia and Chile, all acknowledged humanitarian hot-spots with which they have had no prior relations. And finally, there are also countries which seek to retain congruence in their admission policies with neighbouring countries such as Belgium and France.

While factors such as those outlined above may determine the flows of refugees to Western European countries, others may determine the eventual result of these applications. Material presented above (especially Figures 5.4 and 5.4) has demonstrated how the volume of refugees received and resettled by different countries in Western Europe has varied enormously, with Germany being pivotal within the overall pattern. Such variations have recently been highlighted by national responses to the Yugoslav crisis. Figure 5.9 maps the flows of forced migration created by the disintegration of Yugoslavia. Former Yugoslavs numbering 1.183 million have been displaced within the old international boundaries of that country and a further 556 000 have become refugees by virtue of crossing an international border. As Figure 5.9 shows, there is a clear geographical dimension to the pattern of flight underpinned by distance decay. However, other factors are also at work. Switzerland's response has been shaped by the existence of a sizeable number of Yugoslav labour migrants within that country. The same could also be said for Austria and Germany. The latter has also proved particularly attractive for other reasons. Article 16 of the Constitution guaranteed access to the asylum system for all, Article 19 guaranteed a legal right of appeal; the decision-making procedure could often take years and few of those who failed to win asylum were ever deported (8 per cent in 1989 according to Kemper 1992). In addition 'Germany provides the most generous public support for asylum seekers in all of Europe' (USCR 1993, p.122) comprising housing, clothing, food, schooling, medical care and a social allowance which averages $325 per adult per month. Not surprisingly, in 1991, over 10 per cent of asylum seekers in Germany had arrived in that country from another European state. Figure 5.9 indicates that there are also countries which might be expected to have resettled significant numbers of Yugoslavs because of their geographical proximity but which have failed to do so. Italy is a case in point. It has a highly restrictive admissions policy, it makes strenuous efforts to dissuade asylum seekers, who are, in any case not allowed to work during the determination procedure, and it offers only 45 days' welfare support to new arrivals. Finally there are those countries which are not intrinsically attractive to refugees but which have become major destinations because of their strategic geographical locations as 'waiting rooms' for access to the West. Hungary would be the best example of these.

Clearly, then, the pattern of refugee applications and admissions which has developed within Europe is the product of a variety of factors which include foreign policy considerations, historic ties, recent flows of labour migration, geographical location and actual and perceived generosity towards refugees.

5.5 THE NEW EUROPEAN 'MOTTE AND BAILEY'

Given that Europe has again become not just a resettlement destination but also a mass generator of refugees, how have individual governments and supranational bodies responded? Many would argue that the term 'Fortress Europe' captures the spirit of the European response, but this concept needs to be both unravelled and extended to be of any real value.

5.5.1 UNILATERAL ACTION

Until recently most of the developments on refugee admission within the EU were unilateral actions by individual governments, admittedly governments which were in close contact. These unilateral actions can be grouped as follows:

5.5.1.1 Prevention of access

Some countries have strengthened their borders in order to prevent access. This may take the form of giving border patrols greater powers to determine who should be allowed to make an asylum claim. Examples of this include Austria in 1990 and Switzerland, where over 1 000 000 applicants were turned away in 1992 alone. Alternatively, states may physically tighten border security. In 1992, for example, Poland increased the number of military personnel guarding the border with the former Soviet Union from 360 to 5000. Eventually these unilateral actions lead to bilateral or multilateral agreements on border security and access. M. King (1993), for instance, notes that such arrangements now exist between Denmark, Finland, Iceland, Norway and Sweden; Germany, Austria and Switzerland; Austria and Czechoslovakia; and Germany and Poland. Two other methods of preventing access have also been widely used in Europe. Most countries have now introduced progressively lengthier lists of states from which asylum seekers will not be accepted without visas, and airlines are fined if they carry passengers without such documentation. Carriers Liability Acts—as they are known—were introduced in the United Kingdom, Belgium, Denmark and Germany in 1987 and in Italy in 1989. In parallel to these developments, steps have also been taken in some countries to retreat towards a narrower definition of a refugee. Nobel (1990) notes how Sweden has traditionally accepted *de facto* refugees such as war deserters and those who do not wish to return to their country of origin because of political circumstances there, but how between 1989 and 1991 this broader definition was suspended. Germany, too, abandoned access for war deserters in 1992.

5.5.1.2 Discouragement of asylum seekers

Many countries have engaged in active deterrence even of those applicants who have managed to gain entry to a country. Britain and Sweden have housed asylum seekers on old ferry boats, while both Switzerland and Sweden have used tent encampments to accommodate those awaiting the outcome of the decision-making process. Other countries have chosen instead to reduce the rights and welfare benefits of those awaiting a decision. France, for example, no longer allows applicants to work during the determination procedure, Sweden has reduced the daily welfare allowance and the United Kingdom has withdrawn rights to public housing. In some cases, countries are also making preliminary decisions about the likely outcome of an application and according different treatment to those considered unlikely to be granted asylum: the January 1992 amendments to the Aliens Act in the Netherlands thus allow the state to detain those with 'manifestly unfounded' claims in a secure unit.

5.5.1.3 The decision-making procedure

Under pressure from increasing numbers of applicants, all European countries have reviewed the administrative procedures used to reach a determination, with a view to speeding them. The Verhafen laws of 1988 in Switzerland and their amendments in 1990 were specifically designed to achieve this, as were Belgium's 2×5 per cent rules. Most have also reviewed their procedures with a view to distinguishing between 'economic migrants' and 'refugees'. Recognition rates have thus fallen across Europe, such that only 0.7 per cent of applicants in Finland are awarded full convention status. Instead a growing proportion are being granted conditional refugee status such as 'Exceptional Leave to Remain' in the United Kingdom, '*Asilo*' in Spain, '*Assimilé à Refugié*' in Belgium and 'B' and 'C' status in Scandinavia. Such statuses usually limit and disadvantage the individual, yet in 1992 43 per cent of all applicants in the United Kingdom were given 'Exceptional Leave to Remain'.

5.5.1.4 Return of unsuccessful applicants

As was noted above, in the 1980s many European countries did not take action against those who had failed to acquire Convention status and deport them. In the 1990s this position has changed somewhat. A number of European countries have reneged on their 1951 commitment to *non-refoulement*. Britain has forcibly returned Vietnamese asylum seekers from Hong King, Italy has returned Albanians and France has deported recognized Convention Refugees (Joly and Nettleton 1990). Belgium even chartered aircraft in 1992 to deport people in bulk.

5.5.2 MULTILATERAL ACTION

Although Europe has yet to attain harmony on many issues, refugee policy is perhaps one of the areas where harmonization is most fully developed. The prime multilateral action has been the ideological retreat from an exilic bias. During periods when refugees from the East were few in numbers and symbolic in nature, permanent resettlement in a Western country was the preferred outcome. Increasingly, in the 1990s, Europe is switching its emphasis towards direct humanitarian and peace-keeping intervention in the source area in order to anchor potential refugees and forestall flight, a concept termed 'preventive protection' by the UN's High Commissioner Sadako Ogata. The safe-havens in northern Iraq which were offered Kurds during and since the Gulf War and were sanctioned by UN Resolution 688 are clear examples of this tendency, as are the British and French governments' current positions on former Yugoslavia which is that resettling former Yugoslavs overseas is to aid and abet ethnic cleansing. While such measures are increasingly justified by reference to human rights violations, some commentators are less generous. Frelick (1993, p.9) argues that 'while the rhetoric of "Operation Provide Comfort" was humanitarian, and the military was... mobilised for purposes that were, in part, humanitarian, something else was going on: the prevention of a refugee flow'. He goes on (p.13), 'The trend towards preventing refugee flows jeopardises the most fundamental principles of refugee protection—the right of refugees to flee their countries, [and] to seek asylum from persecution in other countries.'

Other multilateral actions taken by the EU countries have been more formal. One of the first priorities was seen as putting in place a regime in which asylum seekers could make only one application for asylum within the EU and in which it would be clear which country was responsible for processing this. The Dublin Convention of 1990 achieved this. It eradicated the phenomenon of the 'refugee in orbit'. Instead, asylum seekers can now only make an application to that country which allowed entry or issued a visa. An alternative country can opt to process the application if it involves family reunion or extenuating circumstances.

The fundamental stumbling block which has prevented the emergence of an all-encompassing and unified European asylum policy is succinctly expressed by Hailbronner (1990, pp.346–7). He states

Irrespective of a uniform base under international law, namely the 1951 Geneva Convention, admission of refugees to European territory has been and still is determined by ideological and political factors... A decisive reason for their reluctance to agree to a treaty-based obligation to grant asylum was the inherent restriction of political decision-making through the concept of an individual right. This might result in a reduction of a State's sovereign rights to control immigration and to decide upon the admission of aliens.

Despite this, certain states have come together to harmonize some aspects of policy. In June 1985 Belgium, Luxemburg, the Netherlands, Germany and France agreed the Schengen Accords which have since been followed by a supplementary convention in 1990. Italy joined the group in 1990, Spain and Portugal in 1991 and Greece (as an observer initially) in December 1991. Many see the group and the treaties as a potential model for the remainder of Europe (M. King 1993). The treaties aim to open internal borders for goods, services and people while at the same time introducing shared immigration and asylum policies. Visa policy would be harmonized and considerably extended, police controls at external borders tightened and a new Schengen Information System would collect and collate immigration and asylum data to allow the common exclusion of individuals. Even those third-state aliens with visas would have a very limited duration of stay and might have to prove they possessed a return ticket and means of financial support. Finally, refugees would have to submit their asylum applications at an external border of Schengen territory or within that territory. Given the Dublin Convention and Carriers Liability Acts, neither of these possibilities seems viable. What concerns some commentators most about Schengen, however, is the lack of accountability of the group (see Cruz 1991).

Contrary to the sentiments of European harmonization what is actually taking place within Europe is highly divisive. All countries are attempting to make their borders less permeable and exclude the majority of those who wish to gain access to their sovereign territory. In addition the Schengen group is erecting joint barriers around an inner keep or motte while forming agreements with third parties to defend an outer perimeter or bailey against the perceived threat from the East. The countries between, such as Hungary and Poland, while benefiting from collusion with Schengen to some extent, are having to pay a considerable price for their inclusion in the outer circle. Hungary is widely seen as the gateway to the West from Romania, the Ukraine and the former Yugoslavia, but in practice it has become a buffer zone in which people are held prior to possible admission to the West.

5.6 CONCLUSIONS

This chapter has argued that while Europe is experiencing pressure from asylum seekers from the South and East and is feeling some discomfort from this, the situation needs to be set in a broader context. Within a global context, Europe's plight is not severe, nor is it particularly unusual. What is perhaps unique is the extent to which Europeans in the postwar period have externalized and been able to distance themselves from refugee issues, which were increasingly stereotyped as Third World problems. What we are now witnessing is the collective shock of Europe as it realizes that the refugee crisis cannot permanently be held at arms-length and that like almost all other countries in the world, European nations are vulnerable to its effects. What has, however, been lost in the cries for ever more restrictive admission regimes and ever tighter border controls is the humanitarian dimension. Those European refugees seeking admission are being excluded, marginalized and criminalized at a time of unprecedented need and turmoil within Europe. Early evidence (*Economist* 2 October 1993) suggests that the new refugee regimes are achieving their goals in deterring applicants, but at what cost? As Europe's introspection makes it focus more on narrow self-interest, refugees from outside Europe are being marginalized and ignored, the extreme right in Russia is feeding on unfulfilled aspirations and the atrocities in the former Yugoslavia continue. This depressing picture in unlikely to change until Europe lifts its eyes to the horizon, considers its plight in a rational and world context and rediscovers its humanity and its global responsibilities.

Part 2

INTERREGIONAL MIGRATION PATTERNS: NATIONAL PERSPECTIVES

6 Migration in Belgium: Temporal Trends and Counterurbanization

MICHEL POULAIN

6.1 DATA SOURCES AND THEIR WEAKNESSES

The National Register is an administrative file held centrally on a computer which contains all the administrative characteristics of the population of Belgium. This population register is updated daily with changes that occur in the population, particularly changes in place of residence. All changes of residence must be declared to the authorities at the migration destination within eight days when the resident moves from one basic administrative unit (commune) to another or to the authorities of the place where the resident lives, if the migration has taken place within the same administrative unit. All basic demographic variables are entered into the register, which forms the principal source for population data in Belgium. During recent censuses, questions about previous residence (in 1961 and 1970) or place of residence one year ago (in 1981) were asked. However, the experience was unsuccessful because of the high level of non-response. This was why these questions were not asked in the most recent 1991 Census from which it was planned to analyse migration by linking the individual socio-economic information in the census to the migration information available in the National Register.

There is no major problem in accessing data from the National Register as long as they remain anonymous and statistically aggregated. It is important nevertheless to check the accuracy of the information provided. The main problem involves individuals who have more than one possible residence. For example, a young person who has just left home has the choice of registering an independent address or keeping that of his or her parents. A second case is the household which has two residences but which, for tax avoidance, reported residence at only one dwelling. The final example is of an old person who lives in an institution because of infirmity but who keeps his or her former residence for administrative purposes. These cases apart, the individual has a strong incentive to register a change of address without delay, because many social benefits depend on residence. A survey carried out on the migration histories of 500 couples (Poulain et al. 1991b) confirmed the quality of the register. In the majority of cases, the administrative address corresponds to the usual residence of those registered and information extracted from the National Register makes possible an analysis of the spatial migration characteristics of the population.

Population Migration in the European Union Edited by Philip Rees, John Stillwell, Andrew Convey and Marek Kupiszewski. © Editors and Contributors. Published 1996 John Wiley & Sons Ltd.

6.2 LONG-TERM TRENDS IN MIGRATION

It is important to appreciate which different spatial divisions can be used with sources of administrative data in Belgium. With the reform of the Belgian state on 1 January 1995, the country has been divided into three regions: Flanders in the north, Wallonia in the south and the Brussels region in the centre. Flanders is further subdivided into five provinces and 22 administrative *arrondissements*, while Wallonia comprises five provinces and 20 *arrondissements*. Each *arrondissement* is further divided into communes, which number 589 for the whole of the country, and which form the basic administrative units. The Brussels region is divided into 19 communes. As well as these territorial divisions, the country contains three linguistic communities: the Flemish community (Dutch speakers), the French community (French speakers) and the German-language community. No data can be used to describe these communities in detail because they overlap the administrative units. As a result, the analysis of the characteristics of spatial migration in Belgium will use regions, *arrondissements* and communes.

To examine long-term change in the level of migration of the Belgian population, only interregional migration between different *arrondissements* can be used. In order to do this, the data must be standardized for population size and age structure. Change in the standardized migration ratio is indicated by the line labelled 'M' in Figure 6.1 which starts from a value of 1000 for the year 1948. The ratio is computed by dividing the observed number of interregional migrations by the result of multiplying the number in each age group by the age-specific migration rate computed from the 1970 Census (Poulain and Van Goethem 1982). At first, the level of migration remained constant but then rose between 1952 and 1961. A sharp fall of 15 per cent appeared between 1962 and 1967. Thereafter, migration decreased in a monotonic fashion from 1970 to 1990, when it was 20 per cent lower than the level in 1948. Finally, in the last two years for which data are available, migration began a rise which only future observations can confirm or invalidate.

Taken as a whole, the trends conform with those observed elsewhere, as in France, where migration has decreased over the intercensal periods 1968–75, 1975–82 and 1982–90 (Courgeau and Pumain 1993) and as in the Netherlands where an annual time series showed a peak in migration in 1973 and a trough in 1979 (Kuijper and Noordam, 1992). Despite the existence of these similarities, we lack a proper explanation for the trends. Neither the rate of inflation nor the price of property or of building appears to account for the trends. The only explanatory factors that we believe could play a part are related to a continuous improvement in transportation and communications, which extends the distance for a daily journey to work and also to the higher level of social welfare which has reduced the need to change residence in order to take up another job. Finally, could there be a specific migration regime characteristic of times of crisis? That regime would be characterized by a weak level of global migration, whereas during periods of favourable economic growth migration would be higher.

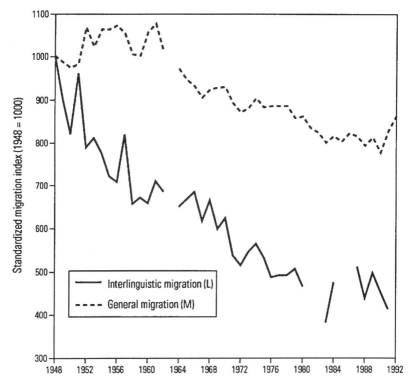

Figure 6.1 Change in the standardized index of total migration (M) and the index of inter-linguistic migration (L), 1948–92

6.3 SEX AND AGE VARIATIONS

Does the level of migration vary by age and sex? The distribution of changes of residence during the year 1992 allows us to answer by looking at the rates of migration shown in Figure 6.2.

The age factor for geographical mobility has the following broad features. The maximum level of migration, of over 20 per cent, occurs for men between ages 24 and 27 and for women between ages 22 and 26. There is a local minimum at age 15 for both boys and girls and a global minimum for both sexes around age 70, at a level 10 times lower than the maximum observed for young adults. Attention can be drawn to two details. First, we note very slight local peaks at age 65 for men and 60 for women, and we can ascribe these to retirement. But the size of the peaks are minimal in Belgium compared with the situation in other countries such as France (Cribier 1994). Second, from age 70, the migration rate rises as a result of increasing independence (through widowhood) and as a result of admission to institutions for the elderly. This rise is shown very clearly in Figure 6.3. The migration rate increases by a factor of three between 70 and 90 years of age and is clearly stronger

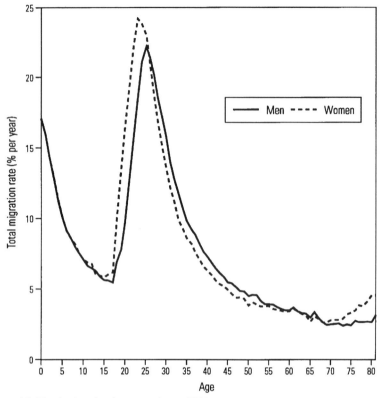

Figure 6.2 Total migration by sex and age, 1992

for women because of their higher rates of widowhood (their spouses dying at younger ages).

Given that the overall level of migration has diminished over the past three decades, what has happened to the age factor in migration? A comparison is possible between data from the census of 1970 and that of 1992. In the two cases, the two sexes are combined and five-year age groups are used (Figure 6.4).

The changes recorded between 1970 and 1992 are as follows, with the all age levels of migration falling by 6 per cent between the two years:

1. Children under 15 years of age and their parents aged 30 to 45 retain the same level of migration;
2. Adolescents and young adults experience a sharp decrease in migration propensity (the decrease is 20 per cent between ages 20 and 25);
3. Migration in the third age, and more particularly between 50 and 80 years, also declined (a maximum decrease of 20 per cent between 65 and 70); and finally
4. There is a rise of 20 per cent in migration after age 85, a rise which is independent of the increase in the numbers of persons at these ages.

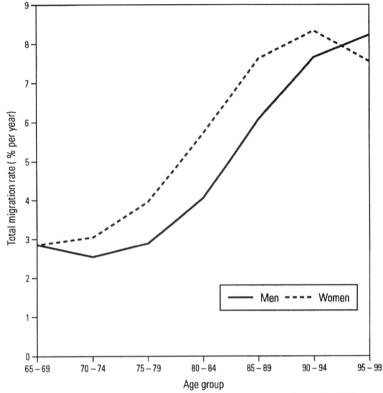

Figure 6.3 Total migration rate by sex and five-year age groups from 65, 1992

To interpret these changes in the propensity to migrate by age, the following points can be put forward, without claiming that they provide a definitive explanation or that the effects are particularly clear. Between 1970 and 1992 there was a shift upwards in the age of leaving home and in the age of first marriage. The unemployment level among young people aged under 25 has risen sharply, as has the higher education participation rate at the same ages. By contrast, the reduction in migration between 50 and 80 years of age, during a period of life when few factors justify movement, can be seen as a sign of improvement in living conditions. Changing residence has come to be seen as an inconvenience to be avoided. Finally, there has been a stronger push for the elderly to move into rest and nursing homes after age 80.

6.4 THE IMPACT OF DISTANCE

The basic relationship is simple: the greater the distance separating places of origin and destination, the lower the number of registered migrations. Half of the changes of residence in 1992 took place within the same commune, the distance of migration being, in this case, generally less than 10 kilometres. A more detailed analysis of the distribution of old and new residences shows that a substantial fraction of

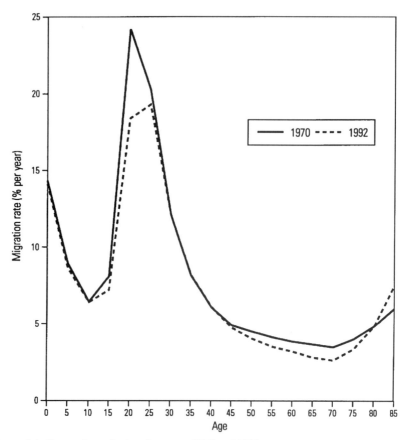

Figure 6.4 Comparison of migration rates, 1970 and 1992

intracommunal migrations take place over a distance of less than one kilometre, and this represents an adjustment of residence within the same neighbourhood. Figure 6.5 details, for males only, migration divided into three types: *intracommunal* or local; *intraregional* or within the same *arrondissement* with a maximum migration distance of 30 kilometres; and *interregional* or between *arrondissements* with migration distances of up to 300 kilometres. A half of changes of residence occurs at local level, a quarter's involve regional mobility and a quarter is made up of interregional moves between *arrondissements*.

Can evidence be put forward for differences in migration rates by age for the three types of migration? One method involves determining the parameters of a gravity model which uses a Pareto function to define the relationship between migration intensity and distance:

$$M_{ij} = k \, P_i \, P_j \, d_{ij}^{\,b}$$

where Mij is the migration flow between zones i and j, Pi and Pj are the population

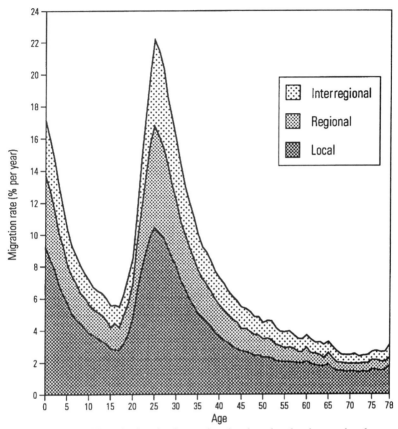

Figure 6.5 Decomposition of migration by age into local, regional or interregional components, males, 1992

sizes of zones i and j, d_{ij} is a measure of distance between the two zones and b is a friction parameter which measures the negative effect of distance on migration (see Poulain 1980 for further details). The more negative the value of b, the more the number of migrations declines as the distance of the move increases. Table 6.1 compares the b parameter measuring the friction of distance across age groups and between the periods 1979–82 and 1989–92.

For each of the two periods, the youngest ages (under 15) are most affected by distance. This is explained by the association of these migrants with new households which adjust their housing to a growing family through a short-distance migration, especially when becoming home owners. The same factors explain the higher values observed for those migrants between 30 and 45 years of age. However, for this age group, as for the 15–29 age group, other kinds of migration, mostly by individuals rather than families, play a part in addition to those migrants forming new households. Above 45 years of age, the strength of the distance effect decreases: migrants feel free to migrate over longer distances. Comparison of the

Table 6.1 Variation in the distance decay parameter by age group, 1979–82 and 1988–92

Age groups	1979–82	1988–92
0–14	−1.27	−1.31
15–29	−1.21	−1.24
30–44	−1.20	−1.26
45–59	−1.05	−1.09
60+	−0.97	−1.08
All ages	−1.17	−1.22

two periods shows that the friction of distance rises for all age groups at the same time as the level of migration is falling. Fewer long-distance migrations were being made in the later period. Only migrations over short and medium distances retain their importance, notably those towards pleasant rural villages, the Belgian coast or the Ardennes, for which the distance of migration is in the order of 100 kilometres.

6.5 MOVEMENT BETWEEN LINGUISTIC COMMUNITIES

As the curve labelled 'L' in Figure 6.1 demonstrates, movement between Dutch-speaking Flanders and French-speaking Wallonia has fluctuated more widely over the course of the study period. There was a steady decrease until the start of the 1980s, while the most recent data suggest a stabilization of the migration exchanges between the north and the south of the country. The level of interlinguistic community migration recorded in the 1980s was only half of that registered in 1948. It is clear that the division of Belgium into linguistic regions, spatially defined in 1963 and confirmed by the federalization of Belgium on 1 January 1995, has only put into concrete form a separation of the two linguistic communities which was clearly present in the data on interlinguistic migration for earlier years. Migration flows across the linguistic frontier are six times lower, at equivalent distances and for similar population numbers, as those that take place within the same linguistic region. This estimate was arrived at by introducing into the gravity model a multiplicative variable l. This takes the form of a binary variable having a value of 1 if the zones considered belong to the same linguistic region and a value of 0 when they do not. The estimated coefficient associated with the l variable is close to 6 for migration data on flows between *arrondissements* in 1975 (see Grimmeau 1992 for further analysis of this phenomenon).

6.6 URBANIZATION OR COUNTERURBANIZATION

The Brussels region constitutes the main urban region of the country. It is possible to carry out an analysis following the process of urbanization in Belgium by examining the migration flows between that region and its two neighbouring provinces, Walloon Brabant to the south and Flemish Brabant to the north (Figures 6.6 and 6.7).

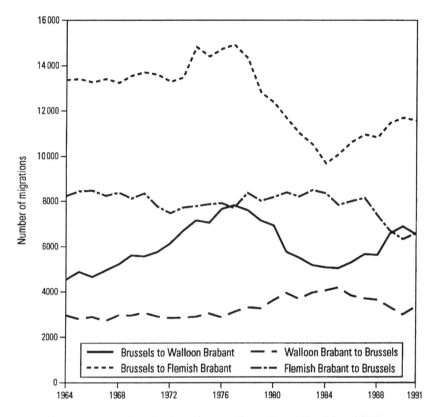

Figure 6.6 Evolution of migration flows between Brussels and Flemish and Walloon Brabant, 1964–91

The evolution of migration flows between Brussels and the two neighbouring provinces reveals very clear and similar trends. From 1964 to 1978 migrations labelled 'return to the countryside' were high in number, particularly between 1974 and 1978. This period proved a turning point: the oil crisis of 1973 and subsequent economic restructuring began to have an effect, one of which was the closure of the country to large-scale immigration. From 1979 to 1984, the decline in the number of counterurbanizing migrations was steep. For Flemish Brabant the number of in-migrations from the capital region decreased from 15 000 to fewer than 10 000. The number of migrations from Brussels to Walloon Brabant fell from 8000 to 5000. During the same period, there was a rising trend of migration into Brussels, most marked from Walloon Brabant where the migration flow increased from three to four thousand, of which only a part represents a true 'return to the city'. From 1985, migration flows adopt a new trend with an increase of 2000 in-migrations to Flemish Brabant and slightly fewer to Walloon Brabant. By 1990, a new maximum in counterurbanization had been reached.

There is no doubt that counterurbanization is tightly linked to economic trends.

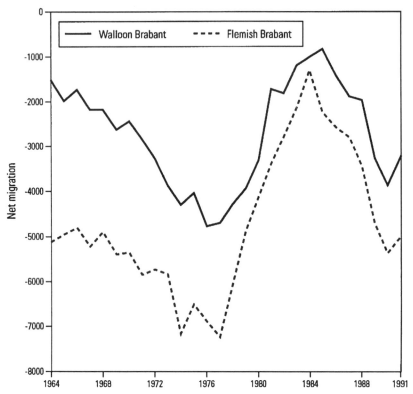

Figure 6.7 Net migration between Brussels and its neighbours, computed as in-migration to Brussels, 1964–91

When economic conditions are buoyant, the counterurbanization flow increases, while economic difficulties reduce this type of migration flow. In order to analyse in more detail such relationships, Figure 6.8 plots together three indices closely linked with the process of counterurbanization: the average price of a dwelling in Belgium, a construction costs index and the level of interest rates. Very briefly, the covariation between migration and the economic indices can be summarized as follows. The strong rise in counterurbanizing migration observed at the start of the 1970s is paralleled by a rise in the price of property and fairly closely by the construction cost index. The rapid rise in interest rates in 1979 is followed immediately by a rapid shrinkage in counterurbanizing migration. In reaction to this the price of property and construction costs decrease. However, it was not until 1986 and a new calm in the money markets that counterurbanization flows began to rise again. Following the law of supply and demand, the cost of property rose again along with construction costs, which, with a renewed rise in interest rates in 1990, could be the basis of a new decrease in the rate of counterurbanization.

It is worthwhile looking in more detail at the age selectivity of migration into and out of urban areas. Migration movements linked to the processes of urbanization

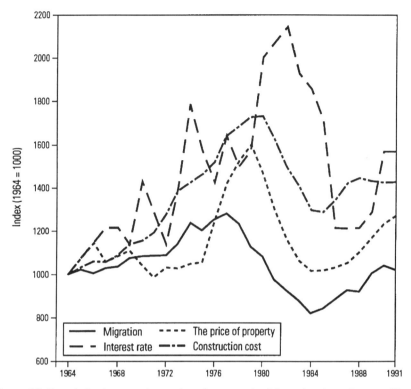

Figure 6.8 Covariation between the number of counterurbanizing migrations, the cost of buying property (houses and building plots), the cost of construction and the interest rate, 1964–91

and counterurbanization are not identical across age groups. As Figure 6.9 shows, in the case of a typical city such as Charleroi, urban areas generally gain from the migration of young adults, aged 18 to 24, and lose from the migrations of persons from age 35. These observations match a migration history which sees young persons start their adult life by migrating to urban areas and then return to the countryside as part of young families when they purchase a residence. The consequences of such a migration pattern are many: the concentration of young adults in urban centres, the impoverishment of cities through the exodus of higher-income households, those remaining behind being unable to afford to buy villas or small farms in the countryside, and a reduction in the population, counted as individuals, of urban areas but an increase in the count of households.

This process of urbanization/counterurbanization is not confined to the Brussels agglomeration. The accompanying maps detail the Belgian communes with a positive net migration balance for ages 15 to 24 (Figure 6.10) and for ages 25 to 39 (Figure 6.11). The first map picks out the principal urban agglomerations, while the second map identifies the fringes of the same urban regions to the east and west of Antwerpen and to the south of Charleroi and Liège (Van Hecke 1991).

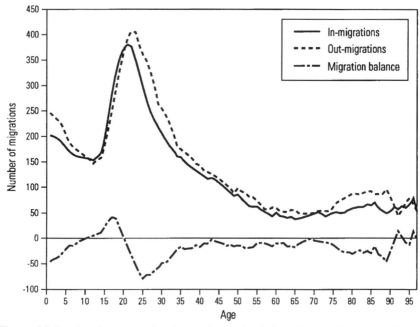

Figure 6.9 In-migrations, out-migrations and migration balance by age, Charleroi, 1988–93

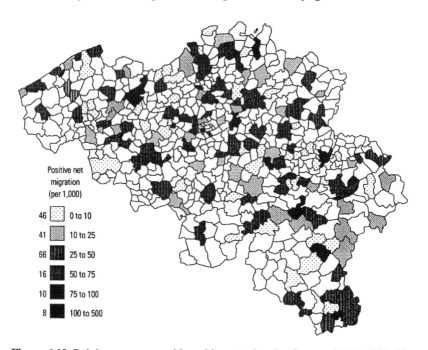

Figure 6.10 Belgian communes with positive net migration for ages 15–24, 1988–92

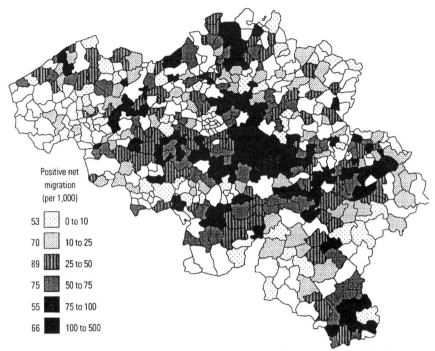

Figure 6.11 Belgian communes with positive net migration for ages 25–39, 1988–92

6.7 ZONES OF ATTRACTION AND ZONES OF REPULSION

Independently of the processes of urbanization/counterurbanization, is it possible to pick out zones of particular attraction or repulsion in the heart of Belgium? Before answering that question, we will set aside here the major role of Brussels (discussed earlier) and will analyse separately migration between Flemish *arrondissements* and between Walloon *arrondissements*.

Both to the north and south of the country, the zones of counterurbanization surrounding Brussels, Flemish Brabant and Walloon Brabant gain migrants from Brussels but lose migrants to the rest of Flanders and Wallonia respectively. At the heart of Flanders, the migration balance of the Hal-Vilvorde *arrondissement* is the most negative, just as that of Nivelles is in the middle of Wallonia. These observations show that the peri-urban areas closest to Brussels have reached a degree of saturation which contributes to the rising price of property in those areas. This saturation leads to population displacement into other *arrondissements* further from Brussels, those of Namur and Soignies in Wallonia and Mechelen and Leuven in Flanders (Van Hecke 1991).

Figure 6.12 is a map of Belgium without Brussels, Flemish Brabant and Walloon Brabant depicted, which shows those areas attracting or repulsing migrants in the rest of the country. In the North, Antwerpen, Aolst, Hasselt and Kortrijk have net

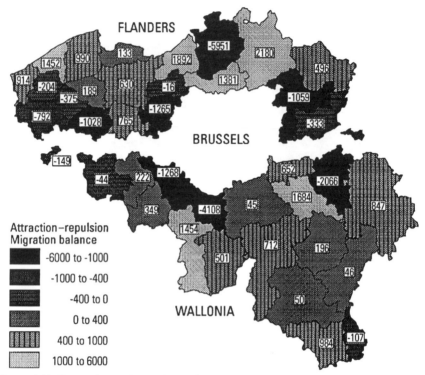

Figure 6.12 Zones of attraction and repulsion in Flanders and Wallonia, 1988–92

migration losses while Turnhout, Mechelen and adjacent *arrondissements* benefit from net in-migration. In the South, Charleroi, Liège and Soignies are zones of migration loss in contrast to Huy, Verviers and Waremme in periphery of Liège, and Thuin and Philippeville to the south of the Charleroi agglomeration which are zones of attraction. Thus, even when internal migration outside of the influence of Brussels is investigated, it is the process of counterurbanization which forms the principal feature of the migration behaviour of the Belgian population.

6.8 CONCLUSION

The existence of a National Register in Belgium provides time series data that enable the extent of the decline in the propensity to migrate since 1948 to be quantified. Age and gender differentials have been examined and geographical character-istics of migration flows have been determined at different spatial scales. The phenomenon of counterurbanization has been shown to be the dominant trend in internal migration, both in relation to Brussels and to areas of Flanders and Wallonia outside the influence of the capital region.

7 Changing Patterns of Net Migration in Denmark: an Explanatory Analysis

SVEN ILLERIS

7.1 DATA AND SPATIAL FRAMEWORK

Denmark is, like the other Scandinavian countries, in a particularly good situation as regards migration data. From the 17th century, parsons have registered births and deaths in each parish, thus enabling us to estimate migrations. The first census was taken in 1769, and from 1925, it has been compulsory to register all changes of address at the registers of population which were set up in all communes. Since 1970, the registration has been based on the personal number which all residents have. This makes it possible to combine the register of population with registers of firms, of dwellings and of schools, so censuses are no longer necessary. This system means that population data are very reliable and that the number of unregistered persons may be considered very small. It is very difficult to exist without a personal number, which is required, for instance, for medical treatment and for opening a bank account.

While official statistical data are the source of all tables and figures in this chapter, the spatial framework uses the administrative system established by the 1970 local government reform: the 14 *amter* (counties) are used which form the NUTS level 3 regions. Their average surface area is 3500 square kilometres and their average population is 300 000. Typically, each *amt* consists of three to four labour-market regions. The Copenhagen region is a special case. Here the labour-market region consists of two core communes, Copenhagen and Frederiksberg, which administratively also perform *amt* functions: the *amt* of Copenhagen, forming a totally suburbanized ring, roughly between five and 20 kilometres from the city centre; and the *amter* of Frederiksborg and Roskilde, forming a peripheral zone roughly 20–50 kilometres from the city centre, with a mixture of exurban settlements and rural land. The boundaries of these areas are shown in Figure 7.4. In this chapter, the commune of Copenhagen is further subdivided into the inner city (the old centre and the 19th-century multi-storey extensions) and the outer districts formed by early 20th-century suburbs, in order to examine trends in the capital region in more detail.

7.2 THE INTERREGIONAL MIGRATION PATTERN

The population geography of Denmark is characterized by the dominance of the

Population Migration in the European Union Edited by Philip Rees, John Stillwell, Andrew Convey and Marek Kupiszewski. © Editors and Contributors. Published 1996 John Wiley & Sons Ltd.

Copenhagen region (Table 7.1). In provincial Denmark, one may distinguish between the more urbanized regions (the islands of Zealand and Funen as well as Eastern Jutland) and the peripheral regions of South, West and North Jutland and some southern islands.

Table 7.1 Population of Danish *amter* 1970–93

Amter	9 Nov. 1970	1 Jan. 1981	1 Jan. 1993
Copenhagen Region	1753	1740	1725
West Zealand	259	279	286
Storstrøm	252	260	257
Bornholm	47	48	45
Funen	433	454	465
South Jutland	238	251	251
Ribe	198	214	221
Vejle	306	327	334
Ringkøbing	241	264	269
Århus	533	576	610
Viborg	221	232	230
North Jutland	456	483	487
Denmark total	5065	5124	5181

Ever since the mid-19th century, the dominating characteristic of interregional net migration was from provincial Denmark to the Copenhagen region. As illustrated by Figure 7.1, this pattern still prevailed in the 1950s and 1960s.

Figure 7.2 shows that in the early 1970s, a major turnaround took place. The net migration into the Copenhagen region ceased; in the 1970s, there was a net migration in the opposite direction, while in the 1980s interregional net migration flows have been very small.

The role of internal and international migration for the total population change is highlighted in Table 7.2, which shows the contribution of these components in selected sub-periods. Table 7.2 shows that regional population development is, of course, influenced by natural growth. This was still substantial in 1966–9 (though the fertility decrease had already started in 1967). Its gradual decline led, for Denmark as a whole, to negative figures in most of the eighties, but since 1990 natural growth has again become slightly positive. The most interesting thing about natural change is the very stable regional differences. It has always been lower in the islands than in Jutland (where it never became negative). The distinguishing factor is the variation in fertility: in this respect there are long-standing differences between the islands (especially Storstrøm *amt* in the south east) and Jutland (especially Ribe and Ringkøbing *amter* in the west). Because of their stability over time, the regional differences in natural growth rates influence the regional differences in total population change much in the same way, through ups and downs.

107

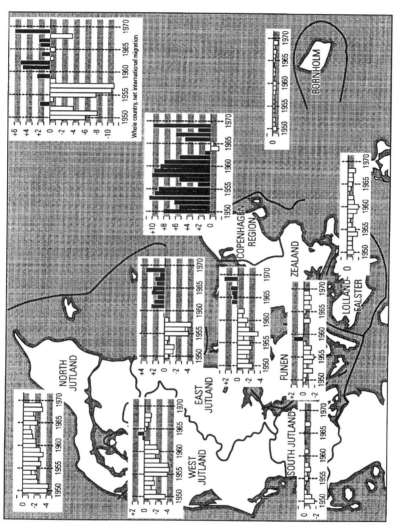

Figure 7.1 Net migration (in thousands) between groups of *amter*, 1950–69

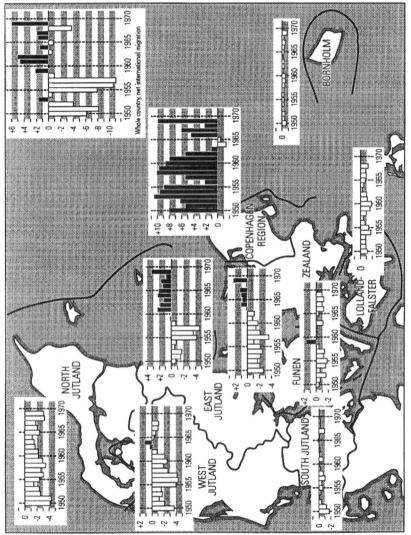

Figure 7.2 Total net migration (in thousands), 1970–92

Table 7.2 Population change and its components by *amter*, 1966–92

Annual rates per thousand inhabitants

Amter	Internal migration						International migration			
	66–9	76–8	80–2	84–6	87–9	90–2	80–2	84–6	87–9	90–2
Cop. region	2.8	-3.9	-0.6	-1.5	-0.5	0.3	-0.3	1.6	0.6	2.1
W. Zealand	2.6	6.5	1.2	4.4	1.2	0.8	0.0	2.1	1.0	2.5
Storstrøm	-2.4	4.7	1.4	2.2	0.7	1.4	0.1	1.7	1.2	2.0
Bornholm	-9.3	1.8	-1.4	-1.6	-4.3	-3.5	-4.9	0.8	-0.8	1.3
Funen	-2.6	1.7	1.3	1.4	1.9	1.6	0.2	1.4	0.9	2.1
S. Jutland	-1.4	0.7	-1.4	-1.9	-0.4	-2.3	0.1	1.5	0.8	1.7
Ribe	-0.4	2.5	0.0	-0.9	-1.4	-2.6	0.2	1.4	1.2	2.1
Vejle	-1.1	1.6	0.4	0.7	0.2	0.6	0.0	1.5	0.6	1.6
Ringkøbing	-1.4	1.8	-1.4	-1.2	-2.3	-2.8	-0.3	1.4	0.5	1.5
Århus	-3.9	0.3	1.4	2.7	2.4	1.9	0.2	1.6	0.2	2.0
Viborg	-4.0	1.6	-1.6	-1.6	-2.5	-2.6	0.0	1.7	0.3	1.8
N. Jutland	-4.6	1.7	-0.1	-0.5	-0.5	-1.2	0.1	1.7	1.0	1.8
Denmark	0.0	0.0	0.0	0.0	0.0	0.0	-0.1	1.6	0.7	2.0

Annual rates per thousand inhabitants

Amter	Natural change						Total change					
	66–9	76–8	80–2	84–6	87–9	90–2	66–9	76–8	80–2	84–6	87–9	90–2
Cop. region	5.7	0.5	-1.9	-2.3	-1.0	0.1	9.2	-2.5	-2.8	-2.2	-1.0	2.6
W. Zealand	5.1	1.1	-1.0	-1.1	-0.6	-0.2	8.1	8.8	0.2	5.4	1.5	3.1
Storstrøm	2.8	-1.1	-3.2	-3.6	-3.1	-3.2	0.8	4.4	-1.7	0.3	-1.3	0.2
Bornholm	3.7	0.8	-1.3	-2.1	-1.4	-2.7	-5.2	3.3	-7.6	-2.8	-6.6	-4.9
Funen	5.5	1.6	-1.0	-1.0	-0.7	0.6	2.8	4.1	0.5	1.8	2.1	4.2
S. Jutland	7.6	3.5	1.3	0.4	0.6	1.6	5.8	6.0	0.0	0.0	1.0	0.9
Ribe	9.2	5.0	3.0	2.1	2.7	3.7	8.8	8.8	3.2	2.6	2.6	3.2
Vejle	7.1	3.4	1.0	0.0	0.8	1.7	6.3	6.2	1.4	2.1	1.6	3.9
Ringkøbing	10.5	6.1	3.4	2.3	3.2	3.4	9.2	8.8	1.7	2.5	1.4	2.1
Århus	7.5	4.2	1.2	0.9	1.9	3.1	11.7	5.3	2.4	5.2	4.5	7.0
Viborg	6.5	2.9	0.8	0.1	0.8	1.0	2.8	5.4	-0.8	0.1	-1.4	0.2
N. Jutland	7.2	2.9	0.8	-0.4	0.2	1.0	2.6	5.6	0.8	0.8	0.8	1.7
Denmark	6.4	2.1	-0.3	-0.8	0.0	0.9	6.7	3.0	-0.4	0.8	0.7	2.9

Note: Cop. region = Copenhagen region

If we turn to the influence of net migration on total change, the picture varies much more from period to period. In the 1960s, the net migration from the provinces to the Copenhagen region influenced total regional population change heavily (though the latter was modified by the differences in natural growth, as already mentioned). This pattern reflects a century-old trend, now only modified by an overspill into the *amt* of West Zealand. International migration played only a small role, except for some net migration into the Copenhagen region. In the 1970s, the dramatic turnaround took place: the internal net migration was now from the Copenhagen region to all of provincial Denmark. Combined with the decline in natural growth, it resulted in a population decrease in the Copenhagen region. The adjoining *amter* of West Zealand and Storstrøm benefited most from the net migration flows, while the growth of population in Jutland was caused primarily by natural growth. The role of international migration was still modest, a small plus everywhere.

In the 1980s, internal net migration flows were smaller and rather unstable. As a result of their small size, they have influenced total regional population change less than they did traditionally. In recession periods (the early 1980s and since 1987), there was virtually no net migration between the Copenhagen region and the rest of the country, whereas the boom of the mid-1980s witnessed a renewed net migration out of the Copenhagen region. The business cycle variations will be discussed later. A constant pattern was negative net migration from the most peripheral *amter* and—in contrast to the 1960s—positive net migration into the more urbanized intermediate regions of Zealand, Funen and Eastern Jutland; the second largest Danish city, Århus, flourished.

While the influence of internal migration thus declined, international migration has become a more important component, especially in the 1990s. A rather surprising fact is that the relative surplus of international net migration has been more or less the same everywhere. This means, however, that the renewed population growth in the Copenhagen region—after 15 years of decline—is almost totally due to international net immigration. Actually, most of the international migration consists of three exchange flows:

1. The migration of labour is unrestricted between Denmark and both the EU and the Nordic countries. These flows are rather modest, constant and, in the long run, balanced in both directions.
2. In the late 1960s and early 1970s, a good deal of immigration from Mediterranean and Asian countries took place, especially from Yugoslavia, Turkey, and Pakistan. However, this type of immigration was more modest than in most West European countries. Since 1973, it has only been allowed for members of families already in Denmark, but this alone has meant some net immigration. The immigrants have primarily settled in the Copenhagen region.
3. In the 1980s and 1990s, a net immigration of refugees and asylum seekers has been permitted, especially from Iran, Sri Lanka, Iraq, Vietnam and the former Yugoslavia. The number is relatively much smaller than in Germany but has become a political problem. The government is responsible for their integration and has placed them all over the country.

7.3 AGE VARIATION IN INTERREGIONAL MIGRATION

The age pattern of intercommunal migration is clear (Table 7.3) and has remained more or less unchanged for many years: the bulk of all migration (in 1990, 57 per cent) takes place between the ages of 15 and 29, with very little migration after the age of 65 (2 per cent of all migrants). There is little difference in gender, though female migration declines a little earlier than male migration. The total number of changes of address is almost three times higher and has a slightly different age distribution: the peak in the 15–29 age bracket is less pronounced (52 per cent of all changes), and there is a small secondary peak of migrants aged 65 and over (5 per cent of all changes). Thus, there is a small flow of intracommunal old-age migration which undoubtedly is connected with moves into nursing homes rather than with retirement.

Table 7.3 Age-specific migration rates, 1990

Age group	Intercommunal migrants	All changes of address
0–4	6.5	18.7
5–9	4.1	12.8
10–14	3.2	9.8
15–19	11.0	27.6
20–4	22.3	53.9
25–9	12.9	32.8
30–4	7.5	20.3
35–9	4.5	13.0
40–4	3.6	10.1
45–9	3.0	8.0
50–4	2.5	6.6
55–9	2.0	5.6
60–4	1.8	5.1
65–9	1.3	4.8
70–4	0.9	4.4
75–9	0.8	5.2
80–4	0.6	6.6
85–9	0.6	8.6
Total	6.1	16.5

In order to highlight the regional pattern in age variation, Table 7.4 shows net migration in age groups in two contrasting areas, the Copenhagen region and the peripheral area of Viborg and North Jutland *amter*. Table 7.4 shows an age pattern which is rather stable: net migration out of the less urbanized regions and into the Copenhagen region takes place in the age brackets of 15–24 and is undoubtedly caused by the need to move to education and first jobs in the big cities. Net migration in the opposite direction primarily takes place in the late twenties and thirties, accompanied by children. This flow consists of young families taking up jobs requiring an education not offered in small towns and rural districts. The variations

Table 7.4 Internal net migration by age group in selected areas and years, 1965–90

Age group	Copenhagen region					Viborg and North Jutland *amter*				
	1965	1977	1981	1985	1990	1965	1977	1981	1985	1990
0–14	−2328	−3388	−1392	−2183	−1073	194	755	72	477	118
15–19	3518	1211	1514	1608	1350	−1683	−461	−523	−529	−431
20–4	3148	1157	2372	2419	2733	−1567	−508	−846	−903	−1073
25–9	−999	−1303	−408	−914	140	7	483	130	149	−177
30–44	−1367	−2547	−1063	−2067	−1195	143	494	−13	448	182
45–64	−504	−1326	−893	−1377	−1629	30	149	125	234	148
65+	−213	−400	−252	−309	−572	39	61	47	−37	86
Total	1255	−6596	−122	−2823	−256	−2827	973	−1008	−156	−1147

between the selected years involve all age groups: in 1965 and 1981, young people's net migration from the peripheral region and into the Copenhagen region was very large, and the opposite net migration of people over 25 and children was modest. In 1977, young people's net migration out of the peripheral region and into the Copenhagen region was modest, while the opposite migration of persons over 25 and children was large. The years 1985 and 1990 show more or less inbetween situations.

7.4 FACTORS BEHIND THE INTERREGIONAL MIGRATION

There is no reason to doubt that interregional migration is mainly caused by factors connected with education and jobs, though no major study has been conducted in Denmark. The following discussion is based on Court (1989) and Illeris (1988; 1990). The supply of jobs in the main sectors of the economy is illustrated by Table 7.5. Here a simplified division of the country into four main regions is applied, as well as a simplified sectoral classification. Due to changes in the administrative division, in the classification of economic activities and in information-gathering methods, the data from 1970 and earlier are not totally comparable with the 1982 and 1990 data. Still, the main trends shown by the table are beyond doubt.

Table 7.5 highlights the dramatic changes in the regional distribution of jobs that have taken place over the last decades: the increase in employment has primarily occurred in Jutland, while employment in the Copenhagen region has been more or less constant in absolute numbers since 1970 and the rest of the islands have kept a constant share of national employment. The shift from the Copenhagen region to Jutland has first and foremost occurred in manufacturing industries, where the Copenhagen region has lost roughly half of its jobs in 30 years. But the increase in public service employment up to 1982 was primarily to the benefit of provincial Denmark too. This fact is connected with the 1970 local government reform, which through amalgamation of small communes made it possible for the new ones to offer child care, education for young people and other services that previously had been the privilege of bigger towns. The development of private services—including such 'metropolitan' sectors as business services—has followed the general trend of employment and population. And the decline of agricultural employment has, of

Table 7.5 Regional distribution of employment, 1960–90

Region	Year	Agriculture	Manufacturing + construction	Public services	Private services + not indicated	Total
Copenhagen region	1960	7	44	49	47	39
	1970	7	37	46	45	38
	1982	6	30	40	42	36
	1990	6	26	37	41	34
Islands	1960	30	19	17	17	20
(W. Zealand,	1970	28	20	18	17	20
Storstrøm, Bornholm,	1982	27	21	19	17	19
Funen)	1990	27	21	20	17	20
East Jutland	1960	17	16	14	15	15
(Vejle, Århus)	1970	17	17	15	16	16
	1982	17	19	17	17	17
	1990	16	20	18	18	18
Peripheral Jutland	1960	46	21	20	21	25
(S. Jutland, Ribe,	1970	49	25	22	22	26
Ringkøbing, Viborg,	1982	50	31	24	24	28
N. Jutland)	1990	50	33	25	24	28
Total	1960	370	760	240	640	2010
thousands	1970	240	830	420	800	2290
	1982	190	640	800	910	2540
	1990	140	690	800	1010	2650

course, gone against the general trend by only affecting provincial Denmark. The conclusion is that the turnaround in the interregional migration pattern, from net migration into the Copenhagen region to the opposite or at least a neutral net migration, is connected with the dramatic shift of manufacturing out of Copenhagen and with the above-average increase in public services in provincial Denmark.

The business-cycle fluctuations mentioned earlier are not highlighted by this rather crude table. Suffice it to say that recessions (1974–5, 1980–3 and from 1987) have hit provincial Denmark worst, simply because agriculture and manufacturing are the most vulnerable sectors in bad times, and they are overrepresented in provincial Denmark. On the other hand, booms (1976–9, 1984–6) have also favoured provincial Denmark. Services, which are overrepresented in the Copenhagen region, are less sensible to business-cycle variations. These facts explain the increasing migration into the Copenhagen region during recessions and out of the Copenhagen region during booms.

7.5 POPULATION CHANGE BY SIZE OF SETTLEMENT

An important question is the migrational fate of the various levels of the urban hierarchy in terms of net migration. Do people move to or leave big cities, small towns, rural districts?

A detailed examination of this question will not be taken up here, but is illustrated by Figure 7.3 which shows the development of a proxy variable, namely total population change. (As stated above, differences in natural growth tend to remain stable, so the changes in total population change are likely to be due to changes in migrational behaviour.) Communes have been classified into groups according to the number of people in their biggest town. The Copenhagen region is shown as a whole.

Figure 7.3 shows how the population of the Copenhagen region dropped under the national average around 1970. From 1975 to 1979, there was a period of complete counterurbanization: the smaller the settlement, the higher the rate of population growth. From 1980, the medium-sized towns with 20 000–500 000 inhabitants have grown fastest, and the Copenhagen region has been the worst performer. But the differences between the size classes are now small, indicating little net migration between them.

7.6 MIGRATION WITHIN THE COPENHAGEN REGION

Until 1856, Copenhagen was contained in four square kilometres inside its old fortifications. Since then, housing and population has spread like a centrifugal wave. At the same time, the population of older areas has decreased, as children grow up and move away. Gradually, the inner city has attracted a new component, namely students and other young people, but they tend to move away as soon as they marry and have children. The distribution of population inside the Copenhagen region in 1970, 1981 and 1993 is illustrated by Table 7.6.

Table 7.6 Population in the Copenhagen region 1970–93

Area	9 Nov. 1970	1 Jan. 1981	1 Jan. 1993
	(Thousands)		
Copenhagen commune			
Inner City[1]	336	259	244
Outer districts	287	235	223
Frederiksberg commune	102	88	87
Copenhagen *amt*	615	625	604
Frederiksborg	259	330	346
Roskilde	153	203	221
Copenhagen region	1753	1740	1725

Note: Including 2000–3000 persons with no fixed address

According to Figure 7.4, which shows net migration in the core, ring and peripheral zones of the Copenhagen region since 1970, the centrifugal wave-pattern still prevailed in the 1970s: large net migration out of the core communes and into the peripheral *amter*. However, from the late 1970s, this pattern changed: the core communes became net receivers of migrants, while the net migration into the peripheral *amter* was dramatically reduced. Net out-migration was taking place

115

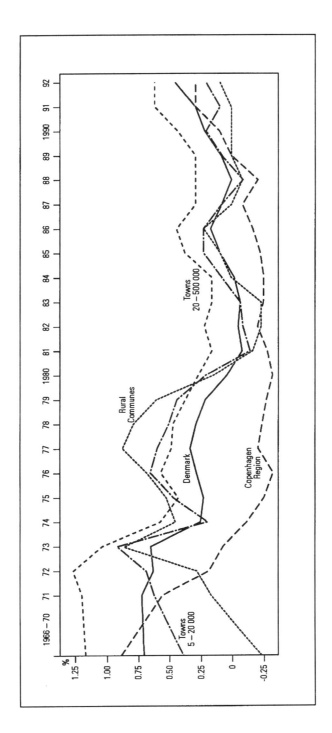

Figure 7.3 Annual population change rate by type of municipality, 1966–92

from the suburban ring (the *amt* of Copenhagen).

As elsewhere, natural growth has influenced population change in the Copenhagen region (Table 7.7). The birth surplus decreased in peripheral zones and the birth deficit increased in the core until the first half of the 1980s and then took a more positive direction. These developments happened in more or less parallel ways everywhere in the region, however. The explanation of the difference between core and periphery is above all the different age structures.

The variations in population change between the various parts of the region are primarily due to the migration pattern. The 1976–8 period represents the traditional pattern, with heavy net migration from the core, and to a small degree from the suburban ring, to the peripheral zones, though these flows had already started to decline. International migration only played a minor role. In the 1980s, we observe a different pattern emerge. Now the migration pattern of the inner city

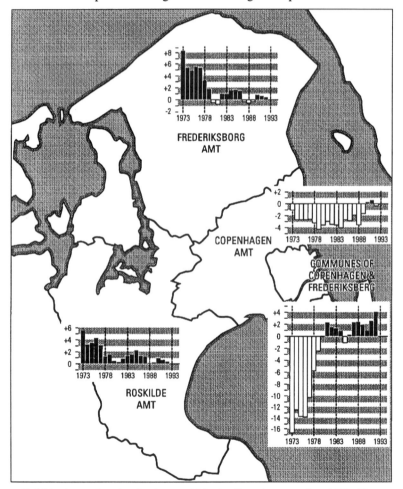

Figure 7.4 Total net migration (in thousands) in the Copenhagen region, 1973–92

Table 7.7 Population change and its components, 1973–92

Area	Annual rates per 1000 inhabitants									
	76–8	80–2	84–6	87–9	90–2	76–8	80–2	84–6	87–9	90–2
	Internal migration					International migration				
Cop. Inner City¹	−18.6	1.8	−0.2	3.9	1.9	0.8	0.1	3.7	0.9	3.5
Cop. Outer Districts	−18.2	−0.7	−6.0	2.0	−1.3	1.0	0.1	1.0	1.0	2.3
Frederiksberg Comm.	−8.5	11.8	3.0	5.6	10.2	−0.5	−0.6	0.6	−0.2	2.6
Copenhagen *amt*	−5.3	−5.0	−6.1	−4.2	−1.4	0.7	−0.4	0.9	0.3	1.7
Frederiksborg	13.6	0.3	2.6	−1.7	0	1.1	−0.6	2.3	0.6	2.0
Roskilde	13.2	3.2	6.7	1.8	1.4	1.7	−0.4	1.5	0.8	1.7
Copenhagen region	−3.9	−0.6	−1.5	−0.5	0.3	0.9	−0.3	1.6	0.6	2.1
	Natural growth					Total population change				
Cop. Inner City¹	−11.2	−12.9	−12.0	−6.5	−5.2	−29.0	−11.0	−8.6	−1.7	0.2
Cop. Outer Districts	−3.6	−4.6	−5.0	−5.6	−2.2	−20.8	−5.2	−10.0	−2.6	−1.1
Frederiksberg Comm.	−8.9	−10.7	−9.6	−9.0	−6.7	−17.9	0.5	−5.9	−3.7	6.0
Copenhagen *amt*	4.1	1.3	0.2	0.6	1.3	−0.5	−4.0	−5.1	−3.3	1.7
Frederiksborg	5.9	2.5	1.9	2.5	3.0	20.5	2.2	6.7	1.4	4.9
Roskilde	5.9	2.7	1.9	2.8	3.6	20.7	5.6	10.2	5.4	6.7
Copenhagen region	0.5	−1.9	−2.3	−1.0	0.1	−2.6	−2.8	−2.2	−1.0	2.6

Note: Including persons with no fixed address

and especially the commune of Frederiksberg have turned positive. This means that the two core communes from 1981 to 1991 received 8000 in-migrants net instead of losing 165 000, as they would have done had the 1973–5 tendency (not shown in the table) continued. The balance of the outer districts of the commune of Copenhagen, on the other hand, remained negative. The net migration into the peripheral *amter* of Frederiksborg and Roskilde decreased substantially. From 1981 to 1991 they received 110 000 fewer net migrants than they would have got had the 1973–5 tendency continued. In the periods 1984–6 and from 1990, international net immigration contributed significantly to the total population change.

One might say that the outward growth wave and the thinning out thereafter almost came to a stop about 1980—though a small wave into the peripheral *amter* and some thinning out in the older suburban ring continued to operate. A completely new phenomenon was the net migration into the inner city and the commune of Frederiksberg. In the case of the inner city, it consisted partly of international immigration, primarily from Turkey, Yugoslavia, Pakistan and Morocco.

There are, however, fluctuations in the pattern of the last decade: the net flows from the suburban rings into the peripheral *amter*, were strongest from 1983 to 86 (a boom period). They were considerably weaker in the early 1980s as well as in the early 1990s (recession periods). Furthermore, the improved migration balance of the region against the rest of the country in recession periods, which has already been mentioned, has contributed to increased gains in the core communes and reduced losses in the suburban ring in these periods.

7.7 AGE VARIATIONS IN INTRAREGIONAL MIGRATION

Table 7.8 shows that the age pattern in net migrations is relatively stable: those aged 15–24 move from the suburban ring and (except in the 1970s) the periphery into the core communes, while people in their late twenties and thirties, with their children, move from the core and the suburban ring out to the periphery (and, as mentioned earlier, to provincial Denmark). The improved balance of the core communes in the 1980s, compared to the 1970s, is caused both by increased net in-migration of young people and by reduced net out-migration of people in their thirties and over, plus children.

The migration pattern has a strong influence on the age distribution of the population. Table 7.9 shows the particular distribution of the core communes of Copenhagen and Frederiksberg, compared to the whole country. There are relatively more young people in the 20–4 age bracket in the core of Copenhagen than in the Danish population as a whole, and also relatively more elderly people over 60 (but the latter surplus diminishes as the old generations in the core of Copenhagen die). On the other hand, there are relatively fewer people in the economically active 25–59 age bracket, as well as children. A change has occurred in the 1980s, where the core has got a relative surplus up to the age of 40, especially of unmarried and divorced persons.

7.8 FACTORS BEHIND MIGRATION IN THE COPENHAGEN REGION

The traditional migration pattern in the Copenhagen region, as in other major urban regions, could be explained by two factors: the outward wave of migration was partly pulled by the construction of new housing on the ever-moving periphery of the built-up area and partly pushed by the size reduction in the households who lived in the older stock of housing. The fundamental changes which took place around 1980 require new explanations, except for the suburban ring where the 'thinning out' continues. Why has a 'turnaround' occurred in the inner city, which now has a positive migration balance in Copenhagen as well as in other big European cities? And why has the net migration to the periphery decreased so much? Several hypotheses have been put forward. In the following section, they will be discussed briefly, continuing the discussion in Illeris (1983).

In the wake of the second oil price crisis, it was a widespread notion that people concentrated in the inner city in order to save heating and transport costs – both of these being cheaper in the multi-storey houses of the inner city, with short distances to many jobs and good public transport, than in the one-family houses of the periphery. However, as the oil prices have gone down without any real return to the old pattern of migration, this hypothesis can be discarded.

Another popular hypothesis points to changing preferences and 'gentrification' as the main cause: due to a new preference for truly urban, high-density environ-

Table 7.8 Internal net migration by age group, 1973–90

Age group	Copenhagen and Frederiksberg commune				Copenhagen *amt*				Frederiksborg and Roskilde *amter*			
	1973	1981	1985	1990	1973	1981	1985	1990	1973	1981	1985	1990
0–14	−8037	−1658	−3002	−2809	−498	−186	−191	807	4013	452	1010	929
15–19	1046	2582	2686	2768	−154	−395	−300	−517	145	−673	−778	−901
20–4	−412	4142	4904	5888	−355	−1156	−1563	−1503	1351	−614	−922	−1652
25–9	−5990	−882	−2128	−1516	−63	−73	−51	733	3295	547	1265	923
30–44	−4673	−775	−2971	−3273	−1118	−275	−328	982	2822	−13	1232	1086
45–64	−1980	−383	−788	−857	−353	−535	−937	−910	833	25	248	138
65+	−897	−743	−861	−929	151	140	72	−86	371	351	480	443
Total	−20937	2283	−2160	−728	−2390	−2480	−3298	−494	12830	75	2635	966

Table 7.9 Age distribution of population in core communes, 1973–92 (%)

Age group	1 Jan. 1973 Copenhagen and Frederiksberg	Denmark	1 Jan. 1982 Copenhagen and Frederiksberg	Denmark	1 Jan. 1992 Copenhagen and Frederiksberg	Denmark
0–4	4.9	7.3	4.0	5.7	5.0	5.9
5–14	9.5	15.7	7.7	14.2	6.4	11.0
15–19	5.5	7.4	5.2	8.0	4.2	7.0
20–4	9.1	7.7	9.3	7.3	10.6	7.3
25–39	19.0	20.7	23.1	22.9	28.0	22.6
40–59	24.7	23.0	20.0	22.0	21.0	25.9
60+	27.4	18.2	30.8	19.8	24.8	20.3
Total	100.0	100.0	100.0	100.0	100.0	100.0

ments and proximity to many people and services, well-to-do and especially child-less households should now move 'back to the city'. There is no doubt that this has happened in some cases, in Copenhagen as well as in other cities, and the relative surplus of persons in the 25–39 age bracket which has emerged in the 1980s (compared to the national population) may be interpreted to support the gentrification hypothesis. However, there is a good deal of evidence to indicate that this is rather the exception than the main cause of the stabilization of the inner-city population: the continued net out-migration of people over 25 (the potential 'gentrifiers') and the continued deterioration of the social status of the inner-city population compared to the national average.

Thus the rate of unemployment in November 1990 was 11.4 per cent in the commune of Copenhagen against 8.7 per cent in Denmark as a whole, while in November 1980 it was only 7.7 per cent in the commune of Copenhagen against 7.1 in Denmark as a whole. Similarly, the mean taxable income in 1990 in the commune of Copenhagen was exactly the same as in the country as a whole, while in 1980 it was 7 per cent higher. The mean taxable income of persons who moved out of the commune of Copenhagen in 1990 was 17 per cent higher than the income of in-migrants. Finally, the commune of Copenhagen has above-average rates of criminals as well as diseases and deaths by suicide, alcoholism, drugs, and lung cancer (Illeris 1984). In all probability, the cheap old housing stock still attracts more 'social losers' than 'gentry'.

Indeed, we have to drop the notion of all-embracing mass changes of preferences such as a 'green wave' in the 1970s followed by gentrification in the 1980s. In general, the shift from a 'Fordist' to a 'Post-Fordist' society is supposed to be connected with more segmented markets and individualized tastes. This is probably also the case in the residential sphere: preferences for low densities and for dense urban environments may very well exist in different groups of the population and both be realized when people can afford it.

A third suggested explanation for the stabilization of the inner-city population is international immigration. Clearly it has contributed—we already observed that in 1990–2 the growth of the population of the whole region was due to this factor. Furthermore, immigrants have a higher fertility than Danish citizens. However, the total number of aliens in the inner city of Copenhagen by 1992 was only 24 000 or 10 per cent of the population (against 3 per cent in Denmark as a whole), a modest increase of 4000 persons since 1982—not enough to explain the changed trend of population.

A fourth hypothesis focuses on the construction of new housing, partly in urban renewal areas and partly on abandoned harbour, railway, industrial and similar sites. As regards old housing areas, for many years it has been an objective of urban renewal to reduce densities in the 19th-century areas—only recently has this objective been relaxed. Consequently, the statistical district where most urban renewal has taken place, Inner Nørrebro, has seen its population decrease from 57 000 in 1970 (before the renewal started) to 34 000 in 1992, after the new housing had been built. Of course the process has contributed to a more positive population development during the rebuilding phase of the eighties than during the demolition phase of the 1970s, but its total effect has been a clear reduction of population.

Altogether, the number of dwellings in the core communes has, after a decrease in the inner city in the 1970s, hardly changed in the 1980s (Table 7.10). Table 7.10 leads, however, to a fifth hypothesis: it might be the very modest construction of new housing in the periphery in the 1980s that was responsible, not only for the deceleration of net migration into these *amter* but also for the stabilization of the population of the core. In this hypothesis, the notion is that it is not changed preferences and hence reduced demand that has caused the slow-down of new peripheral house building but economic barriers that have impeded it. When people cannot afford to have new houses built, they have to remain in the old ones! The economic barriers could be the long periods of recession (1980–3 and again from 1987), high real rates of interest, reduced inflation and hence reduced value of home ownership as an investment and, finally, less favourable taxation and mortgaging rules for private housing from 1987.

This hypothesis probably explains the variation in the migrational balance of the peripheral *amter*. Indeed, in the boom period in the mid-1980s, when house building increased somewhat, net migration into the periphery as well as out of the older

Table 7.10 Number of dwellings in the Copenhagen region, 1970–92

Area	1970	1981	1984	1987	1990	1992
			Thousands			
Copenhagen commune						
Inner City	160	148[1]	149	148	148	147
Outer districts	126	125[1]	130	130	130	130
Frederiksberg commune	47	49	49	50	50	51
Copenhagen *amt*	216	260	264	269	276	279
Frederiksborg	87	122	127	133	139	141
Roskilde	52	75	78	85	89	91
Copenhagen region	686	790	798	815	832	839

Note: [1] 10 000 dwellings in the commune of Copenhagen are not accounted for

and newer suburban rings increased too. If this hypothesis is correct, net migration into the periphery may pick up again if and when economic conditions for house building improve.

The conclusion must be that the observed changes in the intraregional migration pattern since 1980 have been caused by several factors such as gentrification, international immigration and reduced economic and legal stimuli for the building of new private housing in the periphery. These factors combine in a unique way in each metropolitan region, however, so the explanation found in the Copenhagen region cannot be generalized without an examination of each case.

8 Interregional Migration Patterns and Processes in Germany

HANSJÖRG BUCHER and HANS-PETER GATZWEILER

8.1 THE INFLUENCE OF MIGRATION ON REGIONAL POPULATION DYNAMICS IN THE EIGHTIES

The contributions of the individual demographic components (natural change, net interregional migration and net international migration) to the development of regional populations in Germany have been rather diverse. In the 1980s, migration turned out to be the most important component of population development at the scale of Regional Policy Regions (*Raumordnungsregionen*). These 97 regions are special subdivisions of the Federal Republic, defined by functional criteria, particularly accessibility to places of high centrality. In more than two-thirds of all regional policy regions, migration is the crucial component that determines whether a population increases or decreases. When the regions show a population increase, this is mostly due to migration gains. Regions with large attractive metropolitan centres, such as Frankfurt, Stuttgart and Munich, owe their considerable population increase to high migration gains (Figure 8.1). During the second half of the 1980s, migration gained in importance. The high number of resettlers (*Aussiedler*) from Eastern Europe, together with the strongly growing number of asylum seekers, led to a population increase in almost all regions.

8.2 INTERNAL INTERREGIONAL MIGRATION IN THE EIGHTIES

Internal interregional migration is here defined as a relocation of usual residence between regional policy regions. The following description of internal interregional migration in the 1980s emphasizes three aspects: gross and net interregional migration flows, the selectivity of interregional migration and the migration between the western and eastern states (*Länder*) of Germany after unification.

8.2.1 GROSS AND NET INTERREGIONAL MIGRATION

Migration used to be higher in the western regions of Germany than in the eastern, the former German Democratic Republic (GDR), although the differences have narrowed over time (Figure 8.2). Migration across the East German/West German

Population Migration in the European Union Edited by Philip Rees, John Stillwell, Andrew Convey and Marek Kupiszewski. © Editors and Contributors. Published 1996 John Wiley & Sons Ltd.

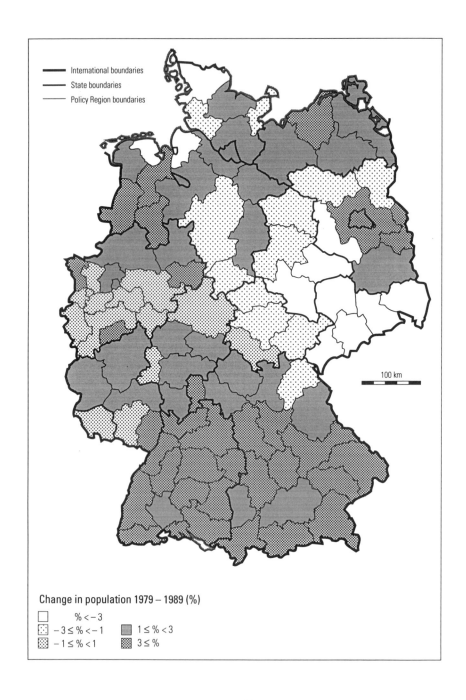

Figure 8.1 Regional population change, 1979–89

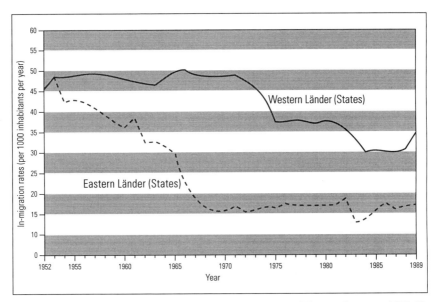

Figure 8.2 Gross interregional in-migration rates in Western and Eastern Germany, 1952-89

border has not been taken into account, though. This means that internal interregional migration is defined as a change of place of residence within the national territory in question. East–west as well as west–east migrations have been counted as internal interregional migrations only since 3 October 1990, when the two parts of Germany were unified. The higher level of migration in the western regions is mainly a product of the freedom of choice of place of residence and the greater number of housing opportunities. In the former GDR, the level of migration was determined mostly by the development of regional housing supply. Migration for education or work-place reasons was much less important.

During the 1980s, a diverse mixture of regions with migration gains and migration losses can be seen in western Germany. Two gradients are visible, one related to settlement structure and one of a geographic nature. Highly agglomerated regions were more likely to register migration gains. Peripherally located and sparsely populated regions, on the other hand, suffered migration losses. During the 1980s, internal interregional migration in the western part of Germany was principally migration from the countryside to the urban agglomerations and caused by regional disparities (Figure 8.3).

In East Germany the important destinations for interregional migration were the Greater Berlin area (East Berlin) and a number of cities which were the seats of regional or local administrations. Migration losses, on the other hand, were concentrated in the north of East Germany with its mainly agrarian structure and in the south, in the industrialized and environmentally deprived agglomeration area of Halle–Leipzig–Dessau, and in towns which were not the seat of any administration. In contrast to West Germany, interregional migration in East Germany could not be characterized as a migration from countryside to urban agglomeration.

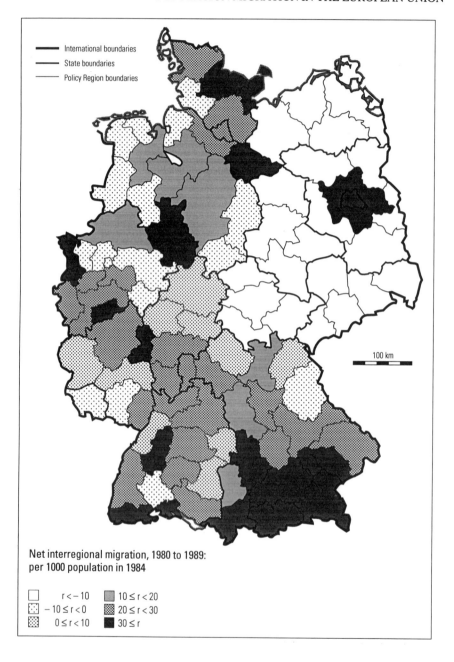

Figure 8.3 Net interregional migration rates, all ages, 1980–9

8.2.2 SELECTIVE INTERREGIONAL MIGRATION

It is a characteristic feature of interregional migration that it is selective with regard to features like age, stage in the family cycle, education, occupation and income. Those features are closely linked to different expectations regarding the living conditions in a region, as well as to different modes of behaviour. Age-specific selectivity of interregional migration within the western part of Germany as a consequence of unequal living conditions becomes obvious when we compare the age-specific migration balances of persons aged 18–29 years and 50 years and over (Figures 8.4 and 8.5).

The 18–29 age group tends to migrate toward urban areas. Migration gains in this age group are found in regions which have a university and employment for qualified people. Interregional migrants in the age group 50 years and over generally migrate from polluted urban areas to the amenity-rich areas along the coast, in the countryside away from large cities and in the Alpine Foreland.

8.2.3 MIGRATION BETWEEN THE WESTERN AND EASTERN PARTS OF GERMANY

Ever since the events of the late 1980s that led to German unification, the difference in living and working conditions between the western and the eastern part of Germany has been the decisive factor stimulating internal migration in Germany. In 1989, after the Wall came down and the GDR collapsed, a total of about 338 000 East Germans migrated to the Federal Republic of Germany. In 1990, their number had risen to 395 000. Since there was hardly any migration from west to east, the migration loss to East Germany was extremely high.

However, in 1991, the migration from east to west decreased by a third compared to the year before. There were a total of 250 000 out-migrations, ie 145 000 fewer than in 1990. The number of average monthly out-migrations decreased from 33 000 in 1990 to 21 000 in 1991. At the same time, the west to east migration, ie the in-migration from the western part of Germany to the eastern part, increased. This means that the migration loss from the eastern part of Germany to the western diminished by one-half, to about 170 000 people, compared to the year before (Figure 8.6).

Taking the age population and sex structures into account, it is safe to assume that the out-migrations from the eastern part of Germany were undertaken mainly by younger families, while mostly men migrated to the east. In 1990, 67 per cent of all in-migrations from the west were men aged between 18 and 50. In 1991, 70 per cent of all in-migrants were male. It remains to be seen whether this west to east migration can be counted as permanent or whether a large part of these men are only temporary migrants, ie living apart from their families for a limited period of time. Apart from the permanent east–west migrations, there are also about 500 000 commuters to be taken into account who live mainly in the former border regions. The percentage of commuters in the work-force amounted to 4 per cent in 1991. This group displays a high propensity for migration.

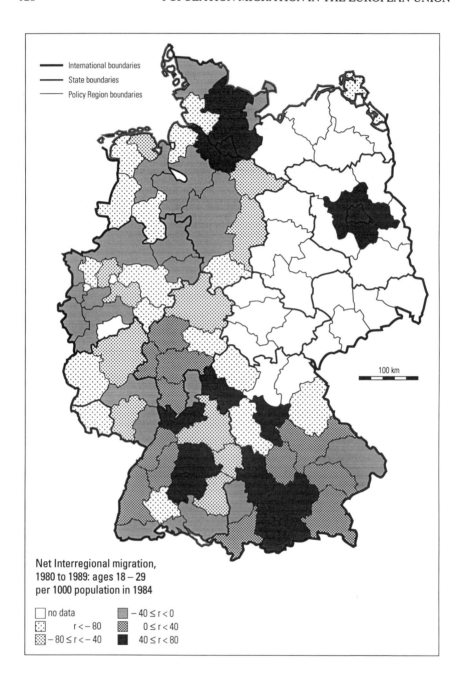

Figure 8.4 Net interregional migration rates, ages 18–29, 1980–9

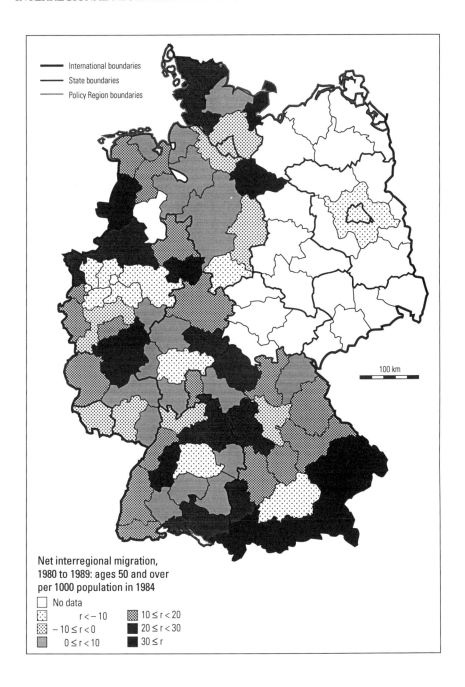

Figure 8.5 Net interregional migration rates, ages 50 and over, 1980–9

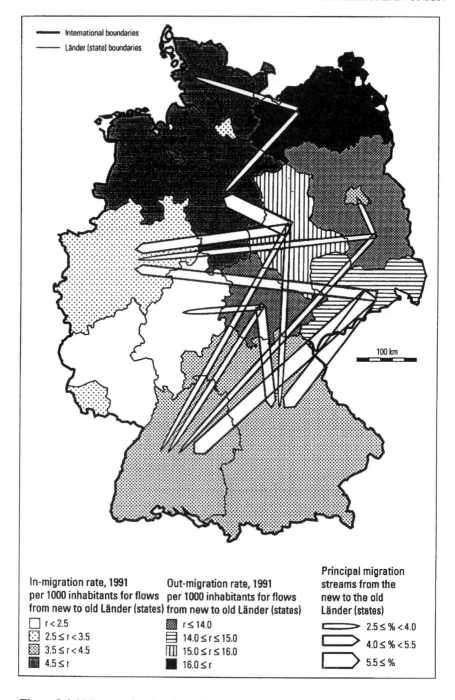

Figure 8.6 Main out-migration flows from eastern to western *Länder*, 1991

Although a decrease in the flow of internal east–west migration is clearly visible, an end of the westward-bound internal flow of migration is not yet in sight. The loss or impending loss of jobs, the still considerable difference in income between east and west, the precarious state of the environment in the east and the insecurity reigning in the housing market produce a high readiness to migrate. In particular, people in employment who are expecting to lose their jobs in the near future and those who are dissatisfied with their income show an above-average willingness to migrate to the western part of Germany.

8.3 INTERNATIONAL MIGRATION IN THE EIGHTIES

As far as international migration is concerned, ie migration across the borders of Germany with other countries, the same factors are at work: the differences in the level of development, the distribution of values like property, social justice, human rights and so on create a potential for migration. Millions of people are apparently no longer willing to await the outcome of collective efforts to diminish the development lag and to improve their living conditions. They are trying to improve their individual situation by emigrating to countries of the developed world (Hoffmann-Nowotny 1992). This approach to an explanation is mainly valid for the most recent migrations from Central and Eastern European countries (including the former Soviet Union) as well as from non-European countries (legal/illegal immigrants for political or economic reasons).

International migration into the western part of Germany has been growing steadily since the middle 1980s, and has led to considerable migration gains. The highest number of immigrants in the history of the FRG, 1 651 000, was recorded in 1991. Compared to 1985, the number of immigrants more than trebled (Figure 8.7). The pattern of regional gains through international migration remained largely unchanged during the 1980s. There were particularly high migration gains in the large urban areas of Munich, Stuttgart, Rhine–Neckar, Rhine–Main, Cologne–Bonn, Düsseldorf and Hamburg.

8.3.1 IN- AND OUT-MIGRATION OF FOREIGN NATIONALS

During the last five years, an annual average of 550 000 foreigners migrated to the western part of Germany. Political changes in Eastern Europe increased the flow over the period. About 200 000 people sought political asylum in 1990; in 1991, their number had increased to more than 300 000. During the 1980s the majority of asylum seekers came from European countries, mainly from Turkey. In the last few years they came from Eastern and South-eastern Europe, at first mainly from Poland, later primarily from the former Yugoslavia (Figure 8.8). In East Germany, international migration had been regulated by treaties. Foreigners were allowed to reside in the GDR in order either to work or to receive an education/vocational training. They played a very minor role in population change.

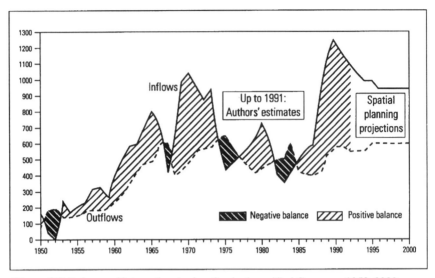

Figure 8.7 Balance of international migration in the unified Germany, 1950–2000

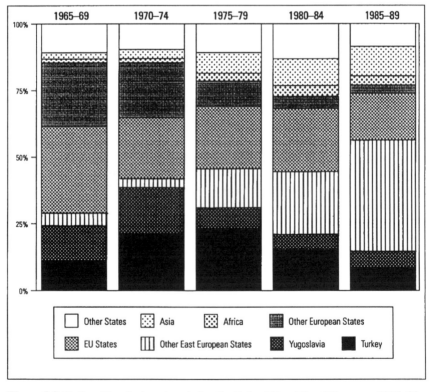

Figure 8.8 Nationality of migrants entering the Federal Republic of Germany, 1965–89

8.3.2 IN- AND OUT-MIGRATION OF GERMANS

The international migration of Germans is dominated by the resettlers (*Aussiedler*) from Eastern and South-eastern Europe as well as—up to 1991—resettlers from East Germany. The migration balance fluctuated between 30 000 and 60 000 people during the 1980s. In 1988, the balance increased dramatically. More than 200 000 resettlers came to Germany from Eastern Europe. The number of resettlers from the eastern part of Germany also increased to about 43 000. The events of 1989 finally went beyond the scope of all previous experience. According to the Federal Board of Equalization, 38 000 resettlers from Eastern Europe and 344 000 resettlers from the eastern part of Germany migrated to the Federal Republic of Germany in 1989. In 1990, there were another 400 000 resettlers from Eastern Europe, and 395 000 migrants from the former East Germany counted as east–west migrants from 3 October, 1990. The number of resettlers from Eastern European countries in 1990 was thus ten times higher than in 1985.

8.4 ASSUMPTIONS CONCERNING TRENDS IN MIGRATION TO 2000

In the next section, likely trends in the medium-term development of migration in Germany will be described. They are based on the assumptions of the first regional population forecasts for Germany. These forecasts are based on a new multi-regional population projection model. The most important features of the projection model and its migration submodel are introduced here.

8.4.1 STRUCTURE OF THE MIGRATION SUB-MODEL

The basic structure of the new multiregional population projection model consists of two submodels: a natural change model (demographic model) and a migration model. The migration model in turn consists of an internal interregional migration submodel and an international migration submodel. The internal interregional migration model contains four migration group-specific submodels corresponding to the behaviour of homogeneous groups of migrants. The basic structure of each submodel connects a migration generation model with a migration distribution model. For each time interval, the migration generation submodel estimates the volume of migration from each region by multiplying age-group specific out-migration rates by the number of people in that age group. Subsequently, the migration distribution model distributes these out-migrants to all other regions (Figure 8.9).

Migration flows are separated in terms of whether the regions of origin and the regions of destination belong to the western or eastern part of Germany. Thus we can distinguish four different migration flows: from western to western regions, from eastern to eastern regions, from eastern to western regions and from western to eastern regions. The model variables—out-migration rates, interregional out-

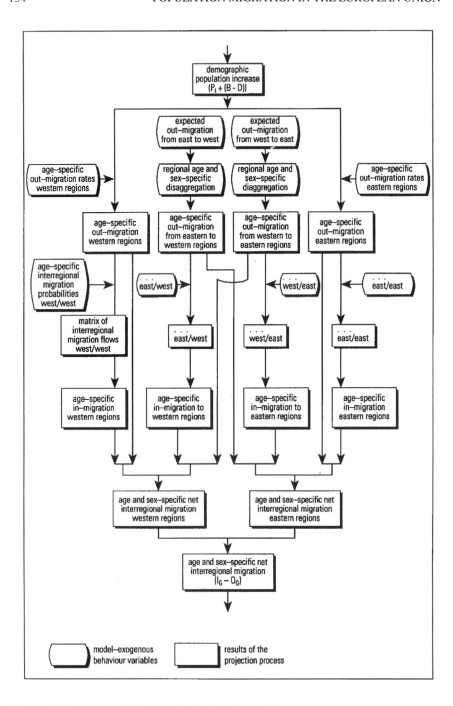

Figure 8.9 Structure of the interregional migration model

migration probabilities—are linked to these various migration flows in different ways. For the origin-destination combinations west–west and east–east, out-migration is generated by out-migration rates, whereas the total number of out-migrants from east to west, and from west to east, are fixed numbers. The numbers are derived from assumptions about how soon disparities in working and living conditions between regions in the western and eastern part of Germany can be reduced. The out-migration forecast is then disaggregated for the requirements of the projection model.

Interregional out-migration probabilities can be estimated only from observed annual migration flows. For the other combinations, hypothetical migration flows had to be estimated under a set of assumptions by using an unconstrained gravity-regression model before interregional out-migration probabilities could be derived. The international migration model is based on a particular set of assumptions concerning trends in migration between Germany and Western Europe, Eastern Europe and countries outside of Europe. The expected total numbers of immigrants and emigrants were disaggregated to produce an age-and sex-specific net international migration for each region. Having added together net internal interregional and net international migration, we obtain the total net migration, and the migration projection for the first time interval is complete. The projected population by age and sex for the first time interval is obtained by adding together the natural increase in population and the total net migration. The projection process is then repeated for the next time interval.

8.4.2 INTERNAL INTERREGIONAL MIGRATION

The hypotheses adopted for the medium-term development of internal interregional migration in unified Germany are, corresponding to the basic structure of the migration model, discussed in three parts: (1) the volume of migration; (2) east–west and west–east migration and (3) interregional migration.

8.4.2.1 The volume of gross migration in the western and eastern parts of Germany

The continual reduction in the volume of interregional migration, which has been observed for years now in the western part of Germany, will most likely continue. There are hardly any regional socio-economic disparities left which could serve as a trigger for migration. Cohort investigations of mobility confirm this (Birg 1992). Migration has decreased from cohort to cohort (classified by year of birth). This means that the trend towards reduced migration is produced mainly by the younger age groups, whereas the migration of the elderly shows a stable level over time (though on a much lower level). The need to be settled in one place seems to be more important than the need for mobility (Geissler et al. 1992).

As far as the eastern part of Germany is concerned, the volume of migration will most likely decrease in the short term. All eastern regions face a difficult economic situation and hence regional job opportunities are limited. Furthermore, the 'national social network' supports people at their current residence, making migration necessary. In addition, many people are bound to their present place of residence by social relations and by property ownership. In the medium term, however, the volume of migration is likely to increase and reach a higher level than it ever did in the former East Germany. An increase in migration is to be expected because regional labour markets, newly developing as the structure of the economy changes and economic recovery starts, will recruit labour selectively.

8.4.2.2 Migration between the western and eastern parts of Germany

As long as the difference in material living conditions between east and west persists, the population of the eastern part will be motivated to move to the west. The population of the western part, on the other hand, will be unwilling to move to the east. The easterners' willingness to migrate turns into an actual migration as soon as there are jobs (and affordable housing) available to them in the west. Since the job and housing market even in the west is under severe pressure, the selective effect of internal migration will become even stronger. Young adults who are motivated, qualified and career-oriented will look for work where they are most likely to find any, and that will be, for quite some time, in the west. Only economic recovery, which is to be expected in the east in the middle or at the end of the 1990s, will put a stop to this flow of migration.

8.4.2.3 Interregional migration flows in the western and eastern parts of Germany

The interregional pattern of migration flows in the western part of Germany is likely to remain stable in the medium term. This is a consequence of stability in the location of economic activity and hence the settlement structure as well as a low level of regional inequality. Whether the large and medium-sized agglomeration areas in the south will remain preferred destinations of migration for out-migrants from the eastern and northern parts of Germany will depend on the state of the housing market and environment, both of which are under pressure as a result of population growth. Symptoms of a growing attractiveness of north and west German business locations and agglomerations for both enterprises and the work-force might herald a possible south–north migration during the 1990s (Geissler *et al.* 1992).

The future interregional migration pattern in the eastern part of Germany cannot be an extrapolation of former trends because conditions have changed radically. The future interregional migration pattern will be determined by future regional differences in living conditions. Those will be determined in their turn by the varying degree to which they are affected by changes in structure of the economy in eastern states. Opportunities for economic recovery in the east are affected by regional locational advantages. It is likely that Thuringia, Saxony and Saxony–Anhalt as well as Greater Berlin will become destinations of interregional migration in the eastern part of Germany.

8.4.3 INTERNATIONAL MIGRATION

Three international migration flows need to be distinguished: with European Union (EU) countries, with European countries outside the EU and with non-European countries. The migration flows between Germany and these groups of countries can be described as follows.

8.4.3.1 Migration with EU countries

During the second half of the 1980s, the international migration balance with EU countries was small but positive. The Single Market is unlikely to effect changes in the medium term, since the freedom to move between member states has been one of the Union's principles for some time. Hence, it is quite unlikely that the Single Market will produce a migration flow (in-migration to Germany). This might change only if regional income and job situations were to become more disparate within the EU which at present is not the case.

8.4.3.2 European countries outside the EU

In the medium term, continuing strong inflows from Turkey and, to an increasing degree, from Central and Eastern European states can be expected. Experts estimate the following inflows from these countries, including the former Soviet Union (Knabe, 1992). In-migrants of German descent might number three million people between 1991 and 2000. During this decade, about two to three million people of non-German origin might be expected as in-migrants. Large numbers might come from the former Yugoslavia (one million), Poland and the former Soviet Union (0.5 million each).

8.4.3.3 Migration with non-European countries

Assumptions concerning non-European migration are subject to the greatest uncertainty. To a large extent, they depend on the future legal framework for 'immigration policy'. In view of the expected intra-Community migration and the impending rush from Central and Eastern Europe, which has to be partly accepted for political reasons, policy makers will probably do whatever it takes to limit migration from non-European countries. In the medium term, the in-migration stream will mainly consist of asylum seekers, originating in Third World countries.

8.5 THE INFLUENCE OF MIGRATION FOR REGIONAL POPULATION DYNAMICS IN THE FUTURE

The assumptions concerning migration discussed above, together with forecasts for fertility and mortality which are mainly based on recent trends, lead to the following

Table 8.1 Components of population change, 1990–2000

Components of population change	Federal Republic of Germany	Western regions	Eastern regions
	(1000s)	(1000s)	(1000s)
Population 1990	79 112.8	60 548.5	18 564.3
Natural change	–947.4	+27.5	–974.9
Net interregional migration	0.0	+902.6	–902.6
Net international migration	+4927.8	+4326.6	+601.2
Population 2000	83 092.4	65 804.7	17 287.7

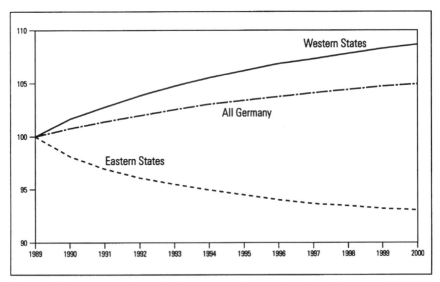

Figure 8.10 Population change in the western and eastern *Länder* of Germany, 1989–2000

projection results. The population in the Federal Republic of Germany will not decrease slightly, as has been predicted in former forecasts; instead it will increase strongly by 5 per cent, which means 3.9 million in absolute numbers. In the year 2000, more than 83 million people will live in Germany, compared to 79.1 million at the beginning of the 1990s (see Table 8.1).

However, population developments in the eastern and in the western parts of Germany run counter to each other (Figure 8.10). The increase in population in Germany is a product of the strong increase in the western part alone, some 5.3 million in absolute numbers or 8.7 per cent. In the eastern part of Germany, however, a population decrease is expected of 6.9 per cent There will be 1.3 million fewer inhabitants in 2000 than there were in 1989.

Regions show considerable differences in forecast population. Except for the Greater Berlin area and its surrounding regional policy regions, all other eastern

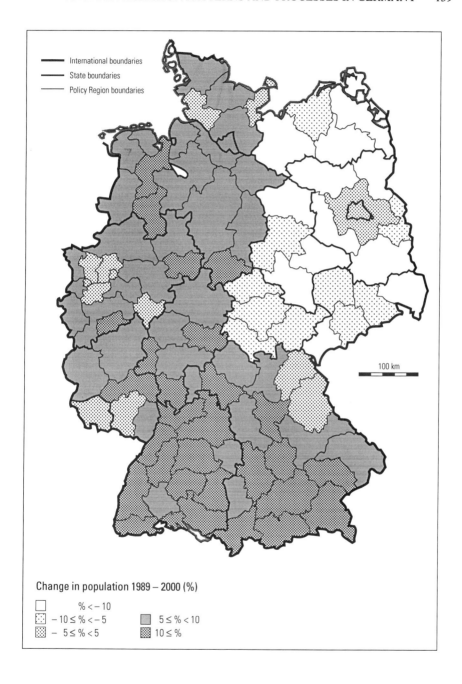

Figure 8.11 Regional population change, 1989–2000

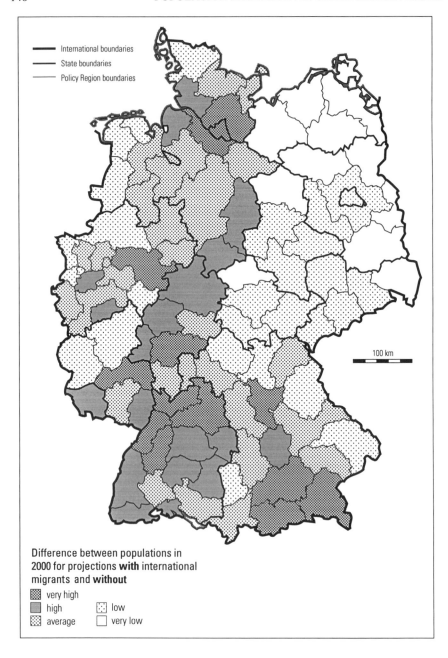

Figure 8.12 Spatial effects of international migration, 1990–2000

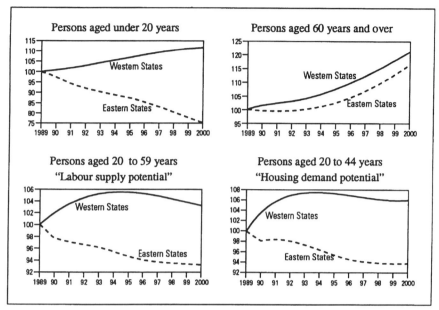

Figure 8.13 Age structure change in the western and eastern *Länder* of Germany, 1989–2000

regions can expect anything between a slight and a strong decrease in population. In the western part, regions with a strong increase in the number of inhabitants are to be found mainly in southern Germany (Figure 8.11).

The most important component of the population development in the 1990s will be migration, particularly international migration. In 78 out of 97 regional policy regions, migration accounts for the increase in population. In 40 regions it more than makes good the forecast natural decrease.

All regions will receive their share of the forecast international migration (five million people), although the numbers will vary (Figure 8.12). The western part of Germany alone will absorb about 90 per cent of the international migration gain. In the eastern part, the remaining international migration gain will comprise 0.6 million people. In many regions, the gain will not be high enough to compensate for natural population decrease and the loss resulting from east–west migrations. In most western regions, however, migration gains coincide with a temporarily positive natural, age-specific population growth. Therefore, compared to the 1980s, many regions switch from being population losers to being winners.

Changes in the age structure of regional populations will also be considerable and again, the developments in the eastern and the western part will sometimes run counter to each other (Figure 8.13). The decrease in fertility and the continuing east–west migration in the 1990s will lead to a drastic reduction of the numbers of inhabitants under the age of 20 in all regions of the east. The average reduction will be 25 per cent. On the other hand, the 'echo-effect' of the baby-boom generation of the 1960s has been leading to an increase in the numbers of births in the western part of Germany. Together with migration gains, this will lead to an increase by the year 2000 of about 12 per cent in the under 20-year olds. This increase is concentrated in southern German regions.

The number of people aged between 20 and 60, the potential work-force, is decreasing in the east, and this reduces the pressure on the job market. In the western part, however, an estimated extra two million people, compared to 1989, will boost the labour-force up to the middle 1990s. With respect to people over 60, developments in the east and the west seem comparable. Their number will increase more than 20 per cent in the western part of Germany and about 17 per cent in the east. The degree of population change varies considerably among regions. A very strong to extremely strong increase of older people during the 1990s will be experienced by many rural regions in north-east and north-west Germany and in almost all of southern Germany.

The most important demographic component during the 1990s will be international migration. Apart from the numerical effect it will have on the population and the structural effect on the age structure, international migration also has a spatial distribution effect. Foreign in-migrants display a marked preference for highly agglomerated regions and for the metropolitan centres. Thus, international migration leads to a concentration of population. On the other hand, natural change and internal migration lead to a deconcentration process at present. Therefore, the relative weight of the individual components will decide in which direction the settlement structure is to develop.

The newly developed population projection model was employed to assess regional differences in the importance of international migration for the population development. This was achieved by comparing two projections based on different assumptions concerning the international migration process. The first projection was based on the assumptions described above for the components of change. The second projection was based on the fictitious assumption of a 'closed society' (ie no migration crossing the international borders of Germany). The differences between the results of these two variants measure the quantitative effect of international migration. It is composed of the accumulated international migration balance plus the secondary effect of natural change and internal migration of the international in-migrants. The regional dispersion of the quantitative effect shows several gradients, each equally strong (Figure 8.11): (1) a settlement-structure gradient, leading from the highly agglomerated down to the rural structured regions, (2) a geographic gradient from the west to the east and (3) within the western part of Germany, from the south to the north. The total quantitative effect of international migration can be allocated to the regional categories as follows (the number in brackets represents the total population share of those categories): regions with large urban agglomerations, 62.9 per cent (53.4); regions with incipient agglomerations, 25.7 per cent (29.7) and rurally structured regions, 11.5 per cent (16.8).

8.6 CONCLUSIONS, CONSEQUENCES FOR FEDERAL REGIONAL PLANNING

The projection of population development creates two issues for regional planning:

1. How can the expected high international migration gains be integrated spatially?
2. How can the ongoing east–west migration, especially of the younger population groups, be stopped?

The forecast of very high population losses, especially of young people, in all regions in the former GDR highlight a vital regional demographic problem that could lead to a further reduction of the development potential in the eastern part of Germany. An increased consciousness of this problem will be required of the politicians, the planners and the public.

Regional planning in the Federal Republic gives priority to objectives relevant to people. The main objective of regional planning is to create equivalent living conditions in all districts of the nation, ie to reduce regional inequalities. This requires a three-point programme which involves the improvement of economic structure and employment opportunities, the improvement of infrastructure and, finally, the improvement of the quality of the environment. The economic structure of deprived areas could be improved by the creation of additional jobs for qualified workers, while those jobs already in existence must be protected. In order to improve the supply of infrastructure for the population, the capacity, efficiency and accessibility of existing infrastructure must be increased. The quality of the environment, especially in industrial regions, should be optimized by a compromise between the economic and ecological potential of the area.

These objectives of regional planning do not require the implementation of a regional population policy, nor do they suggest the direction such a policy should take. In principle, regional population policy is severely limited. The provision for free development of the personality (Article 2GG) protects the freedom of parents to decide on how many children they want and when. The right of free mobility ensures that all German and EU citizens may live and work where they want to. This has two implications for regional planning. First, pure population policy objectives do not exist. A population, large or small, is not inherently good or bad; the population structure, its dynamics and distribution can be evaluated only in relation to other objectives. Second, any objectives and measures that seek to direct population development must therefore be seen against the background of national policy as a whole and within a framework that protects the basic human rights of individual development and free mobility. Measures that affect freedom of movement must be rejected, even if their implementation would help to produce the population distribution and structure required to attain a national objective. From the point of view of Federal regional planning, the projection results stress the central need for establishing equivalent living conditions in the western and eastern parts of Germany.

9 Greece: Population Change Components and Internal Migration

GEORGIOS PAPADAKIS and JOHN STILLWELL

9.1 INTRODUCTION

The population of Greece (Ellada) on 1 January 1992 has been estimated by the National Statistical Service of Greece (NSSG) to number 10.28 million people and to have grown consistently from the beginning of the previous decade. However, it has remained one of the least populated states of the European Union (EU), with a density of 77 inhabitants per square kilometre in 1991, virtually half the EU average of 153 (European Commission 1994).

The Nomenclature of Territorial Units for Statistics (NUTS) was created by the Statistical Office of the European Commission to provide a single, uniform regionalization for the production of regional statistics. There is a three-level hierarchy of regions in each Member State and Greece is divided into 13 development regions at the level of NUTS 2 (Figure 9.1) and into 51 *nomoi* at NUTS 3. At the NUTS 1 level, these territorial subdivisions are grouped into four macroregions: Voreia Ellada, Kentriki Ellada, Nisia and Attiki. Over one-third of the population lives in Attiki, the region that contains Athens, the administrative, financial, industrial and cultural centre of Greece, while a further one million inhabit Thessaloniki, the country's second-largest city and capital of Kentriki Makedonia. Regional contrasts in population density are considerable at the NUTS 2 scale: in Attiki, there were 910 persons per square kilometre in 1991 while in one of the most mountainous regions, Dytiki Makedonia in Voreia Ellada, a density of only 31 inhabitants per square kilometre was recorded. In contrast, Ionia Nisia, the islands region in the west of the country, had a density of 84 persons per square kilometre.

This chapter aims to utilize statistics recently produced by the NSSG in 1994 to track national and regional population change in Greece since the beginning of the 1980s and to identify the relative importance of the natural change and net migration components of change in explaining regional trends. A new set of total population estimates for NUTS level 2 regions has been produced by the NSSG for the beginning of each calendar year since 1981. These rebased estimates include adjustments to take into account the results of the 1991 Census. It is relevant to draw attention to the differences between these rebased population figures and the original estimates that were used in the calculation of residual net migration estimates in the

Population Migration in the European Union Edited by Philip Rees, John Stillwell, Andrew Convey and Marek Kupiszewski. © Editors and Contributors. Published 1996 John Wiley & Sons Ltd.

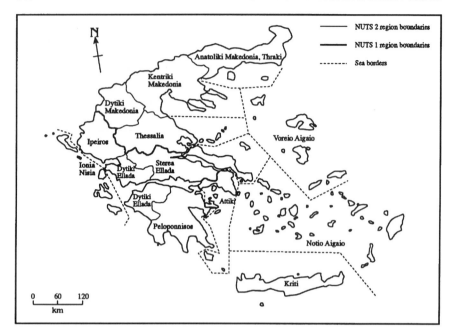

Figure 9.1 NUTS 1 and 2 regions of Greece

1980s. The revised estimates present an entirely different pattern of regional net migration to that indicated by the data published by Eurostat in the 1980s (Eurostat 1989, for example), where three of the Greek regions, Voreio Aigaio, Peloponnisos and Thessalia, are recorded as having the highest rates of net migration loss of all NUTS level 2 regions in the EU.

Annual totals of births and deaths from 1980 to 1992 have been provided with the population estimates in machine-readable form and the natural change and residual net migration components of regional population change are examined in the third section of the chapter, where correlation analysis is used to quantify the importance of each component in explaining population change. By definition, the estimates of net migration that are generated contain not only the balance of in-migration and out-migration flows between each region and all other regions in Greece but also the balance of immigration versus emigration for each region from elsewhere in the world outside Greece.

As in certain other EU countries, there remains a paucity of data on migration flows within Greece during the 1980s with which to confirm the accuracy of the derived residual net migration balances and to provide more detailed evidence of the processes influencing the redistribution of the population. Although some data on internal migration are available from the 1981 Population Census as a result of a five-year migration question, there is no direct mechanism for monitoring internal migration between censuses. The REGIO database and the regional publications of Eurostat contain no information on interregional migration since 1984, when a spe-

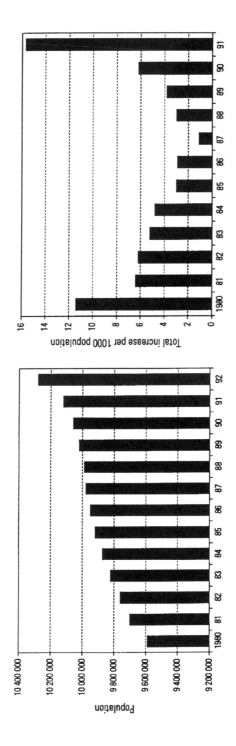

Figure 9.2 National population change, 1980–92

cial sample survey of 1.5 per cent of households was conducted. Thus, in advance of the publication of interregional migration data from the 1991 Census, the fourth section of the chapter contains an analysis of the urban–rural contrast in net migration patterns for particular types of area and investigates the age structure of net migration using data from the 1981 Census. Some conclusions are presented in the fifth section. In order to provide a context for the analysis of regional change and the trends in population components, the development of the country's population as a whole over the 1980s is outlined and a classification of NUTS 2 regions in Greece based on their growth profiles is proposed in the section which follows.

9.2 NATIONAL AND REGIONAL POPULATION CHANGE

The population of Greece increased by 7.2 per cent between 1980 and 1992 (Figure 9.2) to reach a total of 10.28 million by the beginning of 1992. While growth was continuous during this period, rates of annual change declined during the first half of the decade from over 11 per thousand in 1980 to around one per thousand in 1987. Since then, the annual rate of population change has increased to a high of over 15 per thousand in 1991. National population growth in 1991 was therefore greater than in any of the previous years of the period in question.

The regional distribution of the population in January 1992 (Figure 9.3) illustrates the importance of the two regions, Attiki and Kentriki Makedonia, that contain the two main urban centres, Athens and Thessalonika. While half the country's population is resident in these two regions, in no other region does the population exceed 7 per cent of the national total.

While the population in 1992 was higher than in 1980 in all the NUTS 2 regions of Greece, certain regions grew at different rates than others. An examination of the time series of regional population change rates suggests that the Greek regions can be classified into three categories.

The first group consists of five 'high growth' regions: Kentriki Makedonia, Notio Aigaio, Sterea Ellada, Dytiki Ellada and Kriti (Figure 9.4a). In each of these regions, the rate of population change is positive and remains consistently above three per thousand throughout the period. The second group also contains five regions: Ionia Nisia, Thessalia, Ipeiros, Peloponnisos and Attiki (Figure 9.4b). This set of 'medium-growth' regions is characterized by having lower rates of growth and at least one year of annual change close to zero. In the case of Attiki, the population change is negative in this year. The third group contains the remaining 'low-growth' regions—Anatoliki Makedonia and Thraki, Voreio Aigaio and Dytiki Makedonia (Figure 9.4c)—where the data for most years indicate relatively low rates of gain or loss.

One of the most striking features of each of the regional time series schedules is the increase in population that has occurred in the latter part of the period and in 1991 in particular. The spatial incidence of growth in 1991 has been mapped in Figure 9.5 and indicates that among the Greek regions, it is the islands of Notio Aigaio that have recorded the highest growth of over 20 per thousand. The region

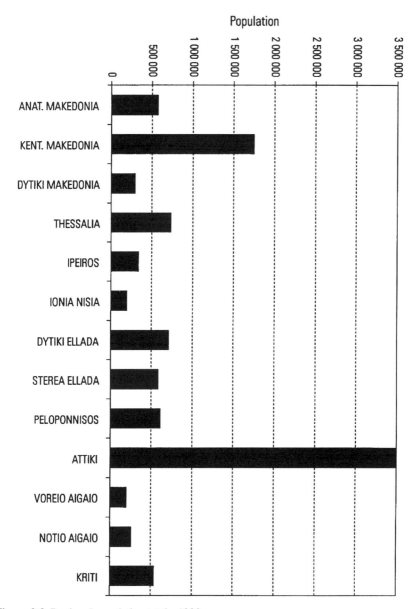

Figure 9.3 Regional population totals, 1992

which experienced the greatest population change rate (21 per thousand) during the whole period was Voreio Aigaio. This region consists of islands, the largest of which are Lesbos, Chios, Samos, Ikaria and Limnos (Figure 9.5). The growth of the population of Voreio Aigaio between 1980 and 1992 has resulted in a transformation of the population structure as indicated by the age pyramids illustrated in Figure 9.6.

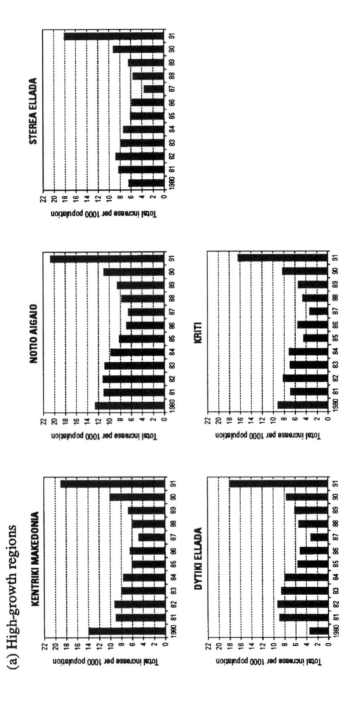

(a) High-growth regions

Figure 9.4(a)   Annual population change rates by region, 1980–92

151

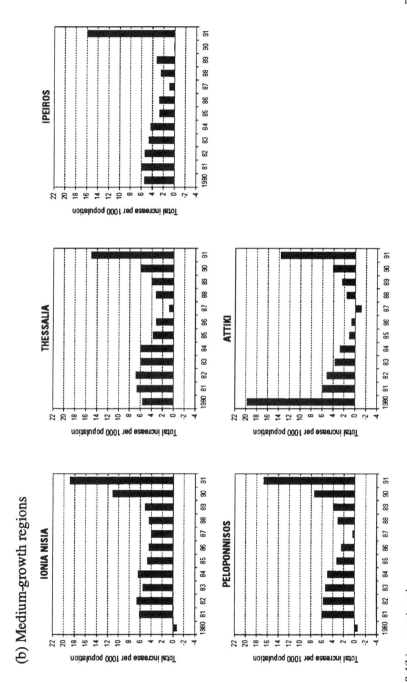

(b) Medium-growth regions

Figure 9.4(b)   *continued*

152

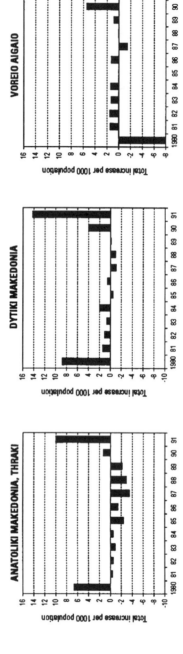

(c) Low-growth regions

Figure 9.4(c) *continued*

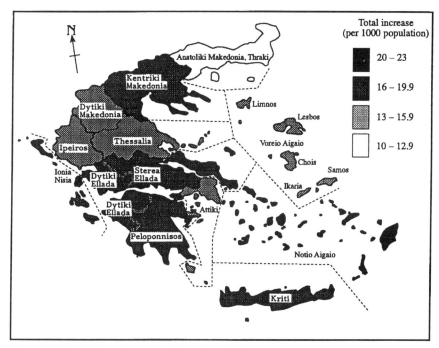

Figure 9.5 Population change rates by region, 1991

In 1980, the age pyramid shows fewer inhabitants in the age groups between 25 and 44 years. This age range contained 21 per cent of the region's population, whereas the same age range for Greece as a whole contained 26 per cent of the population. It is likely that the 'kink' in the 1980 pyramid is due to the migration from Voreio Aigaio to Athens that occurred during the 1970s. In addition, the male statistics are influenced by the inclusion of military personnel. During the 1980s, return migration from the mainland urban areas was commonplace, and this is one reason for the increased numbers in certain age groups in the 1992 age pyramid, particularly for males. A further interesting feature is the narrowing of the base of the pyramid between 1980 and 1992. In 1992, for example, there were more women aged 75–9 years than there were young female infants aged 0–4 years.

9.3 COMPONENTS OF CHANGE

A useful approach in regional demographic analysis is to consider which of the components of population change is primarily responsible for determining the evolution of the population. Vital statistics provided by the NSSG allow the calculation of annual natural change rates ($nc_i(t,t+T)$) as:

$$nc_i(t,t+T) = [B_i(t,t+T-D_i(t,t+T)] / [(P_i(t)+P_i(t+T)/2)]$$

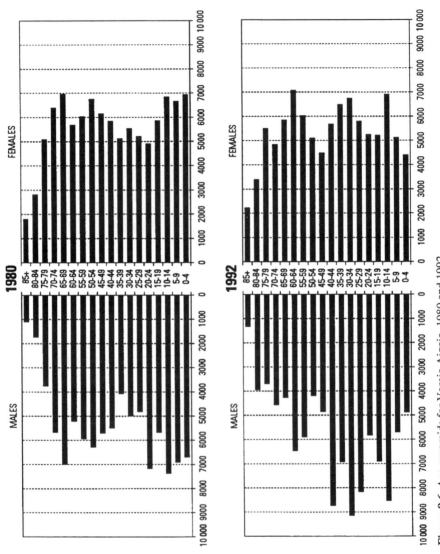

Figure 9.6 Age pyramids for Voreio Aigaio, 1980 and 1992

and net migration rates ($nm_i(t,t+T)$) as:

$$nm_i(t,t+T) = \{[P_i(t+T-P_i(t) -B_i(t,t+T-D_i(t,t+T)]\} / [(P_i(t)+P_i(t+T) \ /2]$$

where:

$B_i(t,t+T)$	is the number of births in region i in year t to t+T;
$D_i(t,t+T)$	is the number of deaths in region i in year t to t+T;
$P_i(t)$	is the population of region i at the beginning of year t,t+T; and
$P_i(t+T)$	is the population of region i and the end of year t,t+T (or the beginning of the following year).

In this case, rates have been computed using an at risk population assumed to be the average of the population at the beginning and end of each twelve-month period.

The decline in the annual rate of natural increase that has occurred in Greece since 1980 (Figure 9.7) is explained primarily by reductions in levels of fertility and is consistent with trends in other Southern European states like Spain, Portugal and Italy (Siampos 1991). The annual natural increase rate fell from over 6.0 per thousand in 1980 to 1.1 per thousand in 1987, increased marginally in 1988 and then continued to decline to a low of 0.6 per cent in 1991. Greece is therefore fast approaching a situation of a zero natural increase. At the national level, the estimate of residual migration reflects the balance of international migrants arriving in and departing from Greece. Throughout most of the period, the net flow remains positive but is negligible in terms of volume. However, since 1987, there has been a consistent rise in the net flow of immigrants. This is a trend which, in view of the low rates of natural increase, is responsible for determining the growth in population.

Greece has therefore become a country of net immigration with the rate reaching 15 per thousand by 1991. According to Siampos (1991), the population of foreign citizenship has gradually increased from 195 000 in 1980 to 217 000 in 1989, with an unknown number of clandestine immigrants. Although the current pattern of international migration for Greece is thus characterized by net immigration, it should be recognized that the country has experienced substantial emigration flows to other parts of the world during the 20th century. Up to the late 1950s, annual emigration flows were dominated by movements to the USA, Canada and Australia (Giaoutzi 1983). From then until the energy crisis in 1973, Germany became a favoured destination (Moussourou 1984) and migrant remittances reached $470 million in 1971 alone (Glytsos 1993).

Official sources of data with which to identify the origins of immigrants or return migrants to Greece in more recent times include the 1981 Census and a 3 per

156

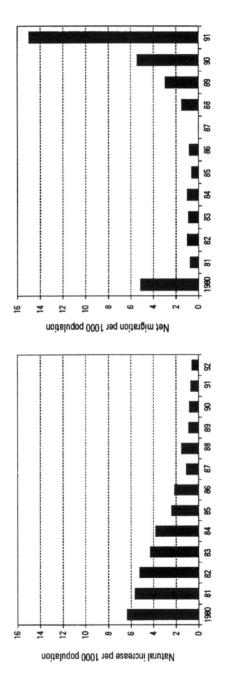

Figure 9.7 Natural change and net migration rates, 1980–91

cent sample survey in 1985/86. Both these sources, providing immigration information for the periods 1976–81 and 1980–5 respectively, illustrate the importance of European countries of origin. In the earlier period, 64.4 per cent of immigrants came from Europe and 15.9 per cent from the USA and Canada; in the more recent period, 61.9 per cent originated from Europe and 19.9 per cent came from North America. In both these periods, the flows from Europe were dominated by migrants from West Germany. No comprehensive official data is yet available to establish the reasons for the sharp increase in net immigration since 1989. It is likely that the wave of immigrants coming from Albania is important, involving ethnic Greeks returning from southern Albania for political as well as economic reasons and Albanians escaping from their native country to Greece in the face of economic collapse. In the first six months of 1991, 24 000 Albanians migrated to Greece (OECD 1992). In 1992, 202 996 Albanians entered Greece, while 201 064 were deported (Petrakou 1993). Another major flow of immigrants is that of 'Pontians', ethnic Greeks returning from the Pontus region around the Black Sea. It is estimated that 40 000 Pontians arrived in Greece between 1988 and 1992.

9.3.1 REGIONAL NATURAL INCREASE

The time-series rates of natural change from 1980 to 1992 indicate that most Greek regions have experienced either declining rates of natural increase or increasing rates of natural decline. In some regions, a transition from natural gain to natural loss has occurred. The regional rates schedules (Figure 9.8) are presented using the classification based on population change trends. In the first group, Kentriki Makedonia, Notio Aigaio, Dytiki Ellada and Kriti all experience change similar to the national trend of declining rates of net gain. Sterea Ellada, however, has undergone the transition from being a region of natural gain in the early 1980s to a region with more deaths than births per thousand population in the second half of the 1980s.

In the second group of regions experiencing lower rates of population gain than those in the previous group, Attiki and Thessalia follow the national trend of declining rates of natural gain, Ipeiros and Peloponnisos both become regions of natural decline during the period and Ionia Nisia experienced increasing rates of natural loss. The final group is comprised of Anatoliki Makedonia and Thraki, whose positive rates of natural change in the early 1980s were replaced by rates of negative natural change in the latter half of the period, and Voreio Aigaio, whose schedule is characterized by rates of natural decline that are the highest for any region in the country.

Thus, patterns of natural change at the regional scale in Greece show considerable variation. By 1991, the highest natural increase rates were recorded in Kriti and Notio Aigaio, whereas the highest rates of natural decline were evident in Voreio Aigaio and Peloponnisos (Figure 9.9).

9.3.2 REGIONAL NET MIGRATION

The time-series schedules of net migration rates for each of the Greek regions

158

(a) High growth regions

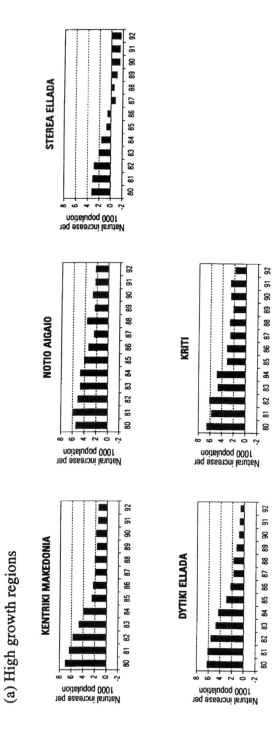

Figure 9.8(a) Natural increase rates by region, 1980–91

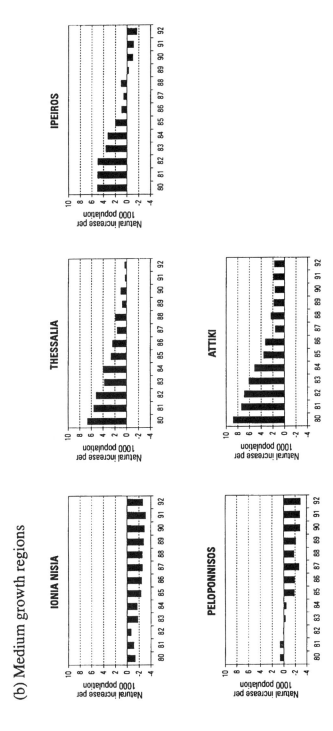

(b) Medium growth regions

Figure 9.8(b) *continued*

160

(c) Low growth regions

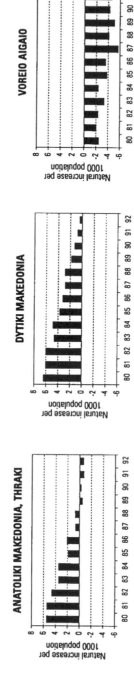

Figure 9.8(c) *.continued*

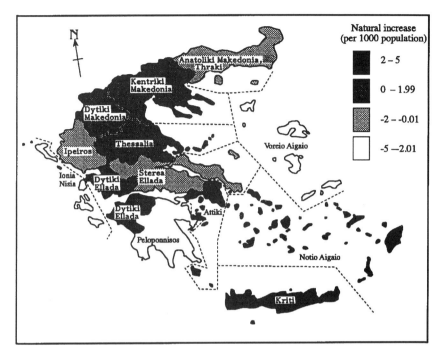

Figure 9.9 Natural increase rates by region, 1991

(Figure 9.10), presented in groups classified on the basis of population change, also illustrate considerable variation. With the exception of Dytiki Ellada in 1980, all the regions in the first group are characterized by positive net migration rates throughout the time period. The net rates for Kriti are lower than those for the other regions in this group, but in all cases there is a distinctive trend towards higher rates of net migration gain towards the end of the period. The second group contains a number of regions with rather differing net migration time series. Ionia Nisia has the highest rates of migration gain of any Greek region in the years after 1981, and Peloponnisos also has strong positive rates after 1980. However, net migration for Thessalia and Ipeiros is negligible throughout the 1980s, and these regions only experience a dramatic change in the first two years of the 1990s. Attiki, on the other hand, has a high rate of net gain in 1980, suffers annual net losses until 1989, but records net migration gains once again in the last two years of the period. Rates of net loss throughout the 1980s also characterize two of the regions in the third group: Dytiki Makedonia and Anatoliki Makedonia and Thraki, but the third region, Voreio Aigaio, records gains in all years except 1980.

The most consistent trend in this set of schedules is the positive net migration rates estimated in each of the regions in 1990 and 1991. It is possible that these net migration schedules reflect trends in international migration as much as in internal migration, but that hypothesis is difficult to prove without access to data at the regional level on either of these two processes. The highest rate of net migration

162

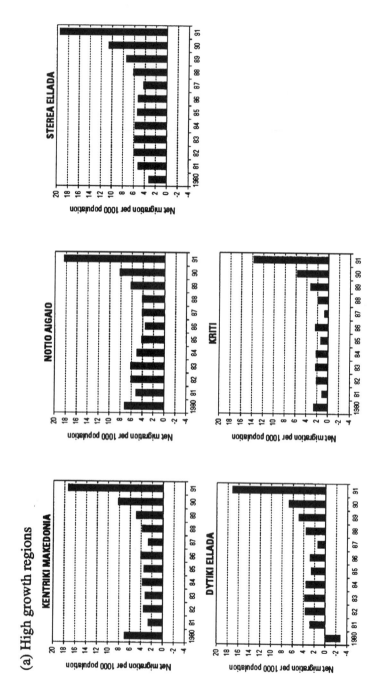

Figure 9.10(a) Net migration rates by region, 1980–91

163

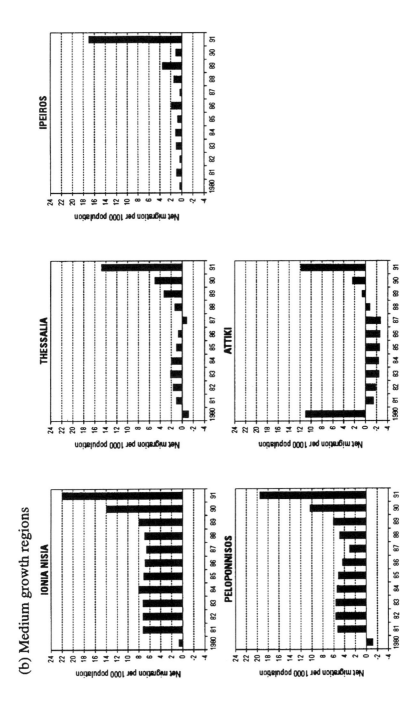

Figure 9.10(b) *continued*

164

(c) Low growth regions

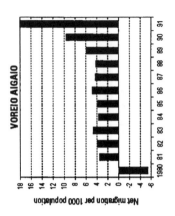

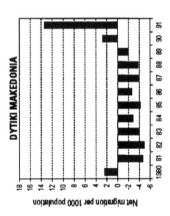

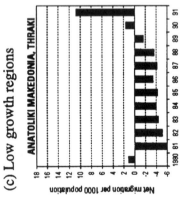

Figure 9.10(c) *continued*

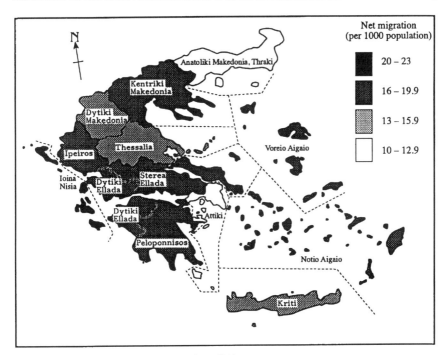

Figure 9.11 Net migration rates by region, 1991

Table 9.1 Correlation coefficients for population change rates (PCR) against natural change rates (NCR) and net migration rates (NMR), 1980–91

Year	PCR against NCR	PCR against NMR
1980	0.87**	0.92**
1981	0.26	0.65*
1982	0.23	0.70*
1983	0.25	0.69*
1984	0.18	0.71*
1985	0.12	0.72*
1986	0.13	0.70*
1987	0.25	0.68*
1988	0.22	0.74*
1989	0.29	0.74*
1990	0.09	0.83**
1991	0.18	0.74*

Notes: ** means significant at 0.01 level
        * means significant at 0.001 level

gain of all the Greek NUTS 2 regions in 1991 (Figure 9.11) occurred in Ionia Nisia, whereas Attiki and Anatoliki Makedonia and Thraki recorded the lowest rates of net gain.

To what extent have the annual rates of population change in the Greek NUTS 2 regions during this 12-year period been determined by net migration rather than natural change?

Pearson's correlation coefficients have been computed between the population change rates and component rates for each year in the time series (Table 9.1). The regional net migration rate is positively correlated with the regional rate of population change in all years and in each case the relationship is statistically significant at a 0.01 confidence level. The correlation coefficients between net migration and population change rates are all over 0.65, whereas coefficients between natural change and population change are all below 0.3, with the exception of the first year in the series where population change rates are highly correlated with both natural change and net migration.

9.4 INTERNAL MIGRATION

Population redistribution within Greece during the 20th century has been dominated by migration shifts from rural to urban areas and by massive flows to the Athens and Thessaloniki metropolitan areas in particular. The civil war, following the end of World War II, forced large numbers of people to migrate to the cities. Thereafter, polarization between core and periphery resulted in the 'severe sociocultural pauperization of the countryside' (Papademetriou 1985) as the Greek government neglected the rural areas and as investment activities were concentrated on the two big cities. Between 1951 and 1961, for example, the two large conurbations attracted over 600 000 people, and between 1965 and 1975, when the predominant flows occurred from rural and semi-urban areas to urban areas, 65 per cent of migration was directed towards the two main metropoli (Giaoutzi 1983). Rural out-migration, caused by the lack of jobs and available land in rural areas and the improved employment and income prospects in urban areas, has been composed typically of younger, unmarried males, a high proportion of whom were the best educated and the most skilled. The effects of this shift from the rural areas have been continuously to reinforce the dependence of the countryside on the country's central cities and to weaken the economic viability of the rural periphery. Some insights into the rural–urban patterns of migration for 1976–81 can be drawn from the 10 per cent sample results from the 1981 Census.

9.4.1 RURAL–URBAN MIGRATION, 1976–81

The 1981 Census (NSSG 1987) distinguishes migration flows into and out of areas classified as urban, semi-urban and rural. *Urban areas* consist of four area types:

1. the Athens and Thessaloniki areas;

2. other cities with population over 50 000;
3. cities with populations between 30 000 and 50 000; and
4. urban areas with populations between 10 000 and 30 000 inhabitants.

Semi-urban areas are divided into settlements with populations between:

1. 5000 and 10 000; and between
2. 2000 and 5000 inhabitants.

Finally, three *rural area* types are identified: those with:

1. 1000–2000,
2. 500–1000, and
3. fewer than 500 inhabitants.

In absolute terms, Athens and Thessaloniki gained almost 100 000 people through net migration during the period, whereas net migration losses were confined to the three types of rural area. A massive loss of over 95 000 occurred from the rural areas with fewer than 500 inhabitants, equivalent to a rate of net loss of 82 persons per thousand. Thus, while Athens and Thessaloniki contained 38.3 per cent of the nation's population by 1981, a further 30.3 per cent were still living in rural areas of Greece with populations of less than 1000. Table 9.2 also indicates that Thessaloniki and the other cities with populations over 50 000 experienced over twice the net in-migration rate of Athens. Rates of net gain were much lower for areas with population between 2000 and 30 000.

Table 9.2 Population, 1981, and net migration, 1976–81, by area type

Area type	1981 population		Net internal migration	
	No.	% share	No.	Rate
Athens	3 027 560	31.1	66 950	22.1
Thessaloniki	705 451	7.2	32 870	46.6
> 50 000	591 123	6.1	28 870	48.8
30 000–49 999	679 781	7.0	19 330	28.4
10 000–29 999	650 143	6.7	2670	4.1
5000–9999	355 280	3.6	3020	8.5
2000–4999	781 370	8.0	1510	1.9
1000–1999	794 456	8.2	−15 940	−20.0
500–999	998 946	10.3	−44 040	−44.1
< 500	1 155 479	11.8	−95 240	−82.4
Greece	9 739 589	100.0	0	0.0

Note: Rates have been calculated using 1981 (end of period) populations and are expressed per thousand population
Source: NSSG (1987)

Almost 1.1 million people moved within Greece during this five-year period. At the same time, there was a total inflow of approximately 0.2 million from abroad (Table 9. 3). Rates of in-migration from elsewhere in Greece decline progressively as area size diminishes, from 156.5 per thousand into Athens to 51.6 per thousand into the rural areas with populations of 500–999. These figures indicate that the migration flows relating to rural areas are not all outflows, suggesting that there is a more complex pattern of movements taking place between areas at different levels in the hierarchy. Evidence from data for earlier periods has demonstrated that although the prevailing trend has been for large cities to grow faster than small cities, migration has taken place from rural to semi-urban areas as well as from urban and semi-urban areas to Athens and Thessaloniki (Giaoutzi 1983). This would account for the continued net gains experienced by the smaller urban and semi-urban areas, who lose less to the bigger cities than they gain from the rural areas.

Table 9.3 In-migration and immigration by area type, 1976–81

Area type	In-migration		Immigration		In-migration/ immigration
	No.	Rate	No.	Rate	
Athens	474 370	156.5	82 210	27.2	5.8
Thessaloniki	105 470	149.5	30 930	43.8	3.4
> 50 000	76 070	128.7	12 490	21.1	6.1
30 000–49 999	87 190	128.3	20 450	30.1	4.3
10 000–29 999	71 030	109.3	13 700	21.1	5.2
5000–9999	40 670	114.5	7500	21.1	5.4
2000–4999	70 980	90.8	14 410	18.4	4.9
1000–1999	51 780	65.2	16 880	21.2	3.1
500–999	51 570	51.6	19 080	19.1	2.7
< 500	62 420	54.0	15 030	13.0	4.2
Greece	1 090 910	112.0	232 680	23.9	4.7

Notes: In-migration refers to inmoves from within Greece
Immigraton refers to inmoves from abroad
Rates have been calculated using 1981 (end of period) populations and are expressed per thousand population

Source: NSSG (1987)

Although Athens recorded the highest rates of in-migration from the rest of Greece, it did not have the highest rate of immigration from abroad, despite attracting 35 per cent of all immigrants to Greece in 1976–81. This distinction went to Thessaloniki, where the rate was 43.8 immigrants per thousand population. The lowest rates of immigration were recorded for the rural areas with the smallest populations. However, the ratio of in-migration to immigration shows that immigration was a relatively important component in rural areas with populations of between 500 and 2000. On the other hand, for cities with over 50 000 inhabitants other than Thessaloniki, the ratio of in-migrants to immigrants was around six to one. The predominance of the flow of migrants to Athens is highlighted by the statistics in Table

9.3 which indicate that the capital city attracted 43.4 per cent of all migrants coming from elsewhere in Greece during 1976–81.

Examination of the age selectivity of migration in Greece based on net migration balances for the aggregate area types (Table 9.4) exposes the importance of those aged 15–24 in the net exchanges taking place. Migrants in this age group accounted for 23 per cent of all internal migration within Greece. A total of 80 000 net migrants were gained by the urban areas and lost from the semi-urban and rural areas. It is also apparent that losses were incurred in rural areas in all age groups, whereas the profiles of both aggregate sets of urban areas showed losses in the 55–64 year-old, retirement age range. In total, Athens and Thessaloniki gained 99 800 whereas the rural areas lost 155 200; the difference was made up by gains of 50 800 by the other urban areas and 4500 by the semi-urban areas.

Table 9.4 Net migration by age and area type, 1976–81

Age group	Athens and Thessaloniki	Other urban areas (> 5000)	Semi-urban areas (2000–4999)	Rural areas (< 1999)
5–9	−2000	6540	3000	−7540
10–14	4900	6730	1690	−13 320
15–24	72 970	7030	−11 680	−68 320
25–34	9380	16 800	3980	−30 160
35–44	4530	9560	2820	−16 910
45–54	5430	2600	1120	−9150
55–64	−1070	−350	1780	−360
65–74	27	720	1380	−2370
75–84	4040	1080	320	−5440
85+	1300	190	130	−1620
Unstated	70	−30	10	−30
Total	99 820	50 870	4530	−155 220

Source: NSSG (1987)

The age profiles of net migration standardized by area population size (Figure 9.12) provide further evidence of the composition of net migration balances for each type of area. Athens and Thessaloniki record the highest rates of net gain in the 15–24 age group; Athens gained over 50 000 net migrants in this age group and Thessaloniki gained nearly 22 000. Rates of net gain were also considerably higher for the elderly than those of middle age, although the absolute numbers were very much smaller than the peak labour-force age group. Unlike the two big cities, other cities with over 50 000 population experienced lower rates in the 15–24 ages but higher rates of gain in almost all other ages up to 75 years.

The rates of net gain in the 15–24 age group were much lower in the areas with populations of between 30 000 and 50 000, and at lower order area types, the net balance became negative. The rate of net out-migration of young persons aged 15–24 from the most rural areas reached 280 per thousand during this period, a total outflow of 38 000 individuals. The net migration rate profiles for both the semi-

(a) Main urban areas

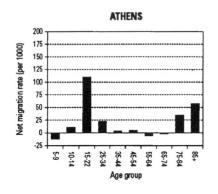
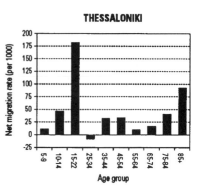

(b) Other urban areas

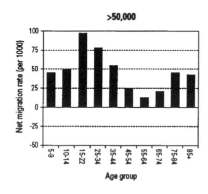
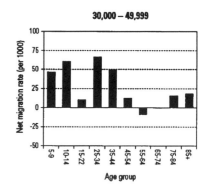

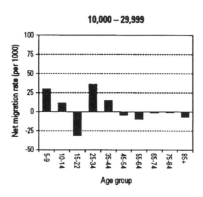

Figure 9.12(a) and (b)   Net migration rates by age and region, 1976–81

(c) Semi urban areas

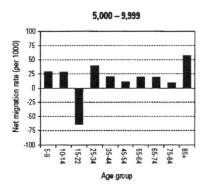
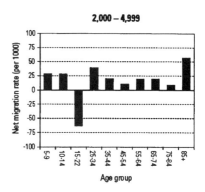

(d) Rural areas

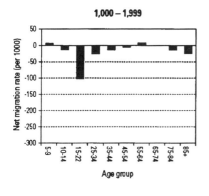
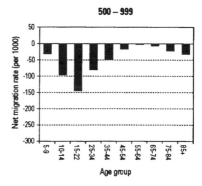

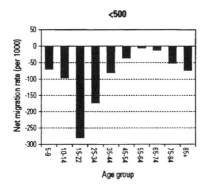

Figure 9.12(c and d) *continued*

urban area types were characterized by net gains for all age groups except that of 15–24 years. In contrast, net losses in the three types of rural area occurred in virtually all age groups.

9.4.2 INTERREGIONAL MIGRATION, 1984

Very few data are available with which to examine trends in migration since the 1981 Census. The most recent information on directional migration within Greece is that published in Eurostat (1989) for movements between the nine former NUTS 2 regions of Greece in 1984. These statistics are of limited value because of their aggregate character and small size of the sample that was undertaken, but they do demonstrate the relative volume of the exchange of population through migration between the former NUTS 2 region containing Athens, Anatoliki Sterea and Nisia, and other former NUTS 2 regions of Greece. Table 9.5 indicates the relative sizes of flows between this particular region and each of the other regions, in comparison with the sum of the flows for each region to and from elsewhere. The total of 55 500 migrants includes 15 700 migrants to Anatoliki Sterea and Nisia from other regions, 17 000 migrants from Anatoliki Sterea and Nisia to other regions. A further 22 900 migrants moved between the other regions, of which the major flow in 1984 was 6000 between Ipeiros in the west and the islands of Nisia Anatolikou Aigaio in the east. This latter flow is particularly difficult to explain and may be the result of sampling error.

9.5 CONCLUSIONS

While the population of Greece has risen steadily since the beginning of the 1980s, and while the Attiki region continues to dominate the population distribution and

Table 9.5 Interregional migration to and from Anatoliki Sterea and Nisia and between all other regions, 1984

Former NUTS 2 regions	Anatoliki Sterea and Nisia		All other regions	
	To	From	To	From
Peloponnisos and Dytiki Sterea	4066	6400	1601	2665
Kentriki and Dytiki Makedonia	3534	2600	4731	5600
Thessalia	2266	1600	1601	2334
Kriti	1467	1800	735	800
Nisia Anatolikou Aigaio	1400	1666	1000	7734
Thraki	1267	1066	2400	1800
Ipeiros	1200	1400	7667	1068
Anatoliki Makedonia	466	466	3133	867
Total	15 666	16 998	22 868	22 868

Note: Anatoliki Sterea and Nisia contains the Athens conurbation
Source: Eurostat (1989)

maintain its primacy, rates of annual growth throughout much of the decade have been less spectacular than in Kentriki Makedonia and certain other regions. A classification of NUTS 2 regions has been proposed on the basis of differing growth rates and has been used to present regional time series of natural change and net migration. Trends in these components are clear at the national level. Natural increase rates have declined steadily during the period, while net immigration has only become important in the 1990s. Greece has become a country of net immigration after having experienced decades of net emigration. At the regional scale, natural change rates have fallen during the decade. However, the annual rates of regional population change appear to be linked with rates of net migration to a statistically significant extent.

The analysis based on the results of the 1981 Census has indicated that massive losses occurred during 1975–81 from the most rural areas, particularly of those aged 15–24, while Athens in particular attracted very large numbers of in-migrants. These results are further evidence of a continuation of trends that have been apparent in Greece during the post-war period. Whether this rural exodus has slowed or ceased to exist during the 1980s remains to be seen when the results of the 1991 Census become available and when a comprehensive analysis of the relationship between rural and urban areas can be undertaken.

ACKNOWLEDGEMENTS

The authors are grateful to George Kotsifakis from the National Statistical Service of Greece in Athens for providing population estimates and vital statistics for the NUTS 2 regions in machine readable form, to Joachim Recktenwald of Eurostat for providing estimates of regional net migration in Greece, and to Professor Maria Giaoutzi at the National Technical University of Athens for her comments on an earlier draft of the chapter.

10 Spain: Return to the South, Metropolitan Deconcentration and New Migration Flows[1]

JUAN ROMERO GONZÁLEZ and
JUAN M. ALBERTOS PUEBLA

10.1 THE HISTORICAL BACKDROP

In order to analyse and fully understand the internal Spanish migration trends in the 1980s, we must first look, briefly, at the intense migration movements of the two previous decades which provide not only the appropriate historical backdrop but also aid the understanding of the recent major phenomena such as the return to rural regions or the loss of growth, if not an actual loss of population, within metropolitan areas.

The 1960s saw what were probably the greatest migration movements of the Spanish population of all time. Through internal migrations alone, nearly 4.5 million people changed their municipality of residence within the same province or between provinces. In the same period, 15 in every 1000 inhabitants changed their municipality of residence each year of which more than 5 per 1000 did so within the same province while more than 8 per 1000 moved province. The provinces are equivalent to the NUTS level 3 regions of Spain (Figure 10.1).

The following decade, the 1970s, saw at least 4.2 million migrants moving residence and it is particularly interesting if we examine the first and second half separately: the period 1970–5 had identical characteristics to the previous decade, while the period 1975–80 saw a deceleration of long-distance migration in favour of those of short distance (MOPU 1988, p.57). The changes after 1975 are important, as much for the clear characteristics which lasted throughout the economic crisis until 1985, as for the long-term behaviour of Spanish migration movements, which increasingly fell in line with the migration evolution of other European countries.

This dramatic movement of population was firstly and fundamentally absorbed by the large urban centres which acted as points of great attraction, secondly by provincial capital cities and other medium-sized cities of more than 50 000 inhabitants and thirdly by towns of between 20 000 and 50 000 inhabitants. Towns with fewer than 20 000 inhabitants registered a net loss of inhabitants (MOPU 1988, p.61). The changing net migration rate patterns at provincial level are illustrated in Figure 10.2.

Population Migration in the European Union Edited by Philip Rees, John Stillwell, Andrew Convey and Marek Kupiszewski. © Editors and Contributors. Published 1996 John Wiley & Sons Ltd.

NUTS 2: Autonomous communities

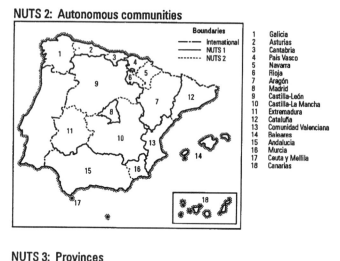

NUTS 3: Provinces

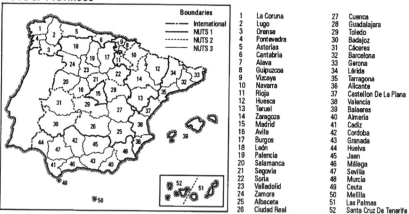

Figure 10.1 NUTS 2 and 3 regions of Spain

However, this information becomes much more significant if we group it by region. As can be seen in Table 10.1 a small number of regions registered high net levels of positive migration, namely Madrid, Cataluña and País Vasco. To this group we can add the Mediterranean regions of Valencia and Baleares on one hand, and on the other, Navarra and Zaragoza to make up the economic axis that joins País Vasco with the Mediterranean axis (MOPU 1988, p.68). The rest of the regions, together adding up to more than 30 provinces, had a continuous loss of population. Those regions with a higher active agricultural population (at the beginning of the 1960s some regions registered over 55 per cent of the work-force in the primary sector) were precisely those regions which registered high rates of net negative migration: Extremadura, Castilla–La Mancha, Castilla-León and Andalucía. The process also affected Aragón and Galicia in a profound way.

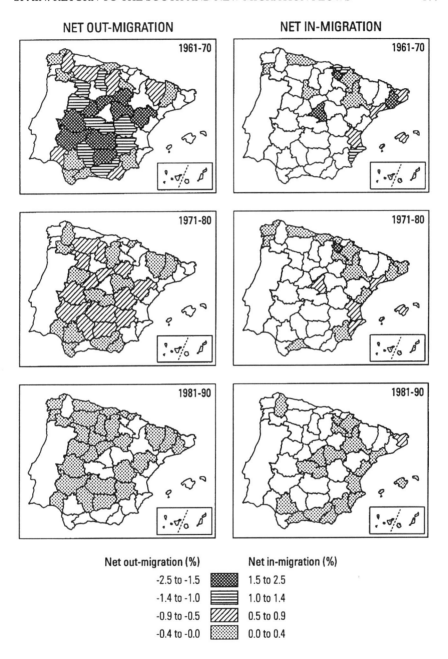

Figure 10.2 Annual net migration rates, 1961–70, 1971–80 and 1981–90

Table 10.1 Net migration by region, 1961–90

Region	1961–70	1971–80	1981–85	1986–90
Madrid	556 443	286 475	4896	40 097
Cataluña	594 180	248 157	−55 719	−2170
C. Valenciana	219 965	186 019	12 693	25 631
País Vasco	174 452	28 663	−28 048	−38 198
Baleares	36 311	31 125	861	24 445
Canarias	24 542	40 818	14 445	26 171
Navarra	14 222	1898	3489	2444
La Rioja	−6833	3445	3217	1704
Cantabria	−1903	3610	−395	−1074
Asturias	12 985	4269	−2927	−3801
Aragón	−25 451	3129	3667	1510
Murcia	−22 536	10 124	9424	7138
Galicia	−55 178	17 414	1200	−12 261
Extremadura	−231 342	−98 194	8613	−18 500
Castilla–León	−288 187	−111 213	−4044	−33 256
Castilla–La Mancha	−308 536	−119 225	38	−18 066
Andalucía	−449 090	−124 706	23 889	−1489

Sources: Period 1960–80, MOPU (1988); period 1980–90, INE (annual)

This movement of population from rural regions to the urban-industrial centres did not occur in a haphazard fashion but by way of two clear systems from south to north. In the first case, which fanned from the lower regions of the Mediterranean, Andalucía and Extremadura, the migration current ran towards Barcelona and its surrounding metropolitan area. In the second case, comprising the two large regions of Castilla and Extremadura, the current ran towards Madrid. Other centres which attracted migrants on a secondary level, such as País Vasco or Valencia, received a large proportion of that population from provinces closer to their respective areas of influence.

The evolution of the Spanish economy, the international context and the regional productive structure clearly explain the unequal volume of migrants, the direction of the currents and the change in this tendency after 1975. Therefore, the migration movements reasonably reflect the three big stages of development (1960–75), crisis (1975–85) and economic recuperation (1985–90) of the Spanish economy. The first coincides with the 15 years when the so-called 'Spanish economic miracle' occurred. The 1959 'Plan de Estabilización' marked the start of a great economic expansion which entailed some production transformations, in turn making the economic expansion visible. These transformations, while changing the economic structure, also produced unequal regional development (VVAA 1990, p.16). The process of industrialization, the development of the construction industry and the growth of the service sector set off the crisis in a traditional manner within agriculture, which had been particularly stable throughout the century. It is therefore clear that the cause of the agricultural crisis was induced by the industrial and service sectors. As a result of the Spanish industrialization process following this change of economic direction from 1959, the rural exodus accelerated at an extraordinary rate. If the rural exodus was intense in Western Europe, in Spain it was even more so because in 1955 the primary sector still accounted for 45 per cent of the country's work-force. In addition, the migration trends not only absorbed the majority of day labourers of southern Spain, Castilla and Aragón, who had provided the abundant and cheap work-force for the traditional *latifundios*, but also, from Andalucía, Castilla and Extremadura important contingents of small farm owners.

The traditional agricultural crisis was propelled by uncontainable forces: the net earnings for a working person in the agricultural sector were 40 per cent lower than in industry; poor living conditions; scarce or nonexistent provision of services and infrastructure; the attraction of urban life and finally, changes in the values of the agricultural society (VVAA 1990, p.16). The process started half way through the 1950s and reached its peak mid-way through the 1960s although lasting until the beginning of the economic crisis in the second half of the 1970s. The movement of the active work-force reached over two million between 1960 and 1975. The intense process of industrialization and urbanization registered an unequal distribution of production and employment. For this reason, spectacular population movements occurred from the rural regions to the industrial localities, basically Madrid, País Vasco, Cataluña and Comunidad Valenciana.

The period 1975–80 can be considered as a bridge to help explain to a large extent the migration movements for 1980–5 which we will be examining later. As a whole, this period contained a profound crisis in both industry and construction with the consequential negative impact on employment. These circumstances explain the notable reduction of interregional migration movements, albeit not on a general level, due to the service sector developing in a dynamic fashion, gaining 10.5 percentage points and finding itself in 1985 with over 50 per cent of the total work-force. This unequal distribution of production and, consequently, occupation affected the territorial regions unequally and was reflected in the slowing down of migration towards the industrial regions, in the appearance for the first time, in País Vasco, of negative migration trends in a region of traditional in-migration, and in the continued migration flows towards those areas or provincial capitals where service industry maintained high levels of activity.

10.2 INTERNAL MIGRATION IN THE 1980s

The study of Spanish internal migration flows based on movement information data can only be assessed using the figures of *Padrones Municipales de Habitantes* (Official Population Rolls for each Municipality). This, therefore, conditions the final definition we use for migration in the eighties as: 'those residential changes that affect any one municipality for a sufficient period of time as to induce the individual to register on the local population roll'. The intermunicipal level of movement, together with the voluntary nature of registration may somewhat bias the final statistics. However, we believe that, in general terms, the sources used reasonably reflect the volume and basic characteristics of the internal migrations that were occurring.

10.2.1 RECENT PATTERNS OF POPULATION CHANGE

The number of people who moved residential municipality during the 1980s, although growing, continued to remain at levels lower than those common in many developed countries. During the decade there is a clear difference between the first period until 1986 characterized by especially low levels of movement: less than 1 per cent of the population moving municipal residence each year reaching a minimum in 1981 of 0.45 per cent; and a second period which starts from 1986 when migration trends increase annually in constant progression to affect 1.76 per cent of the Spanish population in 1990. These two distinct periods in migration patterns coincide exactly with the turning point in the Spanish economy during the 1980s, when there was an economic crisis and structural adjustment up until 1986, followed by a very strong growth situation in the second half of the decade. These conditions undoubtedly favoured at first a restriction of migration tendencies and then, later, the increase in residential changes.

There has been an evolution in the general level of movement of the population coinciding with important changes in the socioeconomic structure of the migrant population which clearly derive from the motives for migration and changing personal circumstances within the life cycle of the family. From this point of view, the age of individual migrating is a critical variable. Concentrating on the recent period of rapid increase in movement, we find that specific age ranges have experienced an increase over and above the overall average. Where this is most marked is in the 25–34-year age group followed by the 65 plus age group and the 35–54-year age group. On the other hand, the mobility of the under 25-year age group and the 55–64-year age group is below the overall average. Increases in migration correspond in particular to the beginning of the working life and the creation of the family, usually in the 25–34-year age group. As well as this, the years following retirement have also seen a notable increase in residential movement. The most obvious reasons for the highest rates among these two groups appear to be: finding affordable housing at the time of creating a family; moving residence with a recently formed family; finding employment at the beginning of the working life; or moving to areas which offer better quality of life after retirement.

Throughout the whole decade there has also been a change in the social structure of the migrant population. Certain social groups have increased their propensity to migrate to the detriment of others. Especially notable among those groups which have increased their residential mobility are the professional and technically skilled classes, as well as office and service personnel. Those groups which have been especially stagnant are industrial workers (qualified and unqualified), construction workers and transport workers. Correspondingly, the proportion of migrants with university or higher education qualifications has increased to the detriment of those with only basic or incomplete education. These changes in themselves reflect, in part, the parallel transformation of Spanish social structure although this is not the only reason. The increased participation in migration among the aforementioned groups also reflects an increasing rate of migration among those groups: eg 23 per cent of all active migrants in 1986 were from the professional and technically skilled classes, although, this group accounted for only 8.6 per cent of the total working population. A similar phenomenon can be seen among office and service personnel who constituted only 23 per cent of the total working population yet contributed to 34 per cent of the active migration. In contrast the agricultural, industrial, construction and transport workers, although constituting 50 per cent of the active population, only contributed to 36 per cent of migrations.

We can therefore conclude that people with a continually greater tendency to migrate in Spain are those with higher education who are integrated into the more economically dynamic sectors of the population: that is to say, those people who are more receptive, negatively or positively, to the information available within the job market, another factor which would also explain the increase in internal migrations in Spain since 1986.

10.2.2 THE SPATIAL COMPONENT

Together with the overall framework of movement and certain components of the migrant population, we must also consider the profound changes in the regions of origin, the direction and destination in the migration movements undertaken. Throughout the decade of the 1980s, and in stark contrast to the previous decades (1970s and more especially the 1960s), the migration movements were over relatively short distances. Throughout the 1980s and without observing any significant alterations between years, 53 per cent of all residential changes occurred without leaving the province (NUTS 3 level) of origin and 62 per cent occurred within the same autonomous region (NUTS 2). The migration changes therefore had a greater impact on the intraregional distribution of population than on the overall interregional distribution on a national level. Simultaneously there have been important changes with regard to those municipalities which have gained or lost population and, as is shown in Table 10.2, there is a clear relationship with population size.

At the beginning of the decade (1980–1), cities with populations between 20 000 and 100 000 were the most attractive to the migrant populations, while smaller

Table 10.2 Relationship between net migration and settlement size, 1980–1 and 1989–90

Size of municipality	Annual per cent migration balance	
	1980–1	1989–90
Up to 10 000	–0.17	0.04
10 000–19 999	0.10	0.36
20 000–99 999	0.27	0.26
100 000–499 999	0.13	–0.10
500 000 or more	0.26	–0.45

Source: INE (annual)

townships (fewer than 10 000 inhabitants, usually rural) continued to be reduced in size and big cities (more than 500 000) also started to experience an overall fall in numbers. It is during this period that the first signs of a change in the migration model can be seen, with a change towards the counterurbanization model proposed by Fielding (1982). By the end of the decade (1989–90) these tendencies became more accentuated: large cities were losing population at an even greater rate and slightly smaller metropolitan areas (100 000–500 000) were joining in the trend. Correspondingly, the centres of population most attractive to people migrating were now quite clearly those large towns of 10 000–20 000 inhabitants. Finally, the rural townships with fewer than 10 000 people achieved a state of equilibrium thanks to an overall slight gain in population numbers; although very small settlements (population less than 2000) continued losing numbers, they were balanced by the stronger gain in the townships of over 2000.

Although there are important regional differences existing to which we will refer later, these results seem to indicate that there were various processes simultaneously affecting the levels of territorial redistribution of the population.

1. A process of short-distance periurbanization was appearing, particularly around the large metropolitan areas.
2. Although more restricted in volume, the return of formermigrants, usually from medium- or long-distance centres favoured greatly the small and medium cities of central and especially southern Spain.
3. A third process, usually at medium intraregional or interregional distances, was directing part of the population to more economically dynamic areas.

It is also essential with regard to these three processes to differentiate between the first and second half of the decade. In the period 1981–5 the process of periurbanization started at the same time that there was an upsurge in older migrants returning to their regions of origin. However, the period 1986–90 saw the increasing process of periurbanization accompanied by revitalized interregional migrations, induced by differential economic growth. The contrast between the two five-year periods is shown in the net out- and net in-migration maps of Figure 10.3.

10.2.3 THE PERIOD 1981–5

During the first five years of the 1980s, a time of economic crisis and low level of migration, the return of older migrants to their regions of origin greatly influenced the overall migration figures. This phenomenon was particularly acute in the large metropolitan areas of Barcelona and País Vasco. From Barcelona people returned particularly towards the south (Andalucía and Extremadura) and from the País Vasco towards Castilla–León. Other areas which had received high in-migration in previous decades stabilized somewhat as a result of out-migration to other areas. This is the case of Valencia, from where most people went to Castilla–La Mancha and Andalucía; or Madrid, from where people went to Castilla–La Mancha, Andalucía or Castilla–León. However, in neither of these two cities can we see an

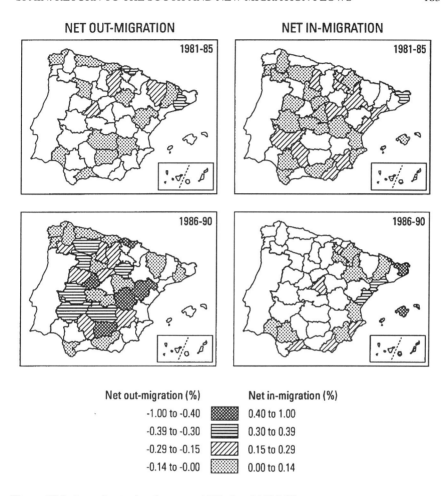

NET OUT-MIGRATION   NET IN-MIGRATION

Net out-migration (%)   Net in-migration (%)
-1.00 to -0.40   0.40 to 1.00
-0.39 to -0.30   0.30 to 0.39
-0.29 to -0.15   0.15 to 0.29
-0.14 to -0.00   0.00 to 0.14

Figure 10.3 Annual net migration rates, 1981–5 and 1986–90

overall decrease in population due to a maintained flow of in-migrants. As we have stated, this aspect of inverse migration flow from industrial to rural regions espe-cially affected Cataluña (Barcelona) and País Vasco (Vizcaya and Guipúzcoa) with an overall reduction of 56 000 and 28 000 people respectively. Other highly indus-trialized and developed regions of northern Spain such as Cantabria and Asturias also registered small reductions in population during this period, albeit part of a continuing process of out-migration which began in the 1960s due to the decline and economic stagnation of the regions.

The poor prospects for procuring employment in the regions of higher in-migra-tion, together with an improvement in the living conditions of more backward areas, traditionally areas of evacuation, reduced the number of people out-migrating from less favoured areas. This, together with the return of a small proportion of the population that had left in previous decades, meant that the age-old tendency of population loss in the rural regions of the south was broken to the extent that, in some cases, the migration balance was equal and in others there were actually some important gains. Andalucía and Extremadura were, without doubt, the two regions which benefited most from this process with a net balance of some 33 000 people between 1981 and 1986. In other cases (Galicia, Castilla–La Mancha and Castilla–León) there was an almost perfect balance between people leaving and arriving.

In conclusion, the first five years of the 1980s are also when other important changes can be seen on the Spanish migration map. During the 1960s and at the beginning of the 1970s the large metropolitan areas had been the destination of interregional migrants, but now these centres started losing their attraction even to the extent of losing population, while other areas of in-migration started gaining force. As we have already seen, until the second half of the 1970s, together with the aforementioned four centres, the whole of the Catalan and Valencian Mediterranean coastline along with the Balearic and Canary Islands had also been attractive to in-migrants. Apart from this fairly homogeneous area only isolated places in the interior, such as Navarra and Zaragoza in the Ebro Valley or Valladolid in Castilla–León, had developed sufficient industrial capacity to attract a migrant population, frequently from a neighbouring region. In the first five years of the 1980s this situation started to change. There was the consolidation of the economic axis of the Ebro Valley as an exceptionally dynamic region attracting in-migration; and the traditionally receptive provinces of Zaragoza and Navarra were clearly joined by La Rioja and Alava, this latter constituting the only area of positive migration within País Vasco. Probably the greatest change to emerge from the 1980s is in the increase in size of the Mediterranean axis. Murcia became an area that received in-migrants as did a part of the Andalucian coastline, particularly Almeria and slightly fewer in Granada and Malaga. Similarly, the Canary and Balearic Islands also appear as one of the main migration destinations.

10.2.4 THE PERIOD 1986–90

The period 1986–90 is characterized by a very strong recuperation of economic growth, especially marked in Madrid and the two axes which make up the 'Y' in modern Spanish development: the Ebro Valley and the Mediterranean coastline in its entirety. This favourable economic situation has had a great impact on migration dynamics, bringing about important variations in the previous patterns.

The phenomenon of returning to rural regions has continued in quantities very similar to those of the first five-year period although marginally smaller for Barcelona and slightly greater for Madrid, Valencia and País Vasco. However, the economic reactivation has notably increased the number of in-migrants arriving in the more dynamic metropolitan areas, creating an overall increase in positive migration in Valencia and Madrid and reducing the overall negative migration of Barcelona. On the other hand, in the case of País Vasco, the relatively weak economic growth has not induced the recuperation of in-migration: losing population has intensified and here we find a net loss of 38 000 people in the period 1986–90.

These differences in the behaviour of the principal metropolitan areas are the result of a combination of three factors: (a) the capacity for growth and generation of employment being inferior in País Vasco; (b) a level of urban development which enables the required socioeconomic conditions for counterurbanization to be realized which is clearly superior in both Madrid and Barcelona and (c) the lifestyles and current economic dynamics of those regions from which the in-migrating population has traditionally come. Within this framework, Barcelona, which has a large proportion of in-migrants from Andalucía and Murcia, is a clear candidate to continue with a high number of out-migrants who return to their areas of origin.

During the same period, the situation of equilibrium or even slight migration gains by areas of traditional out-migration, which occurred during the previous economic standstill, completely disappeared in Galicia, Castilla–León, Castilla–La Mancha and Extremadura. These areas returned to significant migration losses (some 82 000 people in this five-year period). Meanwhile, Andalucia as a whole moved into a state of migration equilibrium. We can therefore conclude that, without doubt, the motivating factor for long-distance migration is the attraction of more developed regions rather than the departure from less favoured regions.

Finally, one last trend in the recent migration evolution is the extension of the in-migration area to include the whole Andalucian coastline within the Mediterranean coastal axis, coinciding even more specifically with major economic growth, and now clearly including Málaga with extensions towards Sevilla and Huelva.

10.3 SHORT DISTANCE MOVEMENTS

We have shown previously how, in contrast to the situation in preceding decades, during the 1980s, particularly in the second half of the decade, short-distance migrations (those which took place within the same province or within the same region) have become the most important flows. Unfortunately, the data sources available do not permit an analysis of what has happened throughout the decade. It is possible to use information on intraprovincial movement only for the period 1988–90. These data enable the calculation of the migration balances for each provincial capital as well as for the other urban areas with more than 100 000 inhabitants in the remainder of each province. Although the data are only for a short time, the period coincides with the years of the greatest general economic growth, particularly strong in the majority of regional economies. The changes in intraprovincial migration flows are now examined during this period of intense economic progress. Following this analysis, the most important findings of the chapter are presented.

The rural areas of interior and northern Spain have continued to lose population. The regional capitals of Castilla-León, Castilla– La Mancha, Extremadura, Galicia, Aragón and part of Andalucía record positive migration balances with the rest of their respective provinces. This very important observation shows that young adults continue to migrate from rural zones into the most important urban centre of each province. In the rural areas there are hardly any other opportunities, and the decline of the agricultural labour force continues. In 1980 there were in Spain some 2.3 million farm workers (17 per cent of the economically active population), but in 1991 there were barely 1.4 million (10 per cent of the economically active). Apart from Madrid (where counterurbanization is at work), only Valladolid and, to a lesser extent, Salamanca, in the whole of interior and northern Spain, show a trend opposite to this rural exodus. That loss of demographic growth gravely threatens the future of farming and at the same time constitutes a very difficult obstacle to overcome in the new context of rural politics that the Common Agricultural Policy has put forward.

The capitals of the provinces located on the two economic axes of the Ebro Valley and the Mediterranean coast with an extension to western Andalucía exhibit a negative migration balance at provincial scale. The economic dynamism of these two axes involving the three production sectors (services, agriculture and industry) and also advanced spatial development (a good urban network and development of communication links) explains the processes of peri-urbanization or more simply a pattern of out-migration from the most populous regional capitals towards other intermediate-sized towns and particularly towards rural centres. The strong economic growth experienced in the Balaeric Islands and the Canaries powered by the tourist sector has resulted in similar migration patterns. These migration processes are reflected in Figure 10.3.

It is equally important to consider the movement of population within a province between urban centres outside the provincial capital. The strong growth in certain economic sectors, different in each case, as well as the different level of development of the urban system, explains why the largest percentage of the Spanish population is found in provinces experiencing net migration flows to the most important urban areas (Figure 10.4).

At least three processes can be observed at work in the intraprovincial and intraregional population movements.

10.3.1 PERIURBANIZATION

This process can clearly be seen at work in the metropolitan areas and the large provincial capitals. The phenomenon has frequently been associated with the improvement of urban transportation infrastructure and is linked to the area within which residences are less than one hour's journey away from work-places. The movement to periurban locations affects high- and medium-income social groups who seek a better quality of life in rural villages or in newly built urban areas in the first or second periurban rings. During the last decade all rural centres have experienced an improvement in accessibility and in the provision of public services which previously were either non-existent or inadequate. A good part of public investment has been directed at the improvement of the network of state schools at primary and secondary level, sporting facilities, health care centres and regional hospitals serving several communes.

10.3.2 OUT-MIGRATION FROM LARGE CITIES RESULTING FROM THE SHORTAGE OF CHEAP ACCOMMODATION

While it is impossible to estimate from Spanish statistical sources how much of the population moved during the 1980s for that reason, it is possible to affirm, with the information available, that the level of such out-migration, especially that of young couples with low or medium incomes, has been significant. This movement is labelled 'migration on marriage'.

One of the most important bottlenecks observed during the 1980s in Spain has been created by the large gap between supply and demand for housing. The rental housing market in Spain is restricted and inflexible, and the price of owner-occupied housing in the large cities is beyond the means of large groups of the popula-

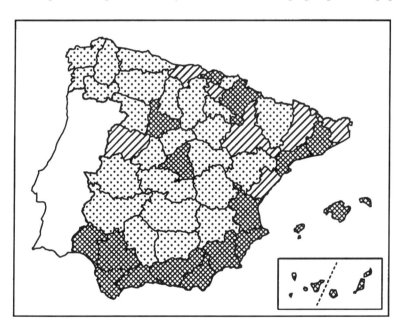

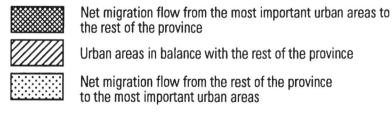

Net migration flow from the most important urban areas to the rest of the province

Urban areas in balance with the rest of the province

Net migration flow from the rest of the province to the most important urban areas

Figure 10.4 Short distance intraprovincial migrations, 1988–90

tion. The gap between supply and demand for housing reached such a size towards the end of the last decade that the central government, in collaboration with regional governments and public and private financial institutions, was obliged to put into operation a housing plan which aims to provide access to housing to young couples and low-income groups. An ambitious housing plan was started which will attempt to build 460 000 housing units during the period 1992–5. The plan underlines the seriousness of the problem, which is marked by a lack of forethought and by the absence of regional or local plans for public housing supply.

10.3.3 ECONOMIC RESURGENCE.

The third process is the most well known and refers more to the economic revitalization of urban areas during the second half of the 1980s than to the consolidation of new non-metropolitan or rural zones of economic expansion. In the two cases, the role of private initiatives has been as fundamental as that of public bodies in a double plan: on the one hand, investment in infrastructure and on the other, a plan for the creation of Development Agencies and support for Local Promotion and Development Initiatives. It would be difficult to explain many population movements during the last decade without reference to regional initiatives to promote new investment, to the processes of restructuring and decentralization of production and to measures of support for local economies.

10.4 CONCLUSIONS

Cabré *et al.* (1985, p.61), while providing an account of migration flows in Spain over the period 1960–75 and reporting on trends which started in the 1977–80 period, have written about the disruption of those trends and of 'territorial reconversion'. After 15 years of economic growth during which profound economic changes have taken place, triggering off interregional population transfers, a very different era has begun. This era has been marked by recession and the start of the decline of the old industrial regions. The most dramatic consequence of the economic restructuring crisis, unemployment, has caused the slowing down and change in secular direction of long-distance migration, and even the appearance or intensification of new flows, unknown or of little importance up to now.

During the last decade the model of long-distance migration broke down. For the first time in their history, the southern regions registered a net gain, particularly in the period 1980–5, the result of former migrants returning. However, the moderate long-distance gains have undergone a new reduction and even disappearance in certain regions during the second half of the decade. Moreover, the analysis of intra-regional movements shows the progressive loss of demographic growth in the least dynamic rural zones of southern and central Spain. The implications of this are well known, and it does not appear that this trend, which seriously threatens the future of both the most remote and intermediate rural areas, will change in the immediate future.

A second important feature has been the net loss of population in large urban areas and large towns in the most dynamic economic areas, in favour of medium-sized towns and even rural centres. Most of the population movements recorded in Spain have been short distance or intraregional. This process is another difference compared to previous decades. The causes of this process of periurbanization or movement of medium distance (improvement of infrastructure and services in rural areas, decentralization of the productive sector, housing) are similar to those given by other authors relating to countries like France or Italy (Champion 1989) and show that Spain, although on a different scale, is progressively approaching the model of counterurbanization which already exists in other countries.

It is probably too early to evaluate the implications of these processes in the sphere of regional economic and urban planning; it is evident that the deep economic recession in Spain since 1990 will have repercussions on the movement of population, but it will be several years before they are fully worked out.

NOTE

[1]A preliminary version of this article was published in *Revista Española de Investigaciones Sociológias,* 1993, **63**, 123–144, Centro de Investigaciones Sociológias, Madrid.

11 Migration in France Between 1975 and 1990: a Limited Degree of Decentralization

BRIGITTE BACCAÏNI and DENISE PUMAIN

11.1 INTRODUCTION

The only source of detailed information on migration in France is the census. An analysis of responses given to the question, 'where were you living at the time of the last census?' gives us an estimate of the number of persons who are living in a different place at the end of an interval of seven years (1975–82) or eight years (1982–90). However, the knowledge acquired in this way about these migrants only provides us with part of the total migration which took place during the intercensal period concerned (Tugault 1973; Courgeau 1988). Other enquiries which attempt to reach a better understanding of the evolution of families, of the labour market (*Enquête Emploi* described in Courgeau 1986), or of life histories (*Enquête Triple Biographie* described in Courgeau 1985) allow us to make the census information more complete and to test it for serious bias.

It has therefore been possible to establish that the total migration of people in metropolitan France (in the sense of change of residence) has achieved a level which is very close to that in neighbouring countries, of the order of 10 per cent per annum (8.5 per cent in the case of 1982–90) (Baccaïni *et al.* 1993). Though rising constantly since the beginning of the 1900s, this migration stopped increasing from 1975 onwards, declined slightly up to 1985 and has remained stable since then (Courgeau and Pumain 1984). This scenario is also characteristic of all geographical and administrative levels, including the *commune* and the *région,* the NUTS Level 2 scale in France (Figure 11.1). It is also found in all age groups.

An understanding of the geographical organization of these movements is very important. Within Europe, France is an area where the population has a low density (104 persons per square kilometre in 1990) and is also the most uneven in its distribution, mainly due to the concentration of population in the Paris area. In a period when natural demographic growth is very weak (0.4 per cent per annum in 1975–90) and external immigration has been markedly reduced by controls (0.07 per cent per annum in 1975–82; 0.1 per cent per annum in 1982–90), the direction and composition of migration flows and the size of these exchanges are revealing

Population Migration in the European Union Edited by Philip Rees, John Stillwell, Andrew Convey and Marek Kupiszewski. © Editors and Contributors. Published 1996 John Wiley & Sons Ltd.

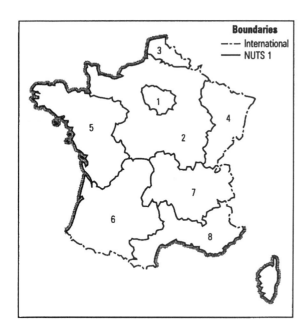

NUTS 1

1   Île de France
2   Bassin Parisien
3   Nord-Pas-de-Calais
4   Est
5   Ouest
6   Sud-Ouest
7   Centre-Est
8   Méditerranée

NUTS 2: Régions

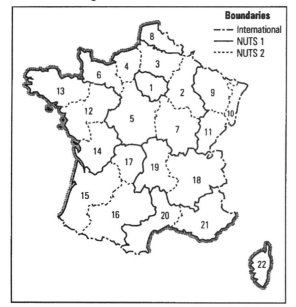

NUTS 2

1   Île de France
2   Champagne-Ardenne
3   Picardie
4   Haute-Normandie
5   Centre
6   Basse-Normandie
7   Bourgogne
8   Nord-Pas-de Calais
9   Lorraine
10 Alsace
11 Franche-Comté
12 Pays de la Loire
13 Bretagne
14 Poitou-Charentes
15 Aquitaine
16 Midi-Pyrénées
17 Limousin
18 Rhône-Alpes
19 Auvergne
20 Languedoc-Roussillon
21 Provence-Alpes-Côte d'Azur
22 Corse

Figure 11.1 NUTS 1 and 2 *régions* of France

components in the evolution of settlement patterns. From these short-term tendencies the experts are doing their best to decipher the likely probabilities in view of these contradictory dynamics. Will the deconcentration of the Paris area, fuelled by centrifugal forces, benefit provincial regions, or will the reinforcement of the metropolitan area by the internationalization of exchanges carry the day? Will the decline of the older industrial areas of the north and east of France, together with 'the rise of the south', bring about a move towards a greater equilibrium of the population, or will levels of development delimited by proximity to the *dorsale nord européenne* (north European urban industrial concentration) produce a renewed movement which favours the north of the country?

Advantages of a different kind are to be found in the larger towns; they are places of employment, diversity and accessibility. On the other hand, smaller towns are nearer to the countryside and are less costly—so will they prevail to any considerable extent? An analysis of recent migration tendencies at the urban and regional levels will enable us to clarify some of these perspectives.

11.2 REGIONAL CONCENTRATION AND LOCALIZED DECONCENTRATION

Between 1975 and 1982, 4.4 million people moved from one region to another in France, and between 1982 and 1990, five million moved. But because many of these movements are compensatory, they only contribute slightly to the redistribution of regional populations, in the order of 100 000 persons annually (the relationship between net migration and total migration being approximately 15 per cent).

The geography of population gains and losses since 1975 has remained extraordinarily stable. The greatest losses may be observed in Lorraine, in the Nord, in Champagne–Ardenne and in the Ile-de-France, while gains were made in the area of the *midi*, in Languedoc–Roussillon, Provence–Alpes–Côte d'Azur, Midi–Pyrénées and Aquitaine. Other areas showing gains were the Centre between Paris and the Loire, and Rhône–Alpes to the east (Figure 11.2).

These totals seem to confirm a continuation of the tendency towards a dispersion of the population from the 'centre' (in terms of economic structure), to the more 'peripheral' regions, though Rhône–Alpes may be considered as part of the 'centre' and the region of the Centre benefits from its proximity to the Ile-de-France. But above all, they illustrate the marked rise in the importance of the 'attractiveness' of an area, a factor which favours considerably the regions of the south. At the same time, the gains made by the regions of the *midi* have shown a slowing down during the periods under study in this chapter. Their levels of net migration were higher between 1975 and 1982 than between 1982 and 1990 (except in Midi–Pyrénées). Conversely, the losses shown in the Ile-de-France were reduced by half, (a loss of 3.6 per cent in 1982–90, compared with 6.4 per cent in 1975–82). Although remaining relatively stable in terms of migratory balance, the differences between regions were progressively reduced during the 1980s, with the exceptions of the Nord,

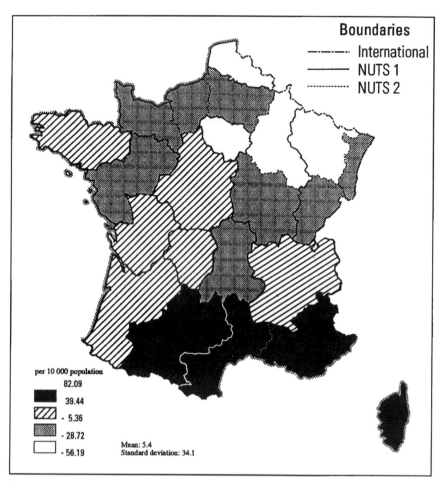

Figure 11.2 Annual net migration rates by *région,* 1982–90

Lorraine and Franche-Comté where the balance continued to deteriorate (Table 11.1).

At a smaller geographical scale, the effects of migration are considerably more complex. One should never forget that today's movements are superimposed upon those which have taken place earlier and which have, for example, rejuvenated the population in most towns and contributed to the ageing of the population in many already thinly populated rural areas. The effects of current migration and current natural population changes, linked to former migratory movements, combine in such a way that at a smaller geographical scale it is possible to see a reinforcement of this division in the population; the urban areas and their peripheries portray an increasing population, while the zones of less dense population continue to collapse.

From the beginning of the 1970s, while migration remained negative in most

Table 11.1 Annual average regional net migration rates by age group, 1982–90

Age	Régions (rates per 10 000)							
	Ile de France	Champagne– Ardenne	Picardie	Haute Normandie	Centre	Basse Normandie	Bour-gogne	Nord–Pas-Calais
0–9	72.5	–44.3	46.3	17.4	80.7	0.7	8.4	–71.3
10–19	– 48.9	–37.6	5.9	–11.7	25.8	–4.1	–0.2	–38.3
20–9	168.7	–90.7	–82.4	–45.3	–43.3	–92.4	–91.7	–98.0
30–9	–52.9	–47.7	36.4	–6.3	55.7	1.4	–0.9	–60.4
40–59	–56.1	–23.5	1.9	–14.1	28.5	6.1	14.6	–34.0
60–4	–202.3	–7.3	19.5	–10.5	89.0	53.6	73.9	–29.7
65–9	–200.9	–11.5	12.1	–3.0	80.2	48.0	53.9	–26.0
70–4	–107.5	–3.3	0.7	3.7	35.7	20.1	15.7	–15.7
75+	–45.1	–4.4	1.3	4.1	13.0	10.6	1.5	–9.5
Total	*–36.4*	*–39.2*	*2.0*	*–8.8*	*32.5*	*–6.3*	*–1.4*	*–51.7*
	Lorraine	Alsace	Franche– Comté	Pays de la Loire	Bretagne	Poitou– Charentes	Aquitaine	Midi– Pyrénées
0–9	51.4	–10.8	–11.0	6.1	8.6	19.4	62.9	70.4
10–19	–101.2	–6.0	–20.3	5.6	12.5	16.0	49.6	55.2
20–9	–72.9	33.5	–85.5	–87.2	–89.6	–122.3	–3.5	25.1
30–9	–37.9	–12.7	–19.2	12.4	7.7	18.0	49.6	53.1
40–59	–29.1	–12.8	–13.4	13.9	28.1	30.1	42.5	38.1
60–4	–21.8	–9.7	3.4	53.1	91.4	87.3	70.4	44.0
65–9	–13.2	–6.6	–1.5	48.3	70.7	70.3	55.2	34.1
70–4	–10.3	0.1	–3.4	28.0	34.3	31.6	30.4	15.0
75+	–56.2	0.8	–6.0	13.3	12.6	6.1	14.0	13.3
Total		*–2.6*	*–23.8*	*0.1*	*7.8*	*6.9*	*39.3*	*40.7*
	Limousin	Rhône– Alpes	Auvergne	Languedoc– Roussillon	Provence– Alpes-Côte d'Azur	Corse		
0–9	25.0	45.9	10.3	97.5	73.3	74.0		
10–19	19.0	18.8	7.5	106.3	51.2	9.0		
20–9	–68.9	51.1	–93.9	34.3	40.7	17.5		
30–9	8.1	33.9	–3.2	88.2	61.4	45.8		
40–59	25.9	7.4	13.5	94.9	45.7	40.9		
60–4	72.9	–8.0	30.1	141.6	76.3	147.2		
65–9	63.5	–3.9	28.0	103.8	77.8	119.4		
70–4	33.2	0.0	14.8	58.7	43.9	39.6		
75+	13.1	8.9	6.5	21.6	16.3	29.5		
Total	*14.2*	*23.0*	*–3.8*	*82.1*	*51.9*	*47.7*		

Source: INSEE 1990

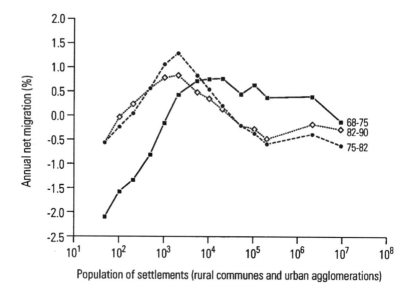

Figure 11.3 Net migration rates by population size of settlement, 1968–90

rural *communes*, it contributed more to population growth in small towns than in the larger urban centres; those towns with populations between 2000 and 20 000 persons showed the highest migratory balances (Figure 11.3). This tendency became accentuated between 1975 and 1982, with migratory balances in general becoming positive for rural *communes* with more than 100 inhabitants, and negative for those urban areas with more than 20 000, with the highest deficits being in the Paris conurbation. Between 1982 and 1990, the picture was similar, but there was a marked reduction in the gaps between towns of different size; the loss of a town's population due to migration slowed down considerably, in particular for the Paris area; actually, it was the larger towns (100 000–200 000) which lost the most.

This type of development seems at first sight to reinforce the concept of counterurbanization. However, a number of detailed analyses have shown that the rejuvenation of rural communes has been limited to those in the peripheries of urban agglomerations, while those communes in the *campagnes profondes* have continued to lose population by migration, even though at rates which are much reduced from those in the main period of *l'exode rural* in the 1950s and 1960s. However, another alternative proposition has been put forward to explain this increase in growth of smaller towns. This theory maintains that the situation is the final phase of a diffusion down the urban hierarchy of the cycle of postwar innovations, which did not begin to reach the smaller towns until the end of the 1960s. This effect would, moreover, be reinforced by the development of satellite towns in the peripheries of the larger urban centres.

The validity of these somewhat contradictory interpretations of the migration balances will be tested over the coming decades. In order to decide between the

Table 11.2 Evolution of the population of city centres and peripheries, 1975–90

| Zones | Population change (% per year) | | | | | |
| | Natural increase | | Total increase | | Net migration | |
	1975–82	1982–90	1975–82	1982–90	1975–82	1982–90
City centres	0.51	0.45	–0.57	–0.33	–0.06	0.12
Suburbs[1]	0.67	0.69	0.26	0.17	0.93	0.86
Rural, periurban areas[2]	–0.06	0.09	1.24	0.86	1.19	0.95
Rural, distant areas[3]	–0.55	–0.48	–0.49	–0.05	–1.05	–0.52

Notes: 1. Other communes belonging to urban agglomerations
       2. Other communes belonging to Zones de Peuplement Industrial ou Urbain (ZPIU) (1990)
       3. Rural communes outside ZPIU (1990)

Source: INSEE, 1982b, 1990.

processes of counterurbanization and metropolization, it is important to refine the analysis of movements by including the size and spatial location of the units concerned (Table 11.2). The diffusion of population from the central areas of towns towards the suburbs and rural peripheries (periurbanization), appears clearly in the migration figures. None the less, the slowdown in the loss of population from city centres, combined with a positive natural population balance attributable in part to the increased numbers of younger adults there, explains the rise in total migration. In contrast, those rural communes a long way from any town continue to lose population, less by migration, however, than by a negative balance between births and deaths.

11.3 LIFE CYCLES AND SPACE

As a result of the selective movements of the population according to age and profession, migrations also have a qualitative effect on population distribution which may be more significant than their quantitative effects. They contribute towards a significant modification of the map showing the ages of the population at different scales. Although very complex in detail, the differential totals show above all the specific importance of two categories of people: those aged 20–9 years, who are the most mobile as students and newly employed, and those aged 60–4 years, who are at retirement age.

On the whole, regions which are benefiting from migration are benefiting in all age groups and the same phenomenon is observed in regions losing from migration. The Ile-de-France, despite its negative total balance, actually shows an influx of young adults of plus 16.9 per cent per annum for the 20–9 age group (Figure 11.4a) and mainly demonstrates its migration deficit in the higher age categories, with an annual mean of minus 10 per cent for the over sixties (Figure 11.4b). Conversely, those regions which are on the whole benefiting from migration, such as the Centre and Aquitaine, are losing young adults in the 20–9 age group.

Looked at as a whole, the rural regions of the western half of France still operate as reservoirs of labour for the more complex economic areas, so they tend to lose

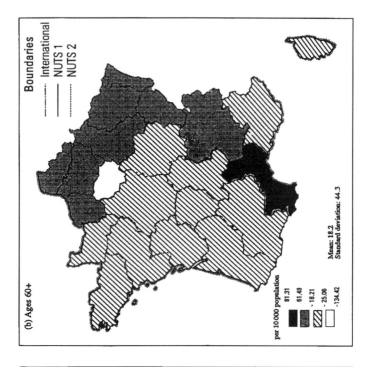

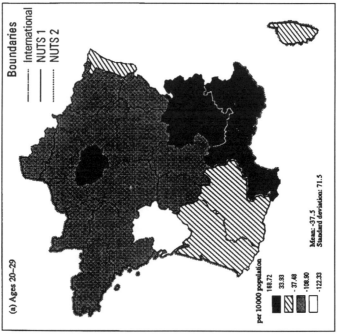

Figure 11.4 Annual net migration rates for selected age groups, 1982–90

young people and to gain retired people (Auvergne, Limousin, Aquitaine, Poitou-Charentes, Bretagne, Pays de la Loire and Basse-Normandie); and one can add to these, those regions on the periphery of the Paris Basin (Picardie, Bourgogne, the Centre and Franche-Comté). By contrast, the Ile de France, Alsace and Rhône-Alpes are regions where the diversifed and innovative labour market both attracts and retains younger workers but which discourage those at retirement age. The regions of the *croissant nord* (Haute-Normandie, Nord–Pas de Calais, Champagne–Ardenne and Lorraine) are losing many of the younger employed and almost as many retired persons, while the regions in the south (Corse, Languedoc–Roussillon, Provence–Alpes-Côte d'Azur and Midi–Pyrénées) primarily attract retired persons but also many of the younger employed.

At the urban scale, this age-specific migration effect appears to be even more marked, exhibiting similar characteristics and contributing strongly to the production of different types of migratory balance: first, that to be seen in the regional capitals (normally in agglomerations of more than 200 000 inhabitants), where the existence of higher education institutions and a labour market explain the commonly observed positive migration balance among younger workers, even in regions which show an overall deficit; and second, that of towns and cities in the *midi* which attract many retired people.

11.4 MIGRATION AND DISTANCE

Distance remains an important obstacle to individual movement. A recent study of migrations which took place between 1925 and 1980, undertaken with data from biographic enquiries (Baccaïni 1991), has demonstrated a highly assymetrical distribution of distances covered by individuals who are migrating. Though migrations took place over an average distance of 85 kilometres, half of these were only over a distance less than seven kilometres. In effect, short-distance migrations (intracommune or to a nearby commune) are very common, whereas movements over very long distances are very much more rare: 54 per cent of migrations are over distances of less than 10 kilometres, while only 4.5 per cent are over 500 kilometres.

11.4.1 A GRAVITY MODEL FOR INTERREGIONAL MIGRATION

In order to analyse the direction of migration streams, it is necessary to screen out the effect of gravitational interaction. A model has been applied to French interregional migration over the intercensal period 1982–90. The results will be compared with those from the preceding period (1975–82), which have already been analysed (Pumain 1986). We have made use of a programme developed by Poulain (1981), using two basic distance-dependent formulae. The distance taken into account is that which lies between the centres of gravity of the regions concerned:

in its Pareto form: $M'_{ij} = k\, P_i\, P_j\, d_{ij}{}^a$
in its exponential form: $M'_{ij} = k\, P_i\, P_j\, e^{bd_{ij}}$

where M'_{ij} is the estimated flow from zone i to zone j; P_i and P_j are the initial

Table 11.3 Goodness of fit and parameter values for gravity models applied to interregional migration, 1975–82 and 1982–90

Statistic and model	Total 1975–82	Total 1982–90	Age group 20–9	30–9	40–59	60+
R²						
Pareto	0.847	0.870	0.845	0.875	0.861	0.829
Exponential	0.830	0.856	0.834	0.862	0.848	0.824
Parameter a						
Pareto	–0.31	–0.40	–0.73	–0.35	–0.30	–0.15
Parameter b						
Exponential	–0.00071	–0.00110	–0.00250	–0.00091	–0.00069	–0.00027

Source: INSEE 1982b, 1990

population of zone i and the final population of zone j; d_{ij} is the distance between i and j and k,a,b are estimation parameters. The model parameters a and b are estimations resulting from a non-linear adjustment by weighted least squares, using iteration. The quality of the adjustment, R^2 (that part of migration flows 'explained' by the model), is calculated with the help of a non-linear correlation coefficient which measures the degree of dependent relationship between observed migration flows and the descriptive variables employed (mass of population; distance between zones). The level of fit reported in Table 11.3 is quite satisfactory, though somewhat better when using the Pareto model than in the exponential form. But it remains necessary to take into account, as Pumain (1986) has already pointed out, the crude nature of regional boundaries, which introduce an important element of heterogenity by comparison with a more refined system of division. In consequence, an adjustment made to the interdepartmental migration flows of the period 1968–75 gave values of R^2 which were superior to 0.92 (Poulain and Pumain 1985).

Interregional migration flows for 1982–90 are now better 'explained' using the effect of populations at risk and distances between regions than was the case for 1975–82, suggesting, therefore, that spatial constraints were stronger or more strongly felt between 1982–90 than in 1975–82. A comparison of different age groups shows that the model gives the best results for the 30–9 age group and is least helpful for the older groups, and this applies to the distance effect whether using the Pareto or the exponential approach. But the differences between one age group and the next, whatever the quality of the adjustment, remain quite small.

11.4.2 VARIATIONS IN SENSIBILITY TO DISTANCE

Parameters a and b of these models underline the importance of the friction of distance, ie the obstacles which distance presents to the migrant. The higher the absolute values of these parameters, the stronger is the effect of distance on migration. It is also a little surprising to note that, contrary to what one might expect from the continuous improvements which have taken place in the means of communication and in the sources of information, which might help people to make moves over long distances, the obstacle of distance became even more marked over the periods 1975–82 and 1982–90. Migrations now take place more frequently between adjacent regions and less frequently between distant regions which was not the case during the previous intercensal periods.

The older people are, the less distance acts as a brake to their migrating. Absolute values of the parameters *a* and *b* become regularly smaller with increasing ages, the eventual gap becoming quite large between the younger age group (20–9 years) and the oldest (59 plus years). Therefore, while a number of studies have shown that levels of migration (ie frequency of migrating) diminish with increasing age, the spatial spread of these migrations has a tendency to increase. The migration fields of young adults in the 1980s are noticeably more constrained than those of their elders, and especially of those at retirement age. This may well be explained, therefore, by the important position held by retirement migration to the south of France (which gives rise to long distance migration by older people) while the migrations of younger adults which are more commonly linked to the family life cycle or to professional reasons (Baccaïni 1991) take place more frequently within a local context, towards nearby regions.

11.5 MIGRATION FLOWS: PREFERRED DIRECTIONS AND BARRIER EFFECTS

In order to demonstrate the regional exchanges of population which have taken place over the two intercensal periods concerned, and within these two age groups, we have made use of the Pareto model, which gives us the most satisfactory results. The gaps between the sizes of observed flows and those calculated using the gravity model demonstrate the characteristics of migration flows after the elimination of the populations at risk (P_iP_j) and inter-regional distances (d_{ij}). The weighted residuals which have to be taken into account are written as follows:

$$X_{ij} = [(M_{ij} - M'_{ij}) / \sqrt{M'_{ij}}]$$

These residuals are consequently indices which characterize preferred directions or barrier effects and are not migrant flows as such. A positive residual shows that a preferred flow exists between the two regions under consideration, the observed flow being stronger than the 'theoretical' flow calculated from the demographic size of the two regions and their relative position in the regional system. Conversely, a negative residual expresses the barrier effect between the regions, as the model overestimates the real migration flows between them.

11.5.1 THE STABILITY OF RESIDUAL FLOWS

When one considers the total number of migrants in all the age groups together, the maps (Figure 11.5) show a high degree of stability between 1975–82 and 1982–90. The pattern of population redistribution from the Ile-de-France towards the regions of the south and the west especially, which appeared over the period 1962–8 and notably between 1975–82, is also confirmed over the most recent period. For at least 30 years, the migration field of the Ile-de-France, which had for a long time dominated the national picture (Courgeau 1970), has kept this assymetrical config-uration. Three regions in particular remain as important *pôles d'attraction* for the Parisian population: the Centre, Provence–Alpes–Côte d'Azur and Picardie. But taken as a whole, the regions in the south (Aquitaine, Midi–Pyrénées, Languedoc–Roussillon) form notable destinations for the people of the Ile-de-France. The pull of the south and of the sun continues to exercise itself markedly over the population of Paris, more there than for any other region.

However, in more detail, the evolution of positive residuals between the Ile-de-France and the provinces shows that, with the exception of the flow to Picardie, all the values have become lower, revealing a slowdown in the number of departures from the Paris region, and this is confirmed by the reduced emigration level from the Ile-de-France between 1982–90 in comparison with the period 1975–82 (Baccaïni, *et al.* 1993). The accentuation of the flow from the Ile-de-France to Picardie is linked to the large-scale deconcentration from the Paris conurbation, towards more and more distant periurban areas, by people who quite frequently continue to commute daily to Paris.

The geographical characteristics of the exchanges of migrants within the provinces have also remained stable between 1975 and 1990, and even since 1954 (Pumain 1986). The most notable flows take place between contiguous regions in the southern and western peripheries of the country, and most of these are two-way (the flows Provence–Alpes–Côte d'Azur and Languedoc–Roussillon; Aquitaine and Midi–Pyrénées; Bretagne and Pays de la Loire). Migration between provincial regions retains, therefore, a largely regional character.

Barrier effects show themselves mainly in the direction of the Nord-Pas de Calais region from most other regions and over both intercensal periods. The region remains unattractive to migrants from most other areas on account of its rundown economic image. On the other hand, the Rhône-Alpes region, which had been able to hold on very successfully to potential migrants towards a number of regions in the north, has perhaps seen a deterioration in this situation, with its ability to attract migrants having become somewhat weakened except with respect to the Pays de la Loire, Lorraine and the Nord. The geographical effects of the barrier have, there-fore, become less complex over the two periods concerned, with many migration deficits which were previously two-way having become one-way during the most recent period.

11.5.2 IMPORTANT CONTRASTS BETWEEN YOUNGER AND OLDER AGE GROUPS

The migration behaviour of the 20–9 age group can be differentiated clearly from

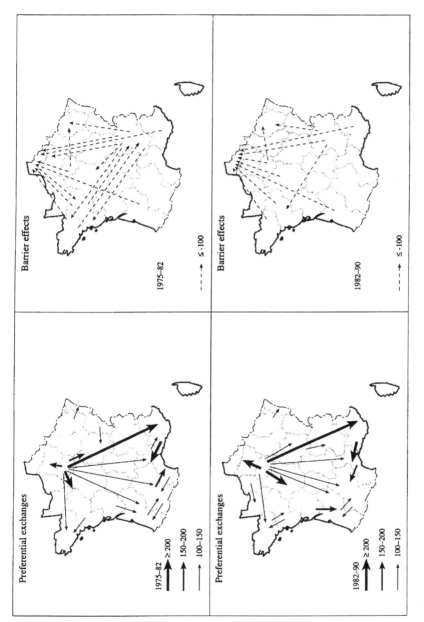

Figure 11.5 Indices relating to gravity model residuals, 1975–82 and 1982–90

204

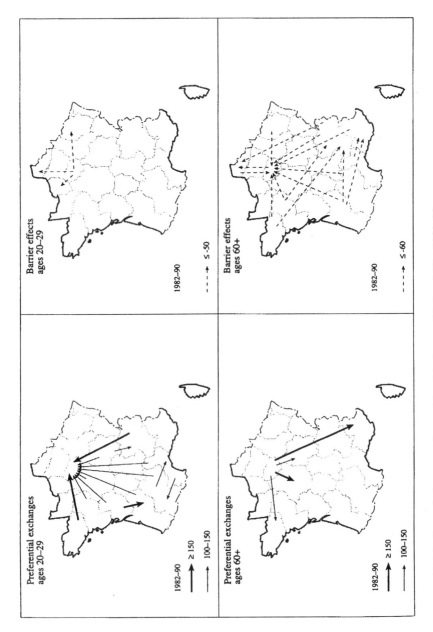

Figure 11.6 Indices relating to gravity model residuals, ages 20–9 and 60+, 1982–90

that of the later age groups (Figure 11.6). In effect, the Ile-de-France represents a very marked and preferred direction for younger migrants coming from many other regions, and particularly from the south and the west: Bretagne, Provence–Alpes–Côte d'Azur, Languedoc–Roussillon, Midi–Pyrénées (which is not to forget the quite large reverse movements from the Ile-de-France towards Provence–Alpes–Côte d'Azur, though these remain much smaller than the flows of the young provincials towards Paris). This age group is now the only one for which Paris has remained attractive over the two intercensal periods, even after eliminating the enormous demographic preponderance of the region. This phenomenon may be explained by the size and diversity of the employment market in the region and also by the large number of institutions of higher education (about half of the total national provision). The geography of the interregional exchanges over the age of 30 years is altogether different to this, even diametrically opposed. The oldest group (59 plus years) by preference moves from the Ile-de-France to Provence–Alpes–Côte d'Azur, to the Centre and to a lesser extent to Bretagne and Bourgogne. For persons between 30 and 59 years, the chosen destinations of those leaving the Ile-de-France are somewhat more varied, but with a particular preference for Picardie (which is not seen for those over 59 years).

Barrier effects present themselves in a complex manner and this complexity increases with age. Between 30 and 39 years, the only migration deficits which can be observed are on the one hand, from the Ile-de-France towards the Nord–Pas de Calais and Lorraine, and on the other between Rhône–Alpes and the Nord–Pas de Calais. One can see a clear reticence on the part of persons over 59 years of age to migrate to the Paris area from Bretagne, Pays de la Loire, Aquitaine, Midi–Pyrénées, Provence–Alpes–Côte d'Azur, Rhône–Alpes, Lorraine and the Nord but also towards certain other regions in the provinces (Bretagne to Rhône–Alpes, Rhône–Alpes to Nord–Pas de Calais, Aquitaine to Provence –Alpes–Côte d'Azur).

The residual method also allows us to identify migration behaviour by particular towns. A detailed study of origin and destination migration flows in 112 *unités urbaines* with populations over 50 000 between 1975–82 has shown the important effect of age-related choices: young persons and especially young adults tend to congregate in large towns, while older people are leaving these towns. Migration is therefore contributing to a rejuvenation of the population of medium- and large-sized towns. Only in the cases of certain towns in the north of the country (Boulogne, Calais, Lens for example), and in most of the towns in the *midi* (apart from Montpellier, Avignon and Arles), have we seen the older age groups form an increased proportion of the urban population through migration.

Urban migration flows are much less selective in the social and professional fields. Only the large university towns are different in these respects, as a result of their role in the training of young people, and of their national role in attracting well-qualified persons. The composition of the outward migration flows of these towns is clearly differentiated from the inward flows by a much higher proportion being made up of professionals and retired persons.

We see confirmed, therefore, a tendency towards the spatial segregation of the population in terms of individual life cycles. On the other hand, we see that the professional composition of flows normally reflects the pre-existing specializations of activity within towns which migration hardly changes (Pumain and Saint-Julien 1989).

11.6 CONCLUSION

The decade of the 1980s in France saw a continuation of the tendencies which had been apparent in the 1970s: migration largely continued to have the effect of redistributing the population of the regions in the northern half of the country towards those in the *midi*, and from the centres of towns towards the suburbs and the rural periurban areas. Counterurbanization remains at this local scale. The analysis of migration flows shows that the regions in the centre of the country and the large towns remain very attractive to the younger elements of the population, while retired people leave in order to regroup in the *midi* and in the smaller towns.

12 Ireland: the Human Resource Warehouse of Europe

RUSSELL KING, IAN SHUTTLEWORTH and JAMES WALSH

12.1 INTRODUCTION

The title of this chapter may appear a little dramatic (in fact its origins lie in a head-line which appeared in the *Irish Times* of 3 March 1989), but in this case the news-worthiness which lies at the heart of journalism refers to a condition which has afflicted Ireland for at least 150 years. Put simply, this condition is the historic inability of the country to create sufficient employment to keep the working popula-tion gainfully employed at a decent, European standard of living. Hence the social history of Ireland is dominated by a constant theme: emigration. What is additional-ly unique about Ireland is that it is the only European Union (EU) country where emigration continued to be a significant phenomenon during the 1980s. While a number of southern European countries, such as Greece and Portugal, have experi-enced rates of emigration in the past which were as high as those which occurred in Ireland, in southern Europe net emigration gave way in the late 1970s and through-out the 1980s to net inward flows, made up both of returning migrants and of immi-grants from regions such as North Africa and the Middle East. In Ireland's case, after a temporary economic boom during the 1970s which produced a short-lived period of net return migration, the 1980s saw accelerating out-migration which, in intensity, approached the rates of loss of the 1950s and early 1960s, when postwar mass emigration was at its heaviest.

Hence, in contrast to most of the other chapters in this book, the Irish case involves a greater emphasis on external migration. This emphasis will concentrate mainly on the so-called 'new emigration' of the 1980s: previous phases of external migration, such as the hundred years between the Great Famine and the end of World War II, the mass exodus of the 1950s and 1960s and the return flows of the 1970s, will be dealt with only summarily in so far as they provide a background context to the emigration of the 1980s. The internal mobility of the Irish population will not be neglected, however. Indeed, internal migration has been in some respects almost as dramatic as external, responding to the powerful forces of mod-ernization and development which have swept across the country—but with markedly uneven regional impacts—since the end of the 1950s.

The structure of this chapter is as follows. First, we shall draw attention to the

Population Migration in the European Union Edited by Philip Rees, John Stillwell, Andrew Convey and Marek Kupiszewski. © Editors and Contributors. Published 1996 John Wiley & Sons Ltd.

unique demography of Ireland and demonstrate to what extent the unusual structural characteristics of the Irish population have conditioned the character of migration processes. Second, we shall deal with emigration, concentrating on the most recent intercensal intervals. Then we shift our focus to internal movements of population before concluding by attempting to speculate on the character of Irish migration in the future. Throughout our analysis we shall refer only to the Republic of Ireland, using the term 'Ireland' to refer to the Republic and not to the entire island (except before 1922). We shall draw on several data sources, including of course the census, and we will present our data at a variety of spatial scales ranging from the national level (for external movements) through the coarse grain of the nine planning regions (equivalent to NUTS 3 units) down to the 26 counties of the Republic (27 if Tipperary is divided into north and south).

12.2 A UNIQUE DEMOGRAPHY

Irish demographic patterns and trends are characterized by volatility and by the curious fact that they are in most respects totally different from those observable in the rest of Western Europe. Ireland's population declined when increases were recorded in other countries, while in the 1970s, when many European countries were experiencing stagnation or decline in their population totals, Ireland's was growing at a rate which approximated that of some parts of the Third World. Ireland's 'deviant' population behaviour is of long standing. The second half of the 19th century was a period of strong population increase in most European countries: in Ireland (the island as a whole) the population declined spectacularly from 8.18 million in 1841 to 4.46 million in 1901. Famine (1845–6) and emigration were to blame. Changes in birth rate had minimal influence for Irish fertility has always been high by European standards and remains so.

For the first 60 years of the present century net emigration continued to cancel out or exceed natural increase so that the population carried on shrinking—from 4.46 million in 1901 to 4.24 million in 1961 (whole island). For the Republic, constituted in 1922, the decline was from 2.97 million in 1926 (the first census of the Republic) to 2.82 million in 1961. Throughout this period too, rates of natural increase remained high; indeed a high birth rate and a declining death rate resulted in a rate of natural increase that was twice as high in the 1970s as in the 1920s (Kennedy *et al.* 1988).

The 1960s heralded a new era of economic prosperity for Ireland as the economy was reconnected to the international system after nearly four decades of isolation. The result was a quarter century of population growth (Figure 12.1) so that the 1986 Census recorded a population (3.54 million) which was more than 25 per cent up on the 1961 figure. The growth resulted from a combination of an increase in the number of marriages—which contributed to a high birth rate even though average family size was declining—and a high incidence of return migration (Walsh 1979). Like other countries, Ireland generally exhibits a lagged response between economic

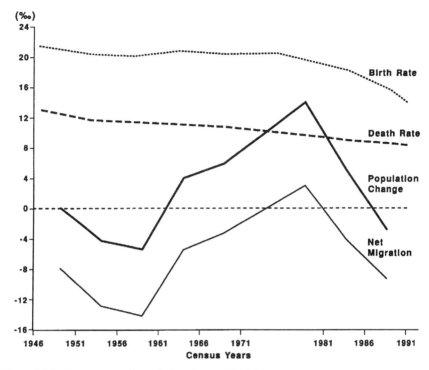

Figure 12.1 Components of population change, 1946–91

performance and demographic change; so that while the highest rates of economic growth were in the 1960s, it was not until the early 1970s that the highest rates of growth (1.6 per cent per annum) occurred in the population. Similarly in the 1980s, even though the economy had been in recession since the beginning of the decade it was not until 1987 that the now rapidly falling fertility level (and consequently natural increase) was overtaken by a rising level of net emigration (Figure 12.1). The results of the 1991 Census (3.52 million) indicate a slight decline (–0.4 per cent) over the figure for 1986.

As the work of the late John Coward has shown (especially Coward 1982; 1989), the pattern of Irish fertility has been almost as unique as the emigration trends just noted. Between the 19th century and the 1960s Ireland was characterized by a very specific, Malthusian regime based on high levels of celibacy, late age at marriage and high marital fertility. Since the 1970s, however, as Ireland becomes the last European country (not counting Turkey) to reach the stage of a demographically posttransitional society, the uniqueness of this fertility regime has broken down. Nevertheless the 20th-century absolute number of annual births peaked as recently as 1980 (74 000), giving Ireland the youngest population in Europe (again, excluding Turkey) with 27.7 per cent of its population under 15 years of age in 1990. During the 1980s the birth rate fell rapidly (Figure 12.1), leading to a 30 per

cent reduction in the annual number of births over the decade. Even so, the reproduction rate is still above replacement level and the average family size remains
significantly above other European countries (Creton 1991). The migratory relevance of these large cohorts of young people, who will not come on to the labour
market until the late 1990s, should not be overlooked; this point will be picked up
later.

12.3 EMIGRATION

12.3.1 A LONG TRADITION

Popular imagery, at least in Britain, stereotypes Irish migration as being confined to
the construction-site workers who came from the poorer parts of the west of Ireland.
This hides the historical and contemporary diversity of the Irish migrant experience
both in Britain and in other areas of the world. There is an extensive literature on
the history of Irish emigration; for some of the more accessible overviews see
Jackson (1963), Kennedy (1973), Lees (1979) and Garvey (1985) and King *et al.*
(1990) for more concise summaries. Descriptions of Irish vagrants and beggars in
the west of England are found as early as the 16th century, while Johnson (1967;
1990) has documented the seasonal 'harvest migration' to Scotland and England in
the 18th century and re-evaluated the impact of the Great Famine on emigration
patterns in the 19th century. The image of Irish migration as a response to poverty
and hunger has some general validity, but in the decades before the famine, emigration was largely made up of more prosperous farmers, artisans and even professionals who came mainly from Ulster; far from being rural Catholic poor, many of these
were radical Presbyterians leaving Ireland for political reasons.

Although in the late 19th century many Irish settled in the port cities of
Liverpool and Glasgow, the main destination until World War I was the United
States, which was attractive to Irish migrants by reason of its economic opportunities and tradition of personal liberty (Collins 1993; Houston and Smyth, 1993). The
British dominions of Australia and Canada were also important destinations. By
1881, over three million Irish-born were living outside Ireland, compared to a total
of 5.18 million living within Ireland.

In the 1920s, the United States instituted immigration quotas and Britain became
the main destination for Irish migrants. A spread of migration destinations inland to
the main concentrations of 19th-century and early 20th-century industry took place;
Irish communities sprang up in textile, coal, iron and steel, and engineering towns
like Manchester, Bolton and Birmingham. For the postwar wave of Irish emigration, at its peak during the 1950s and early 1960s, the geography of destination
changed again, reflecting the distribution of mid-20th century industrial growth in
the London area and the Midlands. Birmingham, Coventry, Leicester and Luton
became important destinations, along with the major concentration emerging in
London. Factory work absorbed the bulk of the Irish migrants in the Midlands; the
construction industry dominated the pattern of Irish employment in London.

Irish migration to Britain has been helped by geographical proximity and by the cheapness of passenger fares on ferries and, latterly, aircraft. Cultural and social barriers to movement across the Irish Sea are also not great. Indeed they are probably less intimidating than would be the case for similar migrant movements between Brittany and Paris or between the south and north of Italy (Hannan 1969, p.195). Even more decisively, the British labour market has always been freely open to Irish migrants, both before and after Irish independence.

12.3.2 AN IRISH MIGRATION CULTURE

The reason we have paid some attention to the historical development of Irish emigration is that Irish migration flows have tended to become self-generating; thus the migration flows of the present can hardly be understood without reference to the past. The Irish example provides convincing evidence for the importance of social networks in the process of migration and for the development of a 'migration culture' in which emigration has increasingly come to be seen as normal rather than exceptional behaviour.

As a mark of the social and economic importance of migration, and prompted in particular by the high loss of population from rural areas, Ireland has been one of the few countries that has thought it necessary to have an official commission to investigate emigration. It comments that 'tradition and example have been very powerful influences' on the development of emigration which has thus become established as a custom. By utilizing personal connections abroad the migrant is able to pass from 'known to known' and 'this path is followed as a matter of course without even looking for suitable employment in this country' (Commission on Emigration 1956, p.137).

Alongside the habit of migration has arisen a 'culture of exile', interpreted in different ways by different observers. Miller (1985, p.165) argues that 'from earliest times the very act of leaving was perceived sorrowfully in Irish culture'. The image of exile was developed from the earliest writings of the Christian era, continued in Gaelic ballads of the 16th and 17th centuries and survives today as a strong and recurrent element in Irish folk and popular music. This predominantly negative image of emigration 'by fate rather than by choice' was all the more firmly established by the nature of the Irish worldview as revealed in the structure of Gaelic. Thus the Irish word for 'emigrant' has strong connotations of isolation from kin and landscape (Miller 1985, pp.105, 121).

In the political arena there is a lack of consensus about the implications of migration and a substantial mismatch between rhetoric and deed. While most politicians have tended to see emigration as an indicator of economic failure (especially when campaigning against an opposition party's policies) and therefore to specify the eradication of emigration as a policy aim, others have argued that migration is inevitable and even desirable. In accord with the Commission on Emigration's remarks (1956, p.140) that emigration had acted as a relief for pressures in Irish society and made it possible for those left behind to live in comfort, the Minister for

Foreign Affairs, Brian Lenihan, said in an interview in the United States in 1987:

I don't look on the type of emigration we have today as being of the same category as the terrible emigration of the last century. What we have now is a very literate emigrant who thinks nothing of coming to the United States and going back to Ireland and maybe on to Germany and back to Ireland again ... It [emigration] is not a defeat because the Irish hone their skills and talents in another environment; the more they develop a work ethic in a country like Germany or the US, the better it can be applied in Ireland when they return. After all, we can't all live on a small island...

Thus there is, even at governmental level, a fatalistic acceptance of emigration, a feeling that emigration is part of the essence of being Irish. This feeling of 'belonging' to Ireland, even when abroad, is probably as strong today as it has been in the past.

12.3.3 EMIGRATION IN THE 1980s

As mentioned earlier, the 1970s was the only relatively long period of sustained net in-migration for Ireland. Even during this decade, when there was a net inflow of just over 100 000 people, there continued to be a high level of gross outmovement, amounting to 176 000, mostly young persons. Indeed when the two-way flows are disaggregated by age groups, there were continued net losses of young adults even during the years of highest overall net return.

Sources for estimating Irish external migration are limited in comparison to many other EU countries. In Ireland very little is known about either the magnitude or the skill/occupation composition of the recent emigration stream; there is no source comparable to the British International Passenger Survey, for instance. The Central Statistical Office (CSO) does issue annual gross and net migration estimates based on an array of indicators (net passenger balance by sea and air, migrant visas issued by the USA, Canada and Australia, new registrants from Ireland with the National Insurance and National Health schemes in Britain, children entering and leaving school rolls), but these indicators, which frequently show divergent trends from each other, give only an approximate prediction. In the late 1980s a further set of estimates was produced by the Irish Labour Force Survey—a large annual sample survey of 45 000 households (Garvey and McGuire 1989). This survey includes, *inter alia*, information on residence one year previously and a separate question on emigration. When the 1986 LFS was cross-checked against the 1986 Census question on one-year migrants, a reasonable correspondence was found. Because of the sample size (less than 5 per cent), grossed-up estimates of total migration flows are only very approximate. However, the LFS does have value in monitoring the changing occupational and regional structure of emigration.

Since 1981 there has been renewed emigration, which reached an annual gross outflow of more than 60 000 in the latter part of the decade, according to CSO estimates. Between 1981 and 1990, there was a gross emigration of more than 360 000. However, over the same period there continued to be a relatively high level of in-migration, amounting to approximately 150 000 over the decade. The volatility of

Irish migration trends was once again demonstrated by figures for 1990–2 which indicate that net emigration has virtually ceased due to reductions in out-migration and a high level of return migration (Figure 12.2).

These trends in external migration are closely linked with the nature and restructuring of the Irish and British labour markets and also, therefore, with unemployment rates (Walsh 1992a). Table 12.1 shows that between 1971 and the mid-1980s the total labour force increased by 17.7 per cent or nearly 200 000 people, mainly due to demographic pressure which was partly fuelled by return migration during 1971–8 and by a steady increase in the female participation rate. However, during 1980–5 the number of unemployed grew quite sharply (Table 12.1). During the second half of the 1980s, the total number of unemployed remained more or less constant due to high levels of emigration. Thus it seems that emigration, at least partly, functions as a response to unemployment, but if openings for emigrants are closed off in the main destination, ie a slump in the job market in Britain, emigration falls and unemployment rises, as happened in Ireland in the early 1990s.

The so-called 'new emigration' of the 1980s has a somewhat different character from the earlier postwar emigration wave of the 1950s and early 1960s (King and Shuttleworth 1988). The traditional perception of the majority of Irish emigrants is of persons who had received low levels of formal education, who were unskilled or in possession of only rudimentary skills and who came from rural, mainly farming backgrounds in the west of Ireland. This perception was broadly true of those who left in the 1950s but not those departing in the 1980s. The shift in the character of migration can be examined under two main heads: educational and socio-occupational background; and geographical origin.

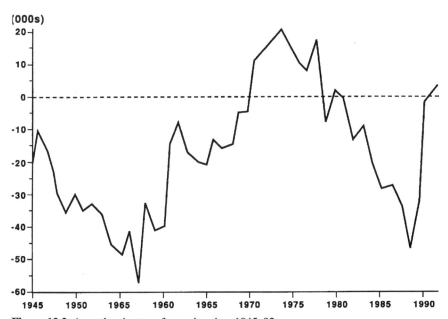

Figure 12.2 Annual estimates of net migration, 1945–92

Table 12.1 Emigration, unemployment and labour market characteristics, 1971 and 1980–90 (in thousands)

Indicator	1971	1980	1981	1982	1983	1984	1985	1986	1987	1988	1989	1990
Total labour force	1110	1247	1271	1293	1307	1307	1305	1308	1312	1310	1293	1303
Total at work	1049	1156	1146	1146	1124	1103	1079	1081	1080	1091	1090	1120
Farming	272	209	196	193	189	181	171	168	164	166	163	165
Industry	320	371	363	354	331	319	306	306	300	300	306	322
Marketed services	299	347	352	353	354	354	356	355	361	371	374	381
Non-marketed services	158	229	235	246	250	249	246	252	255	254	247	252
Unemployed	61	91	126	147	183	204	226	227	232	219	203	183
Unemployment rate (%)	5.5	7.3	9.9	11.4	14.0	15.6	17.3	17.4	17.7	16.7	15.7	14.0
Net external migration	–5	–8	+2	–1	–14	–9	–20	–28	–27	–32	–46	–31

Note: Non-marketed services include defence, public administration and professional services (mainly health and education)

Source: CSO Labour Force Estimates; Sexton *et al.* 1991

The greatest interest has centred on the occupational characteristics of emigrants (Sexton *et al.* 1991). There is evidence that the recent emigrant flows are different in that they involve a significant proportion of qualified persons. While it is not possible to classify emigrants by detailed occupational type or skill level, there is information on their general socio-occupational background as defined by the head of household. Table 12.2 presents this data for 1987–8 emigrants according to the Labour Force Survey. While the main picture to emerge from this table is of a broad leakage of emigrants from all social backgrounds, the figures do show a somewhat greater propensity to emigrate among people from well-off backgrounds and with, presumably, higher levels of education. In contrast to a generation ago,

Table 12.2 Gross migration outflow for 1987–8 classified by the socio-occupational group of the head of household from which the emigrant left

Social group	Gross outflow ('000)	Outflow per thousand population
Farmers	8.1	12.4
Professional	5.5	16.8
Employers and managers	5.0	18.1
Salaried, intermediate non-manual	7.3	14.3
Other non-manual	7.4	18.0
Skilled and semi-skilled manual	13.1	15.6
Unskilled	3.5	15.2
Unknown	6.5	22.4
Total	56.4	15.9

Source: CSO 1988

people from farm households now have the lowest propensity to emigrate. This pattern is corroborated by unpublished data from the British Labour Force Survey which show that since 1981, Irish immigrants have become more 'white-collar', ie more concentrated in the managerial, technical and administrative occupational groups; however these data are only indicative since the Irish only form a small part of the sample.

The discussion can be further refined by considering the relationship between emigration and social mobility rather than social class. Data for 1983–8 cited in Walsh (1992a, p.31) reveal that the propensity to emigrate among the upwardly mobile middle classes (41 per cent) is twice as high as among those of the same class who are downwardly mobile (21 per cent). On the other hand, among those classified as working class (who have a lower propensity to emigrate overall), emigration propensity is higher among the downwardly mobile (26 per cent) than the upwardly mobile (22 per cent). Many of these downwardly mobile working-class emigrants are now (in contrast to the past) of urban origin: they suffer from very low levels of education and have essentially been pushed out of local labour markets by processes such as inner-city deindustrialization and the slump in the Irish construction industry. In fact, about 70 per cent of the most poorly educated migrants who left during 1983–8 had either just lost their jobs or been unemployed for some time (compared to only 33 per cent of those emigrants with third-level education). Many of these unqualified, unskilled emigrants have headed for London where they tend to have difficulty obtaining lasting employment. Inadequately prepared psychologically for emigration and lacking work, a disturbingly high proportion become homeless, disillusioned and alienated. Estimates indicate that in the late 1980s, when the annual gross outflow was between 45 000 and 60 000, around 10 per cent of emigrants to the UK sought assistance from advice centres and night shelters in London and other large cities (Sexton et al. 1991). Those who return to Ireland face a high chance of unemployment again. Overall, 35 per cent of returnees during 1983–8 were unemployed for a significant period after their return.

Problems of a different nature surround the growth in the emigration of the highly qualified during the 1980s. The emigration of graduates has been singled out for special attention (Shuttleworth 1993). Until 1983, less than 8 per cent of graduates emigrated within one year of leaving university or college, according to figures issued annually by the Higher Education Authority. By 1988, the proportion had risen to almost 30 per cent. Then it stabilized and subsequently fell back to around 20 per cent in the early 1990s in the light of more difficult job prospects for graduates in Britain. Such a dramatic loss of around one-fifth of Ireland's highly trained human capital over the past decade has given rise to a vigorous debate in the media and elsewhere about the wisdom (or inevitability) of allowing such an expensive exodus. Optimists such as Brian Lenihan, quoted above, and the planners of the Industrial Development Authority place their faith in the prospect that the majority of these highly educated emigrants will one day return and apply their overseas experience to developing the Irish economy. While there is a good deal of to-ing and fro-ing of skilled migrants, the net trend to emigration remains clear. Moreover the one-year criterion adopted by the Higher Education Authority in monitoring the movement of graduates provides only a snapshot of where they are and what they are doing quite soon after graduation; it ignores the possibility of later migrations which may be motivated perhaps by frustrated career ambitions or high personal taxation in Ireland. Surveys mounted by Shuttleworth (1993) and the individual colleges on cohorts of graduates who left higher education in the 1980s reveal that, five years later, between 40 and 62 per cent of them are abroad or have been abroad and returned. The increasing tendency for Irish school-leavers to go to university in the United Kingdom (including Northern Ireland) can also be regarded as a form of brain drain since these educated emigrants will probably have a lower propensity to seek work in Ireland than Irish graduates who went to university in their own country (King and Shuttleworth 1988–9; Shuttleworth, 1991–2). This brain drain effect should not be overstated, however. Rather it is a case of 'brain overflow' of students unable to find places in the highly competitive higher education system in Ireland or wanting to follow courses not available in Irish universities. It should be remembered that the numbers of 18-year-olds potentially entering higher education in Ireland will continue to rise until the end of the 1990s.

The increasing impact of highly skilled and graduate emigration during the 1980s can be interpreted with reference to two contexts: the context of Ireland's changing position in an international division of labour which is itself changing; and the role of culture and, in particular, social networking which was earlier identified as an enduring feature of the Irish both at home and abroad.

Breathnach and Jackson (1991) maintain that a full understanding of the nature of recent emigration from Ireland can only be understood by considering such migration as a key link in the relationship between a small peripheral region and the core regions of the European and world economy and as a function of the restructuring of international labour markets. With the internationalization of European economic life the most sophisticated and rewarding jobs tend to be concentrated in the major cities of the core countries—London, Paris, Frankfurt, Munich etc. The 'branch-plant' pattern of industrial expansion in Ireland since the late 1960s has meant that much of the employment provided in the new industrial and producer services sectors has been of a routine nature resulting in limited career prospects and low levels of job satisfaction for highly educated and professional workers (Hanlon 1991). This relationship between the low innovative potential of the Irish economy and emigration from Ireland contrasts with other small economies in Western Europe such as Luxembourg and Denmark where career frustration does not seem to be a problem and a mechanism leading to emigration (Mjoset 1992).

What is particularly interesting about the Irish case is the way in which these new macroeconomic relationships between Ireland and the rest of the developed world interface with the traditional 'culture of emigration'. Surveys of graduates have shown that the emigration motives and destinations of this highly trained group have as much to do with lifestyle, family and social network variables as they do with strictly economic factors such as unemployment and high taxation in Ireland (Shuttleworth 1991; 1993). Many emigrant respondents had a family history of migration, with siblings and other relatives abroad; many had also worked abroad as students and fully expected to emigrate as a logical part of the postgraduation life cycle. The results show that these facilitating cultural and personal factors are extremely important in determining migration behaviour. They show how Ireland's long history of mass emigration creates the conditions for further migration by the establishment of social and family networks which enable new emigrants—of whatever educational background—to find work and accommodation relatively easily. In country areas too, this 'embeddedness' of emigration in rural families is still a feature of life in the western regions of Ireland (MacLaughlin 1991). Abroad, this 'networking' approach has been found to be equally relevant in relatively 'new' Irish emigrant communities such as that in Paris (MacÉinrí 1991) as in those in more traditional destinations such as London (Popham 1990) and New York (Corcoran 1991). For this reason the emigration destinations of the 1980s are not that different from those of the past, with the exception of continental Europe which now is the destination of an estimated one in ten Irish migrants, chiefly made up of highly educated young people.

Finally we turn to a brief examination of the spatial patterning of the origins of emigrants during the 1980s, using the NUTS 3 or planning regions of the country as the frame of reference. The geography of Irish emigration during the 1980s was different from previous decades; moreover it changed during the decade of the 1980s as well. Overall, and especially during the first half of the decade, there was a significant shift from rural to urban origins and from western to eastern regions of the country. Sexton (1987) interpreted these spatial changes as symptomatic of the occupational and social changes in the character of emigration discussed above. Table 12.3 shows that, during the 1981–6 intercensal period, the east region, which includes Dublin, had almost the highest rate of net out-migration in the state. CSO annual estimates of net emigration for the same period (Sexton et al. 1991) show an even more remarkable polarization of emigration in the Dublin area: these show that Dublin was the source of over 70 per cent of the total net emigration from Ireland and had an emigration rate 2.5 times the national average.

Several reasons may be suggested for the high rate of emigration from Dublin at this time. First, it contained a disproportionately large share of the highly educated emigrants described above. Many of these well-educated young adults were the offspring of the large middle-class segment of the population which had expanded very rapidly with the tertiary growth of the city during the 1960s and 1970s. Second, at the other end of the social spectrum, Dublin contains a large proportion of working-class families, from which most of the poorly educated and unskilled emigrants come. Third, and closely related to the last point, Dublin's employment base changed in the 1980s. Over the past 30 years the east region has switched from being virtually the only part of the country with employment growth to a situation in the 1980s where almost half the total national net loss of employment was located there (Walsh 1992a). The collapse of Irish-owned small and medium manufacturing employment in the Dublin area has been particularly severe over the past 10–15 years (especially in the inner city), leading to extremely high rates of unemployment in working-class areas of the city (Drudy 1991).

Table 12.3 Changing regional pattern of Irish emigration, 1981–91

Region	Annual net emigration per '000 1981–6	1986–91
East	− 4.7	–6.6
South-east	–4.0	–8.0
North-east	–4.5	–9.1
South-west	–3.7	–7.2
Mid-west	–4.4	–9.2
Midlands	–4.0	–11.3
West	–3.1	–6.9
North-west	–4.8	–9.5
Donegal	–1.2	–8.4
Ireland	–4.1	–7.7

Source: Irish census data summarized by Shuttleworth (1993, p.314)

In the second half of the 1980s the regional pattern of emigration changed again (Table 12.3). Now the east had the lowest rate, although it still accounted for a large proportion of total emigration and the absolute numbers of emigrants from the region increased from 1981–6 to 1986–91. However, in all other regions the rate of net emigration doubled or even trebled between the two intercensal quinquennia. The late 1980s saw significant development of new employment in producer services and selected areas of manufacturing such as electronics which were mainly situated in Dublin and to a lesser extent in Limerick, Cork and Galway—locations close to international airports and to supplies of graduates. These new developments stemmed, but only in a relative sense, the proportion of Irish high-skill emigration originating from these urban areas.

The late 1980s pattern of a return to high rates of emigration from western areas of the country is confirmed by Table 12.4 which shows the regional variation in the economic and migration status of the 1990 cohort of school-leavers one year after leaving school (Walsh 1992b). Dublin has half the national rate of emigration and the north-west twice the national rate; only Dublin and the rest of the east region have below-average rates (note that these new regional units are a slight change over those used in Table 12.3).

A final feature of the migration flow of the 1980s worthy of brief comment was its gender mix. Approximately 58 per cent of the total net emigration was represented by males (cf 47 per cent during the 1960s). Moreover the 1980s' flow was predominantly young—70 per cent aged less than 25 years. The sex ratio of 736 female emigrants per 1000 male emigrants during 1981–6 is the lowest on record except for the intercensal period 1936–46 when there were special restrictions on the emigration of females (Rudd 1987). The following factors may be suggested as contributing to the excess of males in the emigration flows of recent years (Walsh 1987–8). The substantial volume of emigration to the USA, some of which has taken place without adherence to the rules of immigration to the United States, is

Table 12.4 Economic status of 1990 school-leavers by region

Region	At work %	Unemployed %	Emigrated %	In education %
Dublin	37.6	21.8	4.0	36.6
Rest of east	37.8	19.0	5.6	37.6
South-east	35.8	18.1	9.8	36.3
North-east	42.9	13.7	15.6	27.8
South-west	41.2	11.2	8.3	39.3
Mid-west	33.3	15.0	10.6	41.1
Midlands	27.6	24.4	9.0	39.0
North-west	33.0	15.1	16.3	35.6
West	33.1	11.8	8.8	46.3
Ireland	36.7	17.3	8.1	37.9

Source: Annual Department of Labour School-Leaver Survey

male-dominated; this is partly because overseas flows (ie those to North America and Australia) tend to have more males than females and partly because the difficulties of obtaining legal permits to work and reside in the USA have constrained some men to emigrate alone, leaving their wives and families in Ireland. Similarly the high cost of housing in south-east England during the 1980s may have discouraged some husbands from taking their wives and children with them.

12.4 INTERNAL MIGRATION

Faithfully mapping internal migration in Ireland by the census residual method is hampered by the relative importance of external migration which for many areas and many time periods is more important quantitatively than interregional movement within Ireland. The county patterns displayed in Figure 12.3 thus conflate intercounty migration with the external migration flows (emigration, immigration, return migration) of each county. Bearing in mind this interpretative difficulty, the patterns revealed in Figure 12.3 are worthy of comment (cf Walsh, 1990–1; 1991a).

The 1971–81 period, described earlier as the 'decade of return', saw all counties except five (Mayo, Leitrim, Cavan, Offaly and North Tipperary) record positive migration scores. Although the influence of return from abroad is clearly important in this period, there was also a major internal redistribution of population: a west–east shift of population to the Dublin region and a more local-scale decentralization of people from Dublin into the adjacent 'overspill' counties of Kildare, Meath and Wicklow, which had the highest rates of net in-migration of all counties (17.3, 14.3 and 12.6 per thousand per year respectively). A similar but smaller-scale overspill occurred from Limerick City into County Clare, which also attracted an inflow of population to the Shannon airport industrial area (Horner *et al.* 1987, p.26). Return migration from abroad, on the other hand, played a bigger role in the

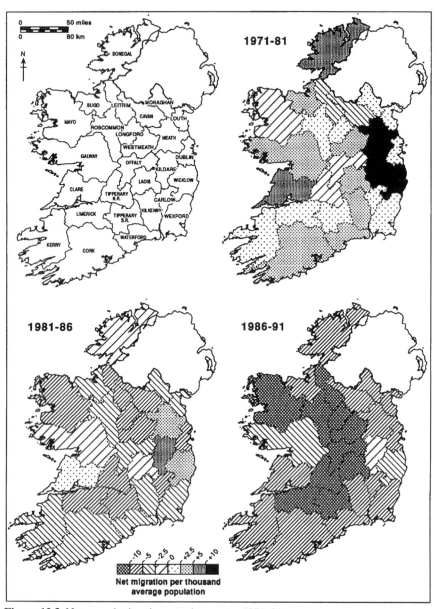

Figure 12.3 Net annual migration rates by county, 1971–91

migratory growth of Donegal (6.3 per thousand per year), a county with a particularly strong history of emigration to Britain.

As Figure 12.3 shows, the 1981–6 and 1986–91 intercensal periods witnessed a
complete reversal of the pattern of the 1970s. In the first half of the 1980s all coun-

ties except four (Kildare, Meath, Wicklow and Clare) had negative migration scores. Residential mobility out of Dublin and Limerick were again the key processes accounting for this periurban growth, although in Clare there was a net in-migration of only 30 persons. For the first time ever, Dublin had the highest net migration loss in the country (–7.4 per thousand per year or 37 200 over the five-year period). It seems likely that most of these emigrated, since there was a net out-flow of 31 800 from the east region despite a net in-migration of 5400 to Kildare, Meath and Wicklow (Horner et al. 1987, p.89). In the most recent period, 1986–91, no single county had net in-migration, the first time that this has occurred since the 1950s. The lowest rates of net loss were from Kildare (– 1.5) and Wicklow (– 3.7). No longer was Dublin the county to experience the greatest rate of net out-migration. During 1986–91, the main counties of migratory loss (more than 10 per thousand per year) formed a broad crescent-shaped belt starting in the north-west (Mayo, Sligo, Roscommon), passing down through the midlands (Longford, Laois, Offaly, Westmeath) and ending in Tipperary and Limerick; such a pattern was also observable for 1981–6.

Table 12.5 gives the same net migration information as Figure 12.3 but at the more generalized level of the NUTS 3 regions. All nine regions gained population by migration during the 1970s, and all lost during both subperiods of the 1980s. This table also shows the combining role of natural increase and net migration in effecting total population change. Declining natural increase is due to significant declines in both marriage and fertility rates (Walsh 1990–1).

Table 12.5 Migration and population change by region, 1971–91

Region	Net migration (per '000 per year)			Natural increase (per '000 per year)			Population change (%)	
	1971–81	1981–6	1986–91	1971–81	1981–6	1986–91	1971–81	1981–91
East	+5.1	–4.7	–6.6	14.3	11.7	8.7	+21.5	+4.6
South-east	+2.1	–4.0	–8.0	11.0	9.5	5.6	+14.0	+2.3
North-east	+0.3	–4.5	–9.1	10.4	9.2	5.2	+11.3	+0.6
South-west	+2.4	–3.7	–7.2	9.6	8.1	7.0	+12.8	+1.2
Mid-west	+2.3	–4.4	–9.2	11.0	9.0	6.0	+14.2	+0.7
Midlands	+1.4	–4.0	–11.3	8.6	8.6	5.3	+10.4	–0.7
West	+2.1	–3.1	–6.9	8.1	7.8	5.1	+10.8	+1.5
North-west	+1.6	–4.8	–9.5	3.9	4.8	2.1	+5.7	–3.7
Donegal	+6.3	–1.2	–8.4	8.1	8.3	5.8	+15.5	+2.3
Total	+3.2	–4.1	–7.7	11.3	9.7	6.8	+15.6	+2.3

Source: Irish census data summarized in Walsh (1990–1, p.95; 1991a, p.118)

Another angle on the measurement of internal (and external) migration is given by the census question which asks respondents to state their 'usual residence one year ago'. The Labour Force Survey also gives the same data annually but on a sample basis. Horner et al. (1987) and Walsh (1991b) have mapped and commented on the spatial patterns of these 'one-year migrants' for the 1981 census. There were 205 000 persons, 5.9 per cent of the population, who had changed their residence during the preceding year; of these 25 000 had moved in from outside the state. There was some increase in residential mobility in 1980–1 compared to 1970–1, for the earlier census had recorded 148 000 one-year migrants, including 25 000 from abroad. Labour Force Survey data for the later 1980s indicate declining internal migration compared to 1980–1. Ignoring those who had a previous residence outside the Republic and standardizing the units as the 27 counties, the figures show a total internal migration trend as follows: 1970–1 123 489; 1980–1 179 183; 1987–8 156 000 and an intercounty trend which similarly rose then fell (1970–1 33 963; 1980–1 47 358; 1987–8 37 000). The inter-county migration in 1987–8 was approximately equivalent to the total net migration out of the state at the same time. During 1980–1, residential mobility was highest in Dublin where 7.6 per cent of the population had changed address over the year and in other urban or periurban counties such as Kildare, Wicklow, Limerick and Galway (all within the range 6.2–7.1 per cent); it was lowest in rural counties such as Leitrim, Cavan, Roscommon, Mayo and Kerry (all below 4 per cent).

Figure 12.4 concentrates on the 47 000 who migrated across a county boundary during 1980–1, ignoring intracounty migrants and people who arrived from outside the state. The three maps show in-movers by county of destination, out-movers by county of origin and the overall balance of net intercounty migration. Overall, about two-thirds of intercounty moves were to a contiguous county, and nearly 30 per cent involve Dublin. In-movers from other counties were most significant in Kildare (27.1 per thousand), Meath (24.6) and Wicklow (22.6)—in other words on the metropolitan fringe of Dublin. In fact 57 per cent of the total in-movers to these three counties (excluding migrants from abroad) were from Dublin. The lowest rates of inflow were recorded in peripheral, mainly rural counties—Donegal, Mayo, Monaghan, Cavan, Kerry, Cork and Wexford. The pattern of out-migration shows the highest intensities in counties of the Midlands: the high contiguity ratios of these counties and their relative proximity to Dublin may be the key factors here. The low rate for County Cork undoubtedly reflects the intervening opportunities offered by Cork City, while the low rate for Donegal reflects its isolation from the Republic and its closer links—both cultural and geographical—to Northern Ireland and Scotland. Intercounty migration rates are rather stable over time, Walsh (1991b, p.104) calculating a correlation coefficient of 0.9 for the pattern of out-migration in 1970–1 and 1980–1 and a coefficient of 0.87 for the corresponding in-migration data. The county-based net migration pattern for 1980–1 (Figure 12.4) shows net in-migration to each of the four counties of the east region and to three contiguous western counties (Galway, Limerick and Clare) which have significant urban centres. Net in-migration to Clare is associated with high levels of movement from other counties to the airport, industrial zone and new town complex of Shannon and with overspill mobility from Limerick City to parts of east Clare. The highest rates of net out-migration are from Wexford and from the central–northern belt of counties stretching from Mayo to Cavan.

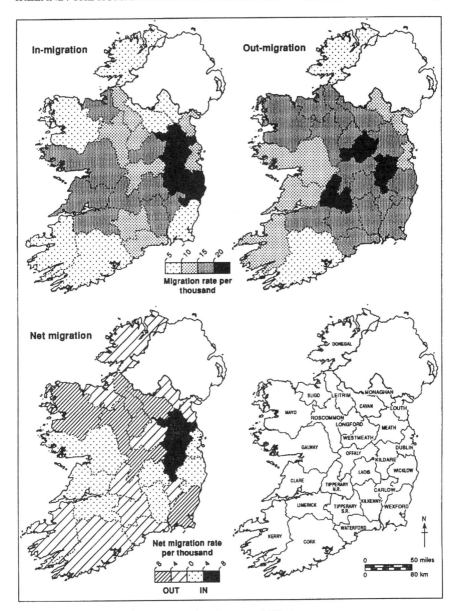

Figure 12.4 Patterns of intercounty migration rates, 1980–1

Figure 12.5 concentrates on the 'Dublin effect'. The map of migrants to Dublin as a percentage of all intercounty out-migrants shows a dual pattern: the intensity of out-migration to the capital being highest in counties close to the capital and in many counties of the west. Dublin accounted for 56.3 per cent of the one-year out-migrants from Wicklow but only 25.5 per cent of the out-migrants from south

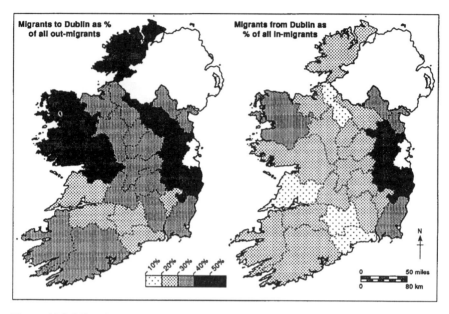

Figure 12.5 Migration to and from Dublin as a percentage of total intercounty migration, 1980–1

Tipperary. The counterflow map shows that Dublin is the main source of migrants to the three adjacent counties, as already noted, and somewhat less so for the other east-coast counties of Louth and Wexford. The Dublin influence is least felt as a source of in-migrants in Leitrim and south Tipperary. The Dublin patterns are also rather stable over time, being broadly consistent with patterns observed in the 1960s and 1970s (Geary *et al.*, 1970; Hughes and Walsh, 1980). Norcliffe (1972) was able to 'explain' by the technique of canonical correlation the dual mobility pattern of high migration interchange between Dublin and its adjacent counties and the strong pull that Dublin exerts over western counties.

There are many factors which influence the scale and pattern of intercounty migration; moreover the strength of these various factors varies from place to place within Ireland. In the counties around Dublin, as already implied, the geographical organization of the property market is a potent factor in the spatial sorting of more local-scale migration flows. Retirement takes migrants from predominantly urban to rural counties, although this factor accounts for only 2 per cent of total inter-county residential moves (Walsh 1987–8). The dominant motives for internal migration are economic and are related to occupational opportunities and aspira-tions (Hannan 1970; Walsh 1984). Among the intercounty migrants during 1980–1, 82 per cent of the males and 58 per cent of females over 15 years of age were mem-bers of the labour force. Therefore many moves can be related to entry into the labour market or to career advancement, especially within large organizations such as banks or sectors of the public service. Table 12.6 shows that the occupational

Table 12.6 Distribution of intercounty migrants 1980–1 according to occupational status

Economic status	Males %	Females %
Total in labour force	66.4	48.4
Agricultural workers	2.6	0.2
Producers, makers and repairers	14.8	2.0
Labourers and unskilled workers	2.9	0.0
Transport and communication workers	3.8	1.8
Clerical workers	6.0	17.3
Commerce, insurance and finance workers	7.2	2.8
Service workers	6.0	5.1
Professional and technical workers	14.8	18.0
Others	7.9	0.8
Seeking first job	0.4	0.3
Total not in labour force	33.6	51.6
Student, at school	10.8	9.6
Home duties	0.0	22.6
Retired	2.2	1.7
Unable to work	1.0	1.0
Others	0.4	0.3
Under 15 years of age	19.2	16.4

Source: 1981 Census data summarized by Walsh (1991b, p.102)

groups which have the highest migration rates are professional and technical, clerical and service workers, and females in the transport and communications category (who are mostly telephone company employees). When account is taken of the composition of the labour force the main occupational groups represented by intercounty migrants are professional and technical workers for both males and females, clerical workers for females and male 'producers, makers and repairers'. The unemployment rate among intercounty one-year migrants is much lower than among one-year immigrants (ie return migrants) and lower than the population as a whole. This arises because, in general, changes of address take place as a result of finding employment rather than in order to look for it.

Although there is a relatively small gender differential overall (53 per cent female, 47 per cent male), there are marked differences when the intercounty flows are disaggregated by age and county. For instance there were 144 females per 100 males migrating in the 15–19 age group in 1980–1; and for 15–19-year-olds migrating to Dublin there were two and a half times as many females as males. Taking the 15–24 age group (the modal group, with 42 per cent of overall migrants), females exceeded males by about 60 per cent in the outflows from several western counties such as Clare, Kerry and Roscommon (Walsh 1991b, p.99). Similar ratios are found in the LFS sample data for annual intercounty migration for 1983–8. Garvey and McGuire (1989, p.12) suggest two reasons for the large discrepancy in numbers of male and female migrants in the 15–24 age group: the greater employment opportunities for women in urban service-sector jobs, and a nuptiality effect whereby

Table 12.7 Rural–urban and urban–rural migration by region, 1985–6 (population aged 1 year and over)

Region	Population ('000)		Rural–urban migration			Urban–rural migration			Net R–U(+) U–R (–)	Migration rate (per '000)	
	Urban	Rural	Same county	Inter- county	% total	Same county	Inter- county	% total		R–U	U–R
East	1134.7	174.1	1796	2015	15.3	1486	4884	30.8	–2559	3.4	36.6
South-east	159.2	216.7	1779	2164	15.8	1444	982	10.3	+1817	+24.8	9.8
North-east	82.4	111.2	1126	1032	8.6	477	318	3.8	+1363	26.2	7.1
South-west	237.7	286.4	1772	2165	15.8	2804	1261	19.6	–128	16.6	14.2
Mid-west	107.4	201.8	634	2155	11.2	1593	1814	16.5	–618	26.0	16.9
Midlands	83.6	172.6	1070	1661	10.9	927	600	7.4	+1204	32.7	8.8
North-west	19.1	62.3	422	676	4.4	250	108	1.7	+740	57.5	5.7
Donegal	28.8	97.8	906	519	5.7	289	100	1.9	+1036	49.5	4.0
West	90.5	196.4	887	2144	12.2	737	914	7.6	+1380	33.5	8.4
State	1943.5	1519.3	10 392	14 531		9707	10 981		+4235	12.8	13.6

Source: CSO special tabulations analysed by Cawley 1991, pp.115–16

women have a greater tendency to relocate following marriage.

Another important factor in generating intercounty migration is education. This factor operates in two senses. First, flows are generated to the main university cities —Dublin, Cork, Galway and Limerick—by first-year students (whose term-time address is regarded as their 'usual' address for census purposes). Upon graduation, students tend to stay in the area of their university (or emigrate) rather than return to their county of origin. Second, educational qualifications (like occupational category) tend to influence propensity to migrate. Thus, during 1990–1 the emigration rate for degree-level graduates was 27 per cent compared with only 14 per cent for certificate and diploma-level graduates. Similarly, for those graduates who obtained employment in Ireland, 64 per cent of degree holders and 45 per cent of certificate or diploma holders were employed in the east region (Walsh 1992b).

A final perspective on the changing pattern of internal migration in Ireland can be given by examining rural–urban trends. Ireland experienced some aspects of the general Europe-wide counterurbanization phenomenon during the 1970s, notably through population retention in and in-migration to rural areas within commuting distance of urban-based employment. Some immigration also took place to more remote areas; this was mainly fuelled by return migration from abroad. During the 1980s evidence emerged of a new wave of migration to urban areas, notably to Dublin and the other four county boroughs (Cork, Limerick, Galway and Waterford) where a combination of service-sector growth, suburban expansion and inner-city refurbishment (the latter stimulated by the 1986 Urban Renewal Act) reasserted the attractiveness of urban life. However, tracing the relevant flows is possible only for one-year migrants identified in the censuses. Here, following Cawley's (1991) analysis of special CSO tabulations from the 1986 Census, we will provide a snapshot of the rural–urban migration balance in the mid-1980s, when towns were defined as settlements exceeding 1000 inhabitants (previously the threshold was 1500). Table 12.7 provides the detailed data, by NUTS 3 region, on which this discussion is based.

For the state as a whole, there was a net rural to urban migration of 4 235 persons during 1985–6, this figure being the balance between much larger gross rural–urban and urban–rural transfers involving 24 923 and 20 688 people respectively. The east, mid-west and south-west regions were exceptions to the general pattern for they experienced net losses from urban areas (Dublin, Limerick and Cork) associated with suburban overspill. The greater tendency to move longer distances with rural–urban moves than with urban–rural migration is revealed by the fact that 58.3 per cent of rural–urban moves were intercounty, but a lower proportion (53.1 per cent) of urban–rural. The disparity between intra and intercounty migration was greatest in the mid-west and west regions, reflecting the importance of Limerick–Shannon and Galway as centres of employment and educational opportunities in attracting longer-distance migrants. The relative flows (rural–urban migrants per 1000 urban population) show that the national figure of 12.8 per thousand is greatly affected by the very low rate (3.4) recorded by the east region which contains 58 per cent of the total urban population of the country. In the north-west and Donegal, by contrast, migration rates were much higher—50 per thousand and above—and clearly made important contributions to the growth of the much more modest urban centres. Thus migration to the smaller towns is limited in absolute quantity but is vital in the context of the growth of those centres. Dublin, on the other hand, absorbed 25 per cent of all rural out-migrants, and two-thirds of rural out-migrants ended up in towns of at least 10 000 population.

Table 12.7 also provides detailed regional information on the counterflow of migration from urban to rural settlements. Although urban–rural migration has been historically far less important than the dominant rural–urban drift, the former is nevertheless well documented for Ireland since the early 1970s; far-reaching social and economic effects have ensued for many former farming communities (Duffy 1983; Gillmor 1988). In 1985–6 over 30 per cent of all urban–rural migration took place in the east region, an additional 19.6 per cent occurred in the south-west, and 16.5 per cent in the mid-west. These moves were associated in the main with subur-ban development of both private and public housing. In the east the bulk of urban–rural movement was intercounty, reflecting the closeness of counties Meath, Kildare and Wicklow to the Dublin urban region. In the south-west, on the other hand, the bulk was within the same county – chiefly County Cork. Donegal and the north-west each accounted for less than 2 per cent of the total Irish urban–rural migration during 1985–6.

When the urban–rural rates are standardized with reference to the rural popula-tion of the reception areas, the regional pattern is found to be the reverse of that reg-istered for rural–urban migration (Table 12.7). Fewer migrants moved from urban to rural areas than in the opposite direction; but the national urban–rural migration index is higher than the rural–urban rate because of the fact that fewer people were living in rural areas than in urban settlements. Dublin was the source area for 18 per cent of all urban–rural migrants; 38 per cent originated from Cork, Limerick, Galway and Waterford and other towns with more than 10 000 people. The smallest towns—those in the 1000–2000 class—made very limited contributions to urban–rural migration (Cawley 1991).

12.5 CONCLUSION

This chapter has made a clear analytical distinction between internal and external migration, but this distinction needs to be qualified. Although, when talking about persistent emigration, we have stressed the special nature of the Irish case, in some senses this feeling of uniqueness is misplaced. Of course if an Irish person crosses the Irish Sea to Britain, he or she crosses a political boundary and thus legally and politically becomes an emigrant. However, this makes a false distinction between 'emigration' and 'mobility' and disguises similarities between Irish emigration and spatial migration within Britain (or within Ireland). The Irish have always had free access to the British job market and numerous studies have shown how trends in Irish migration are closely influenced by labour market opportunities in Britain (Drudy 1986; Hughes and Walsh 1974; Kirwan and Nairn 1983; O'Rourke 1972;

Walsh 1974). The question might well be asked as to how Irish migration to Britain differs from Scottish migration to, say, southern England. In some respects the Scottish migrant is further from home. The essential point is that the processes that bring Irish and Scottish migrants to London or the south-east may be very similar. If Irish net emigration rates (for the Republic) are compared with those for Scotland and for Northern Ireland over the period 1981–9, it is found that all three experienced consistent loss but that the Irish rate of –5.1 per thousand per year was significantly above the rates for Northern Ireland (–3.0) and Scotland (–2.3) (Shuttleworth 1993, p.313).

Given the past history of volatility of Irish migration trends, it is both difficult and dangerous to predict how they might develop in the future. The clearest link, as far as external migration is concerned, is between high levels of emigration and failure to provide sufficient employment opportunities, both in terms of quantity and quality, for the Irish population. Therefore it is important, when looking to the future, to take note of the scale of growth which might be expected in the labour force. The most recent forecasts which take account of demographic pressures from high birth rates in the 1970s and the increasing desires of women to participate in paid employment indicate that the labour force could expand at an annual rate of between 1.5 and 2 per cent over the period up to 2000. With 19 per cent of the work-force unemployed at present (early 1993), the challenge of providing a satisfactory range of employment opportunities to stem further emigration is enormous. Unless there is a strong commitment to a new model of development, one cannot be very optimistic about reducing the scale of involuntary emigration and unemployment, especially among those who have either high or very low educational attainment (Walsh 1992b). Thus high levels of emigration will continue to be a feature of the remainder of the 1990s—so long as there are suitable destinations to migrate to. The relevance of this last point is illustrated by the CSO estimates for net external migration for the past four years (1989 –46 000; 1990 –31 000; 1991 –1000; 1992 + 2000) which show how the migration trend responded closely to the switch of the British economy from late 1980s boom to early 1990s recession. Now that there are some signs of recovery in the British economy, we may expect Irish emigration to rise once again. If net emigration exceeds 20 000 per annum there will be a decline in total population which, on the basis of most recent evidence, will be most severe in rural areas. Steady rural–urban internal migration will probably continue to deplete rural populations, except in attractive districts within commuting distance of the major towns and favoured tourist areas of the south and western coasts.

ACKNOWLEDGEMENT

Had it not been for his tragic death in the Kegworth air disaster in January 1989, John Coward would almost certainly have been the author of this chapter; we dedicate this chapter to his memory.

13 The Pattern of Internal Migration: the Italian Case

ALBERTO BONAGUIDI and VALERIO TERRA ABRAMI

13.1 INTRODUCTION

Over the past 20–5 years in the most developed countries there have been remarkable and largely unexpected changes in the patterns of population redistribution. These countries began to experience a slowdown in the rate of population concentration or a reversal of the migration trends affecting their traditionally attractive regions and larger metropolitan areas. In Europe since the late 1960s or the early 1970s the metropolitan systems have recorded a decentralization process from cores to rings, even in instances when the entire metropolitan areas were still growing. Over time this decentralization process accelerated, and recently in many cases the absolute growth of the metropolitan periphery is not large enough to compensate for the marked population losses sustained by their cores.

In Italy the internal migration pattern shows significant changes since the early 1970s at regional and metropolitan levels. The migratory balance of the southern regions, which in the previous decades had been characterized by a heavy net out-migration, has begun appreciably to improve. The attractiveness of the north-eastern and central regions has risen at the expense of the north-western regions (the so-called 'industrial triangle'), which previously had been the traditionally attractive area of the country. As far as the transformation of the metropolitan system and metropolitan mobility are concerned, the Italian metropolitan areas that seem to be at a more advanced stage are those of Milan and Turin. In these areas the population growth and the decentralization process from the inner part to the metropolitan periphery is recording the same pattern as those observable in many European countries.

The most recent tendencies have not yet been suitably documented. There are signs that in some cases a new pattern is taking shape, while in other instances there seems to be a continuation or intensification of the trends that emerged in the seventies. The aim of this chapter is to outline the recent features of migration behaviour in Italy, its interregional and metropolitan shifts, over the last decade or so, the age selectivity of the new trends and the shifting factors underlying the migration process.

Population Migration in the European Union Edited by Philip Rees, John Stillwell, Andrew Convey and Marek Kupiszewski. © Editors and Contributors. Published 1996 John Wiley & Sons Ltd.

13.2 LONG-TERM EVOLUTION OF INTERNAL MIGRATION

Over the last three decades the internal migration system in Italy has been characterized by significant shifts. From the fifties to the eighties the various components of the internal redistribution process (intraregional, interregional, migration between south and north) have experienced a quite different evolution, so that important changes in the structure of the migration system have progressively taken place. Because these different types of migration are caused by different socioeconomic factors, the changes in the patterns of internal migration are clearly related to a shift in the role of the variables underlying the population redistribution process. Table 13.1 provides figures for selected years on the long-term evolution of the different forms of internal migration in Italy: short-distance (intraregional) migration, long-distance (interregional) migration and very long-distance migration, the migration between south and north.

Table 13.1 Long-term evolution of internal migration in Italy, 1956–87

Years	Total	Intraregional	Interregional (Thousands)	South to North	North to South
1956–7	1349	907	442	116	39
1966–7	1487	978	509	179	82
1976–7	1211	799	412	142	92
1986–7	1141	830	311	104	72

Over the first decade considered (1956–7 to 1966–7), all the components of the Italian internal migration system experienced a rise, but the increase was relatively much more pronounced for long-distance moves, particularly in the very long-distance ones (between north and south). Therefore, in this period, the movement between the most distant and the other regions of the country became relatively more important within the national internal migration context. This evolution can be ascribed to a lack of growth in the depressed part of the country (the south), while the northern regions were characterized by intensive economic development.

During the succeeding decade (1966–7 to 1976–7), a generalized marked decline was observable in all components of the internal migration system (short distance, long distance, very long distance), except for the movement from the north to the south which tended to increase. In the last decade considered (1976–7 to 1986–7), the mobility components show a new and interesting pattern which for some aspects can be considered a reversal to that observed in the first decade. In this period, in fact, long-distance migration declined considerably, while short-distance movement tended to increase.

These first results on the long-term evolution of internal migration look interesting. From the fifties to the sixties the industrialization of the northern regions, combined with a very low level of natural increase, was a potent trigger for massive migration from the depressed southern regions of Italy. In this period, therefore, very long-distance (between south and north) migration tended to increase rapidly, replacing short-distance (intraregional) moves. In contrast, over the most recent period, short-distance migration tended to replace long-distance migration. This means that the economic and employment factors, which are the most important determinants for moving over longer distances are tending now to be replaced by other factors which mostly generate short-distance movement (for housing, family and retirement reasons). In other words, on the whole, the influence of economic factors as determinants of internal migration in Italy has been declining in the recent period.

13.3 RECENT REGIONAL AND METROPOLITAN SHIFTS

The historical framework provided above is essential to evaluate correctly the importance and the extent of changes that occurred in internal migration patterns over the last decade.

In this section we aim to examine the territorial aspects of the migration transition process in Italy and its most recent patterns. According to our experience, as well as to that gained in many developed countries, a valuable description of internal migration patterns may be obtained only if a global approach is used for the analysis. On the other hand, using a global approach implies introducing into the research plan a number of logical (and practical) requirements which are sometimes very difficult to meet.

As far as the spatial aspects of the analysis are concerned, first, in terms of data availability, an origin–destination data set should be used. Second, in terms of a spatial reference framework, the metropolitan dimension should be considered in some way. If, due to the lack of basic information and/or metropolitan/non-metropolitan definitions, these requirements are not met, description and analysis of the internal migration patterns are likely to result in poor conclusions.

In our case, the National Statistical System currently releases suitable origin–destination information and provides Eurostat with an inter-regional origin–destination matrix, reported in the regional Eurostat data base REGIO. Moreover, the interregional matrix is obtained by processing individual records of movers at municipal level (of origin and destination), thus allowing the aggregation of the data to non-administrative territorial clusters of municipalities, including metropolitan areas, as well as intrametropolitan territorial components, namely metropolitan-core and related rings.

As we only wanted to combine the interregional and the metropolitan level of analysis in order to provide a spatially integrated perspective of changing migration patterns, a preliminary step was to incorporate in our research plan a suitable definition of 'metropolitan' scale. Since an official metropolitan classification does not exist, a subjective choice—associated with an inevitable degree of arbitrariness—was necessary. The problem was resolved by choosing the most recent distance-based metropolitan classification (Vitali 1990). Despite its limitations, such a method has the important advantage of being simple and objective, being based only on distance.

On the other hand, this chapter provides quite reasonable evidence that distance is a major variable in describing—though not perhaps in explaining and interpreting—changes in internal migration, even on a metropolitan scale. According to this classification, it is possible to incorporate intrametropolitan shifts in the wider context of metropolitan/non-metropolitan and interregional dynamics.

Very important reversals have occurred in internal migration patterns over the last decade; every territorial scale is considered. Let us first focus on the regional scale and the related interregional network of flows. Table 13.2 sets out some simple regional and summary indicators, namely regional net balances, the intensity (level L of interregional migration) and imbalance of the overall system (efficiency index E), in 1977–8 and in 1987–8 respectively (average figures).

Table 13.2 Regional net migration, 1977–8 and 1987–8

Region	1977–8		1987–8	
	NET	% absolute N	NET	% absolute N
Piemonte	1503	1.5	1602	1.9
Val d'Aosta	191	0.2	622	0.7
Liguria	1150	1.1	–738	0.9
Lombardia	10 439	10.2	10 919	12.8
Trentino Alto Adige	425	0.4	168	0.2
Veneto	4669	4.6	3022	4.4
Friuli	1787	1.7	1311	1.5
Emilia-Romagna	11 050	10.8	9159	10.7
Tuscany	9172	8.9	6799	7.9
Umbria	1387	1.4	1931	2.2
Marche	2306	2.2	2051	2.4
Lazio	7643	7.4	3186	3.7
Campania	–13 913	13.6	–15 640	18.2
Abruzzi	–400	0.4	1425	1.7
Molise	–716	0.7	–141	0.2
Puglia	–8345	8.1	–7521	8.7
Basilicata	–4023	3.9	–1317	1.5
Calabria	–10 510	10.2	–8541	9.9
Sicilia	–10 527	10.3	–8288	9.6
Sardinia	–2438	2.4	–809	0.9
Sum of absolute N	102 594	100.0	85 990	100.0
Efficiency Index (%), E		12.8		14.1
Migration Level, L	399 219		303 992	

Notes: 1. N= net migration
        2. See text for definition of the efficiency index

No doubt the most apparent change is the sharp decline of the interregional system's intensity, ie the decline of the total number of movers (excluding the intraregional movements) over the last decade. Neither quantitative factors—total population keeping fairly stable—nor structural shifts—age structure slightly ageing, can explain a 25 per cent (from 400 000 to 300 000) decline in the interregional migration levels, but intrinsic changes in migration dynamics can. This trend is confirmed substantially if more recent observation years are taken into account (a 20 per cent decline from 1980–2 to 1988–9).

Conversely, in the meantime the system internal imbalance tends to increase. This is usually measured by means of the so-called 'efficiency index'

$$E = \Sigma_i |M_{*i} - M_{i*}| / 2M_{**}$$

where $M_{*i} - M_{i*}$ is the net balance observed in i-th region, while M_{**} is the overall intensity of the interregional migration system. The index E rises from 0.128 (1977–8) to 0.141 (1987–8) and its increase is even stronger (from 0.117 to 0.183) if more recent years (1980–2 to 1988–9) are considered. Although these are rather rough measures of interregional migration—due to the fact that the bi-dimensional origin–destination component of change is neglected—they already give a clear hint that important changes in mobility dynamics are occurring.

The way these changes act may be explored by looking at the percentage distribution of the numerator of the efficiency index, namely $\Sigma_i | M_{*i} - M_{i*}|$.

Look especially at the increasing weight of the positive net balance of Lombardy and of the negative net balance of Campania, each of which may be regarded as symbolic respectively of in-migration and out-migration. This obviously suggests that further attention should be devoted to the changes that occurred in these two regions. However, a first conclusion may be already drafted, despite the strong limitations associated with the nature of the indicators used: namely, that the recent transitional phase may be synthetically characterized by two important dynamics, reversing past trends and acting simultaneously:

1. a clear tendency of interregional migration levels to decrease;
2. a significant tendency of the system towards a situation of increasing imbalance.

But the following question is inevitably: which spatial shifts are behind these dynamics internal to the interregional system? Of course, this question may be answered provided that origin–destination information is available which it does in the case of Italy.

Owing to the reasons mentioned above, it seems particularly worthwhile to focus on changes occurring in the origin–destination patterns from/to Lombardy and Campania. Over a decade, the joint weight of their net absolute balances on the total cross-regional net absolute balances increased from 24 to 31 per cent, thus coming to represent one-third of the total regional net balances in 1987–8, and this was not accidental.

The simple redistribution of origin–destination patterns reported in Table 13.3 provides a clear summary of how spatial migration shifts are acting. Where interregional migration levels decline intensively, Lombardy tends to become more attractive, but it is important to underline that this is due to the relative increase (from 37 to 40 per cent) of short- and mid-distance in-migration flows from the north and the centre of the country, while long-distance in-migration from the

Table 13.3 Interregional distribution patterns for Lombardy and Campania, 1977–8 and 1987–8

Lombardy	From/To North-Centre	
	1977–8	1987–8
Origin	54.1	54.0
Destination	36.8	39.5
Campania	From/To Centre-South	
	1977–8	1987–8
Origin	46.5	52.8
Destination	51.3	55.3

southern regions declines. It is also very interesting to note that the major contribution to this increase is from the bordering regions of Piedmont, Liguria and Emilia-Romagna (from 18.4 to 20.4 per cent). Conversely, the out-migration patterns from Lombardy remain stable with respect to the distance range.

The range-shortening effect appears even stronger for Campania, although in this case in a framework of increasing negative net migration, both in absolute and, especially, relative terms (Table 13.1). Campania becomes less attractive, but in this case, range-shortening affects both outflows and inflows. The short- and mid-distance (towards the central and southern regions) out-migration has increased from 46.5 to 52.8 per cent and, in this case, the major contribution is from the nearest central regions, Lazio and Abruzzi.

The in-migration spatial shifts in Campania also change according to the range-shortening effect. Campania becomes more attractive, although only in relative terms, for mid- and short-distance movers from the central and southern regions (from 51 to 55 per cent), whereas it appears decidedly less attractive, especially for long-distance movers from Piedmont and Lombardy who decline from 35 to 29 per cent of the total inflow.

Thus a further important conclusion is now in order: the decreasing intensity of the overall interregional migration system is basically due to the strong decline, both in absolute and relative terms, of long-distance migration. Meanwhile, mid- and especially short-distance migration tends to increase, particularly in relative terms. The traditional dichotomy between northern and central regions, viewed as in-migration poles, and southern regions, viewed as out-migration poles, does not seem to vanish, but to increase.

On the other hand, these changing patterns may be regarded more as a result of growth of separate subsystems, progressively reducing their interchange, rather than as a result of further imbalance in the system as a whole.

Given this transitional phase in the interregional migration system, it becomes extremely interesting to explore both how the metropolitan spatial dimension interacts with the wider changing framework described above and those changes which are occurring on an internal metropolitan scale. This calls for a metropolitan–non-metropolitan analysis and, on a more restricted spatial scale, for an intrametropolitan analysis of the related shifts. An additional preliminary problem is selecting the metropolitan areas suitable for this integrated analysis. Analysis tends to provide the best results if it is carried out for those metropolitan areas considered to be at a more advanced stage of the migration transition and counterurbanization process.

Reasonable evidence has already shown (Bonaguidi and Terra Abrami 1992) that the Turin and Milan metropolitan areas meet these requirements. This is basically due to the major role played in the past by migration in deeply modifying the spatial population patterns, as well as the related age patterns in those two areas. Since the principal spatial and demographic changes in the Turin and Milan metropolitan areas have been migration-dominated for a long time, the migration transition process exists there at a later, more advanced stage. Thus, analysis has been extended at the metropolitan level with specific reference to these areas to highlight the most significant changing patterns with regard to possible future perspectives on the migration transition process of the system overall.

According to the metropolitan classification chosen, it is possible to distinguish, inside a metropolitan region, Piedmont Lombardy in this case, the metropolitan area *sensu stricto* from the rest of the region (R4). Moreover, it is possible to split the metropolitan area itself into a core and three outer distance rings (from R1 to R3).

Going downwards through the territorial scales, first the metropolitan–non-metropolitan change patterns are examined. On this scale, in order to emphasize the purely metropolitan dimension of interchange, only the metropolitan areas, namely the core plus the three successive rings, are taken into consideration, thereby eliminating the smoothing effect introduced by considering the external interchange of the rest of the region. Table 13.4 sets out inflows, outflows and related net interchanges of each part of the metropolitan area with the northern and central regions, as well as with the southern ones.

It is not surprising to note that the overall metropolitan–non-metropolitan interchanges with the rest of the country strongly decline, thus according to the patterns observed at interregional scale. Nevertheless, it is worth underlining that the intensity of their decline tends to be higher on the metropolitan scale than on the regional scale. This happens for both inflows and outflows for the metropolitan area of Turin and for outflows for Milan.

However, in this regard, the most interesting aspect is how changes occur according to the distance range of migrations. If the interchanges of the overall metropolitan areas with the remaining northern, central and southern regions are considered, it can be seen that the latter declines much more intensively than the former. This applies both to inflows and outflows and to both metropolitan areas. The difference is especially wide for the Turin area (–49 per cent and –52 per cent, respectively for southern inflows and outflows, versus –26 per cent and –28 per cent for north-centre), but also extremely relevant (–35 per cent and –32 per cent versus –20 per cent and –22 per cent) for Milan.

None the less, if the range-shortening effect is on average much stronger for the

238

Table 13.4 Metro/non-metro shifts, Turin and Milan metropolitan areas, 1977–8 and 1987–8

Turin

Zone	North Centre						South					
	1977–8			1987–8			1977–8			1987–8		
	In	Out	Net	In	Out	Net	In	Out	Net	In	Out	Net
Core	5333	9837	−4504	3959	6995	−3036	11 626	9869	1757	5894	4638	1256
R1	1111	2104	−993	805	1517	−712	2233	2119	114	1167	1071	96
R2	875	1285	−410	621	941	−320	1649	1468	181	868	740	128
R3	521	761	−240	412	640	−228	916	790	126	494	420	74
Area	7840	13 987	−6147	5797	10 093	−4296	16 424	14 246	2178	8423	6869	1554

Milan

Zone	North Centre						South					
	1977–8			1987–8			1977–8			1987–8		
	In	Out	Net	In	Out	Net	In	Out	Net	In	Out	Net
Core	11 248	15 038	−3790	8207	11 632	−3425	14 518	6884	7634	7917	4880	3037
R1	2085	3457	−1372	1619	2737	−1118	3443	2589	854	2453	1548	905
R2	2803	3732	−929	2678	3364	−686	3828	2660	1168	3432	2010	1422
R3	2013	3604	−1591	1998	2679	−681	2851	2293	558	2336	1359	977
Area	18 149	25 831	−7682	14 502	20 412	−5910	24 640	14 426	10 214	16 138	9797	6341

Turin metropolitan area as a whole, it appears much less space-selective than for Milan. In fact, if the same metropolitan–non-metropolitan inflows and outflows are disaggregated by core and rings (R1–R3), non-significant differences may be observed between the core and rings of the Turin area, whereas the differences are relevant for the metropolitan area of Milan, where the core's decline is stronger than in the rings, with the exception of the outflows towards the southern regions. It is also worth noting that, in terms of relative net losses, the core of the Milan area increases its share of the total metropolitan losses from the north–centre, whereas its relative net gains from the southern regions decline.

Analysis of differential behaviours between core and rings of the metropolitan areas calls for an analysis of the intrametropolitan dynamics. In this case, the rest of the metropolitan region is considered in order to provide a wider perspective on shifts in short-distance mobility. Table 13.5 sets out the intrametropolitan net balances of each territorial component of these areas, as well as the total level of intrametropolitan mobility.

Table 13.5 Intrametropolitan net migration shifts, Turin and Milan metropolitan areas, 1977–8 and 1987–8

Zone	Turin		Milan	
	1977–8	1987–8	1977–8	1987–8
Core	–7742	–7839	–8820	–12 521
R1	1773	1207	409	43
R2	1366	2485	6267	5238
R3	1904	1392	303	3368
Rest of region	2699	2755	1841	3872
Intrametropolitan Migration Level	29 725	32 873	43 761	49 403

An important point to highlight is that, in a general context of declining longer-distance migration, intrametropolitan mobility increased substantially over the last decade. This happened for both of the two study areas, although for Milan the rise is more intense (plus 13 per cent) than for Turin (plus 10.5 per cent). The slightly stronger intrametropolitan pattern in the Milan area is in accord with stronger centrifugal shifts towards the outer parts of the area itself (Table 13.5). The changes in the intrametropolitan net balances reveal that in fact the outer part (R3 plus R4) of the metropolitan region of Milan gains remarkably, whereas each inner part (core, R1 and R2) loses and the more internal the part, the stronger the related net losses. This further confirms that the Milan metropolitan area is the forerunner of the nation-wide migration transition process.

However, above all, integrating metropolitan–non-metropolitan and intrametropolitan analysis with interregional analysis fosters a global perspective of the recent changes in the territorial patterns of internal migration and leads to a much deeper comprehension of the dynamics behind those changes. According to this integrated picture, it is possible to draw some further important general conclusions.

First, the shorter the distance range of migration, the less internal migration declines. This applies, in decreasing order of rank, to long-distance, mid-distance and short-distance interregional migrations, downwards to metropolitan–non-metropolitan migration. Second, a significant reversal is observable on the intrametropolitan scale, where migration increases. Third, intrametropolitan migration tends to rise according to clearly centrifugal trends. Thus, an increasing range-shortening effect extended to both the interregional and metropolitan–non-metropolitan scale, as well as increasing intrametropolitan migration levels, associated with increasing centrifugal trends, could be regarded as a reasonable short-term scenario for internal migration patterns in the near future.

13.4 AGE SELECTIVITY

In the previous section we have discussed the characteristics of the recent interregional and metropolitan patterns in Italy. However, as long as we consider the aggregate flows without taking into account the demographic and socioeconomic composition of migration, we neglect an aspect of the phenomenon that is considered more and more important for an understanding of the new population redistribution trends. Many studies on a regional and metropolitan scale have, in fact, demonstrated the importance of analysing the age selectivity of movement for an explanation of the recent interregional and metropolitan redistribution trends.

To demonstrate the usefulness of introducing age into the analysis of the interregional migration system in Italy, let us consider two examples. The first one refers to the migratory position of the north-western macroregion (Piedmont, Valle d'Aosta, Lombardy and Liguria) at the beginning of the eighties (Bonaguidi 1990).

This area was particularly attractive during the fifties and the sixties. Its intense industrialization and very low level of natural increase caused a massive migration from the rest of the country, particularly from the depressed south. During the seventies the attraction of this macroregion declined considerably and at the beginning of the eighties the overall level of in-migration was almost the same as that of out-migration. But looking at the age profile of the gross and net migration (Figure 13.1 shows the respective smoothed curves), one may note that zero aggregate net migration is the result of gains and losses at different ages. Marked migration gains are observable at the ages of initial entry into the labour force (15 to 30) but migration losses at all other ages. The losses become more pronounced at the late working ages and initial postlabour ages because of the existence of a retirement peak in the out-migration age profile. In other words, the traditionally attractive area of the country, albeit in decline, tends to maintain a non-negligible capacity to attract and retain the demographically and economically most significant components of the population.

The second example refers, also at the beginning of the eighties, to the age selectivity of two especially significant Italian long-distance migration flows, ie the

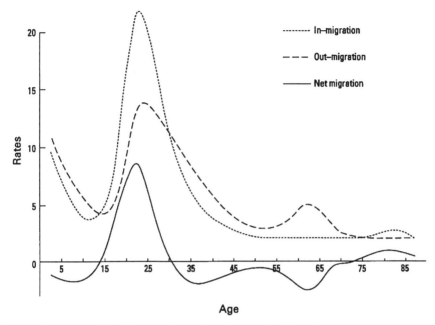

Figure 13.1 Age profiles of gross and net migration rates for the northwestern macro-region, 1980–2

traditional flow from south to the north-west and its counter flow (Bonaguidi 1987). Only male migration is considered. The two age curves (standardized) are shown in Figure 13.2. The overall level of the migration age curve measured by the gross migration rate (GMR) is approximately the same for the two flows, but the profile (age selectivity) is quite different. Migration from the southern regions to the north-western regions clearly appears much more labour dominant and less child and elderly dependent than the corresponding counter flow.

We have previously found that the decline of interregional migration level over the last decade is particularly pronounced in long-distance migration and that the rise in short-distance migration is basically due to an intensification of intrametro-politan centrifugal tendencies. If, as expected, these spatial shifts are age selective, then the introduction of variable age into our analysis will shed more light on the processes under study and the various factors involved.

Of course, a detailed and complete examination by age of interregional and met-ropolitan flows is beyond the scope of this chapter. We will consider, therefore, some flows which can be considered sufficiently representative of the entire sys-tem. More specifically, we will examine over the period 1977–9 to 1989–90 the variation of the age profile of some migration flows particularly significant in the context of Italian internal migration, ie the migration from a southern region (Campania) to the north-centre and the migration from a northern region (Lombardy) to the south, as well as the age selectivity of intrametropolitan

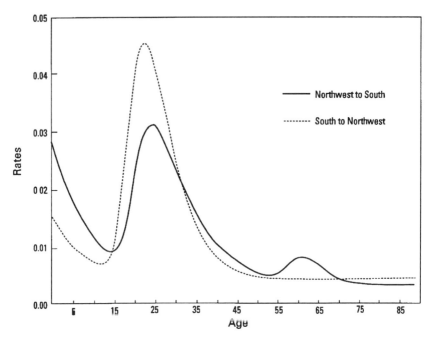

Figure 13.2 Age profiles (standardized) of south to northwest and northwest to south migration rates, 1980–2

(between core and suburban rings) and metropolitan–non-metropolitan migration for the Milan and Turin metropolitan systems.

Figure 13.3 depicts a decline in the propensity to move over all ages from 1977–9 to 1989–90 in the two cases considered. It is rather easy to note that for migration from Campania to the northern and central regions the lowering in the propensity to emigrate is particularly concentrated in the youngest labour-force ages, while in the case of migration from Lombardy to the south the decrease, even if more pronounced in the young labour-force, is also observable in the other components of the curve, in particular in the mid- and late working ages.

Age also plays a crucial role in the metropolitan population shifts. Many studies on metropolitan migration in several countries have, indeed, demonstrated the importance of analysing age-selective metropolitan dynamics (Kontuly and Vogelsang 1988; Winchester and Ogden 1989; Frey 1989, 1992). These studies have contributed considerably to the explanation of the observed metropolitan transition from the historical centralization patterns to the recent decentralization trends.

In the context of the two Italian metropolitan areas considered (Milan and Turin), the short-distance intrametropolitan migration (from the core to the close periphery) shows a typical labour-dominant profile, where the young labour-force component of the age-migration curve is particularly pronounced and no specific pre-retirement and retirement component is observable (Bonaguidi and Terra

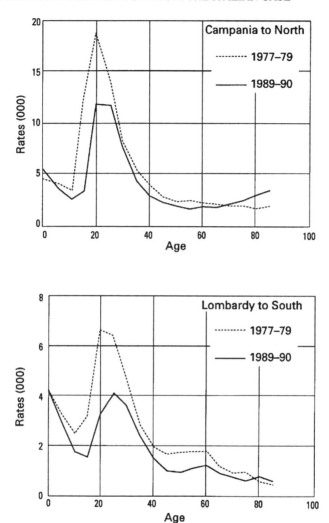

Figure 13.3 Age profiles of migration rates from Campania to north and from Lombardy to south, 1977–9 and 1989–90

Abrami 1992). In contrast, the late working and postlabour age components become relatively important in longer-distance metropolitan mobility, ie in the movement from the central cities to the metropolitan periphery and, in particular, for the metropolitan flows towards the mid-distance regions (northern and central regions). A noticeable rise in the migration rate in the postlabour ages is also observable in very long-distance metropolitan out-migration (to the south).

As mentioned above, the most significant changes in the spatial structure of metropolitan migration over the last decade were a rise of intrametropolitan short-distance migration and a slowdown of extrametropolitan long-distance migration. The increase in intrametropolitan migration, mainly due to the population shifts towards the external parts of the metropolitan system, reflects an intensification of the decentralization process in metropolitan populations.

A recent study of the age composition of these metropolitan shifts (Bonaguidi and Terra Abrami 1992) revealed that the net losses of central cities in short-distance intrametropolitan migration are confined to the young working ages (20–39), while the net losses of central cities in mid-distance mobility are concentrated in the pre-retirement and retirement ages (55 and over). The composition of long-distance migration (originating in the south) is dominated by the younger labour-force (ages 15–29). Over the last decade (1977–8 to 1987–8), the age selectivity of net metropolitan migration tends to be more pronounced. An increase in concentration rate, both in the young labour-force for the (positive) very long-distance migration balance, and in the late labour and postlabour forces for the (negative) mid-distance migration balance, seems to characterize the more recent trend. In the case of the inner city Milan metropolitan area, in 1987–8 the 15–29 age segment represents about 90 per cent of the positive net migration from the southern regions, while more than three-fourths of the negative migratory balance with the northern and central regions is confined to the 55 and over age group.

In short, an interesting integrated system between the population redistribution process across the national settlement context and developments within each element of it becomes evident. The northern metropolitan areas gain less in long-distance interregional migration (from the south), but these reduced gains seem now more 'production-oriented'. These significant segments of population are in turn the main components of the decentralization shifts within the metropolitan systems, while the decentralization of 'non production-oriented' metropolitan population tends to occur over longer distances outside the metropolitan context.

13.5 CONCLUSIONS

Our analysis has illustrated the salient changes in the internal migration system of Italy over the last decade. There has been, first of all, a marked slowdown in the propensity to move over longer distances, particularly between north and south. Secondly, however, this declining migration tends to be slightly more 'efficient' in terms of population redistribution. Thirdly, the increasing migration imbalance is to be viewed more as a new pattern in the migration between the economically and socially more distant areas of the country (north and south) rather than as a process of imbalance of the system as a whole. Fourthly, the rise in short-distance (intra-regional) migration can be related mainly to an intensification of centrifugal shifts from the urban and metropolitan areas.

All these processes are highly selective by age. The reduction in the propensity to move to the north-centre from the southern regions mainly affects the younger labour-forces. Redistribution over longer distances across regions and metropolitan areas tends to be highly dominated by economic 'pushes and pulls' for the younger working-age population. Decentralization of metropolitan populations, particularly towards the outer metropolitan periphery or mid-distance extrametropolitan destinations is largely determined by the postlabour population that is less likely to respond to area employment growth and is more apt to relocate in places with good social services, high amenities and a low cost of living.

The substitution process of long-distance migration by short-distance migration means that, on the whole, the influence of economic factors as determinants of internal migration in Italy is declining because short-distance movement is generally less economically induced.

The diminution of south–north migration does not mean a reduction in the traditional spatial disparities within the country, but is mainly due to the fact that migration is a response to these disparities. The demographic weight of Italy, because of the current trends of natural increase, is tending to shift towards the south. This introduces important implications for the north–south imbalance, which is one of the crucial issues in the country. The different migration pattern of working-age population, still attracted by the economic pulls of metropolitan areas, and that of postlabour population, which accelerates its deconcentration, also have important implications in terms of spatial differentials in the ageing process and distribution of the elderly.

14 The Netherlands: from Interregional to International Migration

HUGO GORDIJN and LEO EICHPERGER

14.1 INTRODUCTION

Internal migration in the Netherlands has been for many years one of the most important determinants of population redistribution (van der Erf 1984). Several social and economic factors have influenced this demographic component. The location of the seaports in the western Netherlands made this part of the country the economic centre of gravity in the first half of the 20th century. Commerce and shipping developed there and attracted internal migrants to the provinces of North Holland and South Holland in particular. This migratory movement was an expression of urbanization, a common phenomenon in several Western European countries, caused by the relative movement of employment from agriculture to industrial activities and services.

Between 1950 and 1960, migration from other parts of the country to the provinces of North and South Holland came to an end. The provinces of Gelderland and North Brabant became the new regions of destination for internal migrants. The phenomenon of suburbanization became stronger than that of urbanization. During the period from 1960 to 1980, a series of subperiods can be identified as follows:

1. 1960–4: the beginning of suburbanization; net out-migration from the cities was small and did not increase much;
2. 1965–9: unguided suburbanization; net out-migration from the cities increased rapidly; this led to net out-migration from the provinces of North and South Holland (the two most urbanized provinces in the Netherlands);
3. 1970–3: suburbanization reached its summit in this period; suburbanization was directed to the smallest villages far from the cities;
4. 1974–9: concentration of suburbanization; net out-migration from the cities decreased and was directed to the municipalities where the government concentrated the building of new dwellings;
5. 1980s: internal migration stabilized at a lower level.

In the next sections we elaborate on the interregional migration and suburbanization taking place in the period 1972–92.

Population Migration in the European Union Edited by Philip Rees, John Stillwell, Andrew Convey and Marek Kupiszewski. © Editors and Contributors. Published 1996 John Wiley & Sons Ltd.

14.2 SPATIAL FRAMEWORKS

For a better understanding of the effect of both types of residential mobility (inter-regional movements and suburbanization), we need a more detailed spatial framework. To examine the effects of migration within and between 'labour markets', we employ the NUTS level 3 regions (Figure 14.1 shows COROP regions), while the effects of migration in terms of suburbanization or reurbanization are analysed at the NUTS level 4 scale of municipalities. These are characterized by their level of urbanization, and three classes; centre, ring and periphery, can be distinguished. No spatial framework is perfect, including that used for this analysis. The major draw-backs include overlapping labour markets, especially in the RANDSTAD (the western highly urbanized area), and 'peripheral' municipalities in the western regions that are quite different from those in the north. We have learned to cope with these disadvantages of our typology.

14.3 RESIDENTIAL MOBILITY

An important indicator for the development of population distribution is overall migration, the total of internal movements (changes of residence) in a country during a given time period. Figure 14.2 shows the development of residential mobility in the period 1960–92. The figure shows clearly that mobility in the Netherlands reaches its peak in the years 1973 and 1974. Thereafter a sharp fall occurs until 1979. The eighties show a small increase in movement, but the level at the beginning of the 1970s is never reached again.

There are large differences in migration by gender and age, particularly the latter. Figure 14.3 shows the typical pattern in the Netherlands which can be observed in many countries (Rogers and Castro 1981). As children, boys and girls have the same migration rates. In adolescence, young women leave the parental home earlier than men; in the Netherlands the difference is about two years. The highest migration peaks occur at ages when working careers start and men and women form unions and live together for the first time. With increasing age the frequency of changes in the working, relational and housing statuses diminishes. After working careers have ended and families have moved on to the 'empty nest' phase, migration slowly rises. In the early seventies a small retirement peak at age 65 is observable. At the end of the 1980s it has almost disappeared due to the dramatic fall of labour participation among older persons. The 'retirement-peak' is spread over the range 55–65 years. At older ages, moves into homes for the elderly and nursing homes are the most important factors causing residential mobility, and probability of migration rises with age. Between the early 1970s and the late 1980s the overall pattern is stable, but some changes are noticeable. Young adults enter the high migration peak later in the late 1980s; their education is prolonged. Both the residential and the labour migration have dropped compared to the high levels of the early 1970s.

The age pattern of international migrants is different from that of internal

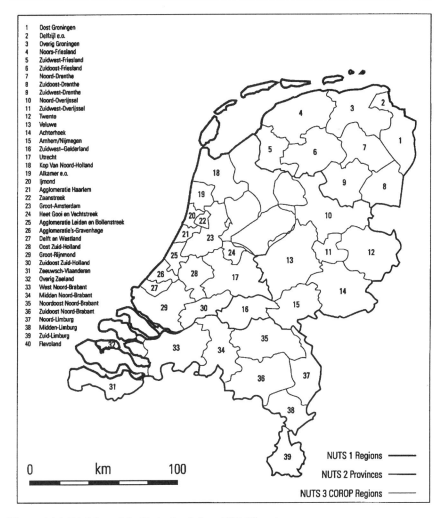

1   Oost Groningen
2   Delfzijl e.o.
3   Overig Groningen
4   Noors-Friesland
5   Zuidwest-Friesland
6   Zuidoost-Friesland
7   Noord-Drenthe
8   Zuidoost-Drenthe
9   Zuidwest-Drenthe
10 Noord-Overijssel
11 Zuidwest-Overijssel
12 Twente
13 Veluwe
14 Achterhoek
15 Arnhem/Nijmegen
16 Zuidwest–Gelderland
17 Utrecht
18 Kop Van Noord-Holland
19 Alkamer e.o.
20 IJmond
21 Agglomeratie Haarlem
22 Zaanstreek
23 Groot-Amsterdam
24 Heet Gooi en Vachtstreek
25 Agglomeratie Leiden en Bollenstreek
26 Agglomeratie's-Gravenhage
27 Delft en Westland
28 Oost Zuid-Holland
29 Groot-Rijnmond
30 Zuidoost Zuid-Holland
31 Zeeuwsch-Vlaanderen
32 Overig Zeeland
33 West Noord-Brabant
34 Midden Noord-Brabant
35 Noordoost Noord-Brabant
36 Zuidoost Noord-Brabant
37 Noord-Limburg
38 Midden-Limburg
39 Zuid-Limburg
40 Flevoland

0   km   100

NUTS 1 Regions ————
NUTS 2 Provinces ————
NUTS 3 COROP Regions ————

Figure 14.1 Division of the Netherlands into COROP regions

migrants. Figure 14.4 shows that international migrants are younger and more likely to be male. If we add the 57 000 emigrants to the 567 000 intermunicipal
migrants and the 986 000 intramunicipal migrants, the result is that total residential
mobility is approximately 1.6 million moves in 1990. The total residential mobility
rate is 7.2 moves in a lifetime, which is an internationally comparable figure, independent of mean size of municipality.

14.4 EXPLANATIONS FOR THE TRENDS IN RESIDENTIAL MOBILITY

The decrease in internal migration and suburbanization can be attributed to several

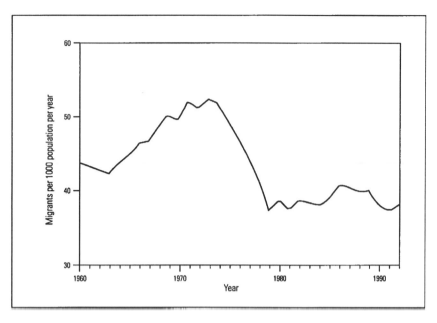

Figure 14.2 Migration in the Netherlands, 1960–92

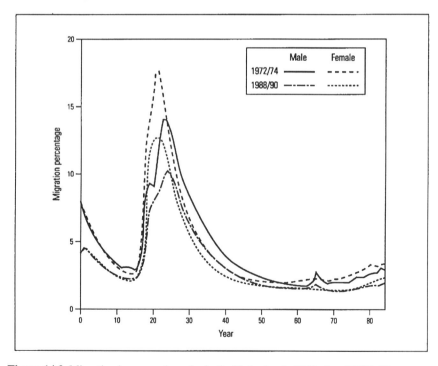

Figure 14.3 Migration by age and gender in the Netherlands, 1972–4 and 1988–90

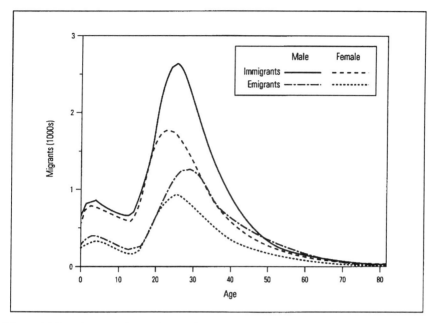

Figure 14.4 Netherlands international migration by age and gender (forecast), 1992

social factors. The Dutch population has changed in number and structure during recent decades. These demographic trends usually occur first in the cities. Changes in demographic structure during the last 20 years manifest themselves in ageing. The proportion of young people diminishes, and the proportion of people in the older ages increases.

Economic development has the strongest influence on interregional residential migration. During the 1970s and the 1980s, socioeconomic development in the Netherlands suffered from a declining business climate. Stagnation of the world economy, due to volatility in currency markets and two successive oil crises, reached a nadir around 1980. This hit the open Dutch economy very hard. Diminishing economic growth had its consequences for the labour and housing markets. The problems in the labour market appeared to be structural. It was not only a question of quantitative differences between supply and demand but also of qualitative differences. The labour market problems were mostly concentrated in the cities. Unemployment during the early eighties was higher in the cities than in the rural areas, which had traditionally been the areas with a high level of unemployment. Due to the economic crisis, purchasing power diminished. It was only in 1985 that purchasing power increased again. Diminishing purchasing power and increasing uncertainty on the labour market were the causes of diminishing demand in the housing market. This, in turn, caused a decline in internal migration. The high level of unemployment in the cities caused a decrease in out-migration from the cities.

Desires with respect to dwellings and the residential environment play an important role in the choice of the municipality of residence (intraregional mobility). The single-family dwelling is most popular. A considerable percentage of households in the Netherlands would prefer a less urbanized place than where they are actually living. Households that can afford it move from the densely populated cities to the smaller cities where single-family homes dominate.

For international migration, the economic motive is predominant in the 'normal' situation (King 1993). Economic upswings are reflected by higher immigration from Turkey and Morocco, for example. Political disturbances and civil wars can suddenly lead to mass migration as can be seen from the large numbers of refugees from Sri Lanka, Iran, Somalia and the former Yugoslavia. In the Dutch case, the colonial past also plays a role. The independence of Indonesia and Surinam gave rise to a large up flow in-migration, and the Netherlands Antilles and Surinam still have strong migration ties with Holland.

14.5 MIGRATION WITHIN AND BETWEEN LABOUR MARKETS

14.5.1 MIGRATION BETWEEN LABOUR MARKETS

At the level of NUTS 3 regions, migration during recent decades shows a change in pattern. During the period 1972–7, when the economy was expanding, the urban-

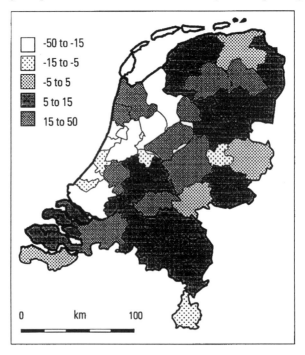

Figure 14.5 Net migration as a percentage of total migration, 1972–9

ized areas (Figure 14.5) in Holland lost a lot of people. The rural regions in Holland and Utrecht, as well as regions with scenic beauty in Utrecht, Gelderland and Drenthe were sought after by migrants. In the period 1987–92, when the economy was experiencing restructuring, the pattern was quite different. The magnitude of change was smaller, the periphery lost people while the centre gained (Figure 14.6).

Behind this overall pattern, very different patterns of migration according to age can be distinguished. Migrants in the 15–24 age group clearly choose the regions in which institutes of education are located, as well as the urban regions of the western part of the country (Figure 14.7). Migration to suburban regions characterizes migrants in the 25–34 age group. The rural areas and areas of scenic beauty are the favourite settlement places for migrants in the 35–64 age group. The same applies for the 65 and older (Figure 14.8) age group, although the presence of retirement homes in the region is also influential for the settlement of senior citizens.

14.5.2 MIGRATION WITHIN LABOUR MARKETS

The Netherlands is a densely populated country with 444 persons per square kilometre. On the European scale, the country is highly urbanized. Some regions are more urbanized than others (Figure 14.9). This section reports on analysis of migratory relationships between municipalities with different degree of urbanization. A

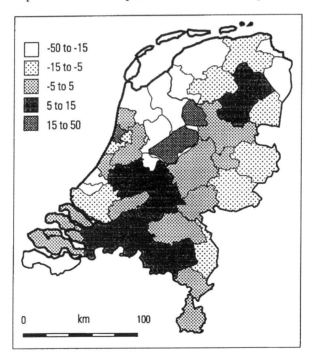

Figure 14.6 Net migration as a percentage of total migration, 1987–92

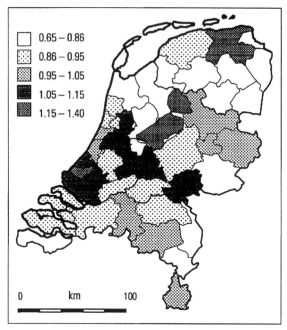

Figure 14.7 Arrival/departure ratio, age group 15–24, 1987–92

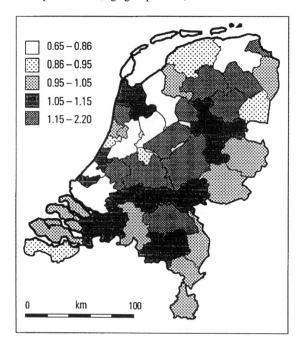

Figure 14.8 Arrival/departure ratio, age group 65+, 1987–92

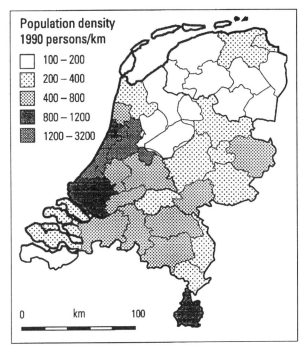

Figure 14.9 Population density by COROP region, 1990

three-way classification has been constructed for urbanized areas: 'centre' (population more than 100 000), 'ring' (commuter municipalities and small towns) and 'periphery' (small villages with a relatively agrarian population). Migration flows within regions among these types of municipalities are shown in Table 14.1, indicating that the outflow from centre municipalities has diminished, but that, simultaneously, flows from periphery to centre municipalities have increased.

The advent of a cyclical process can be observed in the age pattern (Figure 14.10). Youngsters are attracted by the larger cities for their educational facilities,

Table 14.1 Migration between types of municipalities, 1972–92

Period	From centre			From ring			From periphery		
To	Centre	Ring	Periphery	Centre	Ring	Periphery	Centre	Ring	Periphery
					Thousands				
1972–4	9	58	36	26	27	29	18	24	43
1975–7	8	50	29	27	27	27	18	25	42
1978–80	6	43	21	24	23	22	17	21	38
1981–3	6	47	21	28	25	22	18	22	38
1984–6	6	41	24	30	26	25	19	25	43
1987–9	6	40	24	29	28	26	20	26	45
1990–2	7	36	21	28	24	24	19	24	43

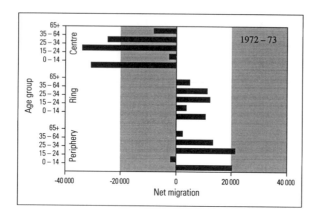

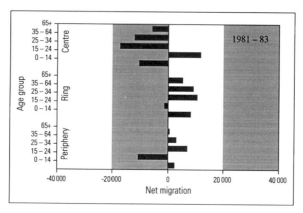

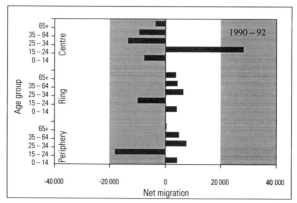

Figure 14.10 Net migration by age group for centre, ring and periphery, 1972–3, 1981–3 and 1990–2

their opportunities for finding a job and the city ambience. After completion of their education, some of them find a job elsewhere; others start a family and find suburbia a better place to raise children, since it provides more space for less money and fewer dangers than the 'big city'.

14.6 SUBURBANIZATION OR REURBANIZATION?

As stated in the introduction, an unguided suburbanization took place in the beginning of the 1970s. After the 1974 Third Report on Spatial Planning, policy was directed to guided suburbanization. The figures clearly show a decrease in suburbanization and in-migration to all rural municipalities. A strong migration flow towards the 'B3' municipalities is obvious. These were the municipalities where, in the 1980s, most of the new dwellings were built with government subsidies. In the 1992 Fourth Report on Spatial Planning, the goal is to intensify land use in inner city areas. The second option is development close to the major conurbations. The main criterion for the selection of building locations is home-to-work accessibility by public transport. The main goal is to reduce fuel emissions and congestion and to save valuable natural areas and open space. For rural areas in the vicinity of large conurbations, a very restrictive policy ('stand-still') was implemented.

Policy is directed thus towards reurbanization. Consumers recognize the numerous attractions of cities but disapprove of the disadvantages of urban living (low quality housing, high prices, insecurity). Reurbanization can only be successful when negative social circumstances in the cities have disappeared. Given an economic upswing, the negative externalities of cities could be reduced. But, in times of economic upswing, people can afford longer commuting journeys and higher house prices. In the Dutch case, a new influx of immigrants into the larger cities can also be expected.

14.7 INTERNATIONAL MIGRATION

Since the 1960s the growing number of foreigners has become an important factor in demographic development. The contribution of international migration to population growth was 15.9 per cent in 1972. In 1991, this contribution increased to 47.8 per cent. Between 1972 and 1991 net international migration into the Netherlands was 648 000. The distribution of the foreign migrants in the Netherlands is not balanced. Forty per cent of the 1.1 million foreigners who were counted on 1 January 1991 in the Netherlands lived in the three large cities, Amsterdam, Rotterdam and The Hague. The remaining 60 per cent lived in the smaller urban conurbations in and next to the western part of the country. This distribution pattern is the result of historical and socioeconomic factors. It follows the industrial development in the 1960s and 1970s. Foreign migrants were recruited in the first place as workers for industry. Furthermore, social factors such as their low education, low income, their

a. Trend scenario

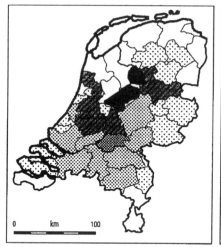

b. 'High-dispersal' scenario

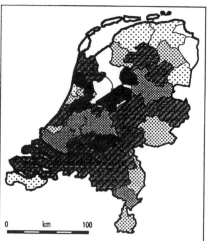

c. 'Low-concentration' scenario

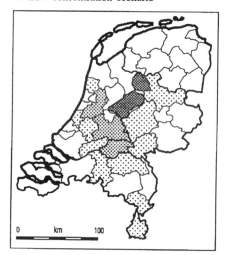

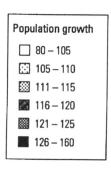

Figure 14.11 Three scenarios for future demographic development, 1992–2015

unwillingness to pay higher rent and their defective knowledge of the Dutch language and customs have contributed to the concentration of foreigners in the cities. At the same time, in certain areas landlords refused to rent dwellings to immigrants. Only the most unpleasant districts were available to immigrants. Moreover, the presence of many foreigners in the cities, and the presence of facilities created by immigrant, attracted new foreign migrants. The fact that the four large cities in the Netherlands have a large proportion of social housing also contributes to the concentration of foreigners in large cities.

14.8 FUTURE SCENARIOS

The impact of a demographic factor on a regional population forecast has two components: the likelihood of a change in the factor and the extent to which the factor influences the outcome of the forecast. Alternative scenarios show that in the long run international migration has the largest impact on the regional population forecasts; fertility is second in importance and internal migration third; mortality is least important. With internal migration we can expect a trend towards the 'stable cyclical' pattern described above. In different periods of their lives, people prefer different environments. There are considerable flows of migrants, but low net migration. Large flows of international migrants can disrupt this tendency. The larger cities have always had a larger share in the accommodation of refugees and other immigrants. Given the limited capacity of cities for growth, a higher influx of foreign migrants will lead to higher outflows of internal migrants towards the ring and periphery.

Two scenarios have been drawn up as alternatives to the trend scenario. In the 'high-dispersal' scenario, we combine high economic growth with a high level of international migration, a high level of internal migration and dispersal towards lower-density areas. In the 'low-concentration' scenario, low economic growth is combined with a low level of international migration, a low level of internal mobility and a concentration of internal migration flows towards higher-density areas. The results (Figure 14.11 gives the growth rates for the three scenarios) show clearly that the level of external migration has a vital influence on the growth of population in the regions of the Netherlands, although in the centre of the country (and especially in the new polders of Flevoland) high growth occurs under all variants.

15 Recent Trends in Regional Migration and Urban Dynamics in Portugal

JOÃO PEIXOTO

15.1 METHODOLOGICAL CONSIDERATIONS

A problem for regional demographic analysis in Portugal is the lack of complete data. While data for natural increase are available on an annual basis, migration data have been largely unavailable. To date, Portugal has not had a system of direct registration of internal migrations and does not have a central register. The data normally used for the study of internal migration come from the census. The situation with regard to international migration is somewhat better. Statistics are available for emigration although these are incomplete as Portugal has always experienced a high proportion of uncontrolled emigration. The time series was interrupted in 1988 because these data had been obtained from those holding 'emigration passports', then discontinued, but resumed in 1992. International immigration data are less complete. The entry of foreigners has only been measured since it became significant in 1974, and have been only available as annual 'stocks' until 1992. Irregular immigration is ignored. The return to Portugal of former emigrants has only been recorded from time to time. This incomplete record from the various possible sources of data makes the use of the 10-year census material absolutely vital. For the most recent period, the 1980s, real understanding of the dynamics of regional migration is not therefore possible without the detailed study of the results of the 1991 Census.

Methodological problems of regional migration analysis in Portugal also arise from the spatial units employed. The adoption of the European NUTS system in 1988 (shown in Figure 15.1) led to the production of a NUTS-based statistical series. For some time, all statistical work had been based upon traditional administrative units which exist across the country, the *freguesias*, *concelhos* and *distritos*. The NUTS 2 units corresponded to the *concelhos* but not to the larger *distritos*. Work on a long time series which does fully correspond to NUTS is being undertaken at present. In addition to this, the division of the country into formal 'urban' and 'rural' zones has never been totally agreed in Portugal. The patterns of regional population and of 'urbanization' are very complex, but this does not of course justify

Population Migration in the European Union Edited by Philip Rees, John Stillwell, Andrew Convey and Marek Kupiszewski. © Editors and Contributors. Published 1996 John Wiley & Sons Ltd.

NUTS 2

NUTS 3

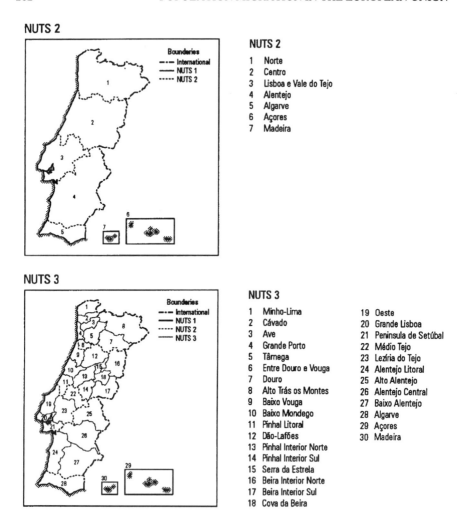

NUTS 2

1 Norte
2 Centro
3 Lisboa e Vale do Tejo
4 Alentejo
5 Algarve
6 Açores
7 Madeira

NUTS 3

1 Minho-Lima	19 Oeste
2 Cávado	20 Grande Lisboa
3 Ave	21 Peninsula de Setúbal
4 Grande Porto	22 Médio Tejo
5 Tâmega	23 Lezíria do Tejo
6 Entre Douro e Vouga	24 Alentejo Litoral
7 Douro	25 Alto Alentejo
8 Alto Trás os Montes	26 Alentejo Central
9 Baixo Vouga	27 Baixo Alentejo
10 Baixo Mondego	28 Algarve
11 Pinhal Litoral	29 Açores
12 Dão-Lafões	30 Madeira
13 Pinhal Interior Norte	
14 Pinhal Interior Sul	
15 Serra da Estrela	
16 Beira Interior Norte	
17 Beira Interior Sul	
18 Cova da Beira	

Figure 15.1 NUTS 2 and 3 regions of Portugal

the lack of an agreed official definition, nor the very low figures for urbanization (around 34 per cent in 1991) which are obtained by using the most common current definition. There is no agreement about the boundaries of complex urban areas. The delimitation of the 'metropolitan areas' of the two largest towns in the country, Lisboa and Porto, has varied according to the researcher. It was not until 1991 that an official definition on this was put forward. As far as the other urban areas are concerned, the problem is similar—each time an analysis of the microregional urban system is undertaken, it is always necessary to produce locally based functional definitions.

15.2 RECENT TRENDS IN REGIONAL DEMOGRAPHIC GROWTH

Even though Portugal is a relatively small country, it still demonstrates marked regional heterogeneity. The main lines of spatial differentiation follow a vertical coastal/interior axis and a second horizontal axis north–south, aside from the autonomous regions of the Açores and Madeira. The coastal regions house most of the population and economic activity and have demonstrated for many years the strongest demographic growth, resulting from the influx of migrants or from natural increase. The distribution of population along the coast is not even, however. The two most important urban *pôles* in the country are Lisboa and Porto. Regional differences result from different 'models' of development. In the northern coastal region (with an extension towards the centre of the country) and including the urban area of Porto, there exist small and medium-sized enterprises which are mostly traditional in character, especially those in the secondary sector. These exist alongside small-scale part-time farming. In the northern and central interior, the economy is based largely upon agriculture, to which are added externally generated revenues, particularly remittances from emigrants but also transfer payments (eg pensions and interest on savings and investments).

In the metropolitan region of Lisboa, the level and extent of modernization are relatively higher than in the north. The southern interior, Alentejo, is essentially agricultural with a predominance of large estates. The southern coastal area, the Algarve, has developed its tourist economy, which has shown very strong growth over the last decade (for more details of regional differentiation in Portugal, see Figueiredo *et al.* 1985; Santos 1985; Ferrão 1985; Gaspar 1987; Amaro 1991, and Reis 1992).

The effects of these different sources of regional differentiation on urban development are clear. While Lisboa demonstrates the usual forms of urbanization associated with most developed societies, in the north and central coastal areas economic activity and especially industrialization are not sufficient to produce high levels of urbanization. An important part of total production here takes place in the 'rural' and/or 'mixed' areas, giving rise to a notably diffuse (Gaspar 1987) or weak pattern of urbanization (Ferrão 1985). As Baptista and Ferrão (1989) also suggest, the degree of endogeneous development, the existence of a marked local potential, is more important in these areas (for the different forms of regional urbanization, see also Ferrão 1985; Gaspar 1987).

Recent analysis of population dynamics for the Portuguese regions highlights their characteristics. Tables 15.1 and 15.2 show the distribution of population in Portugal at NUTS 2 level for 1970, 1981 and 1991, with total increase, natural increase and migration. Table 15.2 shows figures for those NUTS 3 areas which correspond with the most important urban regions: Grande Porto (metropolitan area of Porto), Grande Lisboa and Península de Setúbal (metropolitan area of Lisboa). The north, with approximately 35 per cent of the population in 1970 and 1991, and Lisboa e Vale do Tejo, with 29.4 per cent and 33.4 per cent respectively at the same dates, remain the most populated regions in the country. If one divides the country into coast and interior, the situation becomes clearer. Traditional types of analysis

Table 15.1 Population change and its components by NUTS 2 region, 1970–81 (in thousands)

Regions	Total population[a]		1970–81						Internal migration balance[b]	
NUTS 2	1970	1981	Population growth	%	Natural increase	%	Migration balance	%	1973–81	1979–81
PORTUGAL	8611.1	9833.0	1222	14.2	840	9.8	382	4.4	0	0
Mainland										
Norte	3020.0	3410.1	390	12.9	379	12.5	11	0.4	–5	–2
Centro	1667.2	1763.1	96	5.8	101	6.1	–5	–0.3	–22	–7
Lisboa Vale Tejo	2532.4	3261.6	729	28.8	277	10.9	452	17.8	40	12
Alentejo	587.3	578.4	–9	–1.5	23	3.9	–32	–5.4	–15	–4
Algarve	268.0	323.5	56	20.9	5	1.9	51	19.0	2	1
Autonomous Regions										
Açores	285.0	243.4	–42	–14.7	32	11.2	–74	–26.0	–	–
Madeira	251.1	252.8	2	0.8	23	9.2	–21	–8.4	–	–

Notes: a. Resident population   b. Only mainland
Sources: Total population: INE, Census (1970—Estimated from a 20% sample and 1981); Migration balances: Ministério do Planeamento e da Administração do Território, *Plano de Desenvolvimento Regional*, 1989–1993, Vol. 1, 1989; Population growth and natural increase: calculations by the author

Table 15.2 Population change and its components, and urbanization rates by region, 1981–91

Regions NUTS 2 NUTS 3[a]	Total population[b] 1981	1991	1981–91[c] Population growth	%	Natural increase	%	Migration balance	%	Urbanization rate (%)[d] 1981	1991
PORTUGAL	9 833 014	9 862 540	29 526	0.3	354 104	3.6	−324 578	−3.3	29.7	33.8
Mainland										
Norte	3 410 099	3 472 715	62 616	1.8	224 043	6.6	−161 427	−4.7	21.6	25.4
Grande Porto	*1 117 920*	*1 167 800*	*49 880*	*4.5*	*66 101*	*5.9*	*−16 221*	*−1.5*	*51.1*	*54.5*
Centro	1 763 119	1 721 650	−41 469	−2.4	23 276	1.3	−64 745	−3.7	11.6	19.2
Lisboa Vale Tejo	3 261 578	3 292 108	30 530	0.9	80 775	2.5	−50 245	−1.5	53.3	54.9
Grande Lisboa	*1 853 729*	*1 831 877*	*−21 852*	*−1.2*	*48 356*	*2.6*	*−70 208*	*−3.8*	*71.1*	*72.0*
Península Setúbal	*584 648*	*640 493*	*55 845*	*9.6*	*28 645*	*4.9*	*27 200*	*4.7*	*56.9*	*57.7*
Alentejo	578 430	543 442	−34 988	−6.0	−7979	−1.4	−27 009	−4.7	14.3	16.2
Algarve	323 534	341 404	17 870	5.5	851	0.3	17 019	5.3	24.1	23.4
Autonomous Regions										
Açores	243 410	237 795	−5615	−2.3	17 934	7.4	−23 549	−9.7	13.8	13.6
Madeira	252 844	253 426	582	0.2	15 205	6.0	−14 623	−5.8	17.4	41.9

Notes: a. Only NUTS 3 corresponding approximately to the urban regions of Porto and Lisboa
  b. Resident population
  c. Estimates for the intercensus period
  d. 'Urban centres' of 10 000 inhabitants or more (1991: provisional data)

Sources: Total population: INE, Census (1981 and 1991); Population growth natural increase and Migration balance: INE, estimates; Urbanization rate: calculations by the author, based on INE, Census (1981 and 1991)

made by *distritos* reveal, for example, that the coastal areas had about 78 per cent of the population in 1991, as against 72 per cent in 1970. If we take the urban regions of Lisboa and Porto, we see even more revealing figures. In 1991, the urban region of Lisboa contained about 25 per cent of the national population, while Porto contained 12 per cent.

If one takes the NUTS 2 level data for total population growth during the 1970s, considerable increases can be seen in most regions, with a national average of plus 14.2 per cent. In fact, this period was an exceptional one for Portuguese demography: it included the return of about half a million people from former colonies in Africa; a large return flow of former emigrants, especially towards the end of the decade; and a marked reduction in emigration after 1973. In the 1980s, however, these levels of return migration were considerably reduced. The Portuguese population as a whole experienced only a 0.3 per cent increase. Among the Portuguese regions, it was the Algarve, with 5.5 per cent growth, and Lisboa and the north, with about 1 and 2 per cent growth, which saw the main increases. But population change in these periods is not only explained in terms of external factors. Natural growth alone showed a loss of about two-thirds of its relative value: levels of natural growth fell from plus 9.8 per cent in the 1970s to plus 3.6 per cent in the 1980s. Regional variations of natural increase are also of some significance. The north, which together with the Islands had for a very long time been the population 'reservoir' of the country, saw its natural growth reduced by about half. At the same time, in the 1970s, Lisboa experienced the highest rates of growth which are explained by a very favourable age structure resulting from major internal in-migration streams. This latter effect then gradually reduced through the 1980s. The marked reduction in natural population growth in Portugal during the 1980s has reflected the structural changes in Portuguese demography (Carrilho and Peixoto 1991).

Regional net migration levels also show notable changes from the 1970s to the 1980s. In the 1970s, the positive net migration balance for the country as a whole benefited Lisboa (plus 17.8 per cent) and the Algarve (plus 19 per cent), reinforced by large internal migration flows. But one can also say that external immigration has also benefited other regions, notably the north and the centre, as a result of the turnaround in international migration flows. In the 1980s, the situation was quite different. The country once again lost population by migration, and only one region saw an increase, the Algarve. Losses in the other regions varied from minus 1.5 per cent (Lisboa) to minus 9.7 per cent (the Açores).

One final point to note here is the correlation which one finds between the different components of population growth over recent decades. Peixoto (1990, 1991) indicates that it has been the net migration figures which have 'controlled' total growth. There is a strong correlation between total growth and net migration and an increase in the positive correlation between natural growth and net migration. Migration has induced natural growth by transforming the age structure, reinforcing the mechanisms of total growth, positive or negative, and provoking a form of 'demographic inertia', which explains many of the more recent trends such as that occurring in the urban region of Lisboa.

15.3 INTERNATIONAL MIGRATION AND ITS REGIONAL DISTRIBUTION

In the Portuguese context, it is not easy to separate internal migration from international migration from the statistical point of view. Theoretically it is possible to maintain that they ought to be linked: it is only possible to understand urbanization if one includes both. In the first place, the attraction of the urban areas in Portugal —and the rural exodus—must be seen in a larger context than the national: emigration has taken population from the peripheral areas (usually rural) to urban regions world-wide. As Gaspar (1980) has shown, emigration has contributed to a second form of urbanization, that of financial remittances or cultural influences, which leads to a form of 'urbanization' for those individuals who remain in the peripheral areas.

There has not been much quantitative research into comparisons of internal and external migration in Portugal. One needs to stress that the main difficulty is a statistical one. Alarcão and Morais (1975), in an analysis which regrettably only covers the period 1920–60, considered that the attraction of internal migration had been greater than that of external emigration between 1920 and 1950, but had then only represented a little over a quarter of the total departures between 1951 and 1960. Calculations made later (Peixoto 1990) suggest that the greatest imbalance took place after 1960, during a period of very high emigration. It is generally accepted that in certain regions net out-migration have been dominated by external emigration, while in others internal movement has been more important. In the interior north and the Islands, and also the coastal zones, external migration has been more important, while the interior south has experienced strong attraction of migrants to the Lisboa area. This results from a weight of historic tradition, from existing migration chains, or from the differing levels of influence of Porto and Lisboa. Seruya (1982) and Baptista and Moniz (1985) have quantified these different regional movements, for the periods 1961–74 and 1950–70.

If one looks at the levels of net internal and international migration by regions (*distritos*), as presented by Baptista and Moniz (1985), the differing regional destinations become clear. It is the most rural regions inland which are losing the most population by migration. In the 1950s, total annual losses varied between minus 1 per cent and minus 2 per cent, and during the 1960s, between minus 2.5 per cent and minus 3.5 per cent. Destination differentials are also clear: in the 1960s, the interior north and centre showed between two-thirds and three-quarters of the migrating population choosing to leave the country, while Alentejo showed a majority choosing internal movement. With respect to the absolute figures for external out-migration, the importance of the coastal areas is clear. During the period of greatest emigration, the 1960s and the first half of the 1970s, the interior was the origin of between 20 per cent and 25 per cent of the total population moving away; if one includes the Islands, the proportion rises to between one-third and one-half, and if the 'clandestine' departures were included these figures would be even higher. The remaining outflow from coastal zones includes therefore migration by 'stages' and direct urban-out-migration, situations which are still not well understood (Seruya 1982; and, for data, SECP 1988).

Regional analysis for the 1970s, the period of greatest net immigration, underlines the significance of return migration. According to Amaro (1985), returning migrants have contributed to a form of 're-equilibrium' across Portugal. In effect, they have chosen to go back to their areas of origin. The *retornados* from the old colonies have concentrated mainly in the northern interior region and in the Lisboa area. These gains, together with the marked drop in emigration and the slight fall in internal migration, have collectively contributed to a slowdown in regional divergence in Portugal.

The situation through the 1980s is less well understood. Official data for Portuguese emigration up to 1988 point towards reduced out-flows, but this is not confirmed by recent research based upon international data from destination countries and from the publication of the results of the 1991 Census (Baganha 1991; Peixoto 1992a, 1992b). Positive net external migration into Portugal had been expected over the 1980s, indicating a reduced level of emigration, a continuation of the return of former emigrants and the inward migration of foreigners. The evidence suggests so far that emigration levels appear to be above expectations and that return emigration is lower than expected. The regional character of this new emigration is still to be studied, but it seems to throw doubt on a continuation of convergence between regions in population development. If we analyse the figures for net migration obtained in the last census at a more disaggregated level, it is still the interior north and centre regions, and also the southern areas, which had in relative terms given up most population.

The immigration of foreigners is a new feature of the 1980s. It is true that total numbers remain low in relation to the resident population at about 1 per cent of the total. But their economic and social importance is much greater than their numbers. This immigration, which did not achieve significant size until the second half of the 1970s (then being made up mostly of Africans coming from the old colonies, especially Cape Verde), has increased regularly since then. After 1980 immigrant origins have diversified. The term 'foreigner' in fact covers at least three distinct groups:

1. *Africans*: about 42 per cent of the total in 1991, coming mainly from the old Portuguese colonies, and being generally young, male and unskilled;
2. *Europeans*: 29 per cent of the total, of which the great majority (26 per cent) come from the member countries of the European Union and are skilled professionals or older people, frequently moving on retirement; and
3. *from the Americas*: smaller numbers, coming from Brazil, or being descendants of former Portuguese emigrants to countries like Canada, the USA and Venezuela.

'Foreigners', wherever they come from, tend to choose the main urban zones, ie the same destinations as those of internal migration. About 61 per cent of all registered foreigners were located in the urban region of Lisboa (*distritos* of Lisboa and

Setúbal); 11 per cent located in the Algarve (*distrito* of Faro) and only 7 per cent in the urban region of Porto. The great majority of Africans are found in the Lisboa area; Europeans also choose Lisboa, but more select the Algarve (50 per cent of the British, for example, locate here) and the region of Porto; those from the Americas locate more in the north which confirms the link with previous emigration (for foreign immigration see Esteves 1991; Peixoto 1992b; and, for data, SEF 1991).

15.4 INTERNAL MIGRATION AND URBANIZATION

When analyses of internal migration flows in Portugal are undertaken, the differing characteristics of the urban areas are always underlined. In a study which compares 'place of birth' with 'place of residence' in 1981 (Cónim 1985), the overriding attraction of Lisboa is made very clear when compared with other urban areas, including Porto. More than 50 per cent of the population of the Lisboa zone (the *distritos* of Lisboa and Setúbal) were born outside the region. The other *distritos*, including Porto, only show rates of between 10 per cent and 15 per cent. In addition, an analysis of levels of net migration reveals a positive figure in only four *distritos*: Lisboa, Setúbal, Porto and Aveiro (the latter being very close to Porto). Baptista and Moniz (1985) have shown, using census data for the 1950s, the 1960s, 1973–81 and 1979–81, that the same four *distritos* show positive values over all these periods. The exceptions are net in-migration to Faro (the Algarve) in the 1970s; to certain central coastal areas in the 1960s and towards the end of the 1970s (Leiria and Coimbra), and net out-migration from Lisboa in 1979–81, though, according to Baptista and Moniz, this last situation arises from internal restructuring in the urban region. The values for internal migration, by NUTS 2 regions, shown in Table 15.1, point in the same direction, showing that only Lisboa and the Algarve attract net in-migration.

Portuguese internal migration thus makes differing contributions towards urbanization. The metropolitan area of Lisboa is the only one which shows a typical urban structure, with a strong spatial concentration of population resulting largely from in-migration. The Porto region has, by contrast, a more distinct character, with the partial exception of its central core. This results from the high levels of natural population growth in the region, which has sustained demographic increase and helped the growth of the urban region. The urban structure here, essentially endogenous, is explained by multipliers of largely local origin. It is also these diverse forms which explain the differences in 'levels of urbanization' which one gets when using a simple definition of the phenomenon. If the most common Portuguese definition of 'urban' is used, ie 'urban centres' with more than 10 000 inhabitants, one gets the figures shown in Table 15.2. Even if these values underevaluate the 'urban' phenomenon, they still show the different degree of concentration in the more developed regions, Lisboa (54.9 per cent urban in 1991) and the north (25.4 per cent urban at the same date). This pattern is maintained when one uses the NUTS 3 data for the urban zones of Lisboa and Porto. The urban population in

Lisboa made up 70 per cent of the total in 1991, as against approximately 55 per cent in Porto.

Research on the internal configuration of Portuguese urban regions follows on from that at the regional level. The urban region of Lisboa demonstrates the classic forms of all the great urban poles: an urban core, the administrative sector of Lisboa; a large suburban 'ring'; and a more peripheral zone. It has also followed a classic life-cycle: an urban expansion within its central core this century has led to an internal deconcentration of its population, from centre to periphery (Cruz and Santos 1990), under the influence of the service sector development and population pressure. Later, and especially after 1950, a strong suburban expansion followed, like a spreading oil-spill, along the main axial routes out of the city, both to the north and south of the Tejo River. After 1970, some authors have identified the growth of a second 'suburban ring' (Salgueiro 1992). There has been a progressive filling-in of the interstices between the main suburban axes (Ferreira 1987). In 1981, the urban core comprised 810 000 inhabitants, part of the population of 2 440 000 in the urban region as a whole (at NUTS 3 level). In 1991, the census showed that the city-centre population had reduced to fewer than 700 000 people, while population of the region as a whole had increased to 2 470 000. This decline in the net share in the city centre has occurred over the last few decades, with a peak decline after 1981.

In demographic terms, the 'urban unity' of Lisboa is achieved by the coming together of a large number of daily and periodic journeys to work from the suburbs, with large extension of the urban labour market. In 1981, something like 40 per cent of the employed residents in the suburban areas actually worked in the city centre. The *concelhos* on the northern bank of the Tejo saw about 45 per cent of the employed working in the centre in 1981, while the south bank area, cut off by the river and with more permanent communications difficulties, only had 28 per cent. In the 1970s, the numbers in local employment had increased in all the metropolitan *concelhos*, but these increases did not keep up with the more rapid increases in total population, thus leading to a more marked integration into the urban region as a whole (Salgueiro 1992). The amount of demographic connectivity within the urban region of Lisboa was also reinforced by a marked increase in intraurban migrations after 1970—leading to a restructuring of the population. From this point of view, the most attractive area seems to have been the south bank of the Tejo, due to its more modest property prices (Guerra 1990). Although the unity of the urban agglomeration seems clear, the administrative recognition of the 'metropolitan area of Lisboa' has only taken place recently, delimiting 18 *concelhos*, whose boundaries coincide generally speaking with the above-mentioned NUTS 3 limits (see Gaspar *et al.* 1988 on the housing problems of the Lisboa region, or Baptista 1985 and Ferrão 1988 on the regional economy).

The urban shape of the Porto region is more complex. The city is without question the second city of the country leading, with Lisboa, to an urban 'bipolarization' (Gaspar 1987). It is also the centre of a region with important national and international connections. However, it has shown lower demographic increases than other urban areas, and its population and migration increases have never reached those seen in Lisboa. In 1981, it had about 330 000 inhabitants in the central city area, and 1 120 000 in the urban area as a whole—figures which had changed by 1991 to 300 000 and 1 170 000 respectively. Apart from the central core, the city does not have a clearly defined spatial morphology. Housing and economic activity are dispersed throughout the periphery and other subregional areas, mixed in with a high density of small and medium-sized urban centres. The reasons for this limited amount of growth in Porto are normally to be seen in the high density and traditionally dispersed nature of the regional population, the diffused pattern of the main industries, the proximity of other medium-sized urban centres (eg Aveiro and Braga) and in the weak linkages between the various social groups in the centre and in the hinterland (Gaspar 1987; Salgueiro 1992; Ferrão 1985).

Even within its metropolitan area, Porto shows particular features. On the one hand, the density of population and land use seem to show a normal type of distribution: the most central area becoming more and more a tertiary zone, while transferring the higher densities of population further afield. On the other hand, however, the degree of economic attraction of the centre for most inward-travelling workers is less than in the case of Lisboa. Among the neighbouring *concelhos* in 1981, only 25 per cent of employees worked in the city centre (Salgueiro 1992). In other words, the amount of labour market autonomy in these urban peripheries is much greater than in Lisboa, making it difficult, strictly speaking, to classify them as traditional 'suburbs'. The amount of polarity and extension of the employment area of Porto are therefore also reduced; there is a strong degree of interweaving of minor employment areas throughout the region, given a dense network of economic activities. There is an academic debate in Portugal about whether Porto should be considered a typical 'metropolitan area' or the urban core of a 'multi-centred urbanized region'. However, this has not stopped the 'metropolitan area of Porto' being administratively launched in 1991, at the same time as Lisboa, with a structure of nine *concelhos*, which correspond with the NUTS 3 boundaries.

It is generally accepted that Portuguese urbanization is dominated by the two poles of Lisboa and Porto. There is disequilibrium between the sheer size of these two large urban regions and the much smaller dimensions of the other centres. No other Portuguese urban area exceeded 100 000 inhabitants in 1981 and most had populations smaller than 50 000 (Baptista 1985; Bruxelas 1987). Their spheres of influence are confined to subregional levels, with the exceptions of Coimbra, Braga and Évora (Bruxelas 1987). In the northern coastal area and to a lesser degree the central coastal area (including the periphery of Porto), the many small and medium-sized urban centres are predominantly industrial in character (Bruxelas 1987). As Gaspar et al. (1989) has shown, this spontaneous and somewhat diffuse urbanization currently implies very considerable planning problems: it can lead to a form of spatial 'rupture' in economic, social and physical terms. Towards the interior and partly in the central coastal area, the urban centres adopt more classic forms and show a predominance of the service sector, along with some industry and construction (Bruxelas 1987). The lack of industrial dynamism in these smaller centres is compensated for by their administrative functions or by subregional aid. With respect to the periphery of Lisboa, it is still industry which predominates in the urban landscape. In the Algarve, finally, tourism replaces industry as the key sector supporting urban development, as in Faro.

The complexity of the forms of urban growth in Portugal need not rule out a better understanding of spatial changes in the last few years, and in particular since the second half of the 1970s. Peixoto (1990, 1991) has noted a spatial reordering of Portuguese society since 1973, producing, among other phenomena, the slower growth of the Lisboa urban region. These conclusions arise from observations of the similarity of the pattern of migration behaviour in the regions during successive periods—the average annual rate of migration growth in the various *distritos* in 1951–60, 1961–70, 1971–81, 1973–81 and 1979–81. The values obtained suggest a strong growth of correlation up to 1973, showing a remarkable consistency of internal and external migration patterns, followed by a fall after that date. A look at the average annual rates of migration growth in the urban region of Lisboa for the 1970s reinforces this notion. Growth due to migration seemed, in fact, to diminish notably towards the end of the decade. Even if migration trends to urban areas had not undergone an inversion, the degree of regional concentration into Lisboa and repulsion from peripheral areas seem clearly to have eased towards the end of the decade.

This spatial re-equilibrium in Portuguese society has been underlined by many authors, although they are not all fully in agreement in placing the turnaround in the middle or at the end of the 1970s (Gaspar 1980, 1984, 1987; Ferrão 1985, 1988; Baptista 1985; Baptista and Ferrão 1989; Amaro 1985, 1991; Salgueiro 1992). The main spatial modifications revealed have been a diminution in polarization in the urban regions of Lisboa and Porto; a rise in the attraction of other coastal urban areas (north, centre and the Algarve); a reduction in the degrees of repulsion in some of the interior areas, and local dynamism in certain interior urban centres (especially in the north and centre). This reordering finds its explanation in the profound economic, social, political and demographic changes which Portuguese society has seen since this time. The crisis in the Lisboa region has resulted from a coming together of a variety of factors. These include the world economic crisis, with a special impact upon heavy industry; internal political and social upheavals (the revolution of 1974), with its impact upon production; and the end of its role as 'capital of empire'. Other changes were the advantages held by the economies of the northern and central coastal areas based upon traditional and more flexible types of industry (eg textiles); a policy of redistribution of financial resources begun by the government in 1974, accompanied by administrative decentralization and more local autonomy; the construction of transport infrastructures between the coast and the interior (helped by joining the Economic Community in 1986); the increased difficulty of the European employment market; and the return of emigrants from the colonies.

It is generally accepted that some of the tendencies towards re-equilibrium were prolonged all through the 1980s. One can, however, find signs of a new change in the second half of the decade, with the ending or the reduction of the main constraints upon the Portuguese economy. For example, the Lisboa region was in social and economic crisis until then; however, the renewed signs of life in the capital became more marked during the second half of the 1980s, in line with the strong growth of the Portuguese economy.

The results of the 1991 Census appear to confirm the main spatial trends described above. In the first place, the coastwise movement of the population has continued, although at a slower rate. The interior has seen its potential for growth further compromised by the increased ageing of its population. Second, the attractive power of Lisboa and Porto has weakened. The data for NUTS 3 regions (Table 15.2) show that the urban regions of Lisboa and Porto have even seen a much reduced or even a negative balance in migration. This lack of dynamism in the two main poles may, however, mask two other trends—the internal restructuring of their regions and an increase in the areal extent of their economic influence. Finally, an analysis by settlement size during the 1980s shows that the geographical concentration of population in settlements of more than 2000 and 10 000 inhabitants has continued, as has the reduction of population in the smallest and isolated centres of fewer than 500 inhabitants. This spatial concentration can be confirmed at all regional levels across practically the whole country, coast or interior.

15.5 CONCLUSIONS

The analysis of recent migration dynamics in Portugal must be further developed. In the first place, the results of the 1991 Census can be more fully examined in order to confirm the main trends already observed during the 1980s, including an analysis of the retrospective questions on place of residence in 1985 and 1989. Second, a study is needed of the internal composition of migration flows using the demographic variables of age and sex and the socioeconomic variables profession and skills. Third, it is important to understand better the economic and social motivations of the most recent migrants, even if one accepts (with Baptista and Moniz 1985) that it is difficult to relate short-term economic and social indicators to regional migration change. An understanding of these factors is important for working out reasonable predictions for the future.

Nevertheless, certain conclusions can be reached. The reduction in the degree of national population concentration in the largest Portuguese urban areas seems clear, a start to this having been made in the mid-1970s. Since then, one has seen more redistribution of the population among the minor coastal centres and, in certain cases, to the interior. However, the population disequilibrium between the coast and the interior does not seem to have ended, and marked falls in population in the most rural areas continue. From a theoretical point of view, it is not certain that this means that an urban turnaround took place. The most probable interpretation is that different phenomena have combined, including counterurbanization, reinforcement of local systems of production and a recent urban revival. On the one hand, there has been deceleration in the growth of the urban regions of Lisboa and Porto, as a result of lower natural increase and of migration loss in these places. On the other hand, Lisboa has shown some signs of renewed activity towards the end of the 1980s, including new centrally based development, technological improvement and an extension of its direct influence on its hinterland. At the same time, there has been a continuation of population concentration in the minor urban centres. However one approaches this subject, a change from the strong centripetal trends of the 1960s and the first half of the 1970s seems clear. The uncertainties about the direction of spatial reorganization of Portugal seem to arise from causes which are familiar in other European countries. There is no doubt that the economic, social and technological restructuring during the 1980s has resulted in new urban and migration trends on a wider scale.

16 Migration Between NUTS Level 2 Regions in the United Kingdom

JOHN STILLWELL, PHILIP REES and
OLIVER DUKE-WILLIAMS

16.1 INTRODUCTION

Internal migration has been a key component in shaping the geographical distribution of the population of the United Kingdom. The concentration of 18th- and 19th-century industrial growth was fuelled by the willingness of large numbers of people to migrate from the countryside to the emerging provincial tòwns and cities. The process of suburbanization which characterized most metropolitan areas in the pre- and postwar years involved massive population shifts as the motor car became a popular mode of transport to and from work for the majority of the work-force. More recently, the extended deconcentration of the population beyond the commuting distance to many urban centres has resulted in the massive net migration losses sustained by Greater London and the other large provincial conurbations. There is some evidence to suggest that the rate of counterurbanization is slowing down (Champion 1994), but the big cities are still continuing to lose population in net migration terms.

Analyses of these processes have been reported extensively in the literature together with interpretations of migration occurring at standard region and macro-region scales. However, virtually no analysis of migration patterns in the UK has been conducted hitherto at the scale of the European Commission's NUTS Level 2 regions. There are 35 of these regions (Figure 16.1), of which four are in Scotland, two in Wales and 28 in England. Northern Ireland is treated as a single NUTS 2 region. The boundaries of the English NUTS 2 regions are defined to conform with the former metropolitan counties (apart from Tyne and Wear which is aggregated with Northumberland) and either single shire counties or groups thereof. In Scotland, the Glasgow conurbation is part of a large NUTS 2 region that contains Dumfries and Galloway as well as Strathclyde.

This second tier in the spatial hierarchy which Eurostat has established to collect and publish statistical information is particularly important because NUTS 2 regions are the primary territorial units used in the assessment of areas requiring assistance through the Structural Funds. This spatial scale is therefore important in the European policy context, despite the fact that in the UK, most NUTS 2 regions

Population Migration in the European Union Edited by Philip Rees, John Stillwell, Andrew Convey and Marek Kupiszewski. © Editors and Contributors. Published 1996 John Wiley & Sons Ltd

Figure 16.1 NUTS 2 regions of the United Kingdom

have no administrative credibility or planning function other than that their boundaries are the aggregated boundaries of groups of metropolitan districts or shire counties. The exceptions to this generalization are found in North Yorkshire, Humberside, Cumbria, Lancashire, Cheshire, Lincolnshire, Essex and Kent, where the NUTS 2 region boundaries are consistent with the boundaries of these large shire counties.

In order to identify the patterns of migration that are associated with this system of spatial units, data from two particular sources are used in the chapter. Initially, data on the transfer of patients between doctors in different Family Health Service Authorities (FHSAs) in England and Wales and Area Health Boards (AHBs) in Scotland are used to present a description of annual aggregate migration trends between 1983 and 1992. The FHSA and AHB areas can be aggregated to be consistent with NUTS 2 regions. Thereafter, a comparison of aggregate migration data from the National Health Service Central Registers (NHSCRs) is made with data from the 1991 Census Special Migration Statistics (SMS) and the age and gender characteristics of migration at this spatial scale are investigated using migration data for 1990–1 from the latter source.

16.2 MIGRATION PATTERNS OVER THE 1983–92 PERIOD

16.2.1 NHSCR DATA

The major sources of information about the volume and pattern of population redistribution through internal migration in the UK in the years between population censuses are NHSCRs of National Health Service (NHS) patient reregistrations in England, Scotland and Northern Ireland. The reregistration data in these registers provides useful information on a quarterly basis about changing migration behaviour and has been used to conduct a detailed analysis of internal migration in the United Kingdom during the 1980s (Stillwell *et al.* 1992). Since the NHSCR is a register of individual moves that are made by each migrant, the measure of the migration count is different from that used to record migration in the 12-month period prior to the Census. Since Census 'transition-based' migration is a count of migrants rather than migrations, it is to be expected that, for any particular zonal flow, the NHSCR measure will exceed the Census count. However, this is not always the case because the composition of the two migration counts is different with respect to a number of population subgroups that are included in the aggregate data (infants, students, members of the armed forces, for example). The conceptual and compositional differences between the two data sets are spelt out in detail in Stillwell *et al.* (1992), together with a review of the advantages and shortcomings of the NHSCR data and a comparative analysis of NHSCR versus Census data for 1980–1. The latter suggests that while differences in the levels of migration measured by each source are considerable for certain population subgroups and spatial units, there is a strong association between the aggregate patterns (Boden *et al.*

1992). Certainly the NHSCR data is considered by the Census Office and the Department of the Environment to be of sufficient value to be used in the methodology for generating the net migration assumptions that feed into the main population projection model as summarized by Capron and Corner (1992).

NHSCR time-series data from the registers for England and Wales and Scotland have been assembled together with mid-year population estimates from 1983 to 1992. Data relating to the NUTS 2 regional system can be extracted from this integrated data base using a software package called TIMMIG (Duke-Williams and Rees 1993). This enables aggregate movement counts between NUTS 2 regions to be generated for 12-month periods between mid-1983 and mid-1992, a time series of nine years of data. This aggregate data is used in the following sections to undertake an analysis of year-on-year migration which provides an important context for understanding the more detailed age and gender characteristics which can be identified from the Census data for 1990–1.

16.2.2 INDICATORS OF MIGRATION

The empirical analysis of large migration data sets relies on the researcher selecting from a variety of migration indicators those measures which enable particular behavioural features to be clarified. In the following sections of the chapter, the NHSCR data is used to identify changes in the overall migration propensity, to describe the spatial patterns of net migration, to examine the in-migration and out-migration components that determine net migration balances and to consider particular features of the net zone-to-zone flows. In certain cases, absolute counts are used to emphasize the comparative sizes of the flows concerned; in other instances, flows are expressed as proportions of appropriate populations at risk of migration. Migration rates and time-series indices therefore provide standardized measures of migration that can be used for comparative analysis.

16.2.3 LEVEL OF MIGRATION

Data collected from the NHS registers and extracted through TIMMIG indicates that for the most recent period, mid-1991 to mid-1992, approximately 1.44 million people moved among the 35 NUTS 2 regions of the UK. This total includes students who registered with new doctors at their higher education institutions but excludes armed forces personnel and their dependents who moved between regions, those who might have moved on recruitment to or discharge from the armed forces and those who were committed to or released from prisons and psychiatric hospitals. Expressed as a percentage of the average population at risk during this 12-month period, the total represents a move by 25 in every 1000 persons. The total is some 148 000 or 11.4 per cent more than the previous year, but approximately 223 000 or 13.4 per cent less than in 1987–8 when the overall propensity to migrate was at its decadal peak. It is well known that migration levels generally declined following a peak in 1973 (Ogilvy 1979) to a low in the early 1980s (Stillwell *et al.*

1992). The time-series index of yearly migration between NUTS 2 regions, expressed as a percentage of the 1983–4 base figure (Figure 16.2), highlights the rise and fall of the migration level during the 1980s and suggests that the 1991 Census migration data will reflect migration behaviour at a time when the propensity to move over longer distances was at its lowest level for several years.

Explanations of these fluctuations are likely to be associated with complex changes in labour and housing markets in different parts of the country. In general terms, the nation experienced an economic upswing from the recession of the early 1980s which peaked in the late 1980s. Unemployment differentials had widened and house prices rose rapidly, particularly so in the South East. The migration rate was highest in 1987–8 but then fell rapidly as the boom burst, as unemployment differentials converged and as house price declines after 1988 meant that many people were no longer able to profit from their residential mobility.

16.2.4 NET MIGRATION PATTERNS

The redistribution of the population through migration between NUTS 2 regions during 1983–92 involved over 13 million moves and the net results of this inter-regional migration activity can be summarized by the computation of net migration balances for each region (Figure 16.3). In aggregate terms, the 12 NUTS 2 regions gained population through net migration and 23 regions lost population in this way; the net redistribution involved over one million moves and there were some major 'winners' and 'losers' among the region set. The most emphatic patterns evident from the NHSCR data are the losses sustained by all the major metropolitan regions and the gains recorded by virtually all other regions. In addition to the major metropolitan regions, only Cleveland–Durham, and Bedfordshire–Hertfordshire recorded net losses in England and Wales. In Scotland, Dumfries and Galloway–Strathclyde

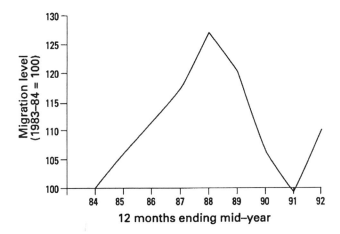

Figure 16.2 Migration level, time series index, 1983–96

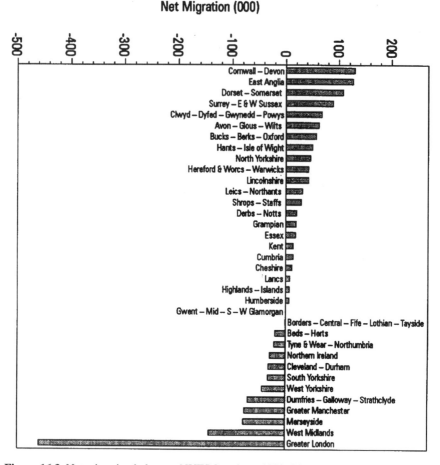

Figure 16.3 Net migration balances, NUTS 2 regions, 1983–92

and Borders–Central–Fife–Lothian–Tayside, the two NUTS 2 regions encompassing urban central Scotland, were both net losers. In addition, Northern Ireland lost nearly 30 000 net migrants during the period.

The role of Greater London is of fundamental importance in the operation of the national migration system. The capital region was responsible for generating 14.5 per cent of all out-migrants and for attracting 11 per cent of all in-migrants at the NUTS 2 region scale during 1983–92. In net terms, Greater London exported nearly 460 000 people during the period. This compares with net out-migration of 142 000 from the West Midlands, 78 000 from Merseyside and 76 000 from Greater Manchester. At the other end of the net migration spectrum, net gains of over 100 000 were experienced by Cornwall–Devon (130 000), East Anglia (127 000) and Dorset–Somerset (108 000).

An indication of the stability of yearly net migration balances during the period

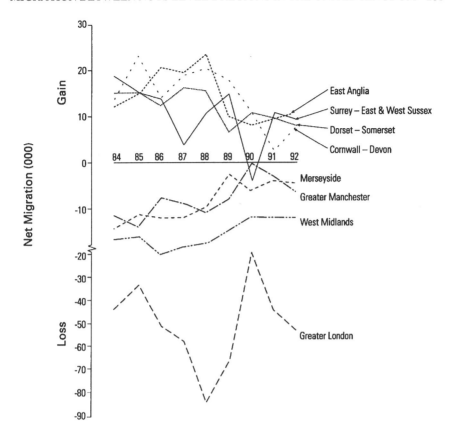

Figure 16.4 Net migration balances, main gaining and losing regions, 1983–92

is evident from Figure 16.4, where the time-series schedules of the four highest gainers and losers are graphed. Greater London has experienced considerable variation with net losses doubling between 1984–5 and 1987–8 and then falling from 85 000 in 1987–8 to 20 000 in 1988–9. These changes are mirrored by the net inmigration to Surrey–East and West Sussex whose net balance actually turned negative in 1987–8, when losses from Greater London were at their lowest. Losses from the West Midlands, Merseyside and Greater Manchester have tended to diminish over time, while gains by the largest gaining regions have also declined, representing a convergence in NUTS 2 regional net migration balances.

Although net migration flows are essential data for central government and local authority planning, the spatial comparison of migration is better undertaken using net migration rates which standardize for the effects of variations in population size among regions. The computation of net rates per thousand population for 1991–2 (Figure 16.5) confirms that Greater London (–7.9 per 1000), West Midlands (–4.9), Merseyside (–3.5) and Greater Manchester (–2.7) remain the prime losers, but

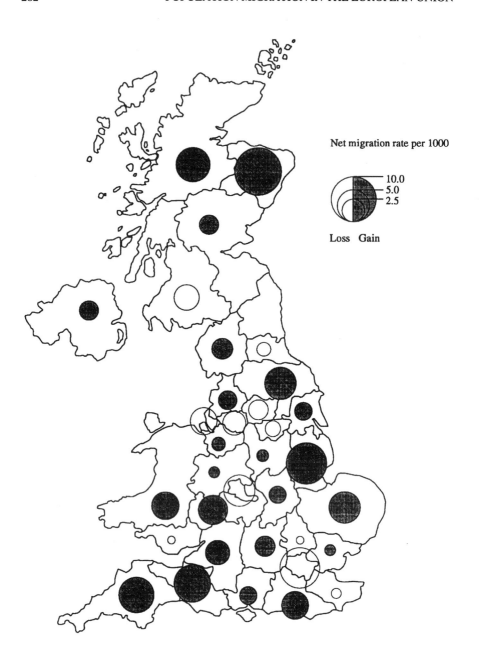

Figure 16.5 Net migration rates, NUTS 2 regions, 1991–2

Grampian (11.0) and Lincolnshire (8.1) record the highest rates of net migration gain. The rural regions of Dorset–Somerset (6.6) and Cornwall–Devon (5.9) both have high rates of net gain, and the Highlands and Islands of Scotland (5.8), together with North Yorkshire (5.0), are also important in this respect.

16.2.5 GROSS IN-MIGRATION AND OUT-MIGRATION

Net migration data is problematic in that, by definition, it conceals the volume of migration taking place into and out of a region. Consequently, a region like Northern Ireland which remains relatively isolated from the rest of the UK, records a net migration rate gain of 1.8 per thousand in 1991–2 as a function of the difference between low rates of gross out-movement (5.2 per thousand) (Figure 16.6) and in-movement (7 per thousand) (Figure 16.7), where the total migration in both directions is less than 20 000. On the other hand, Buckinghamshire–Berkshire–Oxfordshire recorded a rate of net gain of 2 per thousand as a result of the exchange of over 150 000; people left the region at the rate of 37.2 per thousand and entered at the rate of 39.2 per thousand.

In addition to Buckinghamshire–Berkshire–Oxfordshire, the highest rates of out-migration were evident North Yorkshire (34.7 per thousand), Bedford-shire–Hertfordshire (33.3) and Surrey–East and West Sussex (32.2), whereas the lowest rates, other than Northern Ireland, were recorded in Borders–Central–Fife–Lothian–Tayside (14.0), Tyne and Wear–Northumberland (18.7) and Gwent–Mid–South–West Glamorgan (16.2). In-migration rates were highest also in North Yorkshire (39.7), Buckinghamshire–Berkshire–Oxfordshire (39.2) and the Highlands–Islands of Scotland (36.9), and lowest for Gwent–Mid–South–West Glamorgan (16.0) and Merseyside (17.2). As identified in numerous previous studies of migration in the UK and elsewhere, there is a close positive association between the out-migration and in-migration rates for the NUTS 2 system of spatial units.

The relationship between a region's gross out-migration and in-migration can be captured by computing a migration coefficient, the ratio of in-migration to out-migration. This statistic provides a measure of the relative difference between the two flows concerned (Table 16.1); thus, a coefficient of 1.25 indicates that the in-migration flow is 25 per cent greater than the out-migration flow, while a coefficient of 0.75 shows that the in-migration flow is 25 per cent less than the out-migration flow.

The coefficients indicate that for Grampian, the in-migration flow is 47 per cent of the size of the out-migration flow and that there are nine regions where in-migration is over 15 per cent of out-migration. Of the regions recording net losses in 1991–2, Greater London's out-migration exceeds in-migration by over 25 per cent, while the ratio is also greater than 15 per cent in the West Midlands and Merseyside.

16.2.6 INTERREGIONAL NET MIGRATION

While the above indicators of net and gross migration provide valuable summaries

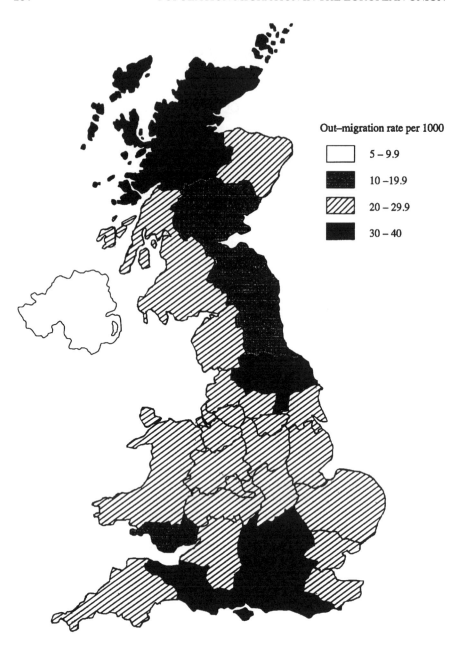

Figure 16.6 Out-migration rates, NUTS 2 regions, 1991–92

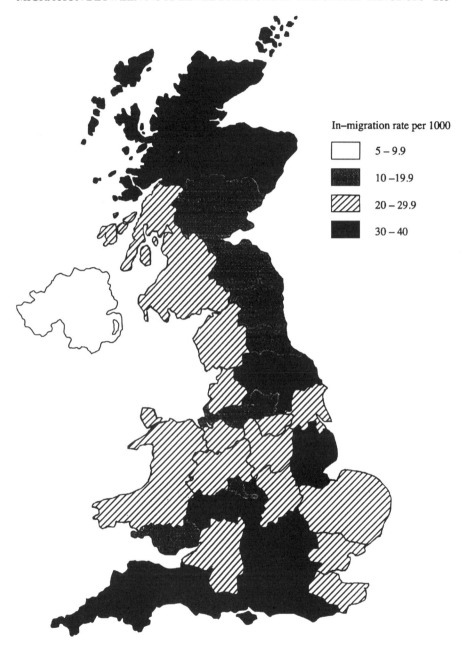

Figure 16.7 In-migration rates, NUTS 2 regions, 1991–2

Table 16.1 Migration coefficients, NUTS 2 regions, 1991–2

Region	Coefficient		Region
	>1	< 1	
Grampian	1.47		
Northern Ireland	1.36		
Lincolnshire	1.28		
		0.74	Greater London
Dorset–Somerset	1.22		
Cornwall–Devon	1.22		
East Anglia	1.21	0.79	West Midlands
Highlands and Islands	1.18		
		0.83	Merseyside
Hereford–Worcester–Warwickshire	1.15		
Clwyd–Dyfed–Gwynedd–Powys	1.15		
North Yorkshire	1.14		
Borders–Central–Fife–Lothian–Tayside	1.13	0.87	Greater Manchester
		0.88	Dumfries–Galloway–Strathclyde
Surrey–E&W Sussex	1.11		
Avon–Gloucestershire–Wiltshire	1.11		
Cumbria	1.09	0.91	West Yorkshire
Humberside	1.07		
Lancashire	1.07		
		0.94	South Yorkshire
Leicestershire–Northamptonshire	1.05	0.95	Cleveland–Durham
Hampshire–Isle of Wight	1.05		
Buckinghamshire–Berkshire–Oxfordshire	1.05		
Cheshire	1.03		
Derbyshire–Nottinghamshire	1.03		
Shropshire–Staffordshire	1.03		
Essex	1.02	0.98	Kent
		0.98	Gwent–Mid–South–West–Glamorgan
		0.99	Bedfordshire–Hertfordshire
Tyne & Wear–Northumberland	1.00		

Source: Unpublished NHSCR data

of migration 'stock' patterns for each region relative to others, they do not enable a full understanding of the directional 'flows' of migration taking place. In order to achieve a concise summary of where the important interregional exchanges have occurred, the net migration flows between the NUTS 2 regions between 1983 and 1992 exceeding 5000 reregistrations can be identified and 'primary' flows (over 25 000 moves) distinguished from 'secondary' flows (10 000–25 000 moves) and 'tertiary' flows (5000–10 000 moves). The pattern of large net movements (Figure 16.8) is dominated by the exodus of migrants to the regions of the south whose boundaries are contiguous with that of Greater London. The net flow from the capital to Surrey–East and West Sussex exceeded 130 000 moves during the nine-year period. Further short-distance deconcentration is evident in the south of England from Essex and Bedfordshire–Hertfordshire to East Anglia and from

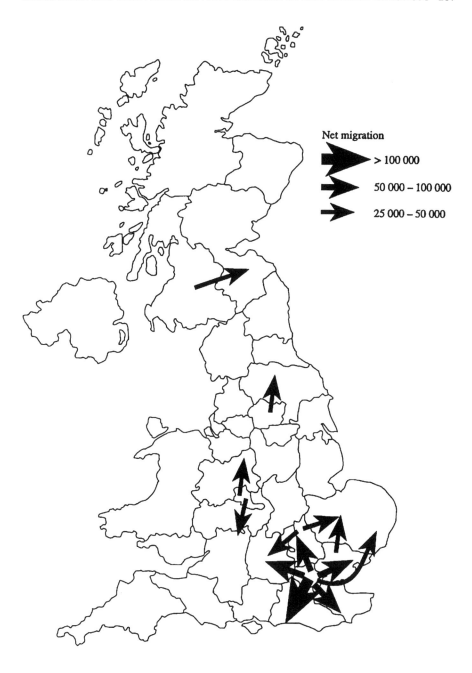

Figure 16.8 Primary interregional net migration flows, 1983–92

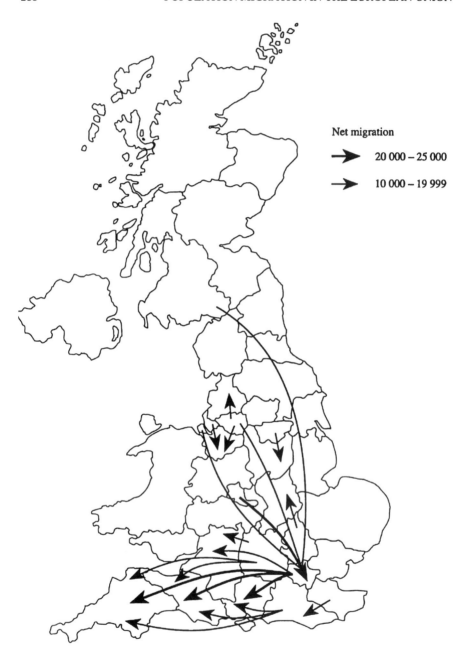

Figure 16.9 Secondary interregional net migration flows, 1983–92

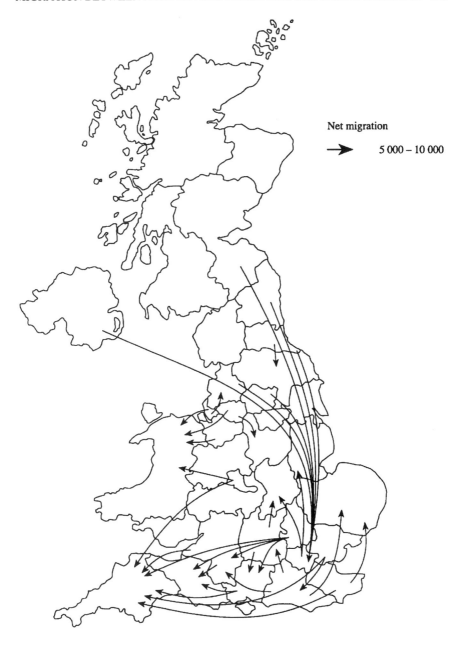

Figure 16.10 Tertiary interregional net migration flows, 1983–92

Bedfordshire–Hertfordshire to Berkshire–Buckinghamshire–Oxfordshire. In the rest of the country, the major net migration flows include those from the major metropolitan regions of the West Midlands and West Yorkshire. In the case of the West Midlands, large net losses occur to both Hereford and Worcester–Warwickshire and Shropshire–Staffordshire, whereas West Yorkshire loses primarily to North Yorkshire. In Scotland, the major net exchange is in an eastward direction from Dumfries and Galloway–Strathclyde to Borders–Central–Fife–Lothian–Tayside.

Certain interesting features of interregional migration in the UK emerge from the patterns of 'secondary' net movement (Figure 16.9). First, there is clear westward counterurbanization drift, involving flows from Greater London to Cornwall–Devon, Dorset–Somerset and Hampshire–Isle of Wight in particular but also from other regions of the South East. Second, longer-distance net migration flows into Greater London from several of the larger provincial metropolitan regions can be identified which illustrate the relative importance of interurban migration in the interregional system. There is further evidence from the patterns of tertiary net migration flows (Figure 16.10) that movements across the north–south divide are predominantly from the urban areas of the north, as well as from Northern Ireland. While the order of magnitude of the net exchanges decreases, the complexity of the flow pattern increases. However, the streams apparent in Figure 16.10 reinforce the trends of decentralization which are also evident in Figure 16.9 and illustrate the predominance of westward movement, not only from the South East to the South West, but also from the West Midlands to Wales and the South West and from regions of the North West into Wales.

16.3 A COMPARISON OF NHSCR AND CENSUS INTERACTION DATA FOR 1990–1

16.3.1 THE DIFFERENCES BETWEEN REGISTER AND CENSUS MIGRATION MEASURES

So far in the chapter, our analysis of the spatial patterns of migration between NUTS 2 regions in the United Kingdom has used data derived from an administrative register. The NHSCR provides quarterly and yearly migration data and is essential for measuring trends in migration. However, the spatial mask available is a limited one, and for finer spatial scales use must be made of migration data from censuses. UK Census Offices have asked a single-year retrospective question on migration (usual address one year ago) in the 1961, 1966, 1971, 1981 and 1991 Censuses. In the fourth section of the chapter migration data from the 1991 Census is used to provide an overview of how migration varies by age. Before embarking on the analysis, it is, however, useful to examine the relationship between migration flows measured using the data from the NHSCR and the 1991 Census respectively. Should we expect them to tell the same story, and do they?

Previous research (Devis and Mills 1986; Boden *et al.* 1992) has established that the two data sources differ in the concept used and the target populations covered. As indicated in section 16.2.1, the NHS data count 'events'; that is, instantaneous 'jumps' from one spatial location to another. Individuals can make more than one jump in a year and these are counted. The retrospective census question, however, measures 'transitions'; that is, differences between the current spatial location and the location at the prior time (one year ago). Individuals can make only one transition per time interval. Other things being equal we would expect the NHS data to record more migration events than the census records migrants making transitions. However, this may not always be the case because of the different population coverage in the two sources. The NHSCR covers the whole civilian population but not the military, while both are included in the Census. Entries and exits to the armed forces are included in the NHS migration counts but not by both origin and destination. No migrations by persons remaining in the armed forces are counted. The NHSCR covers two categories of migrant—those who die in the time interval and those born in the time interval—which are excluded from the census counts.

Finally, students are treated differently in the two sources. Students are recorded at their place of term-time residence in the NHSCR if they have changed the medical practitioner with whom they are registered. Many higher-education institutions require students to reregister with the NHS so that the institution-linked health service can be funded, but institutions that do not provide such a service leave it up to the individual student. Censuses record students at their parental home as usual residence, change in which is the basis for identifying migrants. The 1991 Census, however, did ask for students' term-time address and provides information on usual and term-time address. Stillwell *et al.* (1993, Table 6) showed that when net student in-migration was added to migrant counts, this could produce dramatic increases in migration in the ages 15–19 and 20–4 to areas with large higher-education institutions and losses to the areas without. For example, the in-migration rate per 1000 population for Oxfordshire for 1990–1 was 71 for the 15–19 age groups and 95 for the 20–4 age group using NHS data but 243 and 273 respectively if the Census in-migrant count is supplemented by net student inflow. This is a topic worthy of much further detailed investigation, utilizing a special table published by the Census Offices that cross-classifies students by parental and term-time locations at district scale. It is of particular interest because students are counted at their term-time residence in official population estimates of district populations in the UK.

16.3.2 A COMPARISON OF NUTS 2 INTERACTION MATRICES

Because of the problems of assessing the differences in level of migration reported in NHS and Census migration tables, we concentrate here on the degree of similarity of pattern. In previous analyses comparisons were made between total inflows, outflows and net flows at different spatial scales (standard regions, metropolitan/non-metropolitan regions and Family Practitioner Areas). Here we examine similarity at the more detailed scale or origin–destination flows for NUTS 2 regions.

Both NHS and Census migration data can be aggregated to NUTS 2 regions, but a small number of flows must be excluded from the analysis. Intraregion flows have a different meaning in the two data sets and are set to zero in the analyses. Flows to Northern Ireland are not available in the Census migration tables, and therefore we exclude all flows to and from that province. The comparison is therefore based on 34 of the 35 NUTS 2 regions, yielding a total of 1156 flows of which 34 intra-regional flows play no part, being set to zero in both data sets.

Table 16.2 sets out the correlation coefficients between the 1156 origin–destination flows based on NHS and Census data respectively, for five-year age groups and the two sexes. The correlations are high but not perfect. They are higher than those reported in Stillwell *et al.* (1993) for inflows to 95 Family Health Service Authorities. This is probably a result of using a coarser spatial scale in this analysis.

Table 16.2 Correlations between NHS migrations and Census migrants for flows between NUTS 2 regions by age and gender, 1990–1

Age groups	Persons	Males	Females
0–4 (1–4)	.9372	.9358	.9334
5–9	.9137	.9091	.9111
10–14	.8987	.8810	.8989
15–19	.8638	.8235	.8729
20–4	.9462	.9358	.9488
25–9	.9478	.9369	.9535
30–4	.9523	.9477	.9526
35–9	.9516	.9482	.9505
40–4	.9583	.9537	.9562
45–9	.9583	.9537	.9522
50–4	.9567	.9517	.9490
55–9	.9594	.9529	.9555
60–4	.9710	.9642	.9705
65–9	.9753	.9742	.9671
70–4	.9696	.9571	.9662
75–9	.9622	.9502	.9589
80–4	.9715	.9427	.9704
85+	.9695	.9431	.9667
Total (N=1156)	.9517	.9501	.9524

Notes: 1. The first age group in the NHS data refers to ages 0–4, while the Census data refers to ages 1–4 only.
2. NHS data re-counted in period-ages, while Census data are in period cohorts (one-year time, five-year age intervals).   3. 1156 interactions (34 regions × 34 regions) are involved but 34 of these (intra-regional flows) are set to zero

Source: Computed from NHS movement counts for quarters 2, 3, 4, 1990 plus quarter 1, 1991 and the migrant counts from the 1991 Census, Special Migration Statistics. All data are Crown Copyright. The Census data are from the ESRC/JISC Purchase.

The pattern of correlation across the sexes and ages can be interpreted as follows: male coefficients are lower at most ages than female because of greater registration lags in the NHS and more undercounting in the 1991 Census. Coefficients for age groups beyond age 40 are above the average of 0.95, while below age 25 they are all below this figure. This reflects the different treatment of students and boarding-school pupils in the two statistical systems and the greater difficulties of producing a complete and accurate record for these groups, particularly between ages 10 and 19.

In Table 16.3 are reported more detailed statistics about the relationships between the two migration measures. The first column gives the crude ratio of NHS count to Census count. Overall the former is 23 per cent higher than the latter—in 1980–1 the comparable figure was 24.5 per cent (Boden *et al.* 1992, Table 2.3). The highest ratio is for age group 15–19 (as in 1980–1), the age group at which students leave home and when the maximum discrepancy between the populations covered in the two data sets occurs. Ratios are below average from ages 25 to 45 but then rise above the mean to age 65, after which they follow the average level. The next

Table 16.3 Ratios and regression parameters for NHS migration flows versus Census migrant flows for NUTS 2 regions, by age, 1990–1

| Age Group | Persons | | | Male | Female |
	Ratio NHS/ Census	Regression Constant	Slope	Slope	Slope
0–4	1.29	6	1.11	1.11	1.11
5–9	1.23	5	1.09	1.10	1.06
10–14	1.32	−1	1.37	1.40	1.30
15–19	1.78	21	1.26	1.08	1.37
20–4	1.30	37	1.02	0.86	1.15
25–9	1.20	22	1.02	0.94	1.11
30–4	1.18	9	1.04	1.01	1.07
35–9	1.17	4	1.07	1.05	1.08
40–4	1.16	2	1.06	1.01	1.11
45–9	1.26	2	1.09	1.07	1.09
50–4	1.39	1	1.19	1.16	1.21
55–9	1.39	2	1.18	1.20	1.15
60–4	1.32	1	1.14	1.13	1.14
65–9	1.23	0	1.18	1.19	1.15
70–4	1.26	0	1.23	1.21	1.23
75–9	1.22	0	1.24	1.28	1.20
80–4	1.22	0	1.35	1.30	1.35
85+	1.25	0	1.41	1.50	1.37
Total	1.23	111	1.09	1.03	1.15

Source: as Table 16.2

two columns in Table 16.3 set out the parameters of regression equations linking NHS migration (the dependent variable) to Census migration (the independent variable). To predict an origin–destination movement flow from a census migrant count for the age group 20–4, for example, one needs to multiply the census count by 1.02 and add 37 moves. For 85-year-olds it is necessary just to multiply by 1.41. Slope parameters vary by age in roughly the same way as the crude ratios, though they are mostly lower. On average female slopes and ratios are higher than those for men. This probably indicates that males are even more underrepresented in the NHS migration data than they are in the Census data.

To conclude, our comparison of the two sources of migration data suggests that they give very closely comparable pictures of migration but do differ sufficiently to warrant use of both sources to give a more comprehensive view of UK migration. Neither, however, provides the whole 'truth' and, in particularly, a more detailed analysis of student migration is needed.

16.4 THE AGE AND SPATIAL CHARACTERISTICS OF MIGRATION IN 1990–1

In this section of the chapter we examine the way in which migration varies by age for the two sexes and at different spatial scales, drawing in particular on the fine age classifications which census data provides.

16.4.1 NATIONAL AGE PROFILES OF MIGRATION

Figures 16.11 and 16.12 plot the migration rates for the two sexes and at different spatial scales for Great Britain. The migration rates have been calculated by dividing the number of migrants in a single-year age group by the 1991 Census population of Great Britain at that age, which, although not the ideal population at risk, is the only available one The top curve in Figure 16.12 shows the migration rate for all residents in Great Britain who reported a different address one year before the Census (on 21 April 1990). These include migrants from outside Great Britain, as well as those with origin not stated. The next curve shows the migration profile for residents moving within Great Britain. The bottom three curves plot the migration rates between areas of steadily rising spatial extent: between the 459 districts of Great Britain, between the 66 county/Scottish region units and between the 11 regions (nine in England with Wales and Scotland).

The variation of migration rates for all ages (between 1 and 90 and over) at different spatial scales recorded in the 1991 Census is set out in Table 16.4. Nearly 10 per cent of the Great Britain population reported a change of address from 21 April 1990. Some 88 per cent of migrants originate within the country (GB) from known origins, with 6 per cent coming from outside Great Britain and 6 per cent failing to state their origins. Just over half of migrants (54 per cent) move locally within districts with just

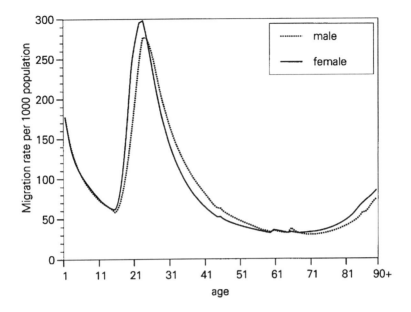

Figure 16.11 Migration rates for migrants resident in Britain by gender, 1990–1

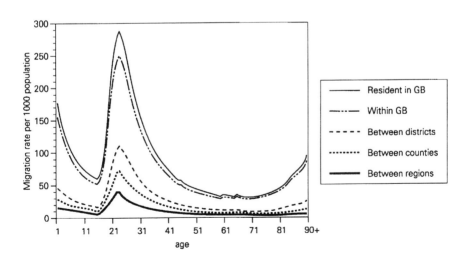

Figure 16.12 Migration rates by age for a variety of spatial scales, Great Britain, 1990–1

over a third moving between districts (459 units). Of these two-thirds move between counties/Scottish regions (66 units) while one-third move between regions.

The age profiles displayed in Figures 16.11 and 16.12 show the familiar features of migration rate schedules, distinguished by Rogers and Castro (1981):

1. *a childhood slope*, in which migration steadily declines from age 1 to age 15;
2. *a labour force peak*, starting with a rapid rise from age 16 to a peak at age 32 followed by steady falls to age 59;
3. *small retirement peaks* at age 60 and 65 (corresponding to official retirement ages for women and men respectively);
4. *a retirement slope* starting at age 68 and continuing until age 90 and over; and
5. *a constant component* across all ages at a level of roughly 30 per 1000 for migrants resident in Great Britain.

These components are associated with significant events during the life course. The childhood slope is closely associated with the declining slope of the labour-force curve, showing the link between children and their migrating parents. The gap between the two slopes is about 28 years, corresponding to the mean age of mothers at birth of their children. The rising slope of the labour-force curve represents the migration of persons into their first non-parental homes (in part associated with a migration to higher education for students recording their term-time address as their usual residence). The peak is associated with rapid changes of status and jobs at the start of adult careers. The retirement peaks are a familiar feature of migration

Table 16.4 Migration rates at different spatial scales, 1991 Census, Great Britain

Migration type	Migration rate per 1000 population		Per cent of total migrants
Resident in Great Britain	98.8		100.0
Within Great Britain	86.6		87.6
Between regions		11.6	11.8
Between counties		21.7	21.9
Between districts		33.6	34.0
Within districts		53.0	53.6
From outside Great Britain	6.2		6.3
From Northern Ireland		0.2	0.2
From outside UK		6.0	6.1
From origin not stated	6.0		6.1

Notes: 1. The migration rates are computed by dividing the number of migrants by the 1991 Census population aged one or over.
   2. The correspondence between the spatial units used in the 1991 Census migration tables and the Eurostat NUTS system is as follows: regions correspond with the NUTS 1 level counties/Scottish regions with NUTS 3 level and districts with NUTS 4 level.

Source: OPCS (1994). 1991 Census Migration Tables (Crown Copyright)

schedules but in the 1991 Census schedule the peaks are relatively minor features, compared with the retirement slope. Less attention has been paid to the retirement slope in previous work because data are normally reported for five-year age groups and often truncated well before age 90.

The migration curves for men and women shown in Figure 16.11 are very similar but the small differences reflect different timings of key life course events. At the childhood ages there is no difference between males and females. Females then begin the rise to the labour-force peak earlier than men, starting at age 16. The peak ages for women are 22 and 23, while those for men are 23 and 24. The gap between the curves widens after the early adult years reflecting the age gap between men and women forming married or cohabiting unions. The small retirement peaks occur, as noted above, at ages around respective official retirement ages. We can anticipate some changes by 2001 in the timing of the female peak as women's retirement age has recently been moved up to 65 for those aged less than 50 in 1994. Overall the differences between the gender curves make little difference to overall measures. The average male migration rate is 100.7 per thousand, while the female rate is 97.1; on the other hand, summing the migration-rates average yields a gross migraproduction rate of 7.7 for males and 7.8 for females.

The migration curves in Figure 16.12 are very similar in shape and timing. However, are there more subtle relationships between the level of migration at different ages and the spatial scale of migration? To discover these relationships it is necessary to look at rates for migrations within districts, between districts within counties, between counties within regions and between regions. The average distance of migration steadily increases from the first category to the last. It is also necessary to standardize each migration schedule by dividing each rate by the total of all age-specific migration rates (the gross migraproduction rate or GMR), and to express the standardized rate at each scale as a percentage of the total standardized migration rate in the corresponding age group. Formally, we define

$$r_k(a) = 100 \; [m_k(a)/\Sigma_a m_k(a))/(m_g(a)/\Sigma_a m_g(a)]$$

where $r_k(a)$ is the ratio of the standardized scale migration rate to the Great Britain standardized rate for age a, $m_k(a)$ is the scale k migration rate for age a. These ratios for each spatial scale fluctuate around a national norm of 100 and are plotted in Figure 16.13. The age profile for all migrants resident in Great Britain would be a straight line across the graph at value 100. The four spatial scales display quite distinctive variations around this line.

Within district migration (incorporating the shortest distance migrations) exhibits above-average migration in the childhood ages up to age 17 when there is a sharp dip to age 23. The ratio then remains below 100 through the labour-force ages to age 55, though a steady rise begins from age 50. The ratio is well above average in the older ages (67 and older). *Between region* migration (incorporating the largest distance migrations) shows an opposite pattern of below-average migration at the youngest ages with highest migrations in the early twenties.

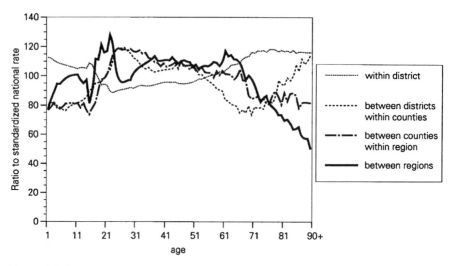

Figure 16.13 A comparison of migration rates for a variety of spatial scales with the national standard, Great Britain, 1990–1

After below-average migration for ages 25 to 29, migration ratios are above average until after the retirement ages, with a minor peak between ages 60 to 66. After age 70 there is a steep fall in the ratio. The elderly do not take as much part in long-distance migration as other age groups. *Between district within county* migration is below average in the childhood ages but then climbs to a local peak around age 27 and stays above average until age 53. The migration ratio is then below average in the retirement ages until the very oldest age. Finally *between county within region* migration has a similar profile to between region migration with above rates in the labour-force years but below average in the childhood and postretirement ages. To summarize, in the young adult, the middle adult and retirement ages, longer-distance migrations are emphasized while at childhood and elderly ages, shorter-distance migrations are more important.

16.4.2 NET MIGRATION PATTERNS BY AGE, 1990–1

In the earlier sections of the chapter we examined in detail the spatial pattern of migration flows between NUTS 2 regions over the 1983–92 period. There are, however, major departures from the average all-age pattern between one age group and the next (Stillwell 1994). Past research (Boden 1989; Rees *et al.* 1989) has suggested that significant differences exist between the pattern of origins and destinations at different ages. The context of the earlier work was a desire to test whether the age groupings for age–destination interactions in the migration model used in the official subnational population projection model could be justified or needed revision. The method used was to group detailed five-year age groups into large clusters using inter-FHSA migration.

Here we use a similar technique to aid description of the patterns of migration by age. The Special Migration Statistics (Table M03) provide flow data between NUTS 2 regions for two sexes and 19 ages. Could these 38 age/sex groups be reasonably clustered into a smaller number that described most of the variation? The shares across destinations and origins were used as the clustering variables. Four clustering analyses (using the default options in the SPSS Cluster procedure) were carried out for males and females, destinations and origins. The five-cluster solution in each case provided a reasonable grouping in each of the four analyses. While the clusters were not exactly the same, the following age groups always formed cluster cores which are clearly associated with life course stages:

1. ages 1–15 and 30–54: the family ages;
2. ages 16–19: the ages of leaving home;
3. ages 20–4: the ages when work careers start;
4. ages 60–9: the ages of retirement; and
5. ages 75–85 plus: the elderly ages (of widowhood and declining health).

The missing ages (25–9, 55–9 and 70–4) joined different clusters depending on whether males or females or origins or destinations were examined. For example, male migrants aged 55–9 were placed in the family cluster when both destination and origin pattern were considered, while 55–9-year-old female migrants joined the retirement age cluster.

Here, in order to examine net migrant patterns, the male–destination clustering is adopted as follows:

1. the family ages: 1–15 and 30–59;
2. the leaving home ages: 16–19;
3. the starting career ages: 20–9;
4. the retirement ages: 60–74;
5. the elderly ages: 75 plus.

Each of these age clusters had a distinct pattern across destinations and origins.

Using this age clustering Table 16.5 organizes the net migration flows for NUTS 2 regions reported in the 1991 Census. To provide some structure to the set of NUTS 2 regions they have been grouped into 'metropolitan' and 'non-metropolitan' categories and divided into 'northern' and 'southern', matching earlier analyses (Stillwell et al. 1992). The story is a familiar one for all age migration (the furthest right column of Table 16.5) already tracked in our NHS migration analyses of metropolitan losses and non-metropolitan gains, and of smaller northern losses and southern gains in aggregate. The dominant pattern is loss of migrants from the largest metropolitan areas and gains in other regions in all sections of the country. Particular heavy losses are experienced by Greater London of twice the magnitude of the other metropolitan areas in total. Note that at NUTS 2 level some non-metropolitan regions (Cleveland–Durham–Gwent–Mid–South–West Glamorgan; Kent)

Table 16.5 Net migration flows by broad age group, 1991 Census

Region	Family 1–15, 30–59	Leaver 16–19	Joiner 20–9	Retirer 60–74	Elderly 75+	Total 1+
SOUTHERN	−2992	3728	12 649	−29	613	13 969
Metropolitan	−40 303	2158	−512	−8037	−3811	−50 505
Greater London	−40 303	2158	−512	−8037	−3811	−50 505
Non-metropolitan	37 311	1570	13 161	8008	4424	64 474
East Anglia	6779	442	1919	1991	522	11 653
Surrey, E & W Sussex	5702	493	1604	730	420	8949
Avon, Gloucs, Wilts	4319	584	2218	420	211	7752
Dorset, Somerset	4610	184	549	1519	331	7193
Cornwall, Devon	5680	210	−699	1413	354	6958
Hereford & Worcs, Warwick	3941	−383	1453	593	440	6044
Hants, Isle of Wight	1852	1154	751	669	339	4765
Lincolnshire	2394	−76	435	1026	263	4042
Berks, Bucks & Oxon	1558	218	1951	−399	403	3731
Derby, Notts	1142	−221	701	33	201	1856
Essex	−525	−187	814	460	283	845
Leics, Northants	1136	−97	−624	101	150	666
Beds, Herts	−1147	−240	2038	−710	201	142
Kent	−130	−511	51	162	306	−122
NORTHERN	7012	−2884	−7528	220	−531	−3711
Metropolitan	−12 450	−1360	−8782	−2975	−2022	−27 589
Tyne & Wear, Northumb	654	128	−704	106	−120	64
S Yorkshire	−672	−173	−1034	−105	−37	−2121
Dumfries & Gall, Strathclyde	−1392	−207	−794	−112	−190	−2695
W. Yorkshire	−1724	−158	−1085	−482	−248	−3697
Merseyside	−1713	−451	−1412	−374	−293	−4243
G. Manchester	−2869	−335	−573	−825	−347	−4949
W. Midlands	−4734	−164	−3180	−1183	−687	−9948
Non−metropolitan	19 462	−1524	1254	3195	1491	23 878
Grampian	2270	278	1065	175	76	3864
N. Yorkshire	2372	524	168	346	239	3649
Borders, Tayside	2815	−233	249	395	206	3432
Clwyd, Powys	2977	−325	−266	834	194	3414
Shrops, Staffs	1735	−249	385	312	311	2494
Cheshire	1688	−194	528	93	143	2258
Highlands & Islands	1410	−151	521	316	98	2194
Cumbria	875	−70	173	210	70	1258
Humberside	1327	−192	−197	212	80	1230
Lancashire	1025	−219	−168	47	21	706
Cleveland, Durham	316	−478	−258	79	49	−292
Gwent, Mid, S, W Glamorgan	652	−215	−946	176	4	−329
Northern Ireland	−4020	−844	−5121	−191	−82	−10 258

Note: 1.The migrant flows include inflows from Northern Ireland but not outflows to Northern Ireland which were not captured in the Great Britain Special Migration Statistics. There is a small bias upwards in the net migration gains to GB regions. The Northern Ireland figures record just the outflows from Northern Ireland.

Source: 1991 Census Special Migration Statistics. Crown Copyright. ESRC/JISC Purchase

also experience net outflows, while one metropolitan region (Tyne and Wear–Northumberland) just achieves a positive balance.

This aggregate pattern is repeated for the *family ages* except that two other regions close to London (Essex and Bedfordshire–Hertfordshire) experience net losses. The *leaving home* age group, 16–19, shows a markedly different pattern from the aggregate. Greater London experiences positive inflows for this age group while a majority of non-metropolitan regions record net migrant losses, and the other metropolitan regions record smaller net losses. The interpretation of this pattern is straightforward: it represents the channelling of a widely dispersed population of students (beginning higher or further education at ages 17, 18 and 19) to a more concentrated set of destinations containing the principal educational institutions. For example, the Lincolnshire region loses 76 migrants at this age even though it is one of the most attractive areas for in-migrants. No major higher education institution is located in Lincolnshire. The *starting career* ages show some of the directional features of the previous age group, with only a small loss of migrants from Greater London and continued losses among some metropolitan regions. The *retirement ages* show a return to the sharp division between metropolitan and non-metropolitan regions and more selectivity with respect to destinations than at other ages. The *elderly age* numbers of net migrants reflect the increase in migration towards the end of life and the sharpest match of net gains and losses with the metropolitan/non-metropolitan classification. At and after retirement migrants are freer to choose destinations than when constrained by job opportunities, and they clearly opt for the pleasanter environments and lower-population density of non-metropolitan regions.

A clear idea of directional preferences in migration can be gained by using the in-migration/out-migration ratios employed earlier in our analysis of NHS migration in 1991–2. Table 16.6 sets out these ratios for the broad age groups and region types. The southern metropolitan profile (ie Greater London) shows dramatic swings from one age cluster to the next, and particularly low migration ratios after retirement. The non-metropolitan regions have ratios well above one (eg 2.48 in East Anglia) indicating their attraction to older migrants.

16.4.3 THE SPATIAL PATTERN OF NET MIGRATION

The overall gains and losses of migrants for a region are made up of complex fields of net in-migration and out-migration flows. Only one region, Grampian, has a field consisting only of net gains. Space precludes presentation of the large number of in-, out- and net migration fields that are present in the NUTS 2 migration system, but it is useful to attempt a summary of their key features. All three types of migration exhibit rapid distance decay. The largest net gains and losses (as well as inflows and outflows) are to nearby, usually contiguous, regions. The only exceptions are the large long-distance migration streams from Greater London to southern non-metropolitan regions outside the south-east.

Based on analysis of the 34 Great Britain net migration fields, we propose a sevenfold classification of regions in terms of the extent and spatial structure of those fields. The classification is mapped in Figure 16.14 and summary statistics are provided in Table 16.7, including the net migration rate and account of the number of gaining and losing net migrant streams within Great Britain. The regions within each grouping are placed in ascending order of the net migration rate, which ranges from a loss of 7.6 per thousand for Greater London to a gain of 8.0 per thousand for the Highlands and Islands.

Table 16.6 Migration coefficients for broad ages and macroregions, 1991 Census

| Macroregion | Broad age group | | | | |
	1–15, 30–59	16–19	20–9	60–74	75+
Southern	0.99	1.11	1.05	1.00	1.04
Metropolitan	0.43	1.46	0.99	0.19	0.26
Non-metropolitan	1.17	1.05	1.07	1.37	1.37
Northern	1.04	0.89	0.95	1.01	0.95
Metropolitan	0.85	0.88	0.88	0.65	0.62
Non-metropolitan	1.21	0.90	1.02	1.38	1.31

16.4.3.1 Large metropolitan regions

Each of these regions loses migrants to two-thirds or more of the NUTS 2 regions of Great Britain. Merseyside gains only from Essex and the West Midlands only from Merseyside and Essex. The other northern metropolitan regions largely gain from other metropolitan regions (eg Greater London) and from Essex and Kent. Only Dumfries and Galloway–Strathclyde departs from this pattern, attracting small surpluses from such areas as East Anglia or Dorset–Somerset, probably to the more attractive rural areas in the region rather than to the central Clydeside conurbation.

16.4.3.2 Older urban-industrial regions

Four of the NUTS 2 regions can be characterized as containing smaller cities and towns with long industrial histories. A majority of the net migrant exchanges of these regions are negative (Table 16.5), but more of them are positive than in group A. These regions gain from some of the group A regions and also from regions in the South East (group C) but lose to the other groups of regions. Their overall net migration rates are close to zero.

16.4.3.3 South-East regions

These regions form a concentric ring around Greater London and experience very

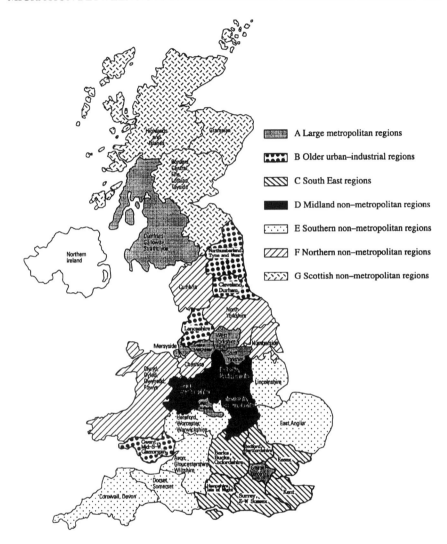

A Large metropolitan regions

B Older urban–industrial regions

C South East regions

D Midland non–metropolitan regions

E Southern non–metropolitan regions

F Northern non–metropolitan regions

G Scottish non–metropolitan regions

Figure 16.14 Interaction pattern groupings, 1991 Census

large net inflows from the capital, from some of the large metropolitan regions and older urban-industrial regions and from some of the other South East regions. Berkshire–Buckinghamshire–Oxfordshire gains from the other South East regions, for example, but then experiences net losses to most non-metropolitan regions in other parts of the country, and the number of losing exchanges exceeds the number of gaining. Within the remainder of the South East there is a distinction between the eastern and western regions. Essex, Kent and Bedfordshire–Hertfordshire experience a majority of net outflows, balanced only by the net gains from Greater

Table 16.7 A grouping of NUTS 2 regions by interaction pattern, 1990–1

Grouping		Net migration Rate (/1000 pop)	Net flows Gains	Losses
A	Large Metropolitan regions			
	Greater London	–7.56	3	30
	West Midlands	–3.90	2	31
	Merseyside	–3.02	1	32
	Greater Manchester	–1.98	6	27
	West Yorkshire	–1.84	7	26
	South Yorkshire	–1.68	9	24
	Dumfries & Galloway, Strathclyde	–1.12	11	22
B	Older Urban–Industrial Regions			
	Cleveland, Durham	–0.26	14	19
	Gwent, Mid-, South-, West-Glamorgan	–0.19	12	21
	Tyne & Wear, Northumberland	0.05	14	19
	Lancashire	0.51	9	24
C	South-east Regions			
	Kent	–0.08	4	29
	Bedfordshire, Hertfordshire	0.09	10	23
	Essex	0.55	3	30
	Berkshire, Buckinghamshire, Oxford	1.95	14	19
	Hampshire, Isle of Wight	2.86	15	18
	Surrey, East-West Sussex	3.71	13	20
D	Midland Non-metropolitan Regions			
	Leicestershire, Northamptonshire	0.46	16	17
	Derbyshire, Nottinghamshire	0.97	19	14
	Shropshire, Staffordshire	1.73	15	18
E	Southern Non-metropolitan Regions			
	Avon, Gloucester, Wiltshire	3.83	23	10
	Cornwall, Devon	4.71	26	8
	Hereford & Worcester, Warwickshire	5.21	22	11
	East Anglia	5.75	27	6
	Dorset, Somerset	6.51	23	10
	Lincolnshire	6.91	29	4
F	Northern Non-metropolitan Regions			
	Humberside	1.43	20	13
	Cheshire	2.36	21	12
	Cumbria	2.60	21	12
	Clwyd, Dyfed, Gwynedd, Powys	3.09	19	14
	North Yorkshire	5.20	27	6
G	Scottish Non-metropolitan Regions			
	Borders, Central, Fife, Lothian, Tayside	1.88	23	10
	Grampian	7.67	33	0
	Highlands & Islands	7.96	30	3

Source: 1991 Census Special Migration Statistics. Crown Copyright. ESRC/JISC Purchase

London. The three western NUTS 2 regions experience bigger gains from Greater London and smaller losses to regions beyond. What these migration patterns reflect is the dynamic development of the rest of the South East through continued suburbanization of both employment and residence, but the concentration of the most successful development to the west of London.

16.4.3.4 Midlands non-metropolitan regions

This cluster of regions contains a number of smaller cities (Leicester, Northampton, Derby, Nottingham, Stoke, Telford) and associated towns containing a wide spectrum of industrial and service industries. These regions gain most from the West Midlands metropolitan conurbation but also from the other metropolitan regions, the older urban-industrial regions and most of the South East. They experience about the same number of inflows as outflows and occupy a truly intermediate position in the country's migration system.

16.4.3.5 Southern non-metropolitan regions

This grouping contains the NUTS 2 regions in England which showed themselves to be most attractive to migrants in the year before the 1991 Census. Note that Hereford and Worcester has been included in this grouping despite its location in the West Midlands standard region.

Each of these regions has net in-migration rates of 3.8 per 1000 or above, ratios of in-migration to out-migration of 1.18 or above and two-thirds of their interactions involving migrant gains. As we have seen earlier these gains come predominantly from the Greater London and West Midlands metropolitan regions (Figures 16.8 to 16.10) but also from the South East regions, the older urban-industrial regions and other large metropolitan regions. The migrant streams involve all the life course stages (Table 16.5), but the retirement and elderly ages contribute 21 per cent to total net gains. The lack of opportunities for young people in some of these regions mean that losses are experienced at the leaver ages (16–19) in Hereford and Worcester–Warwickshire, for example, and in Cornwall–Devon in the joiner ages (20–9). These regions have proved attractive for new enterprise moving out of the more crowded South East and to a lesser extent to long-distance commuters to London, as a result of the improvement of rail links (eg the east coast main line electrification which has made it possible to commute from southern Lincolnshire towns to central London).

16.4.3.6 Northern non-metropolitan regions

These regions serve as the most important destinations of outflows from the large metropolitan regions in northern England and from the older urban-industrial regions. They experience net in-migration, and migration ratios are above one though the rates are lower than for their southern cousins. In-migration results again from a mixture of better employment growth than the metropolitan areas, of the growth of commuting and of migration at retirement. North Yorkshire, for example, plays an important role in nurturing new companies, in providing homes for people who work in the Leeds–Bradford conurbation and on providing attractive urban (Harrogate, Ripon, Northallerton), rural (the Dales, the North York Moors) and coastal (Scarborough–Bridlington) environments for retirees. North Wales plays a similar role for Merseyside, Greater Manchester and the West Midlands. Improved road communications (such as the A55 North Wales coastal route or York southern bypass) make these linkages possible.

16.4.3.7 Scottish non-metropolitan regions

These regions play roles in Scotland analogous to their England counterparts, attracting migrants from central Clydeside and other west central Scotland towns and cities. The two northern most regions, however, play a wider role, attracting migrants from the whole of the UK. Only three of the 66 migrant streams between the Grampian and Highlands and Islands regions and other NUTS 2 regions show a net outflow, and one of these is a loss from Highlands and Islands to Grampian region. Jones (1992) demonstrates for the 1980s the importance of place-specific oil-related developments in creating these flows. Workers from West Central Scotland and other English regions have moved to provide the labour for the North Sea oil industry, both in construction and in servicing activities. Aberdeen in the Grampian region and the Shetlands Isles in the Highlands and Island regions are the centres of oil industry activity. Retirement migration (Table 16.5) contributes only 11 per cent to the gains in these two regions and extended daily commuting is not an important generator of net in-migrants.

16.5 CONCLUSIONS

This chapter has described the principal features characterizing the migration flows among the important policy-related NUTS level 2 regions used by the European Commission in the allocation of regional development funds. The time focus has been twofold: the nine years from mid-1983 to mid-1992 for which a time series of movement data is available and the individual years 1990–1 and 1991–2, the latest for which Census data and Register data were available respectively.

The principal points to emerge from this analysis are as follows. Some are reaffirmations of earlier findings and some offer fresh insight.

1. The migration system is still dominated by flows to and from Greater London. Internal migration continues to empty the UK's capital of population, leaving room for its replacement through immigration.

2. The South East as a whole has taken on some of these London characteristics. The regions within the south-east continue to gain massively from the capital but are themselves losing migrants to non-metropolitan regions further out.

3. Non-metropolitan regions throughout the UK gain through internal migration, in large measure from the metropolitan regions. Although this has been a longstanding pattern (though probably more subdued in the early 1990s than in the previous decade), it still governs the UK migration system. What is perhaps surprising is the long-distance attraction exerted by the two northern Scottish regions which gain migrants from virtually everywhere in the UK. Scotland has continued to experience the net internal migration gain that first appeared in 1989 which was then regarded as simply an end feature of the late 1980s' economic upturn and something that was unlikely to persist in the harsher economic conditions which have occurred in the 1990s.

4. Stages in the life course have long been regarded as influential in determining migration intensities and in explaining the complex variation of migration by age. It has also been observed that the general age profile can vary considerably with region of origin and destination and with origin–destination pair. What is perhaps new is the realization that this reflects different patterns of destination selection at the various life course stages and that at least five of these patterns need to be recognized: family/labour-force origination (ages 1–15, 30–59) leaving home migration (ages 16–19), starting a career migration (20–9), retirement migration (60–74) and elderly migration (75 and over).

5. The most dramatically different of these patterns is that associated with the 16–19 age group when individuals leave home to form new households and increasingly to enter higher education. The participation of this age group in education rather than work has increased dramatically over the past 15 years. Neither of the data sources used in this study adequately capture the migration behaviour of this group, but if we are to develop a capability for projecting migration into the future by means other than simply assuming constancy in migration rates, then further research using new data sources (1991 Census Small Area Statistics Table 100 and the statistics of the Universities and Colleges Admission System) must be carried out.

Part 3

IMPACTS OF MIGRATION ON POPULATION DEVELOPMENT

17 Migration and Policy in the European Union

ANDREW CONVEY and MAREK KUPISZEWSKI

17.1 INTRODUCTION

There is an ineluctable relationship between the existence of migration movements and the resulting policies which are adopted by the authorities of the area concerned towards encouraging these movements, or, more commonly, towards attempting to control or to reduce them. A number of the chapters in this book underline the importance of this situation by referring to the policy context of their study of a particular feature of migration in the European area. This chapter aims to bring together the wide variety of policy issues and responses which may be observed in Europe at the present time and in the recent past and to make an assessment of the extent to which these policies may influence migration movements at present and into the near future.

The most important milestone of policy in recent time has been the Treaty of Maastricht. The fully ratified Treaty on European Union, with associated protocols (to give the actual name of the Treaty of Maastricht), finally came into force on 1 November 1993 and with it a range of agreed provisions which will affect migration behaviour and migration policy in the European area for some time to come. The Treaty opens by stating categorically that, '*every person holding the nationality of a member state shall be a citizen of the Union*', and that among the rights and privileges which this incurs is the right that every such citizen is free to move and reside freely within the territory of the member states, with the Council of the European Union empowered to take the necessary steps to allow this to happen (European Commission 1992a). In many ways, the Maastricht arrangements build upon the provisions allowing for free movement of labour which formed part of the original Treaty of Rome in 1957. This apparently clear situation has, however, been rendered rather more complex by the existence of the apparently somewhat parallel *Schengen* open frontier agreements, which have been entered into at various stages since 1985 by all the original 12 member states other than Denmark, Ireland and the United Kingdom (*Le Monde* 1993). The Schengen Accords finally came into being formally on 26 March 1995 for seven of the 15 EU member states (Belgium, France, Germany, Luxemburg, the Netherlands, Portugal and Spain), even though Germany, the Benelux countries and Spain had been ready to implement Schengen

Population Migration in the European Union Edited by Philip Rees, John Stillwell, Andrew Convey and Marek Kupiszewski. © Editors and Contributors. Published 1996 John Wiley & Sons Ltd.

in full on 1 February 1994. France had also intended to do so on that date but was delayed subject to final internal agreement on the effect of Schengen on the French constitution. Italy, Portugal and Greece, having previously assented to the Schengen Accord, had agreed that they would fully implement Schengen as soon as certain technical difficulties had been resolved. However, problems connected with the final commissioning of the Schengen Information System (SIS)—the main police intelligence network to accompany the Accords—led to considerable delays to this target date. Belgium and the Netherlands had their SIS links in place and France was close to linking up. Germany and the other Schengen countries were not ready, leading to the final delayed implementation in March 1995 (*Le Monde* 1993 and Cane 1994). Certain of the mechanisms by which 'free movement of persons' will operate remain to be worked out in detail, taking account, for example, of the fact that a large proportion of migrants moving within the European area are not formal citizens of the EU and are therefore normally subject to different rules.

The situation was further seriously complicated on 29 June 1995, when France announced that it had decided to maintain its frontier controls with its Schengen neighbours for the present, quoting difficulties in controlling illegal immigration and the movement of drugs, especially at its Benelux borders. This was followed, on 8 July, with an agreement between France and Spain to reinforce their common border, on this occasion quoting terrorist activity in the Basque provinces. However, the other six Schengen states have decided to continue and in addition, the newer EU member states, Austria, Sweden and Finland are negotiating to join. Even Norway and Iceland, not member states of the EU, have opened talks about joining Schengen, in order to allow them to maintain their 40-year old passport union within the Nordic group of countries.

In accordance with the Maastricht Treaty's concept of *subsidiarity*, the field of immigration from non-member states, together with the associated fields of justice and home affairs, remains what is known as an *inter-governmental pillar* of the Treaty, that is to say, the business of individual sovereign member governments working together, although the European Commission is to be associated with decision making and has some limited powers of initiative. The Commission has recently exercised these powers of initiative in producing a major Communication on the question of immigration and asylum (Commission of the European Communities 1994). In the area of immigration, joint positions and joint action may be taken by the Council of Ministers, which can decide that certain measures may be adopted by a qualified majority, though only member states themselves will have powers of initiative in criminal matters. Immigration has effectively been singled out for a 'twin-track' approach, with the Council of Ministers having to decide by a unanimous vote on any proposal coming from the Commission concerning which third countries' citizens will require a visa for entry to the EU area, though qualified majority voting might apply after 1 January 1996. On the other hand, those areas identified as being of 'common interest' to all member governments include the rules about crossing the Union's external borders and the conditions of movement and residence for immigrants. The Single European Act states that:

governments agree to co-operate, without prejudice to the powers of the Community, in particular as regards the entry, movement and residence of nationals of third countries, [and that] nothing in the provisions (of the Single European Act) shall affect the right of member states to take such measures as they consider necessary for the purpose of controlling immigration from third countries, and to combat crime, traffic in drugs and illicit trading in works of art and antiques (European Communities 1989).

The question arises, of course, about how much of this proposed co-operation among member states should actually take place. It may be argued that there should be a growth in the willingness of states to co-operate, given the trans-frontier nature of the act of migrating. On the other hand, the concept of subsidiarity in this field implies that it must be proven in what way and to what degree a given migration situation will have an effect on the EU as a whole, thereby allowing for joint action. It will not be difficult for a member state which is so inclined to argue that a given migration problem is something which affects itself primarily and therefore to take, or seek to take, direct action. Examples of this kind of action are to be seen in the British refusal to join in the Schengen Accord, citing the maximization of a 'unique island situation' as a reason, or the French delay in ratifying Schengen, quoting difficulties in relation to the French constitution; although the French National Assembly had enthusiastically endorsed French adherence to the Schengen Accord in 1989, the question of the relationship which the Accord should have to the French constitution had not been fully resolved, mainly over the question of rights of asylum. Spanish immigration rules clearly distinguish between entry from other member states of the EU and entry from elsewhere, especially from North Africa (BOE 1992; Davidson 1993). On the other hand, a combined effort, such as the development of the Union-wide system of police information exchange (the so-called Europol), is a case where member states clearly feel it is worth working together as a whole (European Commission 1992a).

There may seem to be some degree of anomaly over an apparent overlap between the rules for movement agreed under the Maastricht Treaty and those under the Schengen Accord, as both are seeking to increase the freedom of movement between member states (Carvel 1992a). Schengen probably has its origins in the Fontainebleau Council of the European Communities in June 1984, which adopted the principle of abolishing police and customs formalities at the interior frontiers of the Community area. At the same time, the Single European Act of 1986, in Article 8A, also establishes: *'an area without internal frontiers in which the free movement of goods, persons, services and capital is ensured'*.

There are, therefore, two fairly parallel policy initiatives aimed at increasing the freedom of movement between member states which might seem unnecessary. However, it is probably true to say that the advent of Schengen lay in the need felt by the original five signatories to press on with all possible speed towards the freeing of frontiers, a mood which was then reflected in the decisions agreed for the Single European Act. On the other hand, if both routes towards the same goal are implemented to the letter, a formally illegal internal EU boundary will arise, one which separates Denmark, Ireland and the United Kingdom from the rest. While the

Schengen countries clearly have no intention of stopping inward movements from the other three members of the Union, they are committed to border controls which emulate those being retained by the other three. There also remain many anomalies and variations in the ways in which individual states are putting these rules into practice. For example, the Belgian *Euroinfo* (no.173, March 1993) reported under 'Libre circulation, oui mais...!' that for the Brussels–London return air journey, it was in Brussels airport that the strict controls were to be found, while in London the controls were described as non-existent, perhaps the opposite of what might be expected under Schengen! Such situations may therefore become, in due course, a matter for the European Court to disentangle.

So far as policy towards the question of migration is concerned therefore, it is possible to see two main parallel trends. Policy towards internal EU migration is becoming increasingly liberal in line with the provisions of the Maastricht and Schengen arrangements, though it is important to point out that the question of non-EU citizens moving between member states has not yet been fully resolved, and it has been estimated that these movers number at least eight million (Brochmann 1992). At the same time, policy towards non-EU citizens crossing the external boundaries of the Union becomes increasingly controlled, fuelled perhaps by the increasing severity of certain national policies towards immigrants which in turn may be being pushed by the recent rising levels of xenophobia, if not by extreme nationalism.

17.2 CATEGORIES OF INTERNATIONAL MIGRANTS

It is possible to devise various categories of international migrants. The problem is wider than that. It is impossible to exclude short-term travellers from our considerations, as they are also subject to any migration policies of the country of destination, even if these only request transit visas. After admission, they can try to extend their residence legally or alternatively to overstay and join the group of clandestine migrants. This issue will become even more important as the pressure on national boundaries builds up. Consequently, in this chapter we will classify travellers according to their intended length of stay in the country concerned.

From the temporary point of view, it is possible to distinguish short-term visitors, and mid- and long-term migrants. There are no internationally agreed time thresholds for each of the above categories, but it would seem to make sense to divide them according to the type of visas and permits required. The first category, the short-term visitors, are usually admitted to the receiving country based on either a tourist visa or on a business or scientific visa. These visas are normally valid over a period of several months. A current validity of between three and six months is typical, but the convention implementing the Schengen Agreement (19 July 1990) states that short-term visits should not exceed three months (Schütte 1991). In many cases, based on reciprocal agreements, visas (but usually not restrictions on the length of stay) may be abolished for this category of travellers. Typically, transit passengers, holiday makers, short-time business travellers, researchers, representatives of cultural life and so on fall into this category. They are usually not allowed either to take employment or to open a business in the receiving country.

Mid-term migrants usually intend to stay in the receiving country for more than a few months. Typically they intend to work or study and will require not only visas but also the relevant permits (ie residence and work permits). They are subject to additional restrictions such as registration with the police or administrative authorities and the subsequent reporting of any change of circumstances such as a change of address, passport or marital status. It is not unusual for a migrant belonging to this category to seek to regularize his or her status in the receiving country and to apply for a permanent residence permit and eventually for citizenship, thereby becoming a life migrant. Finally, there is the category of migrants requesting permission to stay for an indefinite period of time—frequently for life. Basically, it is impossible to claim the right of life stay unless a person seeks asylum or is a citizen of a receiving country or can claim the right to obtain citizenship.

17.3 MIGRATION POLICIES

Shifting from one category of migrants to another, or simply joining directly one of the above categories requires an authorization from the receiving countries. In fact, the right to admit or not to admit migrants on to the territory of a given state is considered to be one of the main features of state sovereignty and therefore is a very sensitive issue. From the point of view of international migration policy, each state controls a number of 'gates' which regulate the process of inflow and of settlement of foreigners and which protect against the inflow of unauthorized aliens. These 'gates' are as follows:

1. entry visa requirements,
2. border external controls,
3. long-term work and residence permits,
4. internal controls,
5. permanent residence permits and regularization systems, and
6. naturalization (granting citizenship).

States can to a large extent control the circulation of foreigners by opening or closing some of these gates. Migration policies differ according to the origin of the migrants. Within the EU, three categories of aliens are recognized: (1.) citizens of other EU countries, (2.) citizens of the remaining EFTA countries (these two categories together form a category of citizens of the European Economic Area), and (3.) citizens of third countries. Each category has a different and unequal legal position when passing through the 'gates'.

17.3.1 ENTRY VISA REQUIREMENTS

Citizens of EU member states need no visas to enter another EU country. Citizens of EFTA and most OECD countries enjoy the same privileged position. However, there are a number of non-EU countries' citizens who need to apply for visas even for transit. They need to be able to justify their reason for travel, and they are normally supposed to present appropriate documents, such as a bank statement which proves that they are in possession of a required amount of money per day for their intended stay, and references obtained from the country of destination, insurance policies, return tickets and the like. Costa-Lascoux has shown comparative tables of the conditions one needs to meet in order to enter, obtain asylum, reunite a family, get a temporary stay permit, regularize illegal stay/work and obtain citizenship in France, Italy, the Netherlands and Germany (Table 17.1). She noted that, except in Italy, conditions for the issue of visas varied very much, depending upon the country of origin of the applicant (Costa-Lascoux 1990). It is quite common that, apart from the official restrictions, consular services are able to call upon a whole range of unofficial deterring methods, ranging from abrupt or even rude staff, or only accepting a limited number of applications daily (eg the Italian Embassy in London will accept no more than 100 per day, and none by post (Italian Embassy 1993)), up to the use of very long and protracted procedures. In some cases a high visa fee is collected before the application is even considered, and the fee is then not refundable in the case of refusal. This was, for example, the practice of the UK Embassy in Warsaw before the need for visas between the UK and Poland was finally abolished. In many cases, visa fees are set at a level which is reasonable in the country of destination but is excessive in comparison to the average income of the country of origin. However, the fee level is in many cases based on reciprocal arrangements and may not be a part of migration policy. Citizens of certain countries are subject to detailed scrutiny: for example, the Italian Embassy in London declares that it issues tourist visas on the same day, but citizens of Afghanistan, Albania, Bulgaria, Cambodia, China, Chad, Cuba, Iran, Iraq, Jordan, Libya, Mongolia, Nigeria, Romania, Syria, Sri Lanka, USSR (sic), Vietnam, and Yemen are advised that they should apply well in advance (Italian Embassy 1993). Another element of the policy of closed doors for selected nationals is to impose fines on the carrier which brings in a passenger without valid travel documents. The UK, for example, charges £2000 and France up to FF10000 (SOPEMI 1992). The cross-Channel Hoverspeed Company has had to pay out a total of £484 000 in fines since 1987 when such a regulation was introduced. This practice is intended to make it difficult for asylum seekers to arrive to the country of destination. In fact, it actually abuses the Convention on Asylum of 1951, as it transfers the decision of whether a person will have the chance to apply for asylum to the clerks of a commercial carrier company. The convention which will implement the Schengen Accord specifies that commercial carriers are obliged to check the validity of travel documents of aliens, and in the case of a subsequent refusal to admit an alien to a 'Schengen' country, it is the commercial carrier's responsibility to take him/her back (Schütte 1991).

Within the EU, admission policies differ from one member country to another. For example, all EU countries require visas from citizens of all states of the CIS, Romania and Bulgaria, but citizens of Visehrad countries are much less restricted: Polish subjects, who are the most limited in their freedom to travel, need visas only when travelling to the peripheries of the EU—Portugal, Greece and Ireland. The arrangements are under close scrutiny of the governments involved and change very rapidly.

There is, however, a recognition of the need to develop a common visa policy. At the moment, one of the most important results of these deliberations is a list of countries whose citizens will need visas in order to enter any of the EU member states (SOPEMI 1992). It is an important measure as it is intended to prevent 'shopping' for visas from the most 'liberal' country of the 12. At the same time, to some extent it may of course protect the most liberal countries against an excessive inflow of aliens. The *Conclusions from the Meeting of the Ministers Responsible for Immigration* (Council of the European Communities 1992b) mention that negotiations on common visa policy remain well under way. It is easy to agree the idea of a common list of countries whose citizens will be allowed into EU without visas. Reaching an agreement on the contents of the list will not be as simple. The United Kingdom, for example, wishes to grant visa-free access for short visits to the citizens of Commonwealth countries (Owen 1994), a policy which is fiercely opposed by other EU member countries. France will also have to loosen her traditional links with Maghreb countries.

A rapid reduction in the number of countries whose citizens were required to apply for visas in order to be admitted to EU countries occurred in 1990 and 1991, mainly because of the abolition of visa requirements for Central Europeans. From 1992, however, more restrictions have been introduced, partly because some of the arrangements with Romania and Bulgaria were cancelled and partly because new restrictions have been placed upon citizens of selected Third World countries.

It should be noted that governments of West European countries were reluctant to open borders for citizens of Central European countries and the former USSR. The fear was that such an opening might result in an overflow in Western Europe of unwanted aliens from the East. This policy was in sharp contrast with the Western democracies' criticism of the policies of 'closed doors' implemented by communist governments until 1989 and had to be abolished rather quickly. Consequently, 1990 and 1991 witnessed the reluctant opening of Western Europe, in particular for Czechoslovaks and Hungarians. Poland, despite its leading role in the process of dismantling communism, was treated with more hesitation, both due to the size of its population and to sizeable legal and illegal emigration in previous decades. Citizens of the Commonwealth of Independent States could not and still cannot travel without visas, and their applications are subject to detailed scrutiny. Lifting restrictions on the admission, without visas, of citizens of Central European countries to Western European countries and vice versa was in most cases accompanied by bilateral agreements on readmission of those who were abusing the system. Two or three years ago, these agreements were deemed to be necessary security measures.

They are also important for the future as precedents and extremely useful experiences in the negotiation of the membership of Central European states into the EU.

A much more consistent policy has been elaborated by the Schengen 'group' of countries. They agree that all EU citizens will not be considered to be aliens. They will therefore enjoy a freedom of movement restricted solely by EU legislation. The members of the group had difficulty in establishing a full list of third (non-EU) countries whose citizens do not need to apply for visas. The negotiations may be less difficult than in the case of parallel negotiations run by the EU as the number of members of the Schengen group is smaller, and the United Kingdom, proud of her 'opt-out' and particularly restrictive migration policies, is not a part of the Schengen process. It should be noted that, in the case of persons from countries whose citizens require a visa in order to be admitted on to the territory of one Schengen state, agreement has been reached to issue a visa which will then be valid in all Schengen member countries. This is a very realistic solution and is similar to the one adopted by the Benelux countries a long time ago. Such a visa would be valid for a period of up to three months, and would allow the alien concerned to circulate freely within each of the Schengen states (Schütte 1991).

The problem of aliens residing in one of the signatory countries based on a residence permit has been resolved in a similar way. These are allowed to circulate freely within other Schengen countries, provided that the total length of their residence does not exceed three months. They also have to report their presence to relevant authorities within three days of arrival (Schütte 1991).

There is little doubt that the Schengen 'group' is setting standards for European migration policy. It is likely it will be followed by the other EU member countries, despite the fact that diverse economic and historical links, in particular former colonial ties, make the establishment of common policy quite difficult for some of these countries to accept.

17.3.2 EXTERNAL BORDER CONTROL

In 1960, the Benelux countries abolished border controls at their national boundaries. It then took more than 30 years to extend this practice into other countries. Preparations began some decades ago and the first formal documents were signed in 1985. The countries concerned then proceeded further in two streams—within the Schengen Group and within the EU.

The negotiation of the Schengen Accord has been conducted without the participation of non-governmental or international organizations, and this has been widely criticized (Wierzbicki 1991). The original agreement did not entirely abolish the border check but relaxed it. It also had set the long-term target of abolishing the control altogether by 1990. This deadline was, of course, not met. However, the negotiations continued and a Convention Implementing the Schengen Agreement was eventually signed (as described earlier).

The abolition of border checks clearly reduces the control of states over their territory and puts criminals of various categories in a more favourable situation. The

Convention adopted a number of measures to avoid uncontrolled illegal migration, the international trade in arms or drugs trafficking, and at the same time to improve communication, the flow of information, judicial co-operation and to introduce more efficient transborder policing. One of these measures is the creation of the Schengen Information System (SIS), an on-line data base holding information on persons and goods wanted for one reason or another by the police of member countries. This data base also holds a blacklist of all those who are not welcome on the territory of the Schengen countries. This development is particularly worrying because it will mean that all aliens, as foreigners, will not be protected by local laws on privacy of data; they will be unable to check the contents of information stored in the computers and will therefore be unable to request correction of this information if it is incorrect. The EU is going to create a similar system, the so-called European Information System, which will hold some 800 000–1 000 000 entries on unwanted foreigners (Carvel 1992b).

In July 1991, the former European Community (EC) prepared a Convention on the Crossing of EC External Borders which sought to regulate a number of technical and organizational matters but which also stipulated the creation of EC visas. The signing of the Convention was suspended due to a British refusal to do away with intra-EC immigration controls. The British argued that the geographical situation of their country made it possible to control the inflow of foreigners in a very efficient way. They also argued that there is no identity card system in the United Kingdom and that therefore internal policing is more difficult than in countries where such systems exist. This *impasse* was removed eventually by allowing the UK to maintain its immigration controls (Hopkinson 1991). It is probably more important to note that the EU has now reached agreement on a list of 61 countries, nationals of which will be required to possess visas in order to travel to any of the member countries (Hopkinson 1991).

Recent practice in the EU countries has tended towards a tightening of border checks. SOPEMI (1992) reports that 66 000 foreigners had been refused admission visas to France and that another 11 500 had been turned back at the frontiers. The large number of migrants who cross the French borders illegally now face arrest and deportation. The most spectacular example of this type of policy has been provided by Italy, which turned back some 17 000 Albanians who had arrived in southern Italy in August 1991. Only some 200 who needed immediate hospitalization were actually admitted (SOPEMI 1992). It is worth noting, however, that soon after the deportation of the Albanians, the Italian authorities launched an aid programme worth £27.4 million (Hopkinson 1991), in order to support the crumbling Albanian economy. This combination of a tough approach towards immigrants while providing economic assistance has proved to be successful, at least from an Italian point of view.

The EU, and Western Europe in general, faces a growing number of illegal immigrants who are trying to cross their borders, usually with the mirage of lucrative employment in mind. It seems at the moment that there are two main borders under siege: the Spanish Mediterranean coast, with a new generation of boat people coming from Africa, and the eastern border of Western Europe, with Romanians, Bulgarians and citizens of the former USSR trying to get into Germany and Austria especially (Markiewicz 1992a). In order to give an idea of the volume of these migrations, it is relevant to acknowledge that at present, some 300 000 illegal African immigrants are estimated to be working in Spain (Davidson 1993). Reliable estimates of the inflow into Western Europe from the East are not yet available.

17.3.3 LONG-TERM RESIDENCE PERMITS

Citizens of the EU do not need work permits to get a job in another member state. The freedom to move within the Union means that they may settle and take paid employment anywhere within the member states. However, there are some limitations. Initially, this freedom has been given only in relation to those who were taking employment, but no other category other than employees has so far been mentioned (EEC Treaty, Art. 48). EC legislation extended this right to the employees' families (Callovi 1992) and to those who reached retirement age in a country different from their own. They are allowed to stay in the country in which they have been recently employed. The next step was to allow students, retired persons and others who were not taking up any gainful activity to move freely within EC (Niessen 1992). The right to refuse admission was restricted only to cases where public policy, security or health was threatened in the receiving country. The introduction of common EU citizenship, when and if it comes into effect, will presumably remove these limitations and will open up the last 'gate', the granting of citizenship, thereby removing from EU member countries an important part of their sovereignty. Citizens of EFTA countries also enjoy preferential treatment.

Meanwhile, citizens of third countries are left behind more or less closed (or in some cases slammed) 'gates'. These citizens are usually required to apply for entry visas; they have relatively slimmer chances of getting employment and have many more difficulties in regularizing their stay and eventually of naturalization. As a result, a third-country national residing in a EU member country has neither the right to resettle in another member country, nor even the right to travel freely within the Union (Niessen 1992). The abolition of internal boundaries will make the implementation of the limitations to freedom of travelling rather more difficult to impose, and during the Maastricht Summit Conference a proposal was put forward to change this legislation and to allow third party nationals residing temporarily within one of the country of the Union to travel freely (but not settle or take employment) within the whole of the Union (Niessen 1992). This would be in line with the Schengen Agreement (discussed in 17.3.2).

Association agreements made between the EC and other countries usually varied in the way they made concessions regarding the freedom of movement of people. In this respect, agreements signed in the past with Turkey, Yugoslavia (suspended since 1991), Algeria, Morocco and Tunisia mentioned that there would be no discrimination with regard to employment, social security and social benefits for workers from the countries mentioned above (Niessen 1992; Callovi 1992). These agreements were more liberal than those signed more recently with the Czech Republic, Slovakia, Hungary and Poland, where no provision for protection or non-discrimination of workers has been agreed at all (Niessen 1992). A similar solution has been adopted in recently signed agreements with Romania and Bulgaria. None of these agreements allows for the freedom of movement of people, and all the more specific regulations have been left for bilateral negotiations to resolve.

Temporary work and residence permits (Table 17.1) are normally issued for a specific period of time, in the first instance usually for one year, with the possibility of renewal, (France, Germany, the Netherlands, Italy). The main condition for obtaining a residence permit is stable employment (in Italy at least 24 hours per week). As the length of residence increases, the assurances given to a migrant tend to grow. For example, France offers privileged residence permits for 10 years for those who have legally spent three years in France or for spouses and families of French citizens. Special arrangements have been made for Algerian citizens. In Germany, after five years of uninterrupted residence, an alien may apply for an unlimited residence permit. After another three years (eight altogether), one may acquire the assured residence permit, on the condition that he/she has satisfactory command of German, has adequate housing, sends children to school and adheres to German laws. In the Netherlands, unlimited residence permits may be issued to those who have been there for at least five years, who have had regular employment over this period and who have the prospect of employment for at least one year with a salary at least equal to the minimum salary for a 23-year old and who have adequate housing conditions. In all cases, the protection of national labour markets is the focus of the implementation of such policies, and with the growing number of migrants, the protracted recession and mounting political pressure, these policies may easily become much more restrictive.

17.3.4 INTERNAL CONTROLS

Probably the most important role of internal controls is to protect the internal labour market against the illegal employment of a foreign labour-force. Various countries operate their own policies and little or no international co-operation may be expected in this field. In Germany, in political turmoil because of the increasing influence of the extreme right (going as far as, in one case, to request the reintroduction of concentration camps), (Cook Report 1993), a stringent system has been introduced which requires all workers to possess a social security identification card, to be produced on request by the appropriate authorities, as well as in Social Security Offices. Employers hiring foreign labour have to report this to social security officials. These measures are supported by extensive policing, sometimes accompanied by violation of international agreements and basic civil rights (Markiewicz 1992b).

It is usual that employers hiring illegal foreign labour are subject to forms of liability. In the Netherlands, employers have to cover the cost of any expulsions; in France they have to return all taxes and fees as well as paying fines. If such employers are unable to cover their liabilities, they may even face forfeiture of their

Table 17.1 Conditions for the issuing of work permits and residence permits for non-EU citizens residing in selected EU member states

Member state	Initial conditions and period for which work permit or residence permit is issued	Conditions for the extension of the work permit or residence permit	Conditions for the issuing of permanent work permit or residence permit
France	Initially for one year. Offer of employment confirmed by the Office of Immigration or proof of own resources required.	Extension granted annually.	Work permit valid for 10 years may be issued after three years of residence.
Italy	At the discretion of local authorities (offer of employment of at least 24 hours per week required).	Extension granted annually.	
Germany	Residence and work permits valid for one year.	After the first year, extension of the residence permit granted twice for two years. Extension of work permit possible for two years.	After five years, unlimited residence permit. After eight years of residence, 'special status' on condition of economic self-support, knowledge of German language, children sent to schools, adequate housing and observation of German legislation. Work permit either for five years or unlimited for those who have acquired 'special status'.
Netherlands	Initially for one year.	Extension granted annually.	Unlimited residence permit after five years for those in regular employment, with prospects for further employment for at least another year, with salary at the minimum level for a 23-year old and adequate housing.
United Kingdom	At the discretion of Department of Employment on the condition that the applicant has been offered an employment.	Extension granted at the discretion of Department of Employment on the expiry of previous work permit.	Permanent residence and work permits after four years of uninterrupted employment.

Source: Costa-Lascoux (1990); information from authorities of countries concerned.

assets (Hopkinson 1991). It is quite characteristic that legislation tightening control in these fields has mainly been passed in these countries relatively recently, in 1991 and 1992.

Clearly, these forms of legislation affect not only illegal workers and clandestine migrants but also small companies predominantly in services (tourist industry, catering, restaurants) and in the construction industry, where it is important to keep costs low by saving on wages and social security payments.

In many countries, the police arrest and deport illegal migrants; for example, the UK expelled 4300 migrants in 1992, of whom more than half were illegal. However, the problem of what to do with illegal immigrants frequently remains unresolved. Large-scale deportations are expensive and are often criticized, as has happened with the forced deportation of illegal Romanian migrants from Germany.

17.3.5 PERMANENT RESIDENCE PERMITS AND REGULARIZATION SYSTEMS

There are a number of ways in which one may acquire a permanent residence permit. The first is that a migrant applies on the grounds of prolonged residence and employment. For example, the UK requires from permanent residence permit applicants four years of uninterrupted, legal residence and employment in the country. After a permit is granted, it may still be withdrawn if during the period granted, a migrant stays outside the UK for more than two years. One of the most important streams of permanent migrants is made up of those who reunite with member(s) of their families who are already lawfully residing in the receiving country. In all EU member countries, spouses and juvenile children are admitted, 'juvenile' normally being defined as less than 18 years old, though in Germany it is 16. France, exceptionally, also accepts parents, grandparents and other members of the family.

Despite all these efforts, EU countries still house large numbers of illegal migrants. The actual numbers are not fully known, but the recent legalization programme in Spain processed 133 000 requests for regularization (SOPEMI 1992). Policies aimed at the legalization of clandestine migrants are extremely varied. Some countries, such as Germany or the Netherlands, stand firmly on the position that abusers of the law do not deserve any mercy and they do not allow for regularization of aliens unless they are on German or Dutch territory legally. Other countries, in particular those in the south of Europe, have chosen to allow undocumented migrants to regularize their situation. Programmes of this type were introduced in 1981 in France, in 1985 and 1991 in Spain, in 1987 in Italy and in 1992 in Portugal (OECD 1990; Salt 1991; SOPEMI 1992). In four programmes in these areas, almost 400 000 people have been granted residence permits and work permits (OECD 1990; SOPEMI 1992). Typical of the requirements is that which regularizes the position of an alien who arrived in a country before a specified date and who is able to earn his living either as an employed or self-employed person. Beneficiaries of these programmes have frequently been in a receiving country for a long period of time and are therefore, to some degree, integrated with the 'native' population. There is little doubt that these programmes have helped them a great deal in the integration process and with the stabilization of their professional and family lives.

17.3.6 NATURALIZATION (GRANTING OF CITIZENSHIP)

There are three basic ways of acquiring the citizenship of a country. Citizenship by *jus soli*, meaning that the place of birth determines the citizenship. This criterion is in use in Spain, the Netherlands, Luxemburg and Greece. Some countries (Germany, Denmark, Ireland, Portugal) grant citizenship by *jus sanguinis*, which means that the citizenship of the parents determines the citizenship of a child. In other cases (the UK, France, Italy, Belgium), a mixture of both approaches is often used to determine the nationality of a newly born child.

From the point of view of migration policy, the most important factor is the acquisition of citizenship by naturalization. Taking the citizenship of a host country is a final stage, at least from a legal point of view, of the migration process. In fact, the person who obtains new citizenship is no longer a migrant. Evidently, there remains a large difference between *de jure* and *de facto* integration. Consequently, all countries prefer to have their new citizens as integrated as possible into local communities. This is why, among the most common requirements, there is a long period of residence in the receiving country. The required period of residence differs among the countries of the EU—from five years (France, Ireland, Italy, the Netherlands, the UK) up to 10 years (Belgium, Germany, Luxemburg, Spain). This period is usually reduced when an applicant is the spouse of a citizen of the country where the application is lodged and in certain other cases (Costa–Lascoux 1990). Other conditions are, in the case of France and the UK, recommendations or a certificate of decency and a blank criminal record (in France minor crimes, penalized with less than six months of imprisonment, are condoned). In France, the United Kingdom, the Netherlands and Germany it is necessary to prove assimilation. The most important factor from this point of view is good command of language. Germany and the Netherlands require the renunciation of other citizenship(s), and all countries require an assurance of loyalty to the new homeland.

Germany has a two-tier policy of granting citizenship. On the one hand, it issues German citizenship to everybody who is able to prove even the most distant German ancestry. This is coupled with a policy of 'open doors' for this category of migrants, which generates a large inflow of migrants claiming German roots, even if they do not speak any German at all and have no idea of the history and culture of Germany. The recent massive inflow of migrants from Eastern Europe and the former Soviet Union who declared themselves to be Germans has forced the government in Bonn to introduce a quota system for this category of migrants. On the other hand, Germany is very reluctant to grant citizenship to even second-generation migrants if they are unable to prove their German origin. In many cases, in particular when the applicants have been brought up in Germany, their first language is German and their culture is to large extent Germanized. There are some signs of a change to this restrictive policy, as the new Aliens Law passed in 1990 makes naturalization easier for established and second-generation migrants.

17.4 FURTHER ASPECTS OF POLICIES TOWARDS MIGRANTS WITHIN EUROPEAN UNION COUNTRIES

Once migrants have passed across a EU frontier into their intended destination, whether from another EU member country or from outside the Union, they will then come into contact with other 'secondary' elements of national or Union policy which will affect what they wish to do. Until recently, the question of work permits for EU nationals of another member state (described in detail above in section 17.3.3) remained a recurrent problem. Work permits actually remained necessary for other EU nationals in Spain and Portugal until the implementation of the Single European Market in those countries in January 1993, and they continue to exist everywhere for non-European Union migrants. Of the other 'secondary' elements of policy or regulations which apply to migrants, this section focuses on four which are of great concern to migrants: the equivalence of qualifications; social security provision; health care and policy towards minorities.

17.4.1 EQUIVALENCE OF QUALIFICATIONS AMONG MEMBER STATES

The comparative validity of educational and training qualifications gained in the different member states of the European Union has been a question which has been allied with movement policy for some years. The original Treaty of Rome (1958), which in principle provided for free movement of labour, had set in motion discussions which were eventually to lead to a large measure of agreement in this field. Clearly, it was no use trying to obtain employment at a certain level in another member country if your qualifications were not acceptable there, or if through ignorance or otherwise, they could be used as a pretext for not offering employment. Equally, the EC had always regarded the general improvement of standards in the Community work-force as being essential in its trading competition with the rest of the world, especially with the USA and Japan. By 1989, agreement had been reached to issue a directive on higher education which stated that all nationally-based diplomas successfully obtained after at least three years of full-time advanced study would be recognized throughout the European Union member states. Though some difficulties still remain, major professions such as the law, accountancy and medicine have moved a considerable way towards common agreement about their professional qualifications, already leading to increased levels of mobility of personnel, especially among accountants. In teaching, though agreement has been reached concerning the common acceptance of qualifications, other policy barriers inhibiting large-scale movement remain, especially the fact that in some member states teachers are civil servants (eg in France) and in others (eg the United Kingdom), they are not. The differences in remuneration of teachers between the most generous states (eg Luxembourg) and the least generous (eg the United Kingdom and Ireland) create a situation which in principle might stimulate migration of teachers were it not for the other barrier effects. This kind of situation raises questions of national policy which conflict somewhat with European policy, a problem which remains to be resolved at some future date (Convey 1994). Where other vocational qualifications are concerned, agreement exists for a wide range of over 100 occupations from those in hotels and catering to metalworking:

such information is considered valuable since it provides very useful details in all Community languages with respect to diplomas, certificates and qualifications issued in each member state for a given occupation, and promotes the freedom of movement of workers by helping to create conditions under which they have equal access to employment (European Commission 1990, 1992a).

17.4.2 SOCIAL SECURITY POLICY AND FREEDOM OF MOVEMENT

Social security provision at varying levels has been a long-standing characteristic of employment legislation in all member states of the EU individually. It has also been an important policy plank at the European level since the early days of the European Economic Community (EEC). An EC 'Social Charter' on the Fundamental Social Rights for Workers was adopted at the Strasbourg Council in December 1989. The provisions of this 'charter' have now been enshrined in the 'Social Chapter' of the Maastricht Treaty, which highlights a number of areas for Union-wide initiatives to be taken in order to increase the efficiency of the labour-force. On the question of movement of workers, the Social Chapter of the Treaty highlights four main measures relating to freedom of movement which were started in 1992:

1. to ensure that at least minimum levels of social security protection were afforded to migrating workers;
2. a debate about supplementary retirement schemes in an attempt to ensure wider transfrontier worker mobility;
3. a proposed amendment to existing legislation (EEC 1408/71), in order to ease the co-ordination of existing schemes, both national and European;
4. a communication on the living and working conditions of citizens in frontier regions, especially transfrontier workers (European Commission 1993d).

Meanwhile, the existing internal levels of social security provision throughout the member states, with some appearing to be more 'generous' than others— either in fact or in the popular imagination—are widely held to be factors in the stimulation of migration from one country to another and for migration from outside the Union to selected EU member countries. All member states have social security regulations which, to one degree or another, make a full range of social security benefits available to all inward migrants who have residence and work permits (European

Commission 1991). None of these benefits are formally available to illegal migrants. The degree to which these situations have been factors in increasing mobility is difficult to demonstrate, but they can also easily lead to attempts by certain national politicians to reduce inward migration, on the pretext that incomers would be drawing unfairly upon the national social security system. Perhaps because of this kind of argument, social security and the social protection of workers remain areas where unanimous voting is required under the Maastricht Treaty.

17.4.3 HEALTH CARE AS A FACTOR IN MOVEMENT

Health care provision, especially through regulations covering public health and health and safety at work, now forms part of the Social Chapter of the Maastricht Treaty. Normal medical services have been made available to all EU nationals (and to many others) for some years through the well-known 'E111' system, though this does not normally cater for persons who are staying in another country for more than a year, and it depends upon the persons concerned being social security contributors in their country of residence (European Commission 1993b). Consequently this system, together with the various private health insurance schemes available, while valuable to tourists and occasional travellers, is not especially helpful to migrants. They are normally totally dependent on medical care available through the national social security systems, as described in section 17.4.2 above.

In the fields of public health and of health and safety at work, the Maastricht Treaty is more specific. An enlargement of competence in the area of public health is actually one of the policy innovations in the Treaty. The Council of Ministers will in future be able to adopt Recommendations in this field by qualified majority voting, with the aim of ensuring a high level of human health protection throughout the EU (European Commission 1992b). The Social Chapter includes an action programme containing a series of detailed health and safety measures which supplement existing provisions. Other initiatives have included the updating of a schedule originating in 1962 on occupational diseases and setting out principles for compensation; and agreement in principle was reached in June 1993 on a 1991 Commission proposal that a European Health and Safety Agency should be created (European Commission 1993d). As the main motivating factor for most migrants remains the search for employment, such developments will be to the benefit of legal migrants who are in formal employment, though the same regulations are less likely to be followed by employers who are employing illegal migrant labour.

A further area of increasing importance where health care is concerned rests with the increasing number of retired and older persons who are migrating from one European country to another, frequently in search of the sun, but also by the process of *retour au pays* (return migration). While such movements remained within one country, problems with the provision of public health care and other social security benefits did not arise. However, this has become a problem at the European level, when nationals of one member country retire permanently to another: for example, British and Dutch in the south of Spain or Germans in the *midi* in France. At present, though it is relatively easy for such persons to obtain any appropriate residence permit in the country of their choice within the EU, the authorities of the host country have the right to demand that the migrant concerned has sufficient means to show that he/she will not need to become a charge upon the health and other social services of the host country, other than via private health insurance (Eurinfo 1993a, 1993b). As 1993 was designated as the 'Year of the Elderly', and the number of retired persons, including migrants, continues to rise across Europe, further developments might reasonably be expected in these fields in due course.

17.4.4. POLICIES TOWARDS MIGRANT MINORITIES

Many policies which affect migrant minorities have already been discussed in previous sections of this chapter. There do remain, however, a number of matters which concern the relationships between the population of the host country and inward migrant groups, of which many have received considerable publicity in recent times. Xenophobic attitudes and actions seem to be on the increase. The immigration policies of most EU countries, individually, are evolving from the relatively liberal position which developed during the 1950s–1970s, when the need for extra labour was at its maximum, to a much less inviting character at the present, when the European economy as a whole is undergoing great difficulties, and unemployment is high. The Council of Ministers of the EU, reflecting the opinions of member governments, is also spending a great deal of time on the refinement and co-ordination of immigration policy throughout its area of competence (Council of the European Communities 1992b), and most of these results are leading towards more restrictive immigration policies than hitherto for migrants from outside the EU. Individual governments in member states have the responsibility for combating the racial and other forms of violence towards foreigners which have erupted recently, though any policy responses so far have tended towards restriction of entry rather than the amelioration of conditions within the country (*The Economist* 1992a). Additional strains have been produced by the extreme political situation in former Yugoslavia, producing very large numbers of refugees and asylum seekers throughout the EU area. It is estimated that over the period 1991–2, 60 000 persons a month were entering Germany, which has had no official barriers to asylum seekers, and which has had no law by which the authorities can refuse entry, though after entry it is correspondingly difficult to obtain German citizenship (*The Economist* 1992b). This unmanageable situation in Germany has led to demands for greater restriction of entry, in line with most of Germany's partners.

Where migration between EU countries is concerned, the situation is very different. As already explained, most if not all recent policy and legislation has moved towards the free movement of persons, goods and services, these being the principles underlying the Single Market and the Maastricht Treaty. It is too early to say whether the gradual enlargement of concentrations of retired 'northern' migrants and others in the 'sun belt' of southern France, Spain and Portugal will lead to any forms of tension. At present, the regional economies are in general benefiting from this type of influx, though whether this will continue if migration reduces and these populations get gradually older is open to question. Periodic locally based problems about internal movement are raised in Belgium, where some attempts have been made by Flemish-speaking *communes* to restrict or to stop the inward migration of Walloons (*Le Soir* 1993a, 1993b), and census migration returns in Belgium certainly demonstrate a small amount of movement between the two linguistic zones, the Brussels region apart. In the UK, the Northern Ireland problem has led to widespread relocation of certain sections of the community, especially in the city of Belfast, into concentrations of persons on at least nominal religious grounds. Of course, neither of these two cases can be described as policy, though they do call for policy responses from national governments. All European-level policy on internal migration and movement within the Union remains based upon the presumption that local difficulties such as these will not continue to exist indefinitely or at least will not get further out of hand.

17.5 CONCLUSION

It is clear that migration policy within the area and competence of the EU and its members states remains very complex and is also still in a state of considerable flux. The pushes towards greater controls on movements from the outside, which have been described in this chapter, are in direct competition in policy terms not only with the equally important push towards greater ease of movement within the Union but also with the drive towards greater economic success. The harmonization of legislation and policy seems to be one of the major concerns of the EU member states, and the process of harmonization is apparently gaining in momentum. If, at the same time, the EU were to develop a 'fortress Europe' mentality as far as population migration is concerned, this could well have political ramifications with outside states which go far beyond the question of who gets entry visas and who does not. An enlightened approach which may work gradually to lessen the pressure of inward migration might be for the Union to seek to reduce the 'push' factors existing in third countries and to commence various forms of co-operation with them. These would include the formulation of policies aimed at the management of migration, the development of skills to manage these policies and the more general encouragement of positive public and individual attitudes towards inward migrants. However, such moves would require the development of policies which show considerable foresight, and while there is not much sign of this as yet, it is to be hoped that European politicians will prove capable of moving in such a direction and not to be relying solely upon restrictive moves.

18 Projecting the National and Regional Populations of the European Union Using Migration Information

PHILIP REES

18.1 INTRODUCTION: AIMS AND BACKGROUND

The Treaty of Maastricht[1] contains provisions for the establishment of a Committee of Regions. This reflects a long-running concern among policy makers in both the member states and in European Union (EU) institutions in the development of regions. One of the goals of the European Community (CEC, 1991; 1994) has been to reduce regional differences in well-being (in per caput income and employment in particular). Knowledge of the future population development of EU regions is important in working towards this goal for several reasons. First, population development is a major influence on labour supply (along with changes in activity rates). Second, extremes of population change can have deleterious affects on regional well-being. Drastic population loss can lead to a downward spiral in the demand for goods and services. Alternatively, rapid growth can lead to strains on the regional infrastructure and congestion costs for business and people.

The chapter's principal aims are to review progress that has been made in developing EU-wide projections of regional populations and to assess, in particular, how knowledge about migration (internal and external) has been and should be used in those projections. To achieve this aim, section two of the chapter reviews the models that have been used to project regional populations, section three reviews the assumptions that have been made and how these were developed, while section four examines the results of projections carried out by various organizations in order to draw out implications for future regional demographic distributions of a range of possible migration scenarios and to expose deficiencies that need remedying in the future. The final section summarizes what has been learnt.

In carrying out this review, the chapter draws on papers prepared for two meetings. The first was an international conference on 'Human Resources at the Dawn of the 21st Century' organized by Eurostat (Statistical Office of the European Communities) and the Luxemburg government in November 1991. The second was a workshop on 'Regional Populations Scenarios' organized by NEI (Netherlands Economic Institute) in May 1993 as part of a project, funded by the European Commission (Directorate-General XVI) and Eurostat, to develop 'Long-Term

Population Migration in the European Union Edited by Philip Rees, John Stillwell, Andrew Convey and Marek Kupiszewski. © Editors and Contributors. Published 1996 John Wiley & Sons Ltd.

Population Scenarios for the European Economic Area' as precursor to the 1994 round of regional population projections. These Eurostat meetings reflect the importance accorded to the issue of the future size and distribution of the population of the EU's member states and regions. In the remainder of this introductory section some background information is provided on the likely future development of the population of EU member states, against which the task of regional projection can be set.

Table 18.1 sets out the results of three current projections of the European Community's population based on consistent projections of all member state populations. The Eurostat low projection assumes little change in current fertility levels and conservative improvements in life expectancy (Eurostat 1991a, 1991b) while the Eurostat high projection assumes some increases in fertility (though not to replacement level) and sustained mortality improvements. The ECPOP projections (Rees *et al.* 1992) adopt fertility assumptions midway between the Eurostat low and Eurostat high and very little mortality improvement.

Table 18.1 Projections of the population of the European Union (EUR-12)

Age group	Population (millions)				% distribution	
	1990	2000	2010	2020	1990	2020
EUROSTAT LOW						
0–19	88	82	75	66	25.5	19.6
20–59	189	195	192	184	54.8	54.3
60+	68	75	82	89	19.7	26.1
Total	344	351	349	339	100.0	100.0
EUROSTAT HIGH						
0–19	88	88	94	94	25.5	23.7
20–59	189	198	201	203	54.8	51.2
60+	68	77	87	100	19.7	25.1
Total	344	363	382	397	100.0	100.0
ECPOP						
0–19	87	82	80	71	25.5	21.0
20–59	189	192	188	180	54.8	53.1
60+	68	75	81	88	19.7	25.9
Total	343	350	348	340	100.0	100.0

Sources: Eurostat low and high: Eurostat (1991b); ECPOP: author's computations (using approximately constant mortality levels and fertility levels between the Eurostat low and high scenarios).

The member states of the EU on 1 January 1990 were estimated to contain 344 million inhabitants (including the residents of the eastern *Länder* of Germany), more than ever before. However, projections by Eurostat (1991a), by the United Nations (1991a, 1991b), by NEI (Haverkate and van Haselen, 1990) and by the author (Rees *et al.* 1992) all project that the EUR-12 (the 12 member states of the

EU prior to 1 January 1995) population will peak between 2000 and 2005 under constant or moderately trended fertility and mortality scenarios and decline thereafter.

There is agreement that the European Union population will continue to experience ageing, consequent on previous fertility declines as Table 18.1 shows. The youngest age group (0–19) shrinks in relative size under all three projections, while the elderly (60 plus) increase from a fifth to a quarter of the population. Within the labour-force ages the balance shifts from the younger (aged 20–39) to the older age group (aged 40–59). These changes in the all-age population disguise massive ageing of the population through the three decades. The range of experience is, however, quite large from an increase in the 60 plus population of only 16 per cent in the UK to 61 per cent in the Netherlands, reflecting their different post World War II fertility histories.

This picture of European Union population change masks, of course, considerable variation among smaller, component populations: the populations of the member states and, within member states, of the national regions. These aspects will be taken up in section 18.4.

Forecast populations are the product of two sets of decisions that influence the outcomes of projections. The first set involves the design of the model used to carry out the projection, while the second set involves the development of assumptions about model inputs. In the next section of the chapter, section 18.2, the design of models for projecting national and regional populations of the EU is discussed. Projection assumptions are discussed in section 18.3 and projection results in section 18.4.

18.2 REVIEW OF PROJECTION MODELS

Projections are carried out for European populations by several different agencies: by international statistical offices, by national demographic or statistical offices and by other institutions.

18.2.1 THE COHORT SURVIVAL AND NET MIGRATION MODELS OF INTERNATIONAL ORGANIZATIONS

International organizations have normally adopted a relatively simple methodology for consistent projections across many countries. This methodology involves a cohort survival model for a two-sex population coupled with a female dominant fertility model and an addition of net international migration to each survived cohort. The United Nations carries out projections biennially for all member states and publishes extensive tabulations (United Nations 1991a, 1991b). Eurostat (1991b) has recently carried out a set of projections for European Community member states. The UN projections are based largely on forecasts of the natural components of population, while the Eurostat projections give very careful consideration to future net external migration assumptions as well. More sophisticated methods have, however, been used. The International Institute for Applied Systems Analysis (IIASA) has carried out a series of regional projections for member organizations which included France, Germany, Italy, the Netherlands and the United Kingdom (Rogers and Willekens 1986). The projections included interregional migration flows in a pioneering multiregional projection model. However, the benchmark data bases refer to a variety of years in the 1970s, no account was taken of external migration and only constant rate projections were implemented.

18.2.2 THE NET MIGRATION, MIGRANT POOL AND MULTIREGIONAL MODELS OF NATIONAL DEMOGRAPHIC OFFICES

National agencies have used a spectrum of models ranging from those involving simple cohort survival plus net migration to very detailed multiregional algorithms. The methods adopted by national agencies in the European Economic Area (EU countries plus EFTA members) for projecting regional populations within countries have been thoroughly reviewed by Van Imhoff *et al.* (1994). The authors report the precise demographic intensity measures used by each agency and make recommendations about best practice. More critically, they identify the methods for handling migration between regions within countries. Three approaches characterize EEA countries: (1) use of net migration flows or rates, (2) use of a migrant pool method and (3) a multiregional methodology. Each of these methods faces particular problems.

In the *net migration model*, the number of net migrants in each age–sex group is added to the survived regional populations. For a population of period cohort a, the following equation applies:

$$P^j_a(t+u) = s^j_a P^j_a(t) + N^j_a$$

where P^j is the population of region j in age group a, u is the age and time interval, s is the probability of survival and N is the absolute number of net in-migrants. Note that, in this notation, 'a' refers to period-cohort which changes between projection intervals, not within them.

One of the problems with such a model is that it is difficult to produce a reasonable age distribution for net migration. In addition it is necessary to build in the constraint that the net migration balances of the regions should, for each age–sex group, sum to zero.

The *migrant pool model* involves the application of out-migration probabilities to origin region populations for each age–sex group and the further application of a destination probability. For a typical population the following equation applies:

$$P^j_a(t+u) = s^j_a P^j_a(t) + d^j_a \sum_i o^i_a P^i_a(t)$$

where d^j_a is the probability of an in-migrant in age group a selecting destination j and o^i_a is the probability of the age a population migrating from origin region i.

Note that if the migration probability is restricted to out-migration from the region, as is the case in many national applications, then a logical inconsistency arises: an out-migrant from region i can be assigned as an in-migrant again to the same region.

The *multi-regional model* incorporates the application of an origin to destination migration probability to the origin population:

$$P^j_a(t+u) = s^j_a P^j_a(t) + \Sigma_{i\neq j} m^{ij}_a P^i_a(t)$$

where s^j_a is, in this case, the joint probability of surviving and staying in region i and m^{ij}_a is the joint probability of surviving and migrating from region i to region j. The principal drawback of this elegant and consistent model is in the reliable estimation of the m^{ij}_a probabilities if a fine age and fine spatial classification is employed. Most operational models decompose these probabilities:

$$m^{ij}_a = m^i_a p_A(j|i)$$

where m^i_a is the probability of persons in age group a migrating out of region i. The subscript A refers to a broad age group (including all ages) and $p_A(j|i)$ to the probability of selecting region j as destination given region i as origin. In both the migrant pool and multiregional model, external migration (between the region and other countries) is usually handled using net migration terms.

18.2.3 THE NETHERLANDS ECONOMIC INSTITUTE (NEI) DEMETER MODELS

The problem with using the results of projections carried out by national demographic offices to study national and regional population forecasts across Europe is that you are combining the results of several different models and sets of assumptions. To achieve consistency, the populations of European regions must be projected using an integrated model that simultaneously projects, using the same assumptions, the regional populations of all member states. The Directorate-General for Regional Policy (DG-XVI) of the European Commission funded the Netherlands Economic Institute (Haverkate and van Haselen 1990) to produce regional projections as input to the *Fourth Periodic Report on the Social and Economic Situation and Development of the Regions of the Community* (CEC 1991) and, together with Eurostat, commissioned a further more extensive study as input to the *Fifth Periodic Report* (NEI 1994a, 1994b, 1994c, 1994d). The NEI models have been labelled by the authors with the acronym DEMETER, standing for DEMographic Evolution through Time in European Regions. The NEI 1990 model is labelled DEMETER 2015 after the end date of its projection results, while the NEI 1994 model is given the label DEMETER 2020 reflecting its end-projections year. The NEI DEMETER 2015 (Haverkate and van Haselen 1990) and NEI DEMETER 2020 (NEI 1994a) models used as input to the Fourth and Fifth Periodic Reports project the populations of EU member states and their constituent NUTS Level 2 regions (there are 181 of these in the EUR-12).

The DEMETER 2015 model used five-year projection intervals and ages. The national projections are made through use of a standard cohort survival and female-dominant fertility model with external migration assumptions adopted only for Germany and Ireland in the first two projection intervals, with all other net migration flows set to zero. The regional projections make use of national age-specific fertility and mortality rate schedules adjusted using recently observed regional births and deaths to yield region-specific rates. These are combined with interregion migration rates derived from available national flow tables and national schedules of migration rates by age. At the heart of the model are equations for projecting regional age group populations of the following kind:

$$P^i_a(t+u) = s^i_a P^i_a(t) + \Sigma_{i \neq j} r_a m^{ij} P^i_a(t)$$

where m^{ij} is the probability of migration from origin i to destination j and r_a is the national ratio of the age a migration rate to the average.

The NEI 1994 or DEMETER 2020 model (NEI, 1994a) used single-year ages from 0 to 90 plus and annual time intervals. The structure of the model is similar to the previous DEMETER 2015 model, except that much more detailed scenarios are introduced for international migration (based on Eurostat's national scenarios), mortality (based on an analysis by the Department of Public Health, Erasmus University) and fertility (based on an analysis of gamma curves of fertility by age). For internal migration the previous approach of decomposing interregional migration into level, national age and all-age interregional destination probabilities is retained, though a more detailed analysis of interregional migration rates by age for selected EU member states is carried out. As in DEMETER 2015 forecasts, interregional migration parameters are assumed constant in DEMETER 2020 projections.

18.2.4 THE LEEDS SCHOOL OF GEOGRAPHY ECPOP MODEL

A group of researchers at the University of Leeds were invited by Eurostat to prepare a paper on measuring the impact of intra-Community migration on the demographic structure of regions (Rees *et al.* 1992). To carry out this task a model for projecting the populations of member states and NUTS 1 regions was designed called ECPOP or European Community POPulation projection model.

Migration was decomposed into three components in the projection model: (1) extra-Community migration, (2) intermember state (intra-Community) migration and (3) interregional (intramember state) migration. This necessitated adoption of a hierarchical structure for the model which is illustrated in Figure 18.1. Migration between a member state and the rest of the world outside the European Community is handled through a net migration term, which is distributed across destination regions (eg terms A and B in Figure 18.1, referring to Denmark and the UK respectively). Intermember state migration is projected using a multiregional model and model migration schedules (rates of migration by age). The totals for intermember state out- and in-migration are distributed across origin and destination regions (eg

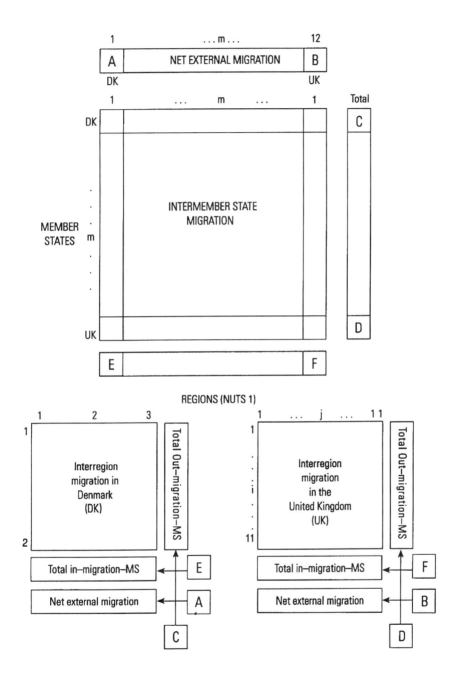

Figure 18.1 The hierarchical structure of the ECPOP projection model for NUTS 1 regions

terms C, D, E and F in Figure 18.1). Finally, interregion migration is projected using a multiregional model and model schedules of migration rates by age.

The model equations for a typical age group are as follows for member state populations:

$$P^{m}_{a}(t+u) = (1-d^{m}_{a})\, P^{m}_{a}(t) + k_{a}N^{m} - \Sigma_{n\neq m}\, k_{a}m^{mn}\, P^{m}_{a}(t) + \Sigma_{n\neq m}\, k_{a}m^{nm}\, P^{m}_{a}(t)$$

where $P^{m}_{a}(t)$ is the population of member state m in age group a at time t, d^{m}_{a} is the mortality probability at age a in member state m, k_{a} is the ratio of the model schedule migration probability at age a to the model schedule average and m^{mn} is the probability of migration from member state m to member state n. The equivalent projection equation for a region j, belonging to member state m, is:

$$P^{i\,(m)}_{a}(t+u) = (1-d^{i\,(m)}_{a})\, P^{i\,(m)}_{a}t + dfem^{j(m)}_{a}\, k_{a}N^{m}$$

$$-dfom^{j\,(m)}_{a}\, \Sigma_{n\neq m}\, k_{a}m^{mn}\, P^{m}_{a}(t) + dfim^{j\,(m)}_{a}\, \Sigma_{n\neq m}\, k_{a}m^{nm}\, P^{(n)}_{a}(t)$$

$$-\Sigma_{i\neq j}\, k_{a}m^{j(m)i(m)}\, P^{i\,(m)}_{a}(t) + \Sigma_{i\neq j}\, k_{a}m^{i(m)j(m)}\, P^{j\,(m)}_{a}(t)$$

where $P^{i(m)}_{a}(t)$ is the population of region i in member state m in age group a at time t, and $d^{i(m)}_{a}$ is the age a mortality probability for region i in member state m. The df terms are distribution factors that share out the net external migration (dfem), the (gross) intermember state out-migration (dfom) and the (gross) interstate in-migration (dfim) to or from member state m to region j. The final two terms parallel those in the national model but refer to migration between regions i and j of member state m.

18.2.5 CONSISTENCY BETWEEN SPATIAL SCALES

Any set of national and regional projections must resolve the issue of consistency. The outcomes of projections (projected populations and their components of change) at different spatial scales must be consistent with each other. When population counts are taken from censuses or registers such consistency follows automatically as long as every individual can be assigned a place of usual residence. The same consistency applies to population accounts which capture flows as well as stocks to yield a picture of population change.

However, when we substitute demographic rates or probabilities for population flows in a projection model, then there is no guarantee that the sum of projected subpopulations will add up to the projected population. Frequently, the sum of regional projected populations is higher than the corresponding national populations. The reason for this is that over time in regional projections the higher-growth regions achieve successively higher weightings.

Therefore, in preparing sets of forecasts for planning purposes, a decision has to be taken on which spatial scale takes priority. Normally, this is the national scale. So, the figures presented in Table 18.1 for the EUR-12 population are sums of the national projected populations. A 'bottom-up' approach has been adopted. Within each member state both national authorities and the NEI team adopt a 'top-down' strategy, adjusting regional populations and components of change to agree with national.

The same procedure can be applied to births, deaths and external migration terms. However, as a result of the adjustment interregional migration terms will now be inconsistent with projected regional population change because there are no equivalent national totals to adjust to. The adjustments also result in a mismatch between the regional demographic rates or probabilities input to the projection calculations and those implied after adjustment.

These difficulties led to Rees *et al.* (1992) presenting both national and regional projected populations independently and hence inconsistently. In Section 18.4, however, a 'bottom-up' approach is used in presenting the result of these variant regional population projections.

18.2.6 FURTHER DEVELOPMENT OF REGIONAL POPULATION PROJECTION MODELS

The discussion above focuses on the mechanisms for incorporating migration which have been used in models for regional population projection. In most projection models great care is taken in the development of plausible scenarios for the future trajectories of mortality and fertility. The mortality probabilities by age will be studied for trend and linear, log-linear or curvilinear functions will be fitted and extrapolated. Alternative fertility scenarios will be developed based on guesses about future behaviour and fitted carefully to knowledge about cumulative fertility in successive cohorts. Little attention has so far been paid to the development of migration scenarios. In the Eurostat national projections high and low scenarios for net external migration to each member state are presented. In the NEI's DEMETER models prior to the 1994 version (DEMETER 2020), most external migration flows were assumed to be zero. Interregional migration probabilities have been assumed constant in all DEMETER models.

In the ECPOP model an attempt is made to develop a mechanism for introducing scenarios for intermember state and interregional migration via destination factors. The argument is that it is the changing propensity of regions to attract or repel migrants that is crucial, and that out-migration propensities will vary less over time. Migration probabilities are trended by applying destination factors:

$$m^{mn}(t+u) = m^{mn}(t)\, fm^{n}(t+u)$$

and

$$m^{i(m)j(m)}(t+u) = m^{i(m)}(t)\, fr^{j(m)}(t+u)$$

where fm^{n} is the factor for destination member state m for updating the migration rate from the projection interval starting at time t+u, and $fr^{j(m)}$ is the equivalent factor for region j in member state m.

Such techniques for developing migration scenarios merely extend the extrapolative methods commonly used in demographic projection. But where does know-ledge come from to inform the creation of time sequences of destination factors for regions? It derives from knowledge about the development trends in regions and the ability of those trends to attract or repel migrants. Crucial development trends are (1) employment change, (2) housing construction, (3) the expansion of higher- education institutions and (4) the creation of new amenities, which affect migrants at different life course stages. Tools for handling migration as flows between origins and destinations are spatial interaction models (SIMs). Such models have been around for over 50 years in crude form (since the work of Stouffer, Zipf and Hägerstrand) and for 25 years in more sophisticated form (since the work of Wilson, Fotheringham, Stillwell, Liaw and others). They have rarely been incorporated into regional projection models. The next generation of projection models for Europe's regions should include, as one option, SIMs and, of necessity, link them to models of regional economic and housing development (as in the Netherlands model—Eichperger and Gordijn 1994).

18.3 REVIEW OF PROJECTION ASSUMPTIONS

As crucial to projection outcomes as model structures are the assumptions about inputs—mortality, fertility and migration. Here we review the assumptions made for member states in national, Eurostat, NEI and Leeds projections, comment on the way these are linked to regional scenarios and make proposals for improvement.

18.3.1 MORTALITY ASSUMPTIONS

The mortality assumptions employed in the projection models reviewed in Section 18.2 are set out in Table 18.2 for selected member states in the form of forecast life expectancies. The assumptions made by national demographic offices are very conservative: all of them assume a slowing down of the rate of improvement in life expectancy. The Eurostat low scenario keeps quite close to these conservative national assumptions, though not as restrained as the DEMETER 2020 low model which assumes virtually no change. The DEMETER 2020 high scenarios envisage moderate improvement in life expectancies, though not as much as in the Eurostat high projections. The ECPOP scenarios select a midpoint between the Eurostat low and high scenarios as their targets, though, for reasons explained later, outcomes are less optimistic.

How do these extrapolations compare with recent historical experience? In general, they assume a marked slowing down in life expectancy improvement, even in the most optimistic, the Eurostat high. For example, in the UK between 1981 and 1990 the average annual life expectancy gain for males was 0.24 of a year and for females 0.19 of a year. The Eurostat high projection assumes gains per year of 0.17 for males and 0.15 for females. Life expectancy experience in 2020 is not outside the range currently observed in the most favoured regions of member states or in

Table 18.2 Mortality assumptions (life expectancies at birth) for selected EU member states: alternative projections

Member state	Male 1990	Male 2005	Male 2020	Female 1990	Female 2005	Female 2020
NATIONAL						
Denmark	71.8	71.9	71.9	77.7	77.8	77.8
Germany	72.3	73.3	73.3	78.8	79.6	79.6
Netherlands	74.0	74.9	75.0	80.3	81.4	81.5
United Kingdom	73.1	74.9	75.8	78.7	80.1	80.7
EUROSTAT LOW						
Denmark	72.0	72.5	72.5	77.7	78.0	78.0
Germany	72.1	72.5	72.5	78.6	79.0	79.0
Netherlands	73.7	74.0	74.0	80.0	80.5	80.5
United Kingdom	72.7	73.5	73.5	78.2	79.0	79.0
EUROSTAT HIGH						
Denmark	72.1	74.4	77.5	77.9	79.9	82.0
Germany	72.2	75.5	78.0	78.7	81.1	83.0
Netherlands	73.9	76.4	78.5	80.2	82.3	83.5
United Kingdom	72.8	76.1	78.0	78.3	81.2	82.5
NEI-DEMETER 2020 LOW						
Denmark	71.7	72.2	72.2	77.4	77.7	77.7
Germany	71.8	72.2	72.2	78.4	78.8	78.8
Netherlands	70.4	71.8	71.8	79.8	80.2	80.2
United Kingdom	72.2	73.0	73.0	77.8	78.6	78.6
NEI-DEMETER 2020 HIGH						
Denmark	71.8	74.3	77.2	77.6	79.7	81.7
Germany	71.9	75.2	77.8	78.5	81.2	82.8
Netherlands	70.5	74.5	77.0	79.9	82.0	83.2
United Kingdom	72.3	75.5	77.5	77.9	80.6	82.0
ECPOP						
Denmark	72.3	73.8	74.8	78.0	79.2	79.9
Germany	72.5	74.3	75.1	78.9	80.3	80.7
Netherlands	74.0	75.4	76.1	80.4	81.6	82.0
United Kingdom	73.2	75.0	75.7	78.6	80.2	80.7
EXTRAPOLATION						
Denmark	72.3	75.3	78.3	78.0	81.0	84.0
Germany	72.5	75.5	78.5	78.9	81.9	84.9
Netherlands	74.0	77.0	80.0	80.4	83.4	86.4
United Kingdom	73.2	76.2	79.2	78.6	81.6	84.6

Notes: 1. The ECPOP figures refer to quinquennia 1990–5, 2005–10 and 2015–20
2. Four member states involved in the Northern Seaboard Study were selected to keep the table size manageable
3. The extrapolated life expectancies assumed an improvement of 0.2 of a year per year through the 1990–2020 period
4. NEI projections: values for 2005—interpolated between 2000 and 2010 values in NEI (1994c); 2020 – assumed to be the 2019 values in NEI (1994c)

Sources: National, Eurostat (1991a); Eurostat low and high, Eurostat (1991b); NEI: Demeter 2020, NEI (1994a, 1994c); Leeds: ECPOP, Rees *et al.* (1992)

more advanced countries (Japan, Switzerland, Sweden). Steady progress is being made against heart disease, strokes and cancers through better treatments, retreat from smoking, improved diet and sensible exercise (Department of Health 1992).

The final panel in Table 18.2 indicates the result of assuming an improvement rate in life expectancy of 0.2 year per year over the 1990–2020 period. Life expectancies rise beyond those of the Eurostat high scenario.

What methods have been used to generate these mortality scenarios? Considerable attention has been paid to likely mortality trends both at national and regional scales. Lopez and Cruijsen (1991) studied post-1950 mortality trends in age-cause-specific death rates in member states using seven broad cause of death categories. The percentage declines observed were used to forecast mortality to 2020, adopting progressive smaller decline ratios in the Eurostat high scenario, while in the low scenario it was assumed that there would be no declines after 2000. To this conventional analysis needs to be added some evaluation of the impact of the HIV/AIDS epidemic on future mortality (Heilig 1991). Critical in the future will be a judgement about whether a heterosexual epidemic is likely or not; UK analysis (Knox et al. 1993; Williams and Rees 1994) suggests that sufficient people are using condoms to prevent an epidemic of African dimensions occurring.

Regional differences in age-specific mortality have been studied both nationally (Coleman and Salt 1992, Chapters 7 and 8; Armitage 1987) and across the Eurostat (NEI 1994a). The NEI DEMETER 2020 projections incorporate the results of an analysis of mortality differentials carried out by Kunst, Groenhof and Mackenbach of the Department of Public Health of Erasmus University (NEI 1994a). They use a log-linear model that incorporates a national age profile, region-specific effects and broad age group and region interactions. The latter term is needed because the pattern of overall regional differentials is not necessarily replicated in each individual age group.

There was no clear direction to change in regional differentials in the countries studied. Although Noin (1993) using national data from Decroly and Vanlaer (1991) has pointed to convergence of mortality experience at country scale in Europe, Kunst, Groenhof and Mackenbach observed regional divergence in Belgium, England and Wales, Denmark and Spain; convergence in Italy and Scotland; and no substantial change in France, the Netherlands and West Germany. In the DEMETER 2020 low projections, no change in regional mortality differentials was forecast, while in the high projections moderate convergence was proposed (NEI, 1994a).

18.3.2 FERTILITY ASSUMPTIONS

Table 18.3 sets out the total period fertility rates associated with or used in the four projections reviewed here. These provide a common set of indices for comparing the nature of the scenarios, even if alternative measures such as completed cohort fertility and average age at childbearing are used to generate the period-cohort fertility rates actually used in the projections.

Table 18.3 Fertility assumptions for selected EU member states

State	Total period fertility rates		
	1990	2005	2020
NATIONAL			
Denmark	1.67	1.80	1.80
Germany	1.42	1.42	1.42
Netherlands	1.59	1.65	1.65
United Kingdom	1.83	2.00	2.00
EUROSTAT LOW			
Denmark	1.66	1.58	1.50
Germany	1.45	1.29	1.30
Netherlands	1.61	1.58	1.50
United Kingdom	1.78	1.66	1.69
EUROSTAT HIGH			
Denmark	1.68	1.94	2.00
Germany	1.47	1.70	1.80
Netherlands	1.63	1.95	2.00
United Kingdom	1.83	2.07	2.19
DEMETER 2020 LOW			
Denmark	1.66	1.58	1.50
Germany	1.45	1.30	1.30
Netherlands	1.61	1.58	1.50
United Kingdom	1.78	1.68	1.69
DEMETER 2020 HIGH			
Denmark	1.68	1.94	2.00
Germany	1.47	1.71	1.80
Netherlands	1.63	1.94	2.00
United Kingdom	1.83	2.07	2.19
ECPOP			
Denmark	1.70	1.76	1.75
Germany	1.47	1.51	1.55
Netherlands	1.66	1.77	1.75
United Kingdom	1.83	1.88	1.93

Notes: The ECPOP figures refer to the five-year periods:1990–5, 2005–10 and 2015–20

Sources: National, Eurostat (1991a); Eurostat, Eurostat (1991b); DEMETER 2020, NEI (1994a, 1994c); ECPOP, Rees *et al.* (1992)

The national projections reported are the central variant adopted for planning purposes in the countries concerned. Most EU countries assume a small rise in fertility, but this rise stops well short of reaching replacement level (2.08–2.10 children per woman). In fact, in their latest, 1991-based projection, the Government Actuary and Office of Population Censuses and Surveys (jointly responsible for

UK national projections) has reduced the long-run fertility level in the UK to 1.9 children per woman.

The Eurostat fertility assumptions are based on two views of future determinants. In the pessimistic view

> Economic growth stagnates, governments are not willing...to extend childcare facilities or to increase family allowances, male partners persist in not equally participating in child-rearing and housekeeping (Cruijsen, 1991, p.20)

while in the optimistic view

> ... everything goes fine. Having children without substantial personal costs becomes a political [goal], governments and private companies [cooperate] in order to create a flexible and highly individualised childcare system, male partners [participate equally in child-rearing and housekeeping] (Cruijsen 1991, p.21).

Under the pessimistic scenario completed, cohort fertility rates continue to decline to an average of 1.5 children per woman by 2000 and thereafter. Even under the optimistic scenario under which there is some fertility recovery, completed fertility only achieves a level of two children per woman, sufficient to maintain numbers at the youngest ages (Table 18.1) but insufficient to prevent decline setting in again after 2015. The ECPOP projections adopt an average of Eurostat high and low scenarios.

The DEMETER 2020 projections adopt the overall total period fertility rates put forward in the Eurostat national projections together with past regional deviations extrapolated so as to produce a degree of convergence over time, with some special adjustments for the regions of former East Germany.

What methods have been used to generate the fertility scenarios? In essence, when forecasting fertility decisions need to be made about the cumulative fertility curves of successive female generations, their asymptotes (completed fertility) and their timing (distribution across the reproductive ages). Some knowledge can be gained from examining the fertility history of successive cohorts currently in the reproductive ages, but ultimately judgements must be made about the future influence of the determinants of fertility in postdemographic transition societies.

Coleman and Salt (1992) provide a definitive list of such determinants in their discussion of British fertility. The first set of determinants are variables that intervene between sexual intercourse and a livebirth. The availability of contraception and abortion is likely to continue to improve across Eurostat nations, and in particular, both technical advances (safer contraceptive pills; femidoms; implanted contraceptives) and social climate ensure firm female control of the process in most sections of Western society. Although a substantial fraction of first births are still unplanned, these do not close the gap between intended family size revealed in surveys (still above replacement in the UK, for example) and actual outcomes. The trend in couple unions is against marriage and towards cohabitation, and fertility in cohabitation is much lower than in marriage because of its less committed and more temporary nature.

Behind these proximate determinants stand underlying causes that influence couples in their decisions to have children or not. The most important trend has prob-

ably been increasing participation of women in the labour-force, partly out of necessity to maintain household incomes in times of recession and partly as a result of the
growth of jobs in the service sector where women compete successfully against men.
There is then a substantial opportunity cost to childbearing and an incentive to have
fewer, faster. Some demographers have gone further to argue for the increasing psy-
chological attractions of working career over home-based childrearing (Keyfitz 1987).

The trends in both proximate and underlying determinants all support a view that
fertility in EC countries will remain well below replacement (Sporton 1993), even
if strong pro-natalist policies were introduced, which Hecht and Leridon (1993,
pp.74–5) consider could only raise fertility levels by 10–15 per cent. Strong immigration into the EU could raise the number of births because of the concentration of
immigrants in fertile age ranges over a single generation, but evidence on trends in
ethnic minority fertility points to rapid decline to host society norms. In terms of
the scenarios set out in Table 18.3, therefore, the lower scenarios (Eurostat low or
DEMETER 2025) are more likely.

In their review of regional population projections in the European Economic
Area, van Imhoff *et al.* (1994) identify only three countries in which region-speci-
fied assumptions are developed (Austria, Germany and the Netherlands). In the
other countries, either regional differentials are assumed fixed or trends in regional
differentials are established (eg Armitage 1987). In the DEMETER 2015 and
ECPOP projections regional fertility rates are derived by adjusting national age-
specific rates to regional births using the following technique:

$$f_a^{j(m)} = f_a^m (B^{i(m)} / \Sigma_a f_a^m P_{af}^{i(m)})$$

where f_a refers to fertility in period-cohort a, applying to member state m or region
j(m) within it, where $B^{i(m)}$ refers to observed regional births and $P_{af}^{i(m)}$ to the population at risk in region i(m) of females in period-cohort a. The national rates are mul-
tiplied by the ratio of observed regional births to births expected if national rates are
applied to regional populations at risk.

It does not make a lot of sense to replicate the detailed Eurostat (1991b) cohort
analysis at regional scale—the necessary data are not available. The strategy pursued
by NEI (1994a) is to represent the schedule of regional fertility rates by age by a simple three-parameter model involving the total fertility rate (area under the schedule),
the mean age of childbearing and the variance in ages. Regional differentials (ratios
of regional to national) in the total fertility rate parameters are established and forecast to converge; the other parameters are forecast at national level. The advantage of
this approach is that future changes in fertility timing as well as level can be accom-
modated. Eurostat (1991b) forecasts that the average age at motherhood will rise from
26.7 years for mothers born in 1945 to 29.3 for mothers born in 2000, for example.

18.3.3 ASSUMPTIONS ABOUT EXTERNAL MIGRATION

The assumptions that need to be made about migration depend both on spatial scale
(national or regional) and projection model adopted. Three types of migration flow
can be distinguished: (1) flows between EU member states and the rest of the

world, (2) flows between EU member states and (3) flows between regions within EU member states. National forecasts of member state and regional populations and Eurostat forecasts of national populations lump together the first and second type and treat them as net migration totals. Flows between EU member states are considered explicitly only in the ECPOP projection model, while interregional migration flows are considered in five national projections (van Imhoff *et al.* 1994) out of 12, and in the DEMETER 2020 and ECPOP models. Each of the flow types is considered in turn.

The assumptions about external migration used in the set of projections considered here are set out in Table 18.4. The national assumptions gathered together in Eurostat (1991b) have mostly been revised upwards (Muus and Cruijsen 1991), in response to the wave of immigration of *Aussiedler* (persons of German ethnic origin living in other east European states) into Germany, and asylum seekers and refugees into most EU states as the communist regimes of Eastern Europe collapsed in the 1989–91 period. Although the 1990–5 period is viewed as one of unusually high immigration, most national projections see the substantial net inflows continuing. So, for example, the UK assumptions have been altered from the zero balance shown in Table 18.4 to an assumption of a net immigration of 50 000 a year up to 2007, and then a diminution to zero by 2015 (OPCS 1993, p.4).

Both Eurostat scenarios envisage permanent net immigration over the three decades to 2020. In the low scenario the number of *Aussiedler* migrating to Germany is expected to decrease rapidly in the rest of the 1990s. As a result of the introduction of more restrictive admission policies co-ordinated through the provisions of the Schengen Agreement and Treaty of Maastricht, the number of asylum seekers is expected to diminish. A stricter application of admission policies for labour migrants and family members will reduce these flows.

Under the Eurostat high scenario, higher numbers of ethnic Germans 'return' to Germany, though decline still sets in and the pressure from asylum seekers, refugees and economic migrants is less successfully resisted. The continuation of conflict in former Yugoslavia contributes to this view.

The national assumptions of DEMETER 2020 are in line with the Eurostat scenarios. The regional distribution of net flows across NUTS 2 regions was calculated by subtracting natural change and net internal migration from population change for 1985–90. The regional distribution of net external migration was shifted up or down to agree with national estimates. In the low scenario this distribution was maintained for the projection period. For the high scenario the assumption was made that international migrants will spread more evenly across the regions, tending towards the overall population distributions (NEI 1994a), the current revision of these DEMETER regional projections. The ECPOP assumptions, as with mortality and fertility, average the two Eurostat scenarios but with one major difference. Estimates of the net migration between EU states are made and subtracted from the net external migration assumptions.

The direct additions between 1990 and 2020 to the EUR-12 population are likely to be substantial under these assumptions: 8.9 millions under the Eurostat

Table 18.4 External migration assumptions for selected EU member states (annual net migration)

Member state	1990–4	1995–9	2000–4	2005–9	2010–14	2015–19
NATIONAL						
Denmark	5	2	0	0	0	0
Germany	272	164	72	50	10	0
Netherlands	37	25	25	25	25	25
United Kingdom	0	0	0	0	0	0
EUROSTAT LOW						
Denmark	5	5	5	5	5	5
Germany	326	100	100	100	100	100
Netherlands	29	20	20	20	20	20
United Kingdom	31	20	20	20	20	20
EUROSTAT HIGH						
Denmark	14	15	15	15	15	15
Germany	574	280	280	280	280	280
Netherlands	50	50	50	50	50	50
United Kingdom	60	60	60	60	60	60
DEMETER 2020 LOW						
Denmark	7	5	5	5	5	5
Germany	650	100	100	100	100	100
Netherlands	46	20	20	20	20	20
United Kingdom	30	20	20	20	20	20
DEMETER 2020 HIGH						
Denmark	9	15	15	15	15	15
Germany	700	280	280	280	280	280
Netherlands	50	50	50	50	50	50
United Kingdom	60	60	60	60	60	60
ECPOP (EXTRA-COMMUNITY)						
Denmark	8	8	8	8	8	8
Germany	385	165	165	165	165	165
Netherlands	39	34	34	34	34	34
United Kingdom	20	14	14	14	14	14

Note: Migration = annual net flow in 1000s

Sources: National, Eurostat (1991a); Eurostat, Eurostat (1991b); DEMETER 2020; NEI (1994a, 1994b); ECPOP, Rees *et al.* (1992)

low scenario, 23.7 millions under the Eurostat high scenario and 15.3 millions under the ECPOP scenario, with additional births of course accruing to these populations.

Which of these scenarios is the most likely? The Eurostat high scenario assumes a level of immigration that is politically unacceptable, and measures are being taken in Germany and elsewhere to control immigration at origin by requiring visas prior to travel. Nevertheless the pressure for migration to settle in the EU is still very high, so we should regard the ECPOP scenario as more likely than the Eurostat low.

18.3.4 ASSUMPTIONS ABOUT INTERMEMBER STATE MIGRATION

One of the aims of both the Treaty of Rome and the Treaty of Maastricht is to ensure freedom of movement for EU citizens among member states. There are now virtually no legal restrictions on this movement. Labour market barriers involving recognition of qualifications are being reduced through harmonization and active policies such as the ERASMUS scheme for student exchanges.

Table 18.5 presents a set of synthetic estimates of intermember state migration in the 1980s based on statistics assembled by Poulain *et al.* (1991), though not a great deal of reliance can be placed on individual numbers. They show the continuing importance of Germany as a destination, the strengths of inflows to the UK and Italy (balanced by an equivalent emigration stream) and the important role of the Benelux countries as receivers of migrants from most origins. The flows from Spain and Portugal are much reduced compared with earlier decades.

There has been a long-term decline in intra-EU exchanges (Simon 1993) from the peak years of the late 1950s, 1960s and early 1970s. The reasons for this decline include population ageing (the older age groups are less mobile), the reduction in demographic pressure in traditional southern emigration countries plus Ireland, the lower economic growth in northern countries of the EU since the oil shock in 1973–4 together with an enhancement to the labour supply in northern countries with the entry of the baby boom generations into the labour-force, coupled with increasing female participation.

What are the prospects for intermember state mobility? Simon (1993) sees three categories of population being most affected by closer integration: young people, the highly skilled and some categories of migrants from outside the EU. Student exchanges among EU member states have been growing as networks of higher-education institutions are extended. The aim of the ERASMUS programme funded by the European Commission is to attain a 10 per cent level of involvement of students (Simon 1993). These exchanges will serve to increase the number of international migrations that occur after graduation. Among the highly skilled in managerial and technical posts, though not as yet the professions, there is evidence of increasing short-term migration. This is a form of circulation linked to the success and spread of international business organizations and will be focused on the most successful economies. Simon (1993) sees ethnic minorities with well-organized family and commercial networks also being involved in this circulatory migration, but this assumes rapid naturalization of extra-EU immigrants.

So, we can conclude that the intra-EU exchanges are relatively small and unlikely to take off in any dramatic fashion. The main argument for including a separate consideration of these flows is therefore conceptual: they are different in kind both from extra-Community and from intrastate migration. Rees *et al.* (1992) accomplish this by converting the Table 18.5 flows into out-migration rates which are embedded in a

Table 18.5 Intermember state migration flows for the EU: synthetic estimates for 1982, 1986–8 (000s)

Origin/Destination	B	DK	D	GR	E	F	IRL	I	L	NL	P	UK	Total out
Belgium (B)	0	0.2	4.1	0.5	1.4	4.1	0.1	3.8	1.0	4.7	0.3	2.9	23.1
Denmark (DK)	0.3	0	2.0	0.2	0.5	0.5	0.2	0.4	0.2	0.3	0.1	2.3	7.0
Germany (D)	3.7	2.0	0	15.5	7.5	7.9	2.2	38.0	0.8	7.9	4.4	19.0	108.8
Greece (GR)	0.6	0.2	19.3	0	0	0.4	0	0.9	0.1	0.6	0	2.6	24.6
Spain (E)	1.2	0.6	26.7	0	0	0.7	0	1.0	0.2	1.7	0	4.0	36.1
France (F)	6.9	0.7	15.1	0	3.0	0	0	6.5	1.3	2.5	0	13.1	49.1
Ireland (IRL)	0.2	0.3	3.0	0	0	0.2	0	0.2	0.0	0.7	0	38.0	42.5
Italy (I)	2.6	2.7	34.5	0.5	0.6	3.5	0.1	0	0.5	1.0	0.1	3.1	49.2
Luxemburg (L)	0.6	0.1	0.8	0.0	0.1	0.5	0.0	0.5	0	0.2	1.1	0.1	4.0
Netherlands (NL)	4.9	0.3	7.5	0.4	1.6	2.2	0.4	1.0	0.3	0	0.5	4.9	24.0
Portugal (P)	0.7	0.1	3.5	0	0.3	0.9	0	0.4	1.4	0.7	0	1.1	9.1
United Kingdom (UK)	2.6	1.7	17.5	2.4	6.2	5.4	19.0	4.6	0.2	5.1	0.9	0	65.5
Total in	24.3	8.9	134.0	19.5	21.3	26.2	21.9	57.3	5.9	25.2	7.4	91.0	443.0
Total net	1.2	1.9	25.2	-5.1	-14.8	-22.9	-20.6	8.1	1.9	1.2	-1.7	25.5	0.0

Note: 1. A zero entry, 0, indicates that no estimate is available, while 0.0 indicates an estimated average of less than 50

Source: 1. The flows are annual average gross flows for the periods 1982, 1986–8 based on information assembled in the report to Eurostat by Poulain *et al.* (1991). Reports from the origin and destination countries were averaged, and estimates made for key missing flows (eg IRL to UK)

'multiregional' model in which the regions are the member states of the EU.

The rates can either be assumed constant in the future (in the absence of a reliable time series from which to extrapolate) or an attempt can be made to develop scenarios. The method adopted is to apply scenario factors, based on conditions at the destination, to the interstate migration rates:

$$m^{mn}(y) = m^{mn}(b) \ (fimm^{n}(y)/100)$$

when (y) refers to the projection period, (b) to the benchmark period and fimm is the time-series factor for migration flows to destination member state n.

Rees *et al.* (1992) define the destination factors. Migration exchanges are assumed to respond to improvements in per caput GNP: they are assumed to increase by 0.4 per cent per year and to be focused on the higher-income countries. By the 2015–20 quinquennium migration rates with Germany and Luxembourg as their destination will have increased by 18 per cent, while migration rates with Greece, Spain, Ireland and Portugal grow by 12 per cent, with rates to the remaining members by 15 per cent. The assumptions are not firmly grounded in analysis—they serve simply to demonstrate that it is not necessary, as has been customary in virtually all national and academic projections involving interarea flows, to assume constancy of migration.

18.3.5 ASSUMPTIONS ABOUT INTERREGIONAL MIGRATION

Current national practice in most EEA countries is to use the latest information about interregional migration in a constant scenario (Van Imhoff *et al.* 1994) or with a small degree of trending. Alternative scenarios are developed in Belgium in its 1992 projections (concerning urban–suburban flows), in Germany (concerning east–west flows) and in the Netherlands with respect to spatial concentration or deconcentration. Policy developments with respect to the future location of the German capital (Bonn/Berlin) are taken into consideration in the German projections; the situation in the housing market influences out-migration in the Netherlands; in the UK the net migration outcomes of the multiregional model used to forecast internal migration are reviewed by local authorities, but adjustments are rarely made (because any regional adjustment will affect other regions).

It is common practice to compute a population projection assuming zero migration, principally in order to assess the effect of using what is often rather unreliable migration data, so both the DEMETER 2015 (Haverkate and Van Haselen 1990) and ECPOP (Rees *et al.* 1992) studies carry out projection based on both constant internal migration and zero internal migration.

It is, however, important to explore alternative scenarios on a Europe-wide scale. The immediate past may not be a very good guide to the longer-term future. One example is the likely level of flows between the eastern and western *Länder* of Germany. In the 1989–92 period, there was a very heavy outflow from the eastern *Länder*, which if it continued would empty these regions. It is expected that economic conditions will improve in the eastern *Länder*, particularly with recovery from the current recession and with the relocation of the Federal capital to Berlin in the 1990s. A second example is in the United Kingdom, where interregional balances have fluctuated in a complex way: migration being connected with the regional diffusion of upswings and downswings in the economy (see Chapter 16).

The ECPOP analysis (Rees *et al.* 1992) developed alternative interregional migration scenarios in response to these concerns using two hypotheses. The first was that in-migration levels to destination regions respond to relative income levels and that the wealthier regions will attract more and more migrants, while the less wealthy become less attractive to migration. Table 18.6 sets out the time-series indices which put this hypothesis into effect and show which regions fall into the

Table 18.6 The income scenario adopted for interregion migration in the EU

GDP/capita category	Level of in-migration (benchmark = 100)					
	1990–5	1995–00	2000–5	2005–10	2010–15	2015–20
High	102	110	115	120	120	120
Medium High	102	104	106	108	108	108
Medium Low	98	96	94	92	92	92
Low	95	90	85	80	80	80

Regions by GDP/capita category (1986–8 average)

High, >20% above EUR-12 mean

Hamburg, Île de France, Bremen, Lombardia, South-east
Hessen, Emilia-Romagna, Berlin, Noord Nederland, Luxembourg

Medium high, 0–20% above EUR-12 mean

Baden-Württemberg, Lazio, Nord Ovest, Nord Est, Bayern, Denmark,
Centro (Italy), West Nederland, Nordrhein Westfalen, Saarland, Centre Est, East Anglia,
South-west, Rheinland Pfalz, Vlaams Gewest, East Midlands, Bassin Parisien

Medium low, 0–20% below EUR-12 mean

Scotland, Est, North-West, Niedersachsen, Yorkshire and Humberside, West Midlands, Zuid Nederland, Schleswig-Holstein, Méditerranée, Sud Ouest,   Wales, Nord-Pas-de-Calais, Abruzzi-Molise, Noreste, Oost Nederland, Madrid, Région Wallonne, Este, Northern Ireland

Low, >20% below EUR-12 mean

Sardegna, Canarias, Sicilia, Noroeste, Sud, Campania, Ireland, Centro (Spain), Sur, Attiki, Kentriki, Continente, Voreia, Nisia

Where no data available, assigned to low category

Azores, Madeira, Sachsen, Sachsen-Anhalt, Brandenburg, Mecklenburg-Vorpommern, Thüringen

Source: GDP/capita figures—Commission for the European Communities, Directorate-General for Regional Policy (1991)

Table 18.7 The counterurbanization/urbanization scenario adopted for interregion migration in the EU

Area/density category	Level of in-migration (benchmark = 100)					
	1990–5	1995–00	2000–5	2005–10	2010–15	2015–20
North						
High	95	90	87	84	84	84
Medium high	98	96	94	92	92	92
Medium low	105	110	112	114	114	114
Low	102	104	109	114	114	114
South/Periphery						
High	105	110	115	120	120	120
Medium	98	96	94	92	92	92
Low	95	90	87	84	84	84

Regions by area and density category (persons per square km (psk), 1988)

North, medium high density (200–499 psk)

Bruxelles, Berlin, Hamburg, Bremen, Île de France, North-West, South-East, West Nederland, Nordrhein Westfalen

North, medium high density (200–499 psk)

Zuid Nederland, Vlaams Gewest, Saarland, West Midlands, Yorkshire and Humberside, Nord-Pas-de-Calais, Oost Nederland, Baden Würrtemburg, Hessen, Sachsen, East Midlands, North

North, medium low density (120–199 psk)

South West, Région Wallonne, Rheinland Pfalz, Schleswig-Holstein, Thüringen, East Anglia, Bayern, Niedersachsen, Luxembourg, Sachsen-Anhalt, Noord Nederland

North, low density (>120 psk)

Denmark, Est, Méditerranée, Centre Est, Brandenburg, Ouest, Mecklenburg-Vorpommern, Bassin Parisien, Scotland, Sud–Ouest

South/Periphery, high density (>200 psk)

Attiki, Madrid, Campania, Lombardia, Madeira, Lazio, Canarias, Sicilia

South/Periphery, medium density (80–199 psk)

Nord Ovest, Emilia-Romagna, Este, Nord Est, Sud, Centro (Italy), Azores, Northern Ireland, Continente, Abruzzi, Noroeste, Sur

South/Periphery, low density (>80 psk)

Sardegna, Noroeste, Nisia, Ireland, Kentriki Ellada, Voreia Ellada, Centro (Spain)

Source: as Table 18.6

different income classes. The second hypothesis proposed that change in the attractiveness of regions to in-migrants is related to population density levels but in different ways in northern and southern member states. High-density, urbanized regions in northern countries become less attractive over time while low-density, less-urbanized regions become more attractive. This is the counterurbanization hypothesis. On the other hand, in southern countries, the relative attraction of high- and low-density regions was felt to be reversed, with the process of urbanization in its final stages. Table 18.7 sets out the time-series destination factors associated with this hypothesis. It should be stressed that both hypotheses presented here are speculative and in need of testing. Testing would involve the construction of a detailed time series of migration data. Such an activity is underway at Eurostat and the Netherlands Interdisciplinary Demographic Institute (NIDI).

So far in the chapter, the methods and assumptions underpinning national and regional population projections in the Eurostat have been reviewed in a critical fashion. We now look at the range of outcomes of these methods and assumptions.

18.4 REVIEW OF PROJECTION RESULTS

The results of the following projections are briefly considered here:

1. Eurostat low, which involves modest improvement in mortality, some further declines in fertility and reduced external immigration;
2. Eurostat high, which involves steady improvement in mortality, rises in fertility though not to replacement, continuing high external immigration (Tables 18.2, 18.4, 18.5).

These set the upper and lower limits on national populations and the controlling scenarios for the regional population projections:

3. DEMETER low, which involves no change in mortality or fertility differentials and constant interregional migration scenarios with reduced external immigration.

4. DEMETER high, which involves convergence between the regions in both mortality and fertility but again constant interregional migration.

5. ECPOP, which involves the average of Eurostat low and high scenarios at the national scale plus specific scenarios for interegional migration: (a) zero, which involves no interregion migration; (b) constant, which involves constant application of benchmark period (late 1980s) interregion migration rates; (c) income, gains and losses in in-migration to destinations dependent on regional GDP/caput levels; (d) counterurbanization/urbanization, gains and losses in in-migration to destinations dependent on regional population density levels.

Table 18.8 The projected populations of the member states of the European Union, 1990–2020 (millions)

Member state	1990	2020	%Change	%Ch.60+	2020	%Change	%Ch.60+
		EUROSTAT LOW			EUROSTAT HIGH		
Belgium	9.9	9.8	−1.8	28.5	11.3	14.0	42.8
Denmark	5.1	5.0	−2.8	23.1	5.9	15.4	38.2
Germany	79.1	73.5	−7.1	27.5	90.3	14.1	49.4
Greece	10.2	10.2	−0.2	33.8	12.3	20.2	52.6
Spain	38.9	38.4	−1.3	34.4	44.7	14.8	48.8
France	56.6	60.0	6.0	41.5	67.8	19.9	55.2
Ireland	3.5	3.3	−6.3	39.9	4.4	24.6	58.0
Italy	57.6	54.3	−5.8	31.8	63.1	9.6	47.4
Luxembourg	0.4	0.4	3.4	44.4	0.5	36.8	62.5
Netherlands	14.9	16.0	7.5	58.5	18.8	26.1	75.1
Portugal	10.3	10.7	3.1	31.9	12.8	23.7	48.3
United Kingdom	57.3	57.4	0.2	16.4	65.3	13.9	30.9
EUR-12	343.9	338.9	−1.5	30.8	397.1	15.5	47.4
		ECPOP-NATIONAL			ECPOP-REGIONAL		
Belgium	9.9	9.7	−3.2	26.4	9.9	−0.9	28.3
Denmark	5.1	5.1	−1.6	24.5	5.0	−3.0	24.8
Germany	79.1	72.8	−7.9	25.2	73.9	−6.6	26.5
Greece	10.0	9.5	−4.8	25.0	10.0	0.0	37.6
Spain	38.9	38.9	−0.2	41.9	38.9	0.0	40.1
France	56.3	60.0	6.6	39.7	60.4	7.3	40.8
Ireland	3.5	3.5	−0.6	32.6	3.5	0.2	32.5
Italy	57.6	54.7	−5.1	32.5	55.3	−3.9	32.6
Luxembourg	0.4	0.4	10.5	50.2	0.4	13.8	54.1
Netherlands	14.9	15.8	6.2	60.8	15.8	6.2	63.5
Portugal	10.3	10.5	1.2	33.0	10.5	1.2	31.7
United Kingdom	57.3	59.0	2.9	15.7	59.7	4.1	16.7
EUR-12	343.4	339.9	−1.0	30.5	343.3	0.0	31.6
		DEMETER LOW			DEMETER HIGH		
Belgium	9.9	9.7	−2.2	28.6	11.3	13.7	42.8
Denmark	5.1	5.0	−3.1	23.1	5.9	15.1	38.2
Germany	79.1	73.2	−7.5	27.5	89.9	13.6	49.4
Greece	10.2	10.2	−0.4	33.8	12.2	20.0	52.6
Spain	38.9	38.3	−1.6	34.4	44.5	14.4	48.8
France	56.6	59.9	5.9	41.5	67.7	19.7	55.2
Ireland	3.5	3.3	−6.1	39.9	4.4	24.9	58.0
Italy	57.6	54.1	−6.1	31.8	62.9	9.2	47.3
Luxembourg	0.4	0.4	2.9	44.9	0.5	36.2	63.3
Netherlands	14.9	16.0	7.2	58.5	18.7	25.8	75.1
Portugal	10.3	10.6	2.8	31.9	12.8	23.4	48.2
United Kingdom	57.3	57.3	−0.0	16.4	65.2	13.7	30.8
EUR-12	343.9	338.0	−1.7	30.8	396.0	15.1	47.4

Source: Eurostat (1991b); NEI (1994a, 1994c); Rees *et al.* (1992)

18.4.1 NATIONAL RESULTS

Table 18.8 sets out national level results. Why do they differ? The Eurostat high scenario's surplus (and that of the DEMETER high) over the low scenario can be apportioned, roughly 50 per cent to higher fertility, 30 per cent to higher immigration and 20 per cent to improved life expectancy.

Although the Eurostat low and ECPOP national scenarios are very close in total population outcomes, this is because the higher fertility and immigration of the latter cancel out the lower mortality of the former. The ECPOP national and regional differ marginally because of both information differences (the higher mortality and fertility of 1988 was used at the regional level rather than the 1989 rates at the national level) and because of disaggregation effects (the ECPOP regional projections are not constrained to the ECPOP national).

What about commonalities between the projections? In particular how do particular countries fare? We can distinguish countries which rank high on all projections, those which rank low and some which change rank. The high group includes the Netherlands, Luxembourg, France and Portugal. The low group includes Germany, Italy, Belgium, Denmark, Spain and Greece. The two countries which have rather different ranks on the Eurostat high projection compared with others are Ireland and the United Kingdom. Ireland exhibits a much higher position on the high scenario than on the others, while for the UK the situation is the reverse. The UK demographic structure does not have as much potential to respond to higher fertility and lower mortality than do the structures of other countries such as Ireland.

The fourth and seventh columns of Table 18.8 show one common element in all projection scenarios—marked ageing of the population. The difference between the Eurostat high scenario and the others also shows the potential for 'super-ageing' of the population if mortality continues to decrease. Past national projections have tended to underestimate this effect.

18.4.2 REGIONAL RESULTS

The DEMETER model is used to produce regional forecasts under high and low scenarios and the results are reported in detail in NEI (1994a, 1994b, 1994c and 1994d). What is clear from those results is the wide range of experiences within each country of population change across the regions (Table 18.9). Within each member state regions are distributed in virtually all the growth categories. Table 18.9 displays the ten highest and ten lowest regions for each of the components of population change as well as the total, drawing on the NEI projections.

It is clear, from the ECPOP projections presented in Table 18.10 that interregion migration produces dramatic shifts in the pattern of population change compared with the natural-increase-dominated projection. Only three regions (Nord-Pas de Calais, Canarias and Azores) appear in the top ten under both the zero and constant scenarios, although five regions (Saarland, Hamburg, Bremen, Emilia-Romagna

Table 18.9 DEMETER projections: highest and lowest regions

Region	Annual pop. change 1995–2000	Region	Natural change 1995
HIGHEST		HIGHEST	
Flevoland	29.5	Flevoland	14.5
Ceuta y Melilla	12.9	Ceuta y Melilla	9.3
Languedoc-Roussillon	10.9	Northern Ireland	8.7
Utrecht	10.8	Campania	8.1
Madeira	10.0	Île de France	7.1
Lincolnshire	9.9	Puglia	7.1
Murcia	8.6	Nord-Pas-de-Calais	6.9
Oberbayern	8.5	Murcia	6.8
Luxembourg (B)	8.4	Canarias	6.8
Noord Brabant	8.4	Utrecht	6.6
LOWEST		LOWEST	
Merseyside	–4.4	Tübingen	–4.3
Thüringen	–6.3	Friuli	–4.3
Magdeburg	–7.1	Magdeburg	–4.5
Leipzig	–7.2	Dresden	–5.2
Mecklenburg/Vorpommern	–7.9	Halle	–5.4
Brandenburg	–8.3	Voreio Aigaio	–5.4
Dessau	–8.7	Dessau	–5.5
Chemnitz	–9.7	Leipzig	–5.7
Halle	–9.9	Liguria	–5.8
Dresden	–9.9	Chemnitz	–6.5

Region	Internal Migration 1995	Region	External Migration 1995
HIGHEST		HIGHEST	
Flevoland	16.6	Ionia Nisia	12.8
Dorset–Somerset	8.4	Ipeiros	9.6
Cornwall–Devon	8.0	Peloponnisos	9.5
Lincolnshire	7.7	Voreio Aigaio	8.5
Languedoc-Roussillon	6.9	Notio Aigaio	8.4
Clwyd, Dyfed, Gwynedd, Powys	6.7	Thessalia	7.5
Valle d'Aosta	5.9	Alentejo	7.4
North Yorkshire	5.7	Algarve	6.0
Dytiki Makedonia	5.3	Madeira	6.0
East Anglia	5.2	Kent	6.0
LOWEST		LOWEST	
Brandenburg	–5.1	Merseyside	–1.0
West Midlands	–5.3	Hampshire, Isle of Wight	–1.2
Lorraine	–5.3	Humberside	–1.6
Ionia Nisia	–5.6	Anatoliki Makedonia	–1.8
Halle	–5.8	Ireland	–2.2
Mecklenburg/Vorpommern	–5.8	Attiki	–2.7
Dresden	–5.9	Açores	–2.8
Greater London	–6.6	Canarias	–3.7
Ipeiros	–7.1	Dytiki Makedonia	–7.2
Arnsberg	–8.3	Baleares	–7.8

Notes: The rates are annual rates per 1000 population

Source: NEI (1994a), Tables 8.2, 8.8, 8.9, 8.10

357

Table 18.10 Top and bottom 10 NUTS 1 regions under variant interregion migration scenarios, % change 1990–2020

Rank	Zero Scenario	% Ch	Constant Scenario	% Ch	Income Scenario	% Ch	CU/U Scenario	% Ch
1	Northern Ireland	25	Nisia	30	Brussel	53	East Anglia	55
2	Ireland	23	Canaries	21	Hamburg	28	South West	55
3	Nord-Pas de Calais	20	Açores	16	South East	22	Wales	49
4	Campania	18	Bayern	15	Luxembourg	22	Schleswig-Holstein	39
5	Azores	17	Nord-Pas de Calais	15	Nisia	20	Bayern	35
6	Île de France	16	Ost-Nederland	14	Berlin	19	Canarias	28
7	Canarias	15	Brussel	14	Hessen	19	Noord-Nederland	23
8	Sur	14	Wales	14	Canarias	16	Luxembourg	22
9	Sud	13	Sur	13	Noord-Nederland	16	Scotland	21
10	Est	11	South West	13	East Midlands	16	Nisia	19
61	Schleswig-Holstein	-10	Hamburg	-11	North	-13	Brussel	-17
62	Nord-Est	-11	Noroeste	-12	Thüringen	-15	Emilia-Romagna	-17
63	Hessen	-11	Emilia-Romagna	-14	Niedersachsen	-15	Berlin	-22
64	Lombardia	-11	Thüringen	-14	West Midlands	-16	Nord-Ovest	-24
65	Saarland	-13	Nord-Ovest	-20	Schleswig Holstein	-16	Saarland	-27
66	Centro	-14	Saarland	-21	Nord-Ovest	-17	Sachsen	-28
67	Bremen	-17	Bremen	-24	Sachsen	-29	Hamburg	-46
68	Hamburg	-18	Sachsen	-26	Saarland	-37	Bremen	-53
69	Nord-Ovest	-20	Brandenburg	-76	Brandenburg	-84	Brandenburg	-77
70	Emilia-Romagna	-21	Sachsen Anhalt	-80	Sachsen Anhalt	-87	Sachsen Anhalt	-81

Notes: CU/U = counterurbanization/urbanization scenario; % ch = % change in population, 1990–2020

Source: author's computations

and Nord-West) repeat in the bottom 10.

Remote peripheral regions dominate the top ten under the zero scenario, while German or north Italian regions take up most positions in the bottom 10. When interregional migration is taken into consideration in the constant scenario, a variety of different regions appear that are attractive to in-migrants such as Bayern, Brussels or Ost-Nederland. The new regions that appear in the bottom 10 include four of the eastern *Länder* of Germany. Although the direction of projected change and their position on the list is probably correct, the magnitude of the population decline projected must be treated sceptically as the out-migration rates involved are very crudely estimated and are likely to reduce rapidly as these regions converge economically with their '*Wessi*' cousins.

The income and counterurbanization lists serve to demonstrate the difficulties of forecasting interregional migration when trends change. For example, the Brussels region heads the income scenario list as the dynamic 'capital' of the European Union, but then appears in the bottom 10 of the counterurbanization list in which an overheated and overcrowded urban economy has sent enterprises and migrants fleeing north to Flanders and south to Wallonia.

Clearly, a great deal of further work is needed to develop detailed regional migration scenarios that reflect the changing developments and pressures affecting individual regions. There is a great deal of qualitative, descriptive and historical analysis of migration within EU member states. The future challenge will be to convert that knowledge into testable hypotheses of migration trends and to develop the consistent space–time series for testing.

18.5 CONCLUSIONS

What are the general conclusions of our review of current practice and recent results in forecasting the regional populations of the EU?

18.5.1 IMPROVEMENT IN PROJECTION METHODS

The models for forecasting EU region populations incorporate relatively sophisticated methods (eg the use of interregional migration rates), but there is room for improvement, should suitable data become available.

The interregional parts of the models could be further developed to become full multiregional modules that recognize the interdependency of origin, destination and age. This improvement will depend on whether a common data base of interregional migration in the form of origin–age, destination–age and origin–destination arrays can be built up. This is an ambition of Eurostat in its work to extend the demographic parts of the REGIO database.

Separate representation of extra-Community, intermember state and interregional migration within member states should be used at NUTS 2 level (as developed at NUTS 1 level in the ECPOP model). The consistency issue raised by operating the model at two levels, national and regional, needs more thorough exploration (building on the work of van Imhoff and Keilman 1991).

It is probably time, in the next round of projections funded by the European Commission and organized by Eurostat, to envisage the conversion of the input data base, the model and the output data base into a publicly accessible tool both for educational purposes and so that national and regional governments, non-governmental agencies and businesses could examine the projections for their own purposes in more detail. A precedent is the Independent Treasury Economic Model (ITEM) Club in the UK which makes available to outside users the model of the British economy used by the UK Treasury (Finance Ministry).

18.5.2 IMPROVEMENT IN PROJECTION ASSUMPTIONS

A great deal of thought has gone into the design of fertility, mortality and external migration assumptions at both national and European levels, but relatively little progress has been made on the internal migration front. The NEI work has always assumed interaction patterns constant over time. The Leeds School of Geography work has been speculative rather than informed by detailed time series analysis. However, the chapters of this book have served to demonstrate that a great deal is now known about the dynamics of internal migration within EU member states. This expert knowledge needs harnessing in future rounds of scenario development for the internal migration component.

18.5.3 REGIONAL POPULATION FUTURES

Most of the discussion of the NEI results (NEI 1994a; CEC 1994) focuses on the common themes across regions—the ageing of the population and the work-force, and the likelihood of the onset of population decline for a substantial set of EU regions. Can we, however, say something about the geography of future population shifts? Looking at Tables 18.10 and 18.11 and drawing on the splendid succession of maps of population change in NEI (1994a), can we identify the winners and losers in the future population redistribution stakes?

Over the 1990–2020 period, the EU population first grows and then begins a decline which brings it back to its starting point (Table 18.1). This means that we can interpret population gains and losses in countries and regions as also being gains or losses in share of the EU total. Gaining countries and their percentage gains under the ECPOP Constant scenario are in rank order: Luxembourg (plus 13.8 per cent), France (plus 7.3 per cent), Netherlands (plus 6.2 per cent), United Kingdom (plus 4.1 per cent), Portugal (plus 1.2 per cent), Greece (plus 0.0 per cent) and Spain (plus 0.0 per cent). The biggest loser is Germany (minus 6.6 per cent), followed by Italy (minus 4.0 per cent), Denmark (minus 3.0 per cent) and Belgium (minus 0.9 per cent). Around these national averages are wide spreads of region gains and losses.

Figure 18.2 summarizes the regimes of demographic change for NUTS 1 regions

Table 18.11 Projected populations of NUTS 1 regions under variant migration scenarios, 2020

Region	1990 Base	2020 populations (1000s)			
		ZE	CO	IN	CU
Belgium	9948	9797	9861	9870	9860
Vlaams Gewest	5740	5638	5617	5539	5589
Région Wallone	3244	3218	3148	2854	3471
Bruxelles/Brussel	964	941	1096	1477	800
Denmark					
Denmark	5135	4913	4980	4992	4992
Germany	79 106	72 882	73 885	74 564	74 573
Baden-Württemberg	9619	9242	10 594	10 763	9741
Bayern	11 221	10 533	12 941	13 277	15 102
Berlin	3410	3104	3303	4066	2651
Brandenburg	2641	2547	631	413	601
Bremen	674	562	515	748	316
Hamburg	1626	1332	1444	2081	883
Hessen	5651	5028	5642	6696	5125
Mecklenburg-Vorpommern	1964	2011	1893	1797	2004
Niedersachsen	7284	6599	7387	6154	8781
Nordrhein-Westfalen	17 104	15 552	15 982	16 185	14 283
Rheinland-Pfalz	3702	3363	3 400	3380	4278
Saarland	1065	923	838	668	774
Sachsen	4901	4447	3607	3495	3541
Sachsen-Anhalt	2965	2765	598	374	575
Schleswig-Holstein	2595	2337	2794	2175	3595
Thüringen	2684	2537	2316	2292	2323
Greece	10 019	10 197	10 023	9840	9838
Voreia Ellada	3174	3269	3108	3084	3012
Kentriki Ellada	2154	2137	2071	2038	1839
Attiki	3796	3845	3678	3645	3922
Nisia	895	946	1166	1073	1065
Spain	38 924	39 447	38 937	38 546	38 551
Noroeste	4464	4030	3915	3873	3825
Noreste	4124	3853	3727	3742	3667
Madrid	4870	5068	5189	5165	5502
Centro	5470	5268	5068	4983	4799
Este	10 466	10 356	10 122	10 122	9958
Sur	8051	9178	9128	8941	8905
Canarias	1478	1694	1788	1720	1895
France	56 305	61 303	60 416	60 014	60 014
Île de France	10 602	12 337	11 809	12 023	11 325
Bassin Parisien	10 212	11 227	11 092	11 062	11 143
Nord-Pas-de-Calais	3944	4724	4548	4473	4477
Est	5000	5548	5388	5306	5359
Ouest	7409	7954	7916	7750	7944

Table 18.11 continued

Region	1990		2020 populations (1000s)		
	Base	ZE	CO	IN	CU
Centre-Est	6636	7169	7105	7099	7101
Méditerranée	6585	6668	6833	6685	6901·
Ireland					
Ireland	3507	4303	3515	3228	3228
Italy	57 579	55 112	55 305	55 169	55 226
Nord-Ovest	6200	4958	4980	5165	4736
Lombardia	8912	7923	8123	8953	9032
Nord-Est	6475	5764	5957	5991	5661
Emilia-Romagna	3922	3088	3385	3729	3238
Centro	5812	4859	5275	5400	5036
Lazio	5171	4949	5097	5285	5738
Campania	5809	6882	6335	5904	6518
Abruzzi-Molise	1602	1529	1567	1477	1462
Sud	6845	7747	7345	6655	6944
Sicilia	5173	5736	5543	5063	5286
Sardegna	1658	1687	1698	1547	1575
Luxembourg					
Luxembourg	378	370	430	460	460
Netherlands	14 893	15 813	15 823	15 790	15 791
Noord-Nederland	1594	1666	1543	1845	1953
Oost-Nederland	3037	3342	3474	2982	3439
West-Nederland	6968	7304	7306	7726	6841
Zuid-Nederland	3294	3501	3500	3237	3558
Portugal	10 337	10 529	10 465	10 387	10 387
Continente	9809	9932	9872	9798	9798
Açores	253	296	294	292	292
Madeira	275	301	299	297	297
United Kingdom	57 310	58 768	59 652	59 868	59 829
North	3084	3045	3125	2683	3051
Yorks. and Humb.	4934	5018	5275	4505	5130
East Midlands	3987	4064	4363	4618	4146
East Anglia	2043	2068	2257	2245	3164
South East	17 418	18 059	17 208	21 311	14 087
South West	4654	4525	5239	5339	7210
West Midlands	5229	5443	5201	4391	4943
North West	6391	6596	6607	5726	5825
Wales	2869	2917	3280	2745	4280
Scotland	5116	5052	5324	4674	6188
Northern Ireland	1585	1981	1773	1631	1805
EUR-12	343 441	343 434	343 292	342 728	342 749

Scenarios:
ZE = zero internal migration   IN = income scenario
CU = counterurbanization/urbanization scenario   CO = constant internal migration

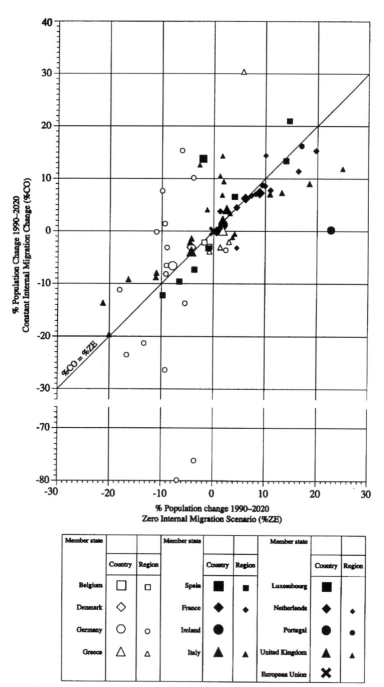

Figure 18.2 Population change, 1990–2020: zero scenario versus constant internal migration scenario

of the European Union over the 30 years from 1990. The graph is a complicated one that needs careful explanation, but it is a very appropriate diagram with which to conclude this volume on migration in the European Union because it captures the essence of the patterns and trends that have been discussed in preceding chapters.

From the projected populations presented in Table 18.11 two indicators were computed. The first is the percentage population change between 1990 and 2020 under the zero internal migration scenario. This is a scenario which expresses an average of the Eurostat high and low scenarios for fertility, mortality and external migration at the NUTS 1 region scale, but in which both intermember state and interregion migration rates are set to zero. This first percentage indicator is used as the horizontal axis of Figure 18.2.

The second indicator is the percentage population change between 1990 and 2020 under the constant internal migration rates scenario. The same assumptions for fertility, mortality and net external migration are adopted as in the zero internal migration scenario, but the intermember state and interregion migration rates are filled in with the best available estimates for the late 1980s which are assumed constant over the projection period. This percentage indicator is used as the vertical axis of the Figure 18.2 graph.

The graph thus reveals the impact of intra-European Union migration on regional population change. Countries and regions lying close to the diagonal line running from bottom left to top right of the graph have similar futures under the two scenarios. Countries and regions lying away from this line of equality have different futures as a result of intra-EU migration. Note that the EU average (by coincidence not design) falls at the zero origin of the graph.

There are a significant number of regions in the European Union which face the prospect of substantial population loss over the next 30 years, recording declines of more than 5 per cent under both scenarios. These are regions in eastern and northern Germany, in north-central Italy and in central and north-eastern Spain. They are characterized by extremely low fertility, rapidly ageing populations and severe net out-migration. Within each of these countries, however, there are other regions with more positive growth regimes which partly compensate and reduce national losses. In Italy, strong positive population change is anticipated in southern regions, principally driven by natural increase and net external in-migration. These regions lie well below the line of equality of the two scenarios, indicating substantial net losses through internal migration. In Germany, the southern regions exhibit population gains under the constant scenario, though all lose through natural change. In Spain, the gaining regions are in southern, coastal and island Spain, where substantial in-migration and natural change are predicted.

Gaining regions exhibit two growth profiles. There is a small set, including Luxembourg, the Brussels region and the South West, Scotland and the North in the UK which are predicted to gain under the constant scenario but experience losses through natural decrease, as with southern German regions, or net external migration.

The other gaining regions are found in the Netherlands, France and the UK but at different positions in the gaining quadrant. The Dutch regions show strong growth under both scenarios and so gain from natural, external and internal components, with the exception of Noord-Nederland. The UK regions (East Anglia, East Midlands and Yorkshire and Humberside) show very little natural or external-based growth but strong growth through internal migration. The French regions are predicted to experience substantial growth under the zero scenario but this reduces under the constant scenario, implying internal migration losses within France to the Méditerranée region but also to other EU member states.

Finally, at the periphery of the European Union we find the most prominent departures from the average demographic future. The islands of Greece (Nisia) show strong growth through internal migration, while the Portuguese region of the Azores islands shows strong natural growth. The Irish Republic and the UK region of Northern Ireland show the two highest percentage gains through natural change in the EU, but these are dramatically reduced when internal migration is taken into account. Northern Ireland experiences interregional losses to other UK regions, while the Irish Republic's losses are through migration to other member states, most prominently the UK.

The European Union, as a whole, faces a future of zero population growth over the medium term and decline over the long term, assuming current trends persist. However, as Figure 18.2 demonstrates, this average future masks a variety of fascinating regional futures which, in part, mirror national prospects but which also show transnational similarities at region scale.

NOTES

1. It is now clear that the term 'European Union', embodied in the Treaty of Maastricht, has been adopted to replace the term 'European Community', which came to be used in the past few years as shorthand for the European Communities (European Economic Community, European Coal and Steel Community, European Atomic Energy Community). Most of the citations to data sources and reports are works produced by, for or with respect to the European Community, so that this term will be retained when reference is made to them. Otherwise the term European Union is used to describe the 12 signatories of the Treaty of Maastricht.

Reference is also made in the chapter to the European Economic Area which comprises the European Community (12 member states or EUR-12) plus the European Free Trade Association (EFTA) members (6 states). Austria, Finland and Sweden joined the EU on January 1, 1995. Iceland, Switzerland and Norway remain outside the EU.

2. NUTS stands for Nomenclature des Unités Territoriales et Statistiques. This is a system designed by Eurostat for the compilation of a consistent series of statistics for the regions of EC member states. The system has four higher levels: NUTS 0 refers to the 12 member states, NUTS 1 to the first tier of large regions in member states, NUTS 2 and NUTS 3 to lower tiers. The functions of regions at each tier vary from country to country. Some may be for purely statistical purposes (eg the NUTS 1 regions of the UK); some may be important local government units in the member state (eg the NUTS 3 regions, départements, in France).

References

Alarcão, A. and Morais, J.P. (1975) *La population du Portugal*. CICRED: Paris.

Amaro, R.R. (1985) Reestruturações demográficas, económicas e socioculturais em curso na sociedade portuguesa: o caso dos emigrantes regressados. *Análise Social*, 21, 87–88–89, 605–77.

Amaro, R.R. (1991) Lógicas de espacialização da economia portuguesa. *Sociologia – Problemas e Práticas*, 10, 161–82.

Anache, M., Fleury, M., Foucher, J. and Santoni, P. (1982) Monter à Paris ou monter en province? *Aspects économiques de l'Ile-de-France* 6, 601–3.

ANHYP (1994) *Valeur immobilière*. Antwerp.

Armitage, R.I. (1987) English regional fertility and mortality patterns, 1975–1985. *Population Trends*, 47, 16–23.

Aubry, B. (1988) Les migrations inter-régionales depuis trente ans. *Economie et Statistique*, 212, 13–23.

Baccaïni, B. (1991) *Mobilité, distances de migration et cycle de vie*. PhD Thesis, University of Paris.

Baccaïni, B., Courgeau, D. and Desplanques, G. (1993) Les migrations internes en France de 1982 à 1990. *Population* 48, 6, 1771–89.

Baganha, M.I. (1991) Portuguese emigration: current characteristics and trends. *Cost Workshop—Migration: Europe's Integration and the Labour Force*. Leuven.

Baldwin-Edwards, M. (1991) Immigration after 1992. *Policy and Politics*, 19, 3, 199–211.

Baptista, A.M. (1985) *Crise e desenvolvimento económico urbano*. IACEP/NEUR: Lisbon.

Baptista, A.M. and Ferrão, J. (1989) Industrialização e desenvolvimento endógeno em Portugal: problemas e perspectivas. *Sociologia—Problemas e Práticas*, 7, 43–64.

Baptista, A.M. and Moniz, F. (1985) *Migrações internas. Algumas observações a partir dos fluxos inter-regionais no período 1973–1981*. IACEP/NEUR: Lisbon.

Barany, Z.D. (1992) Democratic changes bring mixed blessing for Gypsies. *RFE/RL Research Report*, 1, 20, 40–7.

Beiser, M. (1993) After the door has been opened: the mental health of immigrants and refugees in Canada. In V. Robinson (ed.), *The International Refugee Crisis: British and Canadian Responses*. Macmillan: Basingstoke.

Birg, H. (1992) Stellungnahme zur ersten regionalisierten Bevölkeringsvorausschätzung für das wiedervereinigte Deutschland. *Informationen zur Raumentwicklung*, 11/12, 863–76.

Boden P. (1989) *The Analysis of Internal Migration in the United Kingdom using Census and National Health Service Central Register Data*. Unpublished PhD thesis, School of Geography, University of Leeds, Leeds.

Boden, P., Stillwell J.H.C. and Rees, P.H. (1992) How good are the NHSCR data? Chapter 2 in J.C.H. Stillwell, P.H. Rees and P. Boden (eds), *Migration Processes and Patterns: Volume 2: Population Redistribution in the United Kingdom*. Belhaven Press: London, 13–27.

BOE (1992) *Real Decreto 766/1992*. item 15288 in BOE no.156. Ministerio de Relaciones con las Cortes y de la Secretaría del Gobierno, Madrid, 30 June.

Boeri, T. (1994) Labour market flows and the persistence of unemployment in Central and Eastern Europe. *Unemployment in Transition Countries: Transient or Persistent?* OECD: Paris, 13–56.

Bonaguidi, A. (1987) *Alcuni aspetti meno noti delle migrazioni in Italia*. Report no 7, Dipartimento di Matematica e Statistica Applicata all'Economia. University of Pisa.

Bonaguidi, A. (1990) Italy. In C.B. Nam, W.J. Serow and D.F. Sly (eds), *International Handbook on Internal Migration*. Greenwood Press: New York, 239–55.

Bonaguidi, A. and Terra Abrami, V. (1992) The metropolitan aging transition and metropolitan redistribution of the elderly in Italy. In A. Rogers (ed.), *Elderly Migration and Population Redistribution*. Belhaven Press: London.

Boubnova, H. (1992) *East-West commuting*. Paper prepared for the conference, Mass Migration in Europe: Implications in East and West, IAS-IIASA-IF, Vienna, March.

Boudoul, J. and Faur, J.P. (1986) Trente ans de migrations intérieures. *Espaces, Populations, Sociétés*, 2, 293–302.

Breathnach, P. and Jackson, J.A. (1991) Ireland, emigration and the new international division of labour. In R. King (ed.), *Contemporary Irish Migration*, Geographical Society of Ireland Special Publication 6: Dublin, 1–10.

Brochmann, G. (1992) Control vs. control in Immigration Policies: a closed Europe in the making? *Paper presented at the Conference, Mass Migration in Europe*. Vienna, March.

Brubaker, W.R. (1992) Citizenship struggles in Soviet successor states. *International Migration Review*, 26, 269–91.

Bruxelas, M. (1987) *Indicadores de caracterização e evolução do sistema urbano*. GEPAT: Lisbon.

Bundesforschunganstalt für Landeskunde und Raumordnung, *Spatial Monitoring System of the Federal Institute for Regional and Spatial Planning*. Population Projection 1989–2000.

Bundesverwaltungsamt (1993) *Jahresstatistik Aussiedler 1992*, Cologne.

Bundesverwaltungsamt (1994) Photocopied table *Jahresübersicht Registrierung nach Herkunftslander 1993* from current statistics on *Aussiedler*.

Cabré, A., Moreno, J. and Pujadas, I. (1985) Cambio migratorio y reconversión territorial en España. *Revista Española de Investigaciones Sociológicas*, 32, 43–65.

Callovi, G. (1992) Regulation of Immigration in 1993: Pieces of the European Community Jig-Saw Puzzle. *International Migration Review*, 26, 353–72.

Cane, A. (1994) Case of 'déjà vu' on EU Travel. *Financial Times*, 28 January.

Capron, D. and Corner, I. (1992) Subnational population and household projections by Central Government, in *OPCS Occasional Paper 38*, BSPS Conference Papers 1990, Population Projections: Trends, Methods and Uses, HMSO: London, 55–63.

Carrilho, M.J. and Peixoto, J. (1991) Le Portugal. In J.L Rallu and A. Blum (eds), *European Population*, John Libbey/INED: Paris, pp. 393–409.

Carvel, J. (1992a) Please have your passports ready...! *The Guardian (Society):* Manchester, 22 July.

Carvel, J. (1992b) Million 'aliens' face ban on entry to EC. *The Guardian (Society):* Manchester, 3 July.

Castles, S. and Miller, M. (1993) *The Age of Migration*. Macmillan: Basingstoke.

Cawley, M. (1991) Patterns of rural–urban and urban–rural migration. In R. King (ed.), *Contemporary Irish Migration*, Geographical Society of Ireland Special Publication 6: Dublin, 111–21.

CEC, Commission of the European Communities, Directorate-General for Regional Policy (1991) *The Regions in the 1990s: Fourth Periodic Report on the Social and Economic Situation and Development of the Regions of the Community*. Office for Official Publications of the European Communities: Luxembourg.

CEC, Commission of the European Communities, Directorate-General for Regional Policy (1994) *Competitiveness and Cohesion: Trends in the Regions—Fifth Periodic Report on the Social and Economic Situation and Development of the Regions of the Community*. Office for Official Publications of the European Communities: Luxembourg.

Champion, A.G. (ed.) (1989) *Counterurbanization. The Changing Pace and Nature of Population Deconcentration*. Arnold: London.

Champion, A.G. (1994) Population deconcentration trends in the 1980s and their policy implications: Paper presented to the British–Swedish–Dutch Conference on 'Population Planning and Policies', Laxon, Sweden, 15–18 September.

Chesnais, J-C. (1993) Soviet emigration: past, present and future. In *The Changing Course of International Migration*. OECD: Paris.

CIA (1993). *The CIA World Factbook*. Central Intelligence Agency, Langley, Virginia. NISS Wide Area Information Server.

Coleman, D.A. (1992) Does Europe need Immigrants? Population and Work Force Projections. *International Migration Review*, 26, 413–61.

Coleman, D. (1993a) Le monde est-il en mouvement? La migration internationale en 1992. Report presented at the European Population Conference, Geneva.

Coleman, D.A. (1993b) Contrasting age structure of Western Europe and of Eastern Europe and former Soviet Union: Demographic curiosity or labour resource. *Population and Development Review*, 19, 3, 523–55.

Coleman, D. and Salt, J. (1992) *The British Population: Patterns, Trends and Processes*. Oxford University Press: Oxford.

Collins, B. (1993) The Irish in Britain. In B.J. Graham and L.J. Proudfoot (eds), *An Historical Geography of Ireland*. Academic Press: London, 366–98.

Collinson, S. (1993) *Europe and International Migration*. Belhaven: London.

Commission on Emigration and Other Population Problems (1956) *Reports 1948–54*. Stationery Office: Dublin.

Commission of the European Communities (1994) *Communication from the Commission to the Council and European Parliament on Immigration and Asylum policies*. COM(94)23 final. Brussels, 23 February.

Cónim, C. (1985) Migrações internas em Portugal—1981. *Revista do Centro de Estudos Demográficos*, 27, 7–42.

Convey A.L. (1994) Some aspects of teacher mobility in Europe. In W. Tulasiewicz and G. Strowbridge (eds), *Education and the Law. International Perspectives*. Routledge: London.

Convey, A. and Kupiszewski, M. (1994) Migration and policy in the European Union. *Working Paper* 94/5. School of Geography, University of Leeds, Leeds.

Cook Report (1993) ITV, 26 January.

Corcoran, M.P. (1991) Informalisation of metropolitan labour forces: the case of the Irish migrants in the New York construction industry. *Irish Journal of Sociology*, 1, 31–51.

Costa-Lascoux, J. (1990) Les politiques migratoires à l'horizon 1993. *L'Evénement Européen*, 11, 61–77.

Council of the European Communities (1992a) *Conclusions of the Presidency*. European Council in Lisbon, 26–7 June.

Council of the European Communities (1992b) *Conclusions of the Meeting of the Ministers Responsible for Immigration*. Council General Secretariat, London, 30 November (10518/92(Presse 230)).

Courgeau, D. (1970) Les champs migratoires en France. *Travaux et Documents*, 58. Institut National d'Etudes Démographiques: Paris.

Courgeau, D. (1973) Migrants et migrations. *Population*, 28, 1, 95–130.

Courgeau, D. (1978) Les migrations internes en France de 1954 à 1975: I. vue d'ensemble. *Population*, 33, 3, 525–46.

Courgeau, D. (1985) Changements de logements, changements de départements et cycle de vie. *L'Espace Géographique* 4, 289–306.

Courgeau, D. (1986) *Utilisation des données de l'enquête emploi sur les migrations annuelles en France*. Rapport pour la DATAR: Paris.

Courgeau, D. (1988) *Méthodes de mesure de la mobilité spatiale*. Institut National d'Etudes Démographiques: Paris.

Courgeau, D. and Lefebvre, M. (1982) Les migrations internes en France de 1954 à 1975: II Migrations et Urbanisation. *Population*, 2, 341–70.

Courgeau, D. and Pumain, D. (1984) Baisse de la mobilité résidentielle. *Population et Sociétés*, 179, April, 1–4.

Courgeau, D. and Pumain, D. (1993) Mobilité par temps de crise. *Population et Sociétés*, 279, May, 1–4.

Court, Y. (1989) Denmark: towards a more deconcentrated settlement pattern. In G. Champion (ed.), *Counterurbanization: The Changing Pace and Nature of Population Deconcentration*. London: Arnold, 121–40.

Coward, J. (1982) Fertility changes in the Republic of Ireland during the 1970s. *Area*, 14, 2, 109–17.

Coward, J. (1989) Irish population problems. In R.W.G. Carter and A.J. Parker (eds), *Ireland: a Contemporary Geographical Perspective*. Routledge: London, 55–86.

Creton, D. (1991) Fertility changes and the Irish family. *Geography*, 76, 2, 154–7.

Cribier, F. (1992) La migration de retraite des Parisiens vers la province et ses transformations récentes. In E. Lelièvre and C. Lévy-Vroeland (eds), *La ville en mouvement: habitat et habitants*. L'Harmattan: Paris.

Cribier, F. (1994) La migration de retraite des Parisiens: l'apport des enquêtes biographiques par cohortes. *Espace, Populations, Sociétés*, 1994–1, 75–83.

Cruijsen, H. (1991) Fertility in the European Community: main trends, recent projections and two future paths. In Eurostat, *Background Papers on Fertility, Mortality and International Migration under Two Long Term Population Scenarios for the European Community*. Statistical Office of the European Communities: Luxembourg.

Cruz, A.M. (1991) Will the European Community make the 1992 deadline on the abolition of internal border controls? *International Migration*, XXIX, 3, 477–82.

Cruz, M.F.R. and Santos, A.F. (1990) Dynamique populationnelle et croissance urbaine. Analyse de la ville de Lisbonne à partir des derniers Recensements. *Séminaire International Croissance Démographique et Urbanisation*. AIDELF: Rabat.

CSO (1988) *Labour Force Survey*. Central Statistical Office: Dublin.

Davidson, P. (1993) Wave of illegals makes for Spain. *The Independent*, 30 August.

Decroly, J.M. and Vanlaer, J. (1991) *Atlas de la Population Européenne*. Editions de l'Université de Bruxelles: Brussels.

Department of Health (1992) *The Health of the Nation*. HMSO: London.

Devis, T. and Mills, I. (1986) A comparison of migration data from the National Health Service Central Register and the 1981 Census. *OPCS Occasional Paper 35*, OPCS: London.

Dövenyi, Z. (1992) *The role of Hungary in the European migrations of twentieth century*. Paper prepared for the conference, Mass Migration in Europe: Implications in East and West, IAS-IIASA-IF, Vienna.

Drudy, P.J. (1986) Migration between Ireland and Britain since Independence. In P.J. Drudy (ed.), *Ireland and Britain since 1922*, Cambridge University Press: Cambridge, 107–23.

Drudy, P.J. (1991) Demographic and economic change in Dublin in recent decades. In A. MacLaran (ed.), *Dublin in Crisis*, Trinity Papers in Geography 5, Trinity College: Dublin, 17–25.

Duffy, P.J. (1983) Rural settlement in the Republic of Ireland—a preliminary discussion. *Geoforum*, 14, 2, 185–91.

Duke-Williams, O. and Rees, P.H. (1993) TIMMIG: A program for extracting migration time series tables, *Working Paper 93/13*, School of Geography, University of Leeds, Leeds.

Dzienio, K. and Drzewieniecka, K. (1992) Przewidywane zmiany w stanie i strukturze ludnosci w wieku produkcyjnym w krajach europejskich i pozaeuropejskich i w latach 1990–2010 i ich konsekwencje dla migracji zagranicznych. *Studia Demograficzne*, 1, 107, 39–55.

Economist (1992a) At the Gates: if European countries had been quicker to take a tough line on asylum-seekers, they might now be kinder to people fleeing what was once Yugoslavia. London, 5 December.

Economist (1992b) Germany's strains, Europe's fears. London, 5 December.

Economist (1993) Not here, thank you. 2 October, 43–6.

Eichperger, L. and Gordijn, H. (1994) *A Regional Demographic Model for the Netherlands*. National Spatial Planning Agency, Ministry of Housing, Spatial Planning and Environment: The Hague.

Erf, R.F. van der (1984) Internal migration in the Netherlands: Measurement and Main Characteristics. In: H. Ter Heide and F.J. Willekens (eds), *Demographic Research and Spatial Policy: the Dutch Experience*. Academic Press: London.

Esteves, M.C. (ed.) (1991) *Portugal, país de imigração*. IED: Lisbon.

Eurinfo (1993a) Libre circulation; oui, mais...! *Eurinfo* 173, Bruges, March.

Eurinfo (1993b) Le Citoyen Européen retraité. *Eurinfo* 174, Bruges, April.

European Commission (1990) *Interim Report from the Commission to the Council*. (COM(90)225 final). Brussels, 12 June 1990.

European Commission (1991) Immigration of Citizens from Third Countries into the Southern Member States of the European Community. *Social Europe*, Supplement No.1/91. Directorate General for Employment, Industrial Relations and Social Affairs: Luxembourg.

European Commission (1992a) *Comparability of Vocational Training Qualifications*. Final Document, Luxembourg, February.

European Commission (1992b) *The Maastricht Agreement*. ISEC/B25/92, Commission of the European Communities: London, 29 September.

European Commission (1993a) *Social Exclusion—Poverty and other Social Problems in the European Community*. ISEC/B11/93, Commission of the European Communities: London, 6 April.

European Commission (1993b) *Community Travel*. ISEC/B14/93, Commission of the European Communities: London, 11 May.

European Commission (1993c) *The Enlargement of the Community*. ISEC/B15/93, Commission of the European Communities: London, 19 May.

European Commission (1993d) *Application of the Social Charter; Second Report*. ISEC/B25/93, Commission of the European Communities: London, 20 August.

European Commission (1994) *Competitiveness and Cohesion: Trends in the Regions, Fifth Periodic Report on the Social and Economic Situation and Development of the Regions of the Community*. Office for Official Publications of the European Communities: Luxembourg.

European Communities (1989). The Single European Act. *Official Journal of the European Communities*, L 169. Brussels, 30 June.

Eurostat (1989) *Regions Statistical Yearbook*. Office of the Official Publications of the European Community: Luxembourg.

Eurostat (1991a) *Demographic Statistics 1991*. Office for Official Publications of the European Communities: Luxembourg.

Eurostat (1991b) Two long term scenarios for the European Community: principal assumptions and results. Paper prepared for the International Conference, 'Human Resources in Europe at the Dawn of the 21st Century', Luxembourg, 27–9 November. Statistical Office of the European Communities: Luxembourg.

Eurostat (1992a) *Regions Nomenclature of Territorial Units for Statistics NUTS*. March. Statistical Office of the European Communities: Luxembourg.

Eurostat (1992b) *Regional Indicators for the Implementation post-1993 of Structural Policies*. Eurostat: Luxembourg.

Eurostat (1994) *Regions Statistical Yearbook, 1994*. Statistical Office of the European Communities: Luxembourg.

Fargues, P. (1988) La baisse de la fécondité arabe. *Population*, 43, 975–1004.

Fassmann, H. and Münz, R. (1990) Eiwanderungsland Österreich. Gastarbeiter— Flüchtlinge—Immigranten. Institut für Demographie, Österreichische Akademie der Wissenschaften: Vienna.

Fassmann, H. and Münz, R. (1991) European migration patterns and internalization of the European labour market, Paper presented to the European Population Conference, Paris.

Fassmann, H. and Münz, R. (eds) (1994) *European Migration in the Late Twentieth Century*. Edward Elgar Publishing: Aldershot and International Institute for Applied Systems Analysis: Laxenburg.

Ferrão, J. (1985) Recomposição social e estruturas regionais de classes. *Análise Social*, 21, 87–88–89, 565–604.

Ferrão, J. (1988) L'industrie au Portugal – structures productives et sociales dans des contextes regionaux diversifiés. *Annales de Geographie*, 541, 308–29.

Ferreira, V.M. (1987) *A cidade de Lisboa: de capital do Império a centro da metró- pole*. Dom Quixote: Lisbon.

Fielding, A.J. (1982) Counterurbanisation in Western Europe. *Progress in Planning*, 17, 1.

Fielding, A. (1993) Mass migration and economic restructuring. In R. King (ed.), *Mass Migration in Europe*. Belhaven: London, 7–18.

Figueiredo, C. *et al.* (1985) Especialização internacional, regulação económica e regulação social—Portugal, 1973–83. *Análise Social*, 21, 87–88–89, 437–71.

First Book of Demographics for the Republics of the Former Soviet Union 1951–1990 (1992) New World Demographics, L.C., Shady Side, MA.

Financial Times (1992) Strangers in the Land of Unification, 25 November.

Findlay, A. (1995) The future of skill exchanges within the EC. In P. White and R. Hall (eds), *European Population 2000*. Belhaven: London. (In press).

Fleischer, H. and Pröbsting, H. (1989) Aussiedler und Übersiedler. Zahlenmessige Entwicklung und Struktur. *Wirtschaft und Statistik*, 9, 582–89.

Frelic, B. (1993) Preventing refugee flows: protection or peril? In USCR (eds), *World Refugee Survey,1993*. United States Committee for Refugees: New York.

Frey, H.W. (1989) United States: counterurbanization and metropolis depopulation. In A.G. Champion (ed.), *Counterurbanization*. Edward Arnold: New York, 34–61.

Frey, W.H. (1992) Metropolitan redistribution of the US elderly: 1960–70, 1970–80, 1980–90. In Rogers, A. (ed.) *Elderly Migration and Population Redistribution: A Comparative Perspective*, London: Belhaven.

Gachechiladze, R. and Bradshaw, M.J. (1994) Changes in the ethnic structure of Tibilisi's population. *Post-Soviet Geography*, 35, January, 56–9.

Garvey, D. (1985) The history of migration flows in the Republic of Ireland. *Population Trends*, 39, 22–30.

Garvey, D. and McGuire, M. (1989) *Structure of Gross Migration Flows: Labour Force Survey Estimates*. Central Statistics Office: Dublin.

Gasior, K. (1990) Poles in the Soviet Union. *Report on USSR*, 28, 10–16.

Gaspar, J. (1980). *Urban Growth Trends in Portugal*. Centro de Estudos Geográficos: Lisbon.

Gaspar, J. (1984) Urbanization: growth, problems and policies. In A. Williams (ed.), *Southern Europe Transformed: Political and Economic Change in Greece, Italy, Portugal and Spain*. Harper & Row: London, pp. 208–35.

Gaspar, J. (1987) *A ocupação e a organização do território. Análise retrospectiva e tendências evolutivas*. Gulbenkian: Lisbon.

Gaspar, J. *et al.* (1988) L'évolution de la politique du logement au Portugal, *Espaces et Sociétés*, 52–3, 167–82.

Gaspar, J. *et al.* (1989) *Ocupação e organização do espaço. Uma prospectiva*. Gulbenkian: Lisbon.

Gazeta Wyborcza (1992) Rumuni do domu (Romanians go home) 9 December.

Geary, R.C., Hughes, J.G. and Gillman, C.J. (1970) *Internal Migration in Ireland*. Economic and Social Research Institute Paper 54: Dublin.

Geissler, C. *et al.* (1992) Zur Entwicklung der Binnenwanderungen im geeinten Deutschland: neue Paradigmen. *Informationen zur Raumwicklung*, 9/10, 709–20.

Geographical Digest 1992–93 (1992) Heineman Educational: Oxford.

Giaoutzi, M. (1983) Migration patterns in Greece. Paper presented at the UNESCO Conference on Information in Labour Markets: International Comparisons, Groningen.

Gillmor, D.A. (1988) An investigation of villages in the Republic of Ireland. *Irish Geography*, 21, 2, 57–68.

Glytsos, N.P. (1993) Measuring the income effects of migrant remittances: a methodological approach applied to Greece. *Economic Development and Cultural Change*. 42, 1, 131–68.

Golini, A., Righi, A. and Bonifazi, C. (1993) Population vitality and decline. In *The Changing Course of International Migration*. OECD: Paris, 19–36.

Greenwood, M.J. and McDowell, J.M. (1992) *The macro determinants of international migration: A survey*. Paper prepared for the conference: Mass Migration in Europe: Implications in East and West, IAS-IIASA-IF, Vienna.

Grimmeau, J-P, (1992) *Les migrations entre la Flandre et la Wallonie*, Working Paper no. 1992–4, Point d'Appui Démographie, VUB: Brussels.

Grzeszczak, J. (1989) Travailleurs étrangers dans les pays socialistes. In M. Rosciszewski, B. Czyz and J. Grzeszczak (eds), *The State, Modes of Production and World Political Map*. Conference Papers 5. Institute of Geography and Spatial Organization PAS: Warsaw.

Guerra, I. (1990) La péninsule de Setúbal—une région industrielle à la recherche d'une autre logique de développement, *Sociedade e Território*, no especial, 13–22.

Hailbronner, K. (1990) The right of asylum and the future of asylum procedures in the EC. *International Journal of Refugee Law*, 2, 3, 341–60.

Hainsworth, P. (1992) *The Extreme Right in Europe and the USA*. Pinter: London.

Hanlon, G. (1991) The emigration of Irish accountants: economic restructuring and producer services on the periphery. *Irish Journal of Sociology*, 1, 52–65.

Hannan, D. (1969) Migration motives and migration differentials among Irish rural youth. *Sociologia Ruralis*, 9, 2, 191–219.

Hannan, D. (1970) *Rural Exodus*. Chapman: London.

Harrison, P. (1993) *The Third Revolution*. Penguin: Harmondsworth.

Haverkate, R. and Van Haselen, H. (1990) *Demographic Evolution through Time in European Regions (DEMETER 2015)*. Report to the Commission of the European Communities, Directorate-General for Regional Policy. Netherlands Economic Institute: Rotterdam.

Hecht, J. and Leridon, H. (1993) Fertility policies: a limited influence? Chapter 6 in D. Noin and R. Woods (eds). *The Changing Population of Europe*. Blackwell: Oxford, 62–75.

Heilig, G. (1991) The possible impact of AIDS on future mortality. Chapter 5 in W. Lutz (ed.), *Future Demographic Trends in Europe and North America*. Academic Press: London, 71–95.

Heins, F. (1991) Migration patterns within the European Community during the 1980s and outlook for the 1990s. *Report to the EC*.

Hessenberger, M. (1994) *Aussiedler: Migration of people of German origin from the former Soviet Union to the Federal Republic of Germany and the resulting demographic and social problems*. School of Geography, University of Leeds, Leeds.

Hoffmann-Nowotny, H-J. (1992) Die neue Völkerwanderung. Ursachen internationaler und interkontinentaler Migration. *Informationen zur Raumwicklung*, 9/10, 769–76.

Hofman, H.J. and Heller, W. (1992) *Social and Economic Dimensions of the Migration of Aussiedler into the Former West Germany*. Migration Unit Research Paper No.2, Department of Geography, University College, Swansea.

Holt, J. (1991) How has 'Soviet' immigration affected the Israeli labour market? School of Geography, University of Leeds, Leeds.

Hönnekop, E. (1991) Migratory Movements from Central and Eastern Europe: the cases of Germany and Austria. Paper given at the Council of Europe Conference of Ministers on the Movement of Persons coming from Central and Eastern European Countries, Vienna

24–25 January, Council of Europe: Strasbourg.

Hopkinson, N. (1991) *Migration into Western Europe*. HMSO: London.

Horner, A., Walsh, J. and Harrington, V. (1987) *Population in Ireland: a Census Atlas*. University College Dublin: Dublin.

Houston, C.J. and Smyth, W.J. (1993) The Irish diaspora: emigration to the New World, 1720–1920. In B.J. Graham and L.J. Proudfoot (eds), *An Historical Geography of Ireland*, Academic Press: London, 338–65. /

Hovy, B. (1992) Asylum migration in Europe: Patterns, determinants and the role of East–West movements. Paper prepared for the conference, *Mass Migration in Europe: Implications in East and West*, IAS-IIASA-IF, Vienna.

Hryniewicz, J., Jalowiecki, B. and Mync, A. (1992) *The brain drain in Poland*. European Institute for Regional and Local Development, University of Warsaw, Warsaw.

Hughes, J.G. and Walsh, B.M. (1974) Migration flows between Ireland, the UK and the rest of the world. *European Demographic Information Bulletin*, 7, 4, 125–49.

Hughes, J.G. and Walsh, B.M. (1980) *Internal Migration Flows in Ireland and their Determinants*, Economic and Social Research Institute Paper 98: Dublin.

Illeris, S. (1983) Befolkningsudviklingen i den ældre del af Hovedstadsregionen 1973–84. *AKF-nyt*, 4, 22–37.

Illeris, S. (1984) Arbejdsløshed og arbejdsmarkeder i Hovedstadsregionen. Copenhagen: Amternes og Kommunernes Forskningsinstitut.

Illeris, S. (1988) Regional Economic Development and Local Government in Denmark. In S. Illeris (ed.), *Local Economic Development in Denmark*. Copenhagen: Amternes og Kommunernes Forskningsinstitut, 7–23.

Illeris, S. (1990) *Den regionale erhvervsfordeling i 1980'erne*. Copenhagen: Amternes og Kommunernes Forskningsinstitut.

INE (1981–91) *Anuario Estadístico*. Instituto Nacional de Estadística: Madrid.

INE (1986–90) *Migraciones*. Instituto Nacional de Estadística: Madrid.

INE (1992) *Anuario Estadístico 1991*. Instituto Nacional de Estadística: Madrid.

INE (annual) *Annual Statistics on Migration*.

INED (1989) *XVIIIème rapport sur la situation démographique de la France*. Institut National d'Etudes Démographiques: Paris.

INSEE (1982a) *Annuaire Statistique de la France 1982. Résultats de 1981*. Paris.

INSEE (1982b) *Recensement Général de la Population 1982*. Paris.

INSEE (1990) *Recensement Général de la Population 1990*. Paris.

INSEE (1992) *Annuaire Statistique de la France 1991–92. Résultats de 1991*. Paris.

Instituto Nacional de Estadistica (1992) *España, Annuario Estadistico 1991*. Madrid.

Italian Embassy in London (1993) Italian Embassy's recorded telephone message. January, London.

Jackson, J.A. (1963) *The Irish in Britain*. Routledge and Kegan Paul: London.

Johnson, J.H. (1967) Harvest migration from nineteenth century Ireland. *Transactions, Institute of British Geographers*, 41, 97–112.

Johnson, J.H. (1990) The context of migration: the example of Ireland in the nineteenth century. *Transactions, Institute of British Geographers*, 15, 3, 259–76.

Joly, D. and Nettleton, C. (1990) *Refugees in Europe*. Minority Rights Group: London.

Jones, H. (1992) Migration trends for Scotland: central losses and peripheral gains. Chapter 6 in J.C.H. Stillwell, P.H. Rees and P. Boden (eds), *Migration Processes and Patterns: Volume 2: Population Redistribution in the United Kingdom*. Belhaven Press: London.

Jones, K. and Smith, A. (1970) *The Economic Impact of Commonwealth Migration*. Cambridge University Press: Cambridge.

Jones, P.N. (1990) Recent ethnic German migration from Eastern Europe to the Federal Republic. *Geography*, 75, 249–52.

Jones, P.N. and Wild, M.T. (1992) Western Germany's Third Wave of Migrants. *Geoforum* 23, 1, 1–11.

Kemper, F.-J. (1992) New trends in international migration in Germany. Paper presented at the International Geographical Union Population Congress, Los Angeles.

Kemper, F.-J. (1993) New trends in mass migration in Germany. In R. King (ed.), *Mass Migration in Europe. The Legacy and the Future.* Belhaven Press: London, 257–74.

Kennedy, R.E. (1973) *The Irish: Emigration, Marriage, Fertility.* University of California Press: Berkeley.

Kennedy, K., Giblin, T. and McHugh, D. (1988) *The Economic Development of Ireland in the Twentieth Century.* Routledge: London.

Keyfitz, N. (1987) The family that does not reproduce itself. In K. Davis, M.S. Bernstam and R. Ricardo-Campbell (eds), *Below-replacement fertility in Industrial Societies: Causes, Consequences, Policies.* Cambridge University Press: Cambridge.

King, M. (1993) The impact of Western European border policies on the control of refugees in Eastern and Central Europe. *New Community,* 19, 2, 183–99.

King, R. (1993a) European international migration 1945–90. In R. King (ed.), *Mass Migration in Europe.* Belhaven: London, 19–39.

King, R. (ed.) (1993b) *The New Geography of International Migrations.* Belhaven: London.

King, R. (ed.) (1993c) *Mass Migration in Europe. The Legacy and the Future.* Belhaven: London.

King, R., McGrath, F., Shuttleworth, I. and Strachan, A.J. (1990) Irish on the move. *Geography Review,* 3, 3, 23–7.

King, R. and Shuttleworth, I. (1988) Ireland's new wave of emigration in the 1980s. *Irish Geography,* 21, 2, 104–8.

King, R. and Shuttleworth, I. (1988–9) The movement of Irish school-leavers into British higher education: a potential brain-drain? *Geographical Viewpoint,* 17, 75–85.

Kirk, D. (1946) Europe's Population in the Inter-war Years. Gordon and Breach: New York.

Kirwan, F.X. and Nairn, A.G. (1983) Migrant employment and the recession: the case of the Irish in Britain. *International Migration Review,* 17, 4, 672–81.

Knabe, B. (1992) Die künftigen Wanderungsbewegungen zwischen dem geeinten Deutschland und den osteuropäischen Ländern. *Informationen zur Raumwicklung,* 9/10, 777–81.

Knox, E., MacArthur, C. and Simons, K.J. (1993) *Sexual Behaviour and AIDS in Britain.* HMSO: London.

Komisja Rzadowa do spraw koordynacji dzialan miedzyresortowych w zakresie polityki ludnosciowej. (1989) Emigracja zagraniczna ludnosci Polski do krajów kapitalistycznych w latach 1981–1988. *Aneks do Raportu Rzadowej Komisji Ludnosciowej nt. 'Sytuacja demograficzna Polski'.* Warsaw.

Kontuly, T. and Vogelsang, R. (1988) Federal Republic of Germany: the intensification of the migration turnaround. In A.G. Champion (ed.), *Counterurbanization.* Edward Arnold: New York.

Korcelli, P. (1992a) *European migration—the Polish example.* Paper prepared for the conference, Mass Migration in Europe: Implications in East and West, IAS-IIASA-IF, Vienna.

Korcelli, P. (1992b) *International Migration in Europe: Polish perspectives for the 1990s.* Paper prepared for the conference, The New Europe and International Migration, Turin.

Kuijper, H. and Noordam (1992) In 1990 minder verhuizingen binnen Nederland, *Mnstat Bevolking,* CBS, No 1, 12–17.

Kuba Kozlowski, T. (1994) *Asylum seekers and refugees in Poland.* Paper prepared for the conference: Migration issues in Poland within the context of European Integration, OECD–MPPISS. Warsaw.

Kunz, E. (1973) The refugee in flight: kinetic models and forms of displacement. *International Migration Review,* 7, 2, 125–46.

Kupiszewski, M. (1993) Poland as a source of Migration and Travel. A map with a comment. In P. Jordan (ed.), *Atlas of Eastern and Southeastern Europe,* Öster-reichishes Ost- und

Südosteuropa Institut: Vienna.

Kurcz, Z. and Podkanski, W. (1991) Emigracja z Polski po 1980 roku. In W. Misiak (ed.), *Nowa emigracja i wyjazdy zarobkowe za granice*. Polskie Towarzystwo Socjologiczne: Warsaw.

Lanphier, M. (1993) Host groups: public meets private. In V. Robinson (ed.), *The International Refugee Crisis: British and Canadian Responses*, Macmillan: Basingstoke.

Lawless, R., Findlay, A. and Findlay, A. (1982) Return migration to the Maghreb. *Arab Papers*, 10, Arc: London.

Lees, L. (1979) *Exiles of Erin*. Manchester University Press: Manchester.

Le Monde (1993) L'Accord de Schengen? 20 October.

Lipietz, A. (1993) The local and the global transactions. *Institute of British Geographers*, 18, 8–18.

Le Soir (1993a) Un Walen Buiten déloyal. Brussels, 24 February.

Le Soir (1993b) S'installer en Flandres? Il faudrait prouver un 'intérêt'. Brussels, 24 February.

Lewandowska, M. (1991) Imigranci polscy w Republice Federalnej Niemiec w latch 1970–1985. Wyniki badan ankietowych. *Przeglad Polonijny*, 17, 3, 31–56.

Liebich, A. (1992) Minorities in Eastern Europe: Obstacles to a reliable count. *RFE/RL Research Report*, 1, 20, 32–9.

Livi-Bacci, M. (1993) South–North migration. In *The Changing Course of International Migration*. OECD: Paris, 37–46.

Lopez, A. and Cruijsen, H. (1991) Mortality in the European Community: trends and perspectives. In Eurostat, *Background Papers on Fertility, Mortality and International Migration under Two Long Term Population Scenarios for the European Community*. Statistical Office of the European Communities: Luxembourg.

Lutz, W. (ed.) (1991) *Future Demographic Trends in Europe and North America*. Academic Press: London.

Lutz, W., Prinz, C., Wils, A., Buttner, T. and Heilig, G. (1991) Alternative demographic scenarios for Europe and North America. In W. Lutz (ed.), *Future Demographic Trends in Europe and North America*. Academic Press: London, 523–60.

MacÉinrí, P. (1991) The Irish in Paris: an aberrant community? In R. King (ed.), *Contemporary Irish Migration*, Geographical Society of Ireland Special Publication 6: Dublin, 32–41.

MacLaughlin, J. (1991) Social characteristics and destinations of recent emigrants from selected regions in the west of Ireland. *Geoforum*, 22, 3, 319–31.

Markiewicz, T. (1993) Tesknota za Vaterlandem. *Wprost*, 14 March.

Markiewicz, W. (1992a) Przez zielona. *Polityka*, 19 September.

Markiewicz, W. (1992b) Atak na budowe. *Polityka*, 22 August.

Marshall, A. (1992) Refugees pay a high price as Europe raises the drawbridge. *The Independent*: London.

Marx, K. (1976) *Capital* (Vol 1). Penguin: Harmondsworth.

Massey, D. (1984) *Spatial Divisions of Labour*. Macmillan: London.

Migration News (1994a) Department of Agricultural Economics, University of California, Davis, CA, 1, 1.

Migration News (1994b) Department of Agricultural Economics, University of California, Davis, CA, 1, 2.

Migration News (1994c) Department of Agricultural Economics, University of California, Davis, CA, 1, 3.

Migration News (1994d) Department of Agricultural Economics, University of California, Davis, CA, 1, 4.

Migration News (1994e) Department of Agricultural Economics, University of California, Davis, CA, 1, 5.

Mihalka, M. (1994) German and Western response to immigration from the East. *RFL/RL*

Research Report, 3, 23, 36–48.

Miljøministeriet, Planstyrelsen (1989) *Tendenser i den regionale udvikling i Danmark.* Copenhagen.

Miller, K. (1985) *Emigrants and Exiles.* Oxford University Press: Oxford.

Miles, R. (1987) *Capitalism and Unfree Labour.* Tavistock: London.

Mjoset, L. (1992) *The Irish Economy in a Comparative International Perspective.* National Economic and Social Council Report 93: Dublin.

Montanari, A. and Cortese, A. (1993) South to North migration in a Mediterranean perspective. In R. King (ed.), *Mass Migration in Europe.* Belhaven: London, 212–33.

MOPU (1988) *Cambios de la población en el territorio.* Madrid.

Moussourou, L.M. (1984) La sociologie de la migration en Grèce depuis 1960, *Current Sociology,* 32, 2, 89–121.

Muus, P. and Cruijsen, H. (1991) International Migration in the European Community: two scenarios. In Eurostat, *Background Papers on Fertility, Mortality and International Migration under Two Long Term Population Scenarios for the European Community.* Statistical Office of the European Communities: Luxembourg.

Nazareth, J.M. (1988) *Unidade e diversidade da demografia portuguesa no final do século XX.* Gulbenkian: Lisbon.

National Spatial Planning Agency (1966) *Second Report on Spatial Planning.* Staatsuitgeverij: The Hague.

National Spatial Planning Agency (1992) *Fourth Report on Spatial Planning.* SDU: The Hague.

National Statistical Service of Greece (1987) *Results of the Census of Population and Households Taken on 5 April 1981, Volume IV,* NSSG: Athens.

National Statistical Service of Greece (1990) *Statistical Yearbook of Greece 1988.* Athens.

National Statistical Service of Greece (1991) *Statistical Yearbook of Greece 1990.* Athens.

National Statistical Service of Greece (1994) *Statistical Yearbook of Greece 1993.* Athens.

NEI (1993) *Regional Population and Labour Force Scenarios for the EEA.* Interim Report: Population. Netherlands Economic Institute: Rotterdam.

NEI (1994a) *Regional Population and Labour Force Scenarios for the European Union. Part I: Two long term population scenarios.* Netherlands Economic Institute, Department of Regional and Urban Development, Erasmus University, Department of Public Health; Netherlands Interdisciplinary Demographic Institute (NIDI): Rotterdam, June.

NEI (1994b) *Regional Population and Labour Force Scenarios for the European Union. Part II: Two long term labour force scenarios.* Netherlands Economic Institute, Department of Regional and Urban Development, Erasmus University, Economic Geography Institute: Rotterdam, June.

NEI (1994c) *Regional Population and Labour Force Scenarios for the European Union. Part III: Results Population Scenarios.* Netherlands Economic Institute, Department of Regional and Urban Development, Erasmus University, Department of Public Health: Rotterdam, March.

NEI (1994d) *Regional Population and Labour Force Scenarios for the European Union. Part IV: Results Labour Force Scenarios.* Netherlands Economic Institute, Department of Regional and Urban Development, Erasmus University, Economic Geography Institute: Rotterdam, March.

Niessen, J. (1992) European Community Legislation and Intergovernmental Cooperation on Migration. *International Migration Review,* 26, 676–84.

Nobel, P. (1990) What happened with Sweden's refugee policy? *International Migration Journal of Refugee Law,* 2, 2, 265–73.

Noin, D. (1993) Spatial inequalities in mortality. Chapter 4 in D. Noin and R. Woods (eds) *The Changing Population of Europe.* Blackwell: Oxford, 38–48.

Norcliffe, G. (1972) Canonical analysis of the relations between certain aspects of the demographic and urban systems of the Republic of Ireland. *Irish Geography,* 6, 4, 411–27.

Öberg, S. and Boubnova, H. (1993) Ethnicity, nationality and migration potentials in Eastern Europe. In R. King (ed.), *Mass Migration in Europe. The Legacy and the Future.* Belhaven Press: London, 234–56.

Öberg, S. and Wils, A.B. (1992) East–West migration in Europe. Can migration theories help estimate the numbers? *Popnet*, 22, 1–7.

OECD (1990) *Comparative Analysis of Regularization Experience in France, Italy, Spain and the United States.* OECD: Paris.

OECD (1992) *Trends in International Migration.* Paris.

OECD (1993) *Employment Outlook.* Paris.

Ogilvy, A.A. (1979) Migration—the influence of economic change, *Futures*, 11, 5, 383–94.

O'Keeffe, D. (1992) The Dilemma posed by Asylum Policy. *The Independent*, 31 December.

Okólski, M. (1991) *Migratory Movements from Countries of Central and Eastern Europe.* Paper given at the Council of Europe Conference of Ministers on the 'Movement of Persons coming from Central and Eastern European Countries', Vienna 24–5 January. Council of Europe, Strasbourg.

Okólski, M. (1994) *International migration in Poland—trends and characteristics.* Paper prepared for the conference on Migration issues in Poland within the context of European integration, OECD, Polish Ministry of Labour and Social Policy, Warsaw.

OPCS (1993) *Population Trends, 74,* Winter. HMSO: London.

OPCS (1994) *1991 Census Migration Great Britain. Part 1 (100% tables).* Volume 2. HMSO: London.

O'Rourke, D. (1972) A stocks and flows approach to a theory of human migration with examples from past Irish migration. *Demography,* 9, 2, 263–74.

Owen, I. (1994) Lords Hit at EC over visa list plan. *The Financial Times.* 1 August.

Papademetriou, D.G. (1985) Illusions and reality in international migration: migration and development in post World War Greece. *International Migration,* 28, 2, 211–23.

Parekh, B. (1994) Three theories of immigration. In S. Spencer (ed.), *Strangers and Citizens.* Rivers Oram Press: London, 91–110.

Pavlik, Z. (1991) *L'utilisation des recensements pour l'observation des migrations.* Paper prepared for the conference: Chaire Quatelet 1991. The collection and comparability of demographic and social data in Europe, Institut de Démographie, Université Catholique de Louvain, Gembloux.

Peixoto, J.(1990) La croissance urbaine au Portugal: démographie et mécanismes sociétaux au XXème siècle. *Séminaire International Croissance Démographique et Urbanisation.* AIDELF: Rabat.

Peixoto, J. (1991) Migrations et urbanisation au Portugal: concentration, urbanisation diffuse et dispersion. *Séminaire International Phénomènes Migratoires, Urbanisation et Contre-urbanisation.* Amalfi.

Peixoto, J. (1992a) Migrações e mobilidade: as novas formas da emigração portuguesa a partir de 1980. *Colóquio Internacional sobre Emigração-Imigração Portuguesa nos Séculos XIX e XX.* Lisbon.

Peixoto, J. (1992b), Migrations régulières et irrégulières au Portugal. *Seminário Movilidad y migración en la frontera del siglo XXI.* University of Alcalá de Henares.

Petrakou, E.V. (1993) Immigration policy in northern and southern states of the EC with special reference to Britain and Greece, Master's Thesis, Department of Politics, University of Warwick, Warwick.

PHLS (1993) The incidence and prevalence of AIDS and other severe HIV disease in England and Wales for 1992–1997: projections using data to the end of June 1992. *Communicable Disease Report,* 3, Supplement 1, June.

Popham, P. (1990) The London Irish. *Independent Magazine* 101, 11 August, pp. 22–8.

Post-Soviet Geography (1993) Geography of the human resources in the post Soviet realm: A panel. 34, 4, 219–80.

Poulain, M. (1980) Contribution à l'analyse spatiale d'une matrice de migration interne,

Recherches Démographiques 3, Institut de Démographie: Louvain-la-Neuve.

Poulain, M. (1981) Contribution à l'analyse d'une matrice de migration interne. *Recherches Démographiques* 3.

Poulain, M. (1993a) L'Europe de la migration. La croisée des chemins. *Revue Suisse de l'Economie Politique de la Statistisque.* 129, 257–81.

Poulain, M. (1993b) Confrontation des statistiques de migrations intra-Européennes: vers plus d'harmonization. *European Journal of Population/Revue Européenne de Démographie,* 9, 4, 353–81.

Poulain, M., Debuisson, M. and Eggerickx, T. (1991a) *Proposals for the harmonisation of the European Community Statistics on International Migration.* Report to Eurostat. Catholic University of Louvain, Louvain-la-Neuve, Belgium.

Poulain, M. and Pumain, D. (1985) Une famille de modèles spatiaux et leur application à la matrice des migrants interdépartementaux français, 1968–75. *Espaces, Populations, Sociétés,* 1, 33–42.

Poulain, M., Riandey, B. and Firdion, J.-M. (1991b) Enquête biographique et registre belge de population: une confrontation des données, *Population,* 46, 65–88.

Poulain, M. and Van Goethem, B. (1982) Evolution à long terme de la mobilité interne de la population belge de 1948 à 1979. *Population,* 37, 319–40.

Poulton, H. (1992) *Minorities in the Balkans.* Minority Rights Group: London.

Pumain, D. (1986) Les migrations inter-régionales de 1954 à 1982: directions préférentielles et effets de barrière. *Population,* 41, 2, 378–88.

Pumain, D. and Saint-Julien, Th. (1989) Migration et changement urbain en France, 1975–1982. *Revue d'Economie Régionale et Urbaine,* 3, 509–30.

Redei, M. (1992) *Displaced persons in a new host country.* Paper prepared for the conference: Mass Migration in Europe: Implications in East and West, IAS-IIASA-IF, Vienna.

Rees, P.H. (1992) *The future population of Northern Seaboard regions.* Demographic Sector Working Paper prepared for Price Waterhouse. School of Geography, University of Leeds.

Rees, P.H., Stillwell, J.C.H. and Boden, P. (1989) Migration trends and population projections for the elderly. Chapter 12 in P. Batey and P. Congdon (eds), *Developments in Regional Demography.* Belhaven: London, 205–26.

Rees, P.H., Stillwell, J.C.H. and Convey, A.L. (1992) *Intra-Community Migration and its Impact on the Demographic Structure at the Regional Level.* Working Paper 92/1, School of Geography, University of Leeds, Leeds.

Reis, J. (1992) *Os espaços da indústria.* Afrontamento: Porto.

RFE/RL (1993) *Daily Report,* 20 July.

Rhode, B. (1993) Brain drain, brain gain, brain waste: reflection on emigration of highly educated and scientific personnel from Eastern Europe. In R. King (ed.), *New Geography of European Migrations.* Belhaven Press: London, 228–45.

Rijksplanologische dienst (1993) *Regionale bevolkingsprognose.* Ministerie van Volkshuisvesting, Ruimtelijke Ordening en Milieubeheer.

Robinson, V. (1993) North and south: resettling Vietnamese refugees in Australia and the UK. In R. Black and V. Robinson (eds), *Geography and Refugees.* Belhaven: London.

Robinson, V. The evolution of refugee settlement policy in post-war Britain. In M. Kenzer (ed.), *The World Refugee Atlas,* Toronto University Press, forthcoming.

Rogers, A. and Castro, L. (1981) *Model Migration Schedules.* Research Report RR-81-30, International Institute of Applied Systems Analysis: Laxenburg, Austria.

Rogers, A. and Willekens, F. (eds) (1986) *Migration and Settlement: Multiregional Comparative Study.* Reidel: Dordrecht.

Rudd, J. (1987) The emigration of Irish women. *Social Studies,* 9, 3–4, 3–11.

Rzeczpospolita (1992) *Mniejszosci traktowac nowoczesnie, Interview with Geza Entz, Secretary of State for Hungarians Abroad,* 12 August.

Sage, A. (1992) Mackay stresses benefits of co-operation in Justice. *The Independent:*

London, 1 October.

Salgueiro, T.B. (1992) *A cidade em Portugal. Uma geografia urbana.* Afrontamento: Porto.

Salt, J. (1991) *Current and Future International Migration Trends affecting Europe.* Paper given at 4th Conference of European Ministers responsible for Migration Affairs, Luxembourg 17–18 September. Council of Europe: Strasbourg.

Salt, J. (1993) *Migration and Population Change in Europe,* UN Institute for Disarmament Research Paper 19, New York.

Salt, J. (nd) *Tendances actuelles et futures des migrations internationales touchant l'Europe,* Council of Europe: Strasbourg.

Santos, B.S. (1985) Estado e sociedade na semiperiferia do sistema mundial: o caso português, *Análise Social,* 21, 87–88–89, 869–901.

Sarre, P. (1989) Race and class structure. In C. Hamnett *et al.* (eds), *Restructuring Britain.* Sage: London, 124–57.

Schütte, J.J.E. (1991) Schengen: Its meaning for the free movement of persons in Europe. *Common Market Law Review,* 28, 549–70.

Schütte, F. (1994) *Germany's programmes for the training and short-term employment of workers from countries of Central and Eastern Europe.* Paper prepared for the conference 'Migration issues in Poland within the context of European integration'. Warsaw.

SECP (Secretaria de Estado das Comunidades Portuguesas) (1988) *Boletim Anual.* MNE.

SEF (Serviço de Estrangeiros e Fronteiras) (1991) *Relatório Anual,* MAI.

Segbers, K. (1991) Migration and refugee movements from the USSR: causes and prospects. *Report on the USSR,* 15, 6–14.

Seruya, L.M. (1982), Determinantes e características da emigração portuguesa—1960–1979, in H.M. Stahl (ed.), *Perspectivas da emigração portuguesa para a CEE, 1980–1990.* Moraes/IED: Lisbon.

Sexton, J.J. (1987) Recent changes in the Irish population and in the pattern of emigration. *Irish Banking Review,* Autumn, 31–44.

Sexton, J.J., Walsh, B.M., Hannan, D.F. and McMahon, D. (1991) *The Economic and Social Consequences of Emigration.* National Economic and Social Council Report 90: Dublin.

Shuttleworth, I. (1991) Graduate emigration from Ireland: a symptom of peripherality? In R. King (ed.), *Contemporary Irish Migration,* Geographical Society of Ireland Special Publication 6: Dublin, 83–95.

Shuttleworth, I. (1991–2) Trends in Irish student migration 1980–90: the implications of cross-border flows. *Geographical Viewpoint,* 20, 64–73.

Shuttleworth, I. (1993) Irish graduate emigration: the mobility of qualified manpower in the context of peripherality. In R. King (ed.), *Mass Migrations in Europe: The Legacy and the Future.* Belhaven: London, 310–26.

Siampos, G. (1991) Greece. In J.L. Rallu and A. Blum (eds), *European Population, Volume 1: Country Analysis.* Libbey: Paris.

Simon, G. (1993) Internal migration and mobility. In D. Noin and R. Woods (eds), *The Changing Population of Europe.* Blackwell: Oxford, 170–84.

Sommer, B. and Fleischer, H. (1991) Bövelkerungsentwicklung 1989. *Wirtschaft und Statistik,* 2, 81–8.

SOPEMI (1991) *Continuous Reporting System on Migration. 1990.* OECD: Paris.

SOPEMI (1992) *Trends in International Migration. 1992.* OECD: Paris.

SOPEMI (1994) *Trends in International Migration. Annual Report 1993.* OECD: Paris.

Sporton, D. (1993) Fertility: the lowest level in the world. In D. Noin and R. Woods (eds), *The Changing Population of Europe.* Blackwell: Oxford, 49–61.

Strachan, A. and King, R. (1982) Emigration and return migration in Southern Italy. *Occasional Paper* 9. Leicester University Geography Department, Leicester.

Statistisches Bundesamt (1991) *Statistisches Jahrbuch für Bundesrepublik Deutschland.*

Statistisches Bundesamt (1992) *Statistisches Jahrbuch für Bundesrepublik Deutschland.*

Statistisches Bundesamt and Eurostat (1991) *Country Reports. Central and Eastern Europe*

1991. Office for Official Publications of the European Communities: Luxembourg.

Statistical Yearbooks of the Federal Republic of Germany, various years.

Statistical Yearbooks of the German Democratic Republic, various years.

Stillwell, J.C.H. (1994) Monitoring intercensal migration in the United Kingdom, *Environment and Planning A*, 26, 1711–30.

Stillwell, J.C.H., Rees, P.H. and Boden, P. (eds) (1992) *Migration Processes and Patterns: Volume 2: Population Redistribution in the United Kingdom.* Belhaven Press: London.

Stillwell, J., Duke-Williams, O. and Rees, P. (1993) The spatial patterns of British migration in 1991 in the context of 1975–92 trends. Working paper 93/19, School of Geography, University of Leeds.

Stpiczynski, T. (1992) *Polacy w swiecie. GUS:* Warsaw.

Sunley, P. (1992) An uncertain future. *Progress in Human Geography,* 16, 58–70.

Szoke L. (1992) Hungarian perspectives on emigration and immigration in new European architecture. *International Migration Review*, 26, 305–23.

Taffin, C. (1987) La mobilité résidentielle entre 1979 et 1984. In *Données Sociales*, INSEE, 169–75.

Tannahill, J.A. (1958) *European Volunteer Workers in Britain.* Manchester University Press: Manchester.

Thumerelle, P-J. (1992) Migrations internationales et changement géopolitique en Europe. *Annales de Géographie,* 565, 289–318.

Tugault, Y. (1973) *La mesure de la mobilité. Cinq études sur les migrations internes.* Travaux et Documents 67. Institut National d'Etudes Démographiques: Paris.

United Nations (1981) Recommandations en matière de statistiques des migrations internationales, *Etudes Statistiques*, série M, no 58, New York, 5–9.

UN (1991a) *World Population Prospects 1990.* United Nations: New York.

UN (1991b) *The Sex and Age Distribution of Population: The 1990 Revision of the United Nations Global Population Estimates and Projections.* United Nations: New York.

UN (1992) *Economic Survey of Europe in 1991–1992.* United Nations: New York.

UNDP (1992) *Human Development Report 1992.* Oxford University Press, New York.

UNECE (1993a) *International Migration Bulletin,* No 3.

UNECE (1993b) *Rapid Information System. Bulletin,* No 2.

UNHCR (1993) *Information Notes on Former Yugoslavia,* November.

UNHCR (1994) *The State of the World's Refugees.* Penguin: Harmondsworth.

USCR (1993) *World Refugee Survey, 1993.* United States Committee for Refugees: New York.

Van de Kaa, D.J. (1993) European migration at the end of history. *European Review*, 1, 1, 87–108.

Van Hecke, E. (1991) Migrations et dynamique de l'espace belge. Mémoire no.34, *Bulletin de la Société Belge d'Etudes Géographiques,* 60, 159–211.

Van Imhoff, E. and Keilman, N. (1991) *LIPRO 2.0: An Application of a Dynamic Demographic Projection Model to Household Structure in the Netherlands.* NIDI/CBGS Publications 23. Swets and Zeitlinger: Amsterdam/Lisse.

Van Imhoff, E., Van Wissen, L. and Spiess, K. (1994) *Regional Population Projections in the Countries of the European Economic Area.* Swets & Zeitlinger: Lisse.

Vasileva, D. (1992) Bulgarian Turkish emigration and return. *International Migration Review*, 26, 342–52.

Vishnevsky A. and Zayonchkovskaya, Zh. (1992) *Emigration from the USSR: the fourth wave.* Paper prepared for the conference: Mass Migration in Europe: Implications in East and West, IAS-IIASA-IF, Vienna.

Vitali, O. (1990) *Mutamenti nelle aree urbane.* F. Angeli: Milan.

VVAA (1990) La España desigual de las Autonomías. *Papeles de Economía Española,* 45, Madrid.

VVAA (1992) Balance económico de las Autonomías. *Papeles de Economía Española,* 51,

Madrid.

Walsh, B.M. (1974) Expectations, information and human migration: specifying an econometric model of Irish emigration to Britain. *Journal of Regional Science*, 14, 1, 107–20.

Walsh, J.A. (1979) Immigration to the Republic of Ireland 1946–1971. *Irish Geography*, 12, 104–10.

Walsh, J.A. (1984) *To Go or Not to Go: The Migration Intentions of Leaving Certificate Students.* Occasional Paper 2, Department of Geography, Carysfort College, Dublin.

Walsh, J.A. (1987–8) Components of demographic change in the Republic of Ireland. *Geographical Viewpoint*, 16, 45–59.

Walsh, J.A. (1990–1) Population change in the Republic of Ireland in the 1980s. *Geographical Viewpoint*, 19, 89–98.

Walsh, J.A. (1991a) The turn-around of the turnaround in the population of the Republic of Ireland. *Irish Geography*, 24, 2, 117–25.

Walsh, J.A. (1991b) Inter-county migration in the Republic of Ireland: patterns and processes. In R. King (ed.), *Contemporary Irish Migration.* Geographical Society of Ireland Special Publication 6: Dublin, 96–110.

Walsh, J.A. (1992a) Economic restructuring and labour migration in the European periphery: the case of the Republic of Ireland. In M. O'Cinnéide and S. Grimes (eds), *Planning and Development of Marginal Areas.* Centre for Development Studies, University College: Galway, 23–36.

Walsh, J.A. (1992b) Education, migration and regional development. In J.P. Davis (ed.), *Education, Training and Local Economic Development.* Regional Studies Association (Irish Branch): Dublin, 34–49.

White, P. (1986) International migration in the 1970s. In A. Findlay and P. White (eds), *West European Population Change.* Croom Helm: London, 50–80.

Wierzbicki, B. (1991) Europejska polityka wobec uchodzców. *Sprawy Miedzynarodowe*, 4, 71–86.

Willman, J. (1994) Hoverspeed protests to EU over immigration law. *The Financial Times.* 3 August.

Williams, J. and Rees, P. (1994) A simulation of the transmission of HIV and AIDS in United Kingdom regional populations. *Transactions, Institute of British Geographers*, 19, 4, 311–30.

Winchester, H.P.M. and Ogden, P.E. (1989) France: decentralization and deconcentration in the wake of the late urbanization. In A.G. Champion (ed.), *Counterurbanization.* Edward Arnold: New York.

World Bank (1992) *World Development Report 1992.* Oxford University Press, New York.

World Bank (1993) *World Development Report 1993.* Oxford University Press, New York.

Zayonchkovskaya, Z., Kocharyan, A. and Vitkovskaya, G. (1993) Forced migration and ethnic processes in the former Soviet Union. In R. Black and V. Robinson (eds), *Geography and Refugees*, Belhaven: London.

Zolberg, A. (1989) The next waves. *International Migration Review*, 23, 403–30.

Index

Africa
  North   43–5
  West   44–5
Alarcão A.   267
Albania   16, 18, 19, 25
  Greeks from   19, 25
  Albanians in   26
Amaro R.R.   263, 272
Antwerpen
  migration to   101–3
Århus   106, 108, 110, 113
Armitage R.   343, 345
Asylum
  applicants, regional origin   74, 79, 80
  applications   75, 79
  country of application   81 [Fig.]
  the Dublin Convention of 1990   86, 87
Asylum seekers   17–20, 48, 67–88
  cost of administration   78
  decision-making procedure   85
  discouragement of   85
  exceptional leave to remain   85
  in the industrialised world   76
  principal sources   74
  return of unsuccessful applicants   85
  waiting times   78
Asylum seeking
  geography of   67–88
America
  North   21
Aussiedler   21–3, 72, 123, 133, 346
Austria   19, 21, 24
  stock of foreign population   47

Baccaïni B.   191, 202
Baganha M.I.   268
Baldwin-Edwards M.   25
Baltic States   28
Baptista A.M.   263, 267, 272, 273
Barany Z.D.   28
Beiser M.   67
Belgium   7, 8, 17, 24, 91–104
  arrondissements   92, 103
  data sources
  east European population in   25
  migration exchanges with EU   54–6
  migration   91–104
    between linguistic communities   98

by age and sex   93–4 [Fig.]
  communes   102–3 [Fig.]
  counterurbanization   91–104
  distance-decay   97–8
  impact of distance   94–8
  inter-linguistic   93
  intracommunal   96–7
  intraregional   96–7
  interregional   96–7
  local   97 [Fig.]
  long-term trends   92–3
  regional   97 [Fig.]
  temporal trends in   91–104
  zones of attraction   103–4
  zones of repulsion   103–4
  National Register   91
  stock of foreign population   47, 48
  urbanization   98–102
Birg H.   135
Boden P.   290, 293, 298
Bonaguidi A.   237, 240, 243, 244
Bosnia-Herzegovina   19
  Muslims in   26
Border agreements   84–5
Boubovna H.   14, 19, 28, 29
Boundary crossing   14
Brabant
  Walloon   98–101, 103
  Flemish   98–101, 103
Bradshaw M.J.   29
Breathnach P.   216
Brochman G.   314
Brussels   92, 103
  migration with Flemish Brabant
  migration with Walloon Brabant
    99–100
  region   98–101
Bruxelas M.   271
Bulgaria   16, 18, 19, 21, 22, 23, 25
  Turks from 19, 20
  Pomaks from   20
  Bulgarians in   26
Bundesverwaltungsamt   21, 22
Burkhina Faso   44

Callovi G.   320
Campania
  migration to/from   235–6

Campania *(cont.)*
  age profiles of migration   243 [Fig.]
Canada   20
Cane A.   312
Carriers Liability Acts   84–5, 87
Carrilho M.J.   266
Carvel J.   313, 319
Castles S.   39, 40
Castro L.   248, 296
Cawley M.   226, 227
CEC   331
Charleroi
  migration to/from   101–3
Chesnais J-C.   29
CIA World Factbook   27
Coleman D.   33, 342, 344
Collins B.   210
Collison S.   39, 49
Commission
  of the European Communities   1, 2, 3,
    17, 18, 20, 312
Commission on Emigration   211
Cónim C.   269
Contracts for services   23
Convey A.   33, 326
Cook Report   321
Copenhagen   8, 105–22
  commune   114, 116, 117
  factors behind migration in   118–22
  interregional net migration   106–7 [Fig.]
  intraregional migration
    age variation in   118–9
  migration turnaround   106
  population   114, 115 [Fig.]
    age distribution   120
    change   117
  hypotheses about migration in   118–22
Cortese A.   39, 47
Costa-Lascoux J.   316, 324
Council
  of the European Communities   317, 328
Counterurbanization   8
Courgeau D.   92, 191, 202
Court, Y.   112
Coward J.   209, 229
Creton D.   210
Croatia   17, 19, 23, 26
Cribier F.   93
Croats   17
Cross-boundary commuters   24
Cruijsen H.   342, 344, 346
Cruz A.M.   87, 270
Czech Republic   16, 20, 21, 23, 24
Czechoslovakia   14, 15, 16, 18, 19, 25

  former   22

Data
  harmonization   53
  in international migration   53–6
Davidson P.   320
Decroly J.M.   342
DEMETER
  projection models   335–6, 339, 340–53
Demographic discrepancies
  in East–West migration   33–34
Denmark   8, 15, 17, 24
  asylum seekers   110
  east European population in   25
  employment
    business cycle fluctuations   113
    changes in   112–3
    regional distribution   112–3
  immigration   110
  international migration   110
  interregional migration   105–10
    age variation in   111–2
    factors behind   112–3
  migration
    exchanges with EU   54–6
    in Copenhagen region   114–22
  net migration   105–22
    between groups of *amter*   107 [Fig.]
    changing patterns   105–22
    total 1970–92   108 [Fig.]
  population
    age distribution   120
    amter   107 [Fig.]
  population change
    components   109–10
    by settlement size   113–4
    by municipality type   115 [Fig.]
  refugees   110
  stock of foreign population   47
Department of Health   342
Devis T.   290
Diaspora
  and chain migration   30
  Poles   30
  Hungarians   30
  Armenians   30
  Ukrainians   30
Doubling time   43–44
Dövenyi Z.   30
Drudy P.J.   217, 228
Drzewieniecka K.   33
Dublin
  emigration from   217
  migrants to   223–4

Dublin Convention   86, 87
Duffy, P.J.   228
Dzienio K.   33

East–West migration   13–37
  future of   24–34
Economic characteristics,
  east European   31
  west European   31
Economic discrepancies
  in East–West migration   30–3
ECPOP
  projection model   332, 336–8, 339,
  340–53
EFTA   4
Eichperger L.   340
Erf, Van der R.F.   247
Ethnicity   24–30
ERASMUS scheme   348
Euroinfo   328
Europe
  Eastern   13
  Western   13, 21, 44
  Northern   44
  Southern   44
European Commission   311, 313, 326, 327
European Communities   313
Eurostat   172, 331, 332, 343, 344, 345,
  346, 347, 353

Family reunification   48
Fargues P.   44
Fassmann H.   2, 14
Ferrão J.   263, 271, 272
Ferreira V.M.   270
Fertility
  assumptions   342–5
  total period rates   343
Fielding A   42
Figueiredo C.   263
Finland
  stock of foreign population   47
Firstbook of Demographics   27
Flanders   92
  zones of attraction in   104
  zones of repulsion in   104
Fleischer H.   21
Forecasts   9
  of East–West migrants   35–6
France   7, 8, 17, 20, 21, 24
  age-specific migration   197–9
  annual net migration rates   194 [Fig.]
    195
  census   191

concentration
  localized   193–7
  regional   193–7
decentralization   191–206
East European population in   25
enquête emploi   191
enquête triple biographie   191
life cycles   197–9
gravity model   199–200
migration exchanges with EU   54–6
migration
    1975–90   191–206
    and distance   199–201
    barrier effects   201–6
    older age groups   202–5
    permits, conditions of   322
    preferred directions   201–6
    residual flows   201–2
    younger age groups   202–5
net migration by settlement size   196–7
NUTS regions   191, 192 [Fig.]
population gains   193–5
stock of foreign population in   47, 48
variations in sensibility to distance
    200–1
Frederiksberg   105, 114, 116 [Fig.], 117,
  118, 119, 120, 121
Frederiksborg   105, 114, 116 [Fig.], 117,
  119, 121
Frelic B.   6, 86
Frey W.   242
Futures, for regional populations   359–64

Gachechiladze R.   29
Garvey D.   212, 225
Gasior K.   29
Gaspar J.   263, 267, 270, 271, 272
Gazeta Wyborcza   16
Geary R.C.   224
Geissler C.   136, 137
Germans
  in former Soviet Union   29–30
Germany   7, 8, 16–17, 19–24, 44
  constitution   23
  eastern Länder   16, 21, 123, 125, 130
    population change in   138 [Fig.]
    age structure change in   141 [Fig.]
  east European population in   25
  future population
    under 20 years of age   141–2
    potential workforce   141–2
    people aged 60 and over   141–2
  in-migration
    of foreign nationals   131

Germany *(cont.)*
    of Germans   132
    interregional migration, 123–43
  between western and eastern Germany
      136
    selective   127
    volume   135–6
  international migration   131–3, 137
    balance   132 [Fig.]
    nationality   132 [Fig.]
    spatial effects of   140 [Fig.], 142
    with EU countries   137
    with Europe outside the EU   137
    with non-European countries   137
  migrants to   13, 14
  migration
    exchanges with EU   54–6
    eastern to western *Länder*   130
      [Fig.]
    east–west   127–31
    sub-model   133–5
    sub-model structure   134 [Fig.]
    trends to 2000   133–7
  net interregional migration   123–6
    rates   126 [Fig.]
    ages 18–29   128 [Fig.]
    ages 50 and over   129 [Fig.]
  out-migration
    of foreign nationals   131
    of Germans   132
  permits, conditions of   322
  population change
    regional   124 [Fig.], 139 [Fig.]
    components of   138
  population projections   137–43
    consequences for regional planning
      143
  Raumordnungsregionen   123
  regional policy regions   123
  regional population dynamics
    in the future   137–42
    influence of migration on   137–42
  stock of foreign population   47, 48
  support of asylum seekers   83
  western *Länder*   22, 123, 125, 130
    population change in   138 [Fig.]
    age structure change in   141 [Fig.]
Giaoutzi M.   155, 166, 168
Gillmor D.A.   372
Glytsos N.P.   155
Golini A.   45
Gordijn H.   340
Greece   17, 24
  and Macedonia   26

east European population in   25
emigration   155
immigration
  by area type   168
  net   155
in-migration
  by area type   168
internal migration   145–73
interregional migration   172
  to and from Anatoliki and Nisia   172
migration
  exchanges with EU   54–6
  age selectivity   169
natural increase
  correlations   165, 166
  decline in   155
  national   155, 156 [Fig.]
  regional   157, 158–60 [Fig.], 161
    [Fig.]
net migration
  by age   169
    and region   170–1 [Fig.]
  by area type   167, 169
  correlations   165, 166
  national   155, 156 [Fig.]
  regional   157, 161, 162–4 [Fig.],
    165 [Fig.]
NUTS regions   145, 146 [Fig.]
population   145
  regional totals   149 [Fig.]
population change   145–73
  components   145–73
  correlations   165, 166
  national   147 [Fig.], 148–53
  rates by region   150–2 [Fig.], 153
    [Fig.]
  regional   148–53
residual net migration   146
rural–urban migration   166–72
  semi-urban areas   167
  urban areas   166–7
Greenwood M.J.   31
Grimmeau J.P.   98
Grzeszczak J.   16
Guestworker   23

Hailbronner K.   86
Hainsworth P.   72
Hanlon G.   216
Hannan D.   224
Harrison, P.   70
Haverkate R.   335, 350
Hecht J.   345
Heilig G.   342

Heller W. 72
Hofman H.J. 72
Hoffmann-Navotny H-J. 131
Holt J. 21
Hopkinson N. 319, 323
Horner A. 42, 219, 221
Houston C.J. 210
Hovy B. 17, 18, 19
Hryniewicz J. 32, 33
Hughes J.G. 224, 228
Hungary 14, 15, 18–25

Ile de France 8
Illegal migration
    see Migration, illegal
Illeris S. 112, 118
Immigration,
    policy and practice 46–50
Inequalities
    South–North 46
Instituto Nacional de Estadistica 25
International immigrants
    definition 52
International migrants
    categories of 314–5
International Passenger Survey 51
Intra-Community migration
    relationship to population at risk 57
Intra-European migration
    direction and meaning 58–9
    most significant imbalances 59–62
    evolution during the 1980s 61–4
    synthesis 63, 65
Ireland
    components of population change 208
    demography 208–10
    emigrants
        social groups 214
    emigration 207, 210–9
        and gender 218–9
        and social mobility 215
        in the 1980s 212–9
        in the 1990s 228
        networking 217
        of graduates 215
        regional pattern 218
    fertility 209–10
    human resource warehouse 207–29
    intercounty migration
        and age 225
        and gendre 225
        and education 227
        and occupations 225
        rates 223 [Fig.]

internal migration 219–28
    Labour Force Survey 212, 214, 222
    migration culture 211–2
    migration exchanges with EU 54–5
    net migration
        annual estimates of 213 [Fig.]
        by county 220 [Fig.]
    population decline 208
    residential mobility 222
    rural–urban migration 226–8
    spatial scales 208
    unemployment 214
    urban–rural migration 226–8
Israel
    migrants to 21
Italian Embassy 316
Italy 7, 8, 15, 17, 19, 2, 24, 44
    age selectivity in migration 240–4
    east European population in 25
    metro/non-metro shifts 238
    migration
        age profiles 241 [Fig.], 242 [Fig.]
        efficiency index 235
        exchanges with EU member states
            54–6
        internal 231–45
    long-term 232–3
        interregional 233
        metropolitan 233–4
        regional net 234
    northwestern macroregion 240–1
    permits, conditions 322
    regional and metropolitan shifts
        233–40
    restrictive admissions policy 84
    stock of foreign population 47

Jackson J.A. 216
Job opportunities
    in the West 32–3
Johnson J.H. 210
Joly D. 86
Jones H. 306
Jones K. 40
Jones P.N. 72
Jutland 106–113

Kemper F-J. 21, 22, 33
Kennedy R.E. 208, 210
Keyfitz N. 345
King M. 84, 87
King R. 2, 39, 210, 213, 216, 252
Kirwan F.X. 228
Knox E. 342

Kontuly T.   242
Korcelli P.   15, 29, 33
Kosovo
    Albanians in   17, 26
Kuba Kozlowski T.   28
Kuijper H.   92
Kupiszewski M.   14, 33
Kurcz Z.   33

Labour
    migration of, *see* Migration labour
Labour Force Survey   52
Lanphier M.   71
Lees L.   210
Le Monde   311, 312
Leridon H.   345
Lennihan B.   212
Le Soir   329
Lewandowska M.   33
Liebich A.   29
Life expectancies   340–2
Lipietz A.   42
Lisboa   270–3
Livi-Bacci M.   39
Lombardy
    age profile of migration   243 [Fig.]
    migration to/from   235–6
Lopez A.   342
Lutz W.   39, 46
Luxembourg
    east European population in   25
    stock of foreign population   47
    migration exchanges with EU   54–6

Maastricht
    Treaty of, *see* Treaty of Maastricht
Macedonia   26
Markiewicz T.   30
Markiewicz W.   16, 320, 321
Marx K.   41
Massey D.   42
Mass migration   39–40
McDowell J.M.   31
McGuire M.   212, 225
Mediterranean
    a demographic and economic divide
        43–6
Migrants
    nationality   49
Migration
    extra-Union   5, 7
        East-West   13–37
        North-South   39–50
    'gates'   315

illegal   16–17
inter-EU member state   7, 51–65, 349
interregional   7
labour   20–24
long-term   20–24
Marxian perspective   40–43
patterns by age   8
policies   9
South to North flows   45–6
flows between EU countries   51–65
Migration News   17, 34, 35
Migration policies   311–29
    and social security   326–7
    and healthcare   327–8
    towards minorities   328–9
Mihalka M.   34
Milan
    migration patterns   231, 237–40
    intrametropolitan shifts   239
Miles R.   41
Miller K.   39, 41, 211
Mills I.   290
Mjoset L.   216
Moniz F.   267, 273
Montanari A.   39, 47
Montenegrans   17
MPOU   175, 176
Morais J.P.   267
Morocco   44
Moussourou L.M.   155
Münz R.   2, 14
Muus P.   346

Nairn A.G.   228
Nansen F.   69
Nationalism   24–30
Nationalities
    in eastern Europe   27
    in the former Soviet Union   29–30
NEI   331, 335–6, 341, 342, 343, 345, 356,
    359
Netherlands   17, 247–59
    arrival/departure ratios   254 [Fig.]
    COROP regions   249 [Fig.]
    east European population in   25
    economic development   251
    explanations for trends   249–52
    future scenarios   258, 259 [Fig.]
    international migrants   252
        age patterns   248–9, 251 [Fig.]
        gender patterns   248–9, 251 [Fig.]
    interregional migration   247–59
    migration
        between labour markets   252–3

between types of municipalities
255
by age and gender 248–9, 250 [Fig.]
  exchanges with EU 54–6
  trends 250 [Fig.]
  within labour markets 253–7
net migration 252 [Fig.], 253 [Fig.]
  by age 256 [Fig.]
NUTS regions 249 [Fig.]
permits, conditions of 322
population density 255 [Fig.]
residential desires 251–2
residential mobility 248–9
reurbanization 257
spatial frameworks 248–9
stock of foreign population 47, 48
suburbanization 257
NIDI 353
Niessen J. 320, 321
NSSG
  National Statististical Service of Greece
    25, 145, 166, 168
Nettleton C. 86
Nobel P. 85
Noordam 92
Noin P. 342
Norcliffe G. 224
Nordic countries 21
Norway
  stock of foreign population 47
  refugee policy 83
NUTS
  Nomenclature of Territorial Units
    for Statistics, classification 3, 145

Öberg S. 19, 28, 29, 35, 36
OECD 47, 48, 323
Okólski M. 14, 16, 20, 24, 31
Ogden P. 242
OPCS 346
O'Rourke D. 228
Overstayers 14
Owen I. 317

Papademetriou D.G. 166
Pavlik Z. 15
Peixoto J. 266, 267, 269, 272
Podkanski W. 33
Poland 14–25, 28
Poles 21
Policy
  in East–West migration 34–5
Population change

1990–2020, 362 [Fig.]
Portugal 8, 17, 261–74
  east European population in 25
  emigration 268
  immigration 268–9
    of foreigners 268–9
  international migration 267–9
    regional distribution 267–9
  internal migration 269–73
  migration exchanges with EU 54–6
  methodological considerations 261–2
  NUTS regions in 262 [Fig.]
  population change 264, 265
    components of 264, 265
  regional demographic growth 263–6
  regional net migration 266
  retornados 268
  trends in regional migration 261–74
  urban dynamics 261–74
  urbanization 269–73
    rates 265
Porto 271–3
Poulain M. 53, 91, 92, 97, 200, 348, 349
Poulton H. 72
Projected populations
  of member states of EU 354
  of national populations 331–64
  of NUTS1 regions 360–1
  of regional populations 331–64
  of the European Union population 332
Projection
  assumptions 340–53
    external migration 345–8
    fertility 342–4
    improvement in 359
    inter-member state migration
      348–50
    interregional migration 350–3
    mortality 340–2
  methods
    improvement in 358–9
  models 333–40
    cohort-survival 333–4
    consistency 338–9
    DEMETER 335–6
    ECPOP 336–8
    further development 339–40
    migrant pool 334
    multiregional 335
    net migration 333–4
    of international organizations 333–4
    of national demographic offices
      334–5
    results 353–8

Projections *(cont.)*
    DEMETER   353–8
    ECPOP   353–8
    Eurostat   353–8
    national   354–5
    regional   355–8
    population futures   359
Pumain D.   92, 191, 200

Redei M.   14, 15, 19, 29
Rees P.H.   2, 298, 336, 339, 342, 343, 347,
    348, 350, 351
Refugee crisis
    framework   68–70
    globalization   70–1
    in Europe   73
    knocking on the door   71–2
    squaring the circle   72–3
Refugee policy
    harmonization   86
    'motte and bailey'   84–7
    multilateral action   86–7
    prevention of access   84–5
    preventive protection   86
Refugees   17–20
    admission policies   80
    cost of administration   78
    financial assistance   75
    major flows   76
    number   80 [Fig.]
    number in the world   68
    numbers in Europe   75
    population by country   77
    principal sources   74
    source   80 [Fig.]
    waiting times   78
    waves   79
    world perspective   73–8
    Yugoslav   19
Regimes
    demographic   5, 6 [Fig.]
Registers
    for measuring international migration   51
Reis J.   263
Resettlers, *see Aussiedler*
Residence permits
    conditions of   322
    long-term   320–1
    temporary   321
Return
    to country of origin   28–29
Rhode B.   31
Robinson V.   70, 71

Rogers A.   248, 296
Romania   16, 17, 18, 19, 20, 21, 22, 23, 24,
    25
    Gypsies from   19, 17, 28
    Hungarians from   19, 26, 28, 72
    Romanians in   26
Roskilde   105, 114, 116 [Fig.], 117, 119,
    121
Rudd J.   218
Russia   21
Russian Federation   21
Russians in CIS   28
Rzeczpospolita   30

Salgqueiro T.B.   270, 271, 272
Salt J.   15, 20, 40, 49, 72, 323, 342, 344
Santos A.F.   270
Santos, B.S.   263
Sarre P.   46
Scenarios
    constant internal migration   360–4
    counterurbanization/urbanization
        351, 352, 360–4
    future   258
    income scenario   351, 360–4
    zero internal migration   360–4
Schengen
    Accords   87, 311–4, 316, 318, 320, 346
    Information System   87, 312, 319
Schütte F.   23, 316, 318
Seasonal workers   23–4
SECP   267
Segbers K.   28, 36
Serbs   17
Serbia   26
Seruja L.M.   267
Sexton J.J.   214, 217
Shuttleworth I.   213, 215, 216, 218
Siampos G.   155
Simon G.   348
Slovakia
    Hungarian minority   26
Slovak Republic   23–24
Slovenia   23
Smith A.   40
Smyth W.J.   210
SOPEMI   13, 14, 15, 16, 17, 20, 21, 25, 29,
    34, 35, 316, 317, 319, 323
Spain
    agricultutal crisis   179
    east European population in   25
    economic resurgence   188
    evolution of the economy   178–9

industrialization 179
migration
    and the life cycle 180
    and social structure 180
    annual net rates 177 [Fig.], 183 [Fig.]
    currents 178 [Fig.]
    exchanges with EU 54–6
    historical backdrop 175–9
    in 1960s 175
    in 1970s 175
    in 1980s 179–85
    in 1990 184–5
    levels 180
    metropolitan deconcentration 175–90
    return to the South 175–90
    short distance movements 185–8
    spatial component 181–2
    to economically dynamic areas 182
net migration 175–8
    by region 178
    and settlement size 181
NUTS regions in 176 [Fig.]
out-migration from large cities 187–8
Padrones Municipales de Habitantes 179
periurbanization 182, 186–7
population change 180–1
return migrants 182
service sector 179
Sommer B. 21
Soviet Union
    former 16, 21
    refugees in 28
    expected outflow of migrants 72
Statistisches Bundesamt 21, 22
Stillwell J. 277, 291, 298, 299
Stpiczynski T. 25
Strachan A. 42
Sunley P. 42
Sweden 19, 24
    refugee policy 83
    stock of foreign population 47
Switzerland 19
    response to refugees 83
    stock of foreign population 47
Szoke L. 28

Tannahill J.A. 70
Terra Abrami V. 237, 243, 244
The Economist 30, 32, 88, 328
Total fertility rates 44
Traineeships 23

Transylvania 26
Treaty of Maastricht 1, 311–4, 327, 331, 348, 346
    Social Chapter 326–7
Treaty of Rome 325, 348
Tugault Y. 191
Turkey
    migrants to 20
Turin
    migration patterns 231, 237–40
    intrametropolitan shifts 239

Ukrainians 21
UN 33, 52
Underregistration 52
UNECE 17, 19, 21, 34
Unemployment
    in eastern Europe 32–3
UNHCR 19, 67
United Kingdom 7, 8, 17, 19, 24, 44, 275–307
    census migration data 290–4
    comparison
        of NHSCR and census 290–4
        of interaction matrices 291–4
    correlations of migration flows 292
    data sources 277
    differences in measures 290–1
    east European population in 25
    in-migration rates 285
    interaction pattern groupings 303 [Fig.]
        large metropolitan regions 302
        Midlands non-metropolitan regions 305
        Northern non-metropolitan regions 305
        older urban-industrial regions 302
        Scottish non-metropolitan regions 306
        South East regions 302
        Southern non-metropolitan regions 305
    migration
        age profiles 294–7
        and age 294–301
        and life course stages 299
        and spatial characteristics 301–6
        and spatial scales 296–8
        between NUTS 2 regions 275–307
        coefficients 286, 302
        directional preferences 301–2
        exchanges with EU 54–6
        gross in 283

United Kingdom *(cont.)*
   gross out   283
   indicators   278
   in 1990–1   294–306
   level   278–9
   patterns 1983–92   277–90
   ratios   293
  net migration
   balances   280 [Fig.]
   gaining and losing regions 281
     [Fig.]
   flows by age   300
   interregional   283, 287 [Fig.], 288
     [Fig.] 289 [Fig.]
  patterns   279–83, 301–6
   by age   298–301
   rates   282 [Fig.]
  NHSCR data   277–8
  NUTS regions   275, 276 [Fig.]
  out-migration rates   284 [Fig.]
  permits, conditions of   322
  Special Migration Statistics   299–300,
   304
  standardized rates   297–8
  stock of foreign population   47
  student migrations   291, 294
USA   20
USCR   67, 73
USSR   18,
  former 22, 25

Van de Kaa D.J.   30
Van Goethem B.   92
Van Haselen H.   335, 350

Van Hecke E.   101, 103
Van Imhoff, E.   345, 350
Vanlaer J.   342
Vasileva D.   21
Viborg   101, 111, 113
Vishnevsky A.   21, 29
Vitali O.   233
Vogelsang R.   242
Voivodina   26
Voreio Aigaio
  age pyramids   153, 154 [Fig.]
VVAA   178

Wallonia   92
  zones of attraction and repulsion   104
Walsh J.A.   208, 212, 215, 217, 218, 219,
  221, 222, 224, 225, 227, 228, 229
White P.   41, 46
Wierzbicki B.   318
Wild M.T.   72
Williams J.   342
Wils A.B.   35, 36
Winchester H.   242
Work permits   321–2
  conditions of   322

Yugoslavia   18, 23
  crisis   82
  former   16, 17, 19, 20, 22, 25
  forced migration in   83

Zayonchkovskaya Z.   21, 29, 72
Zolberg A.   43